VIOLENCE
and
REPRESSION
in
LATIN AMERICA

VIOLENCE

and

REPRESSION

in

LATIN AMERICA

ERNEST A. DUFF *and*

A Quantitative
and
Historical Analysis

JOHN F. McCAMANT

with **Waltraud Q. Morales**

THE FREE PRESS
A Division of Macmillan Publishing Co., Inc.
NEW YORK

Collier Macmillan Publishers
LONDON

The Free Press
A Division of Macmillan Publishing Co., Inc.
866 Third Avenue, New York, N.Y. 10022

Collier Macmillan Canada, Ltd.

Library of Congress Catalog Card Number: 75-16645

Printed in the United States of America

printing number
1 2 3 4 5 6 7 8 9 10

Library of Congress Cataloging in Publication Data

Duff, Ernest A
    Violence and repression in Latin America.

    Bibliography: p.
    Includes index.
    1. Violence--Latin America--History. 2. Vio-
lence--Latin America--Case studies. 3. Latin
America--Social conditions. I. McCamant, John F.,
joint author. II. Title.
HN260.Z9V53   301.6'33'098   75-16645
ISBN 0-02-907690-0

To Barbara and Sally

CONTENTS

LIST OF
TABLES AND FIGURES

Tables

Figures

PREFACE

The work on ideas that have now been put into this book began when we were visiting professors together for the Rockefeller Foundation University Development Program in Cali, Colombia, in 1966 and 1967. The Latin American location is significant because we decided while teaching Colombian students that we should never make explicit comparisons between Latin American nations and the United States. We would only compare Latin American countries with each other. We found that this limitation did not restrict our discourse because Latin America contains such a rich variety of nations. This book brings to fruition our finding that a comparison of differences among the states of Latin America can yield far more knowledge about the causes of certain phenomena south of the Rio Grande than an emphasis on uniformities.

In Cali we collaborated on an article, "Measuring Social and Political Requirements for System Stability in Latin America," which contained in rudimentary form many of the concepts of the present work. After returning to teach in the United States, one to Virginia to Randolph-Macon Woman's College and the other to Colorado to the University of Denver, we decided that the ideas in the article deserved more work. Political violence had become one of the major themes of research in the late 1960s and early 1970s and we wanted to demonstrate that there was another side to political violence, the less open and eventful but more insidious and destructive repression of political opposition. This book seeks to explain both.

We also developed an additional methodological concern. We believe that historical description and the development of general theory have been too disjoined, to the detriment of both. General theory is necessary to explain historical cases, and historical cases can do much to enrich the general theories. Hence, Part 1 of this book examines the development of general propositions through the analysis of variables, and Part 2 elaborates and applies these propositions to the particular history of the individual countries. Part 3 combines the two approaches. Three of the country studies in Part 2—Bolivia, Paraguay, and Peru—were written by Waltraud Q. Morales, a Ph.D. candidate at the University of Denver whose intimate knowledge of these countries is demonstrated in these passages.

Work on this book has been a tremendous learning experience for us. If we were to start over again, knowing what we do now, we could finish the work in one-third the time and no doubt make many improvements in our methodology. We hope that the readers will also learn from our experience and be ready to improve upon our logic and our methods. Social science is a process, not a product; our greatest accomplishment would be to have laid the basis for further work in the study of violence and repression.

In the several years that we have taken to learn enough to make this study, we have contracted innumerable debts. Our footnotes and bibliography point out many of our scholarly debts, but we owe much more to the many teachers and colleagues who have contributed to our intellectual development. We also owe a great deal to the many students who have stimulated and challenged us. Many have contributed more directly to the research. The coauthor from the mountains would like to thank Eduardo Feller, Mary Jane Hogan, Ken Switzer, and Charlotte Redden for their valuable research assistance and Shirley Taylor for her typing. The coauthor from the piedmont would like to thank Josie Ferguson and Kathy Major for their research assistance and his wife for her typing. Both the Social Science Foundation at the University of Denver and Randolph-Macon Woman's College provided funds that aided our research.

Our errors are our own.

Ernest A. Duff
John F. McCamant

INTRODUCTION

Latin America provides a fascinating study in contrasts. There are countries with long histories of democratic government, and there are countries with harsh and seemingly endless dictatorships. There are coups, civil wars, and revolutions, but there is also peaceful political change as well as enlightened political discourse. There are countries that appear to be modern societies, while a number of others have yet to emerge from the nineteenth century. Many Latin American countries have become intensely nationalistic since the end of World War II, but others still lack any real basis for nationalism.

In spite of its Iberian heritage, Latin America is geographically, ethnically, economically, and politically diverse. Geographically, the islands of the Caribbean have little in common with the nations strung out along the spine of the Andes; the Andean nations possess a set of geographic features entirely different from those of the nations in the Rio de Plata region; and the desert plains of Mexico are in clear contrast with the jungles of Brazil.

1

Economically, the Latin American nations range from Haiti, with a per capita gross national product of approximately sixty-five dollars, to Venezuela, where the gross national product per capita exceeds one thousand dollars.

Several Latin American nations are essentially Indian countries, though politics may be controlled by a non-Indian minority. Bolivia, Paraguay, Guatemala, Ecuador, and Peru fall into this category. Other nations, such as Argentina, Uruguay, and Costa Rica must be classified as overwhelmingly European. Haiti has essentially African antecedents, and Brazil, Panama, the Dominican Republic, Cuba, and Nicaragua all have substantial elements of their populations with African heritage. The rest of Latin America can be classified as "mestizo," but this term covers a multitude of situations, including those nations where mestizos constitute a majority of the population—Mexico, Colombia, Venezuela—and those where mestizos are less predominant.

Politically, Latin American nations can be classed as: constitutionally elected governments—Colombia and Venezuela; traditional dictatorships—Nicaragua and Paraguay; mobilization dictatorships—Panama and Peru; or totalitarian regimes—Cuba. Interesting variants of these types can be found in Mexico, a purported democracy where one party has won more than ninety percent of the vote in every presidential election since 1929; in Brazil, where the military appears to be attempting to introduce a mobilization dictatorship; and in Uruguay, where an ineffective civilian regime finds itself increasingly in thrall to the military. In some Latin American countries, political freedom has often been greater than in the United States. Before the recent military coup, Chile boasted an election system in which political views ranging from neo-Fascist to Communist and Socialist were represented at the ballot box. In many Latin American nations, politics is characterized by a personal contact between politician and constituent, actual or potential, that seems to have been lost in the more "developed" countries of the Northern Hemisphere. At the same time, however, the authoritarian image of Latin American governments, so dear to the minds and hearts of Anglo-Saxons, is firmly rooted in the reality of such nations as Haiti, Paraguay, Nicaragua, and Brazil—among many others.

Political contrasts among Latin American nations continue to amaze both the expert and the amateur. Political culture, interest groups, parties, government machinery, and governmental outputs all vary widely from one country to another. Why should one "underdeveloped" area of the world, in which all the countries were colonized by either Spain or Portugal, where all share a similar literary and intellectual tradition and speak similar languages, exhibit such political diversity? Exploring and explaining this diversity is (or should be) the goal of the political scientist engaged in an examination of Latin America. Why is it that Costa Rica has no army, whereas Cuba is armed to the teeth and Peru buys modern jet aircraft? Why has one family ruled Nicaragua since 1936, whereas governments in Ecuador come and go with astonishing speed? Why does Colombia have two political parties with roots in the nineteenth century, whereas many countries have no parties at all? Why—to get to the specific focus of this book—do the Latin American nations exhibit such great diversity in the amount of political violence and repression? Why do some Latin American nations appear to be ever on the brink of political chaos, whereas others exhibit a great deal of social cohesion? Consider some of the contrasts that fall into this dimension.

The five countries of Central America are often considered together as unstable "banana republics." Yet this small isthmus contains nations with enormous differences in social cohesion. To the north lies Guatemala, with a tradition of harsh dictatorships, a nation that for the past eight years has experienced a cruel war with ill-defined battle lines. People have been shot down with submachine guns on the streets of Guatemala City; a beauty queen and a U.S. ambassador have been murdered, while other people simply disappeared. Mutilated bodies have been found in the rivers, and there are well-substantiated reports of people being tortured to death. The last few years in Guatemala have been, indeed, "nasty, brutish, and short" for many people. But these years have been merely an extension of the situation portrayed by Miguel Angel Asturias in *El Señor Presidente,* the classic study of the traditional dictator based on the life of Guatemalan dictator Manuel Estrada Cabrera. Guatemala has earned the sobriquet, "banana republic."

In Costa Rica, on the other hand, another of the so-called banana republics, there have been no reports of armed violence for the past fifteen years. Political campaigns are carried out with enthusiasm, but without gunfire. The lack of violence in Costa Rica, unlike some Latin American countries, is not due to government coercion. In fact, control of the Costa Rican government has changed hands peacefully from one party to another seven times since 1949. Costa Rican democracy appears even to have weathered the peripheral effects of Watergate, in the person of fugitive financier Robert Vesco. Costa Rica not only has less violence than Guatemala, it also has less political violence and repression than the United States.

Variations in violence and repression are not limited to Central America. Argentina and Paraguay, at the southern end of the South American continent, provide striking contrasts in both violence and repression. Argentina is one of the most violent countries in Latin

America, whereas Paraguay is relatively peaceful. Both nations have had repressive governments, but that of Paraguay, under General Alfredo Stroessner since 1954, has been consistently more repressive than any other regime in Latin America.

Sometimes differences in violence and repression among the nations of Latin America seem inexplicable. We have alluded to the high level of violence in Argentina, which is one of the richest and most modern nations in the Southern Hemisphere. Venezuela, the richest, has also had extremely high levels of repression—under the dictatorship of Marcos Pérez Jiménez in the 1950s—and violence—after the overthrow of Pérez Jiménez and on into the 1960s. For many years books and articles on pre-Castro Cuba began with the seeming paradox that in one of the richest nations of Latin America was occurring some of the greatest violence. The violence was followed by one of the two or three genuine social revolutions the hemisphere has witnessed. At the other end of the spectrum is Ecuador, one of the poorer nations in Latin America and one often perceived as having a turbulent, if not violent, political history. Yet the empirical evidence shows that Ecuador is neither extremely violent nor particularly repressive. Quite obviously, there must be some not readily apparent factors to explain why the richest nations of Latin America are among the most violent, while some of the poorer nations are neither violent nor repressive. Certainly, economic development does not appear to diminish political violence in Latin American nations, nor does it appear to have much effect on the level of repression. One of the most cherished shibboleths of many writers on "development," and one of the operative principles behind the United States' program of foreign economic assistance, seems therefore to be in grave jeopardy. Economic development, or modernization, does not automatically produce political peace, nor does it necessarily produce the kind of society most foreign-aid officials hope for.

On the other hand, being poor does not guarantee low levels of violence and repression. Haiti, the poorest nation in the hemisphere, has had very high levels of both violence and repression over the past twenty years. Paraguay, another poor country, is low on violence but high on repression. Bolivia, too, has high levels of both.

Repression and violence vary in Latin America not only geographically, but temporally as well. Most Latin American nations have had periods of relative peace and open political process, followed by outbreaks of violence or repression or both. The Dominican Republic had practically no violence during the 1950s, but erupted in 1965 with the worst year of violence in all Latin America for the last two decades. Repression also fluctuates within countries over time, although not as drastically as violence, which seems to be a less stable variable. Many Latin American nations do differ considerably, however, in the level of repression from year to year, as government changes bring in rulers who are more, or less, inclined to an authoritarian rule.

Latin America, then, is an area of great political diversity. It is the purpose of this book to explore this diversity, particularly as it relates to variations in violence and repression. We plan to investigate the reasons why some Latin American nations show high levels of violence and repression, appearing to be constantly on the brink of political chaos, while others exhibit a high degree of social cohesion—the absence of violence and repression. In a real sense, we are looking for the basic causes of diversity: Why are some societies in Latin America able to handle social and political confrontations in a more or less peaceful manner, whereas others erupt into violence or suffer under the jackboot of the *caudillo?* Why do apparently similar situations provoke vastly different consequences in these societies?

Two events that occurred in neighboring countries in 1969 illustrate our question. In Córdoba, Argentina, in May of that year, opposition to the policies of the military government reached a peak: churchmen, labor unions, and students took to the streets to demonstrate against the government. The military, which had outlawed political parties and was trying to break the back of organized labor, would not allow even a peaceful demonstration against it, and troops attacked the demonstrators. An unequal, bloody battle ensued, in which more than five hundred protestors were injured and twenty-three were killed.

Across the Andes, in Santiago, Chile, political passions were also high as the question of whether Chile's future course should remain capitalist or become socialist was increasingly debated. In this case, however, parties and labor unions were allowed to demonstrate peacefully and organize freely. When demonstrators became unruly, as they often did, the Chilean *carabineros* seldom injured anyone, and when they made arrests, prisoners were held for only a few days. The question, of course, is why Chile was able to handle the pressures generated by intense political opposition and debate, while Argentina, at almost the same time, wholly failed to resolve differences without extensive violence and bloody repression. Paradoxically, one must also ask why Chile was able to manage change peacefully in 1969, but was unable to do so in 1973.

Similar seeming paradoxes abound. Why did Colombia erupt into violence after the assassination of Jorge Eliécer Gaitán in 1948, while Brazil remained calm through the suicide of Getulio Vargas in 1953 and the sudden abdication of the presidency by Jânio Quadros in 1961? Why was the Trujillo dictatorship in the Dominican Republic so repressive while the Somoza dictatorship in Nicaragua has resorted to very little coercion? Why can the Colombians work out amicable settlements with labor unions, while the Argentines have engaged in continuous confrontation with organized workers for eighteen years?

In any study of violence and repression in Latin America, the most consequential event of the past twenty years is, of course, the Cuban Revolution. No one predicted the violent take-over of the government and the repression that followed. After the revolution, however, many predicted that much of Latin America would follow the same course. Fidel Castro spoke of making the Andes the Sierra Maestra of Latin America; a spate of books appeared in the U.S. predicting imminent violent leftist revolutions throughout Latin America (among these were: *Evolution or Chaos; Latin America: The Zero Hour;* and *The Winds of Revolution*). Ché Guevara, as well as many U.S. academics and journalists, concluded that the objective conditions for Cuban-style revolution existed everywhere in Latin America. Guevara staked his life on that conclusion—and lost; the academics, among others, simply turned their attention elsewhere. But the question remains: Why did violent revolution wrack the island of Cuba in the last half of the 1950s, whereas similar attempts at revolution in other Latin American countries in the 1960s utterly failed?

The basic assumption of this book is that variations in violence and repression between societies, or variations in time within the same society, are caused by certain conditions common to those societies. In the jargon of the social sciences, violence and repression are dependent variables, and they vary with (are dependent on) certain independent variables common to all Latin American nations. A variable is a characteristic observed in any member of a group that differs—in quantity or quality—from one member of the group to the next. Independent variables are those variables that for the purpose of this analysis are not considered to be the consequence of other variables with which we are concerned. Dependent variables are those that we assume are affected or determined by the independent variables. Therefore, although we have indicated that certain independent variables, such as economic development, hold little promise for explaining the geographical and temporal variations in social cohesion, there are other, more subtle, variables that do explain these differences. The social disintegration of Guatemala and the social cohesion of Costa Rica, in other words, are explicable in empirical terms. The variation between Paraguay and Argentina in both violence and repression, the seemingly anomalous situation between Venezuela and Ecuador, the swift alteration in the level of violence in the Dominican Republic, and the Cuban Revolution all have empirical explanations. In fact, all variations in violence and repression in Latin America, whether geographical or temporal, can be explained by a limited number of independent variables.

The explanations, of course, are not as simple as we have made them sound in this brief introduction, nor is the process of finding them ever easy. Three different methods are used in this study to find and support a few tentative theoretical relationships. Part 1 searches for propositions that might explain the large diversity in repression and violence in Latin America through the definition and measurement of separate variables, suggesting the reasons why there might be relationships between them, and testing the relationships by means of statistical analysis. Part 2 applies the propositions supported by the statistical analysis to the historical interpretation of individual national cases. Special and nonquantifiable factors are also discussed. Finally, Part 3 compares the national histories to provide more explicit explanations of traditional personalist dictatorships, social revolution, the decline of social cohesion, and the much slower increase in social cohesion.

PART 1

COMPARATIVE ANALYSIS AND THE DEVELOPMENT OF THEORY

1

THE ANALYSIS
OF SOCIAL COHESION

Consider for a moment that the president of a country declares a state of siege and orders the arrest of opposition leaders, that the confederation of labor unions declares a general strike, that students form a clandestine band, make plastic bombs, and blow up two foreign-owned department stores. These incidents are not difficult to imagine certainly. Indeed, they are typical of social phenomena with which the analysis in this book is concerned.

Do such incidents tell us anything about the society in which they take place or only something about the participants? Do the three kinds of incidents mean something similar, or do they have different meanings? Do similar appearing incidents have the same implications in different countries? Why do some countries have more of one kind of incident than another? Why do some countries have more of all kinds? Which countries should be studied in order to test general explanations?

These questions are basic to any comparative analysis, but they do not have unambiguous answers. Our research was shaped by the choices we made on how best to approach the questions; they were made on the basis of some general feelings about what kind of analysis would be most productive at this stage of our understanding of the problem of violence and repression. Only as we worked on the research and reflected on how it differed from other research, did we begin to articulate direct answers to these questions. If we had answered any one of these questions differently, the whole shape and content of this book would have been changed.

One of the first questions we asked ourselves was whether our research should focus on the participants or on the societies in which the incidents take place. We chose to concentrate on the societies. Most research on violence within the United States has concentrated on the participants. Because the researcher is very limited in what he can do, he must choose whether to work at the societal level or the individual level, but from the point of view of theory, there should be no such dichotomy. It is impossible to study individuals without being concerned about the society from which they come and in which they act. Aristotle summed it up when he said, "Man is by nature a political animal." At the same time, societies are nothing more than individuals acting together in a collectivity.

Social conditions produce social phenomena only through the intervening elements of the individuals' dispositions and behavior as molded by social interactions. Social conditions and interactions develop an individual's disposition and condition his behavior. Any specific individual act is a response to social conditions and to anticipated interactions. What we observe as societal behavior is either aggregated individual behaviors or global behavior, that is, collective action. In social theory, there should be no division between micro and macro behavioral levels, as Figure 1 illustrates.

The president's repression of opposition leaders is an example of global behavior. The president speaks with the authority of the whole society, even if the majority disagree with the act. The decision to arrest the opposition leaders was made by one individual who obtained his position of authority, by fair means or foul, through the structured interaction of that society. To explain this act of repression, a theory would need to specify the social conditions and interactions that produced the disposition toward repressive behavior, how a person with such a disposition became president, the specific conditions and anticipated interactions that led the president to make the decision, and, finally, how the pattern of interactions allowed him, let us assume, to get away with the repressive act.

Figure 1.   Elements of Social Theory

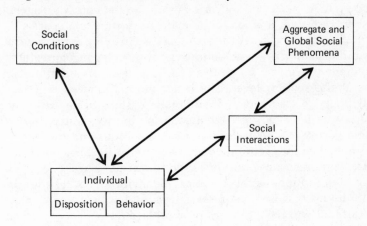

The acts of violence perpetrated by a group of students also reflects many things about the society in which it takes place. These students grew up in that society and learned their values from it. While taking into account possible interactions of supporters or opponents, they are responding to conditions in that society. If their anticipations are correct, other groups will be stimulated to imitate their actions. An aggregation of all such actions in society would indicate to what extent the conditions that led these particular students to their risky action prevail in the society as a whole. The total of the students' actions, then, also says something about the society.

Even though the individual, the interactional, and the social levels of analysis need to be combined to make a theory, the researcher, because of scarcity of time and resources, must choose a part of the problem to work on—and a part to leave out. We can observe and analyze only a few phenomena at once. Journalists, government statistical agencies, and scholarly writers have given us a wealth of information at the societal level, but all analysts have to develop their own individual-level information. Unfortunately, collecting information on individuals requires extensive interviewing, which is always time consuming and expensive. It becomes necessary, therefore, to limit the coverage to a few countries at a particular point in time. Another difficulty also pertains to surveys of individuals: they sometimes lead to inaccurate results because of the tendency of respondents to give what they consider socially desirable answers. In any case, surveying on such politically sensitive subjects as repression and violence is impossible in many locations in Latin America.[1] On the other hand, by using information already collected by various information gathering agencies we were able to cover a much larger expanse of time and space.

We made the choice, then, to work exclusively at the societal level, using information on social conditions and aggregated and global social phenomena. We also made use of information on structured interactions at the societal level. The little information we obtained about individuals is scattered and cannot be systematically analyzed. It is used primarily for purposes of illustration in the country studies of the second part of the book. Individual dispositions and behaviors, however, are taken into account when we present our causal interpretations of why certain social conditions produce certain social effects. Here we made assumptions about human behavior. The testing of these assumptions, of course, requires a different kind of research and analysis, but that will have to wait for another day.

Accepting for the time being, then, that all individual acts have meaning for the society as a whole, what is the meaning of the incidents we mentioned? The jailing of opposition leaders, the general strike, and the bombing of foreign-owned stores are all examples of the use of physical coercion for political ends. One part of society is resorting to force in an attempt to assert its will against another part of society. Individuals have gone beyond the bounds of persuasion, beyond any agreement to disagree, and are saying, in effect, comply or else.

The use of physical coercion in society is nothing new. All societies have been organized through the use of force. Large, complex societies, such as nation-states, may resort to more coercion than smaller, more intimate societies, such as the Eskimo, but some degree of coercion is omnipresent. What is interesting is that societies vary so much in their use of physical coercion. In some, it is relatively absent; in others, violence seems to be the principal form of politics.

We use the term "cohesive" to describe the society in which the government and the opposition apply relatively little coercion. In its ideal form, the cohesive society would be able to make collective decisions and have them obeyed without the application of coercion. Those who disagree with the decision, and disagreement always exists to some extent in complex societies, would obey the decision even

[1]The response to Project Camelot—a U.S. Army-sponsored program to study the causes of revolution and insurgency—indicates the limitations of this method when it was bitterly denounced in the Chilean Senate. See Irving Louis Horowitz, "The Life and Death of Project Camelot," and Kalman H. Silvert, "American Academic Ethics and Social Research Abroad," in U.S. Congress, House of Representatives, 89th Congress, 2nd Session, *International Education: Past, Present, Problems, and Prospects* (Washington: GPO, 1967), pp. 289–303 and pp. 304–314 respectively.

while trying to alter it. The expression of differences would follow certain rules and be channeled through certain structures. It would not be manifested in violent form. The government would not fear disagreement in these circumstances and would preserve the right to disagree.

We have no name for the highly coercive society that lacks social cohesion, though it can be characterized by Hobbes's war of all against all, where "life is brutish, nasty, and short." Our perspective differs from Hobbes's, however. As we look over the history of the nations of the world, we observe that the government is as likely to be the initiator of violence as is the opposition. Often governments do not follow the "general will," but reflect only the particular will of a tyrant, an oligarchy, the military, or some other part of the society. From their position of authority, such groups wage war against the rest of the population, depriving them of their property, their freedom, and their livelihood. To make matters worse, governments, more often than citizens, get away with committing atrocities. We want to move away from the recent academic tradition in the United States, which has studied oppositional violence while ignoring official violence. Our concern with societies, rather than participants, means that we do not need to take sides between the opposition and the government. We focus on the extent to which societies are cohesive or, alternatively, are wracked by violence or repression or both.

What we call "social cohesion," which has often been discussed under other names, has been a classic theme of philosophers and social scientists. Aristotle had something similar in mind in his distinction between true forms of government and perverse forms. More contemporary writers have considered the theme under a multitude of terms: "political order," "integration," "revolution," "nation-building," "homeostatic equilibrium," "solidarity," "degree of stress," "strain," "political stability," "nationalism," "government performance." All these terms apply to the society as a whole. Other writers have discussed the relationship from the individual's perspective using such terms as "anomie," "alienation," "political violence," and "legitimacy."

When we first wrote on this subject, we used the term "system stability."[2] At that time, "political stability" was used by many writers to describe such disparate phenomena as guerrilla warfare and cabinet changes. We used the word "system" to make clear that we were

---

[2]Ernest A. Duff and John F. McCamant, "Measuring Social and Political Requirements for System Stability in Latin America," *American Political Science Review* 62 (December, 1968), pp. 1125–1143.

interested only in the more serious phenomena. The troublesome word, however, was "stability," which implies lack of change: it was a troublesome term because societies have always had to change in order to meet changing circumstances. Societies that failed to change have had more troubles than those that did. So where is the virtue of "stability"? Stability in and of itself has little meaning. It is a term that can be applied to a war where neither party has an advantage, to a dictatorship that has lasted a long time, or to a policy that has been consistently applied. But it has misleading connotations when used to describe the absence of coercion in society, which may have resulted from just the right amount of change. Some systems theorists, in recognition of the problem that societies continually need to adjust to changing environments, have introduced the term "homeostatic equilibrium." They picture societies as having a kind of thermostat that turns the furnace on when things get cold or turns the air conditioner on when things get hot. However, these writers never make clear what the mechanism for automatic adjustment is in societies. We have not noticed that governments always do what is necessary to ease the tensions of society. More often than not, they do the wrong thing, and as a result, societies carry on at all temperatures, sometimes getting too hot and sometimes too cold. Nor have we been able to figure out exactly what was supposed to be in "equilibrium," what was being balanced. "Homeostatic equilibrium" may fit some systems that are analogous to a social system, but applying the term to societies seems to be carrying the analogy too far.

The term "integration" or "political integration" has also been used in the way we are using social cohesion. However, the term "integration" also refers to the number of interactions between individuals, and considerable interaction may lead to friction, causing violence or suppression or some of each. A society based on selective separation, on "live and let live," as is the case with religious groups in the United States and language groups in Switzerland, will not be integrated, but may experience less coercion and be more cohesive.

Revolutions may occur when societies break down entirely, and the study of revolutions has a similar perspective to ours. The concept of revolution, however, varies only dichotomously; societies have either a revolution or have no revolution. We are more interested in revolutionary potential—how close a society is to having a revolution. Revolution, or revolutionary potential, implies something more than we imply by lack of social cohesion. A revolution implies a new beginning. Yet the fact that a society falls apart does not mean it will be put back together in a drastically new way. Some societies live on in violence and in chaos for generations. We are concerned in this study less with social change than with the disintegration of societies.

A consensus exists among all those who use the terms discussed above that societies may differ in the degree in which their members cooperate together in collective action. We have called this dimension— variation in one direction—social cohesion. The question of what is a proper dimension for analysis is a more complex problem than we have implied, however, and consensus is no substitute for clear criteria. The social sciences are full of works that have been confused because the authors have pursued dimensions that were either too broad or too narrow. We originally asked, "Do the three kinds of incidents mean something similar, or do they have different meanings?" We could enlarge the problem by asking whether there are other kinds of incidents with similar meanings. This is the problem of dimensionalization, which concerns the question of what kinds of phenomena should be aggregated into a general concept. If too many kinds of phenomena are thrown together, the concept ceases to be unidimensional. At the other extreme, if the phenomena are defined too narrowly, the concept ceases to be general and instead applies only to specific events.

There are three criteria for answering the question of what kinds of phenomena shall be aggregated: (1) Do they have a quality in common? (2) Do they have common causes? and (3) Do they have common consequences? Whether to aggregate or not to aggregate will then depend on what aspect is considered. At times some phenomena should be aggregated and at other times kept separate. There are no hard and fast rules.

However, social scientists have often tried to use concepts that were obviously too inclusive according to the above criteria. The concepts of stable democracy, political development, and governmental performance have been used to cover what we call social cohesion, but they have at the same time included phenomena that we feel properly belong in a separate dimension. Logically, stable democracy includes at least two dimensions: stability and democracy. If one were asked to illustrate how the concept of stable democracy varies, one might present the following matrix:

	Democraticness	
Stability	Stable Democracies	Stable Nondemocracies
	Unstable Democracies	Unstable Nondemocracies

The concept of stability and the concept of democraticness seem to refer to quite different things. Stability refers to the unchanging nature of the constitutional system, or perhaps the absence of challenges to it. Democraticness refers to the extent of competitiveness or the extent of participation (two dimensions?). Because other forms of government can be stable, it seems the causes of stability are likely to be different than the causes of democraticness. The foreign investor who seeks a stable country, but not necessarily a democratic one, will certainly feel that the consequences of stability are different from the consequences of democraticness.[3]

The most flagrant failure to properly dimensionalize is apparent in the political development literature. The term "political development" seems to encompass every political dimension and some economic dimensions as well. It also seems to be saying that all good things go together, "every day, in every way, better and better"—or, "Yes, on all counts we are definitely superior and are the model for other nations to emulate." The literature fails to ask the basic question of what are the dimensions in which politics vary. Stability and democraticness are thrown together, and redistributive or economic growth-producing policy outputs are added. Combining these dimensions obfuscates the extremely difficult choices that a political leader must make between satisfying consumption of the population and increasing investment, between increasing participation and preventing greater demands for services, between preventing corruption and maintaining the freedom of corrupt politicians, and so on. All good things do not come together. Progress on one dimension may mean retrogression on another. Writers have slid out from under the problem by working on only one dimension and calling it political development. Huntington was only concerned with violence,[4] and Apter was primarily concerned with policies conducive to "modernization."[5] Cutwright focuses on democracy.[6] The concept of political development utterly confuses the dimensionalization question and is useless for political analysis.

Harry Eckstein has done some of the most careful conceptualization in political science. He began with the concept of stable democracy, recognized that the two dimensions are present, and turned to the

[3]Robert Dahl's otherwise excellent study falls down because he has confused the two dimensions and it is never clear whether he is explaining stability or democraticness. Robert Dahl, *Polyarchy, Participation, and Opposition* (New Haven: Yale University Press, 1971).

[4]Samuel Huntington, *Political Order in Changing Societies* (New Haven: Yale University Press, 1968).

[5]David Apter, *The Politics of Modernization* (Chicago: University of Chicago Press, 1965).

[6]Philips Cutwright, "National Political Development: Its Measurement and Social Correlates" in *Politics and Social Life*, ed. Nelson W. Polsby, Robert A. Dentler, and Paul A. Smith (Boston: Houghton Mifflin, 1963) pp. 569–582.

concept of political performance as applicable equally to democracies and dictatorships.[7] He divides governmental performance into four parts: durability, civil order, legitimacy, and decisional efficacy. It is unclear, however, whether we are dealing with one dimension or four. Eckstein seems torn between the search for *the* basic dimension of politics and the recognition of the multidimensionality of politics. We see no point in including decisional efficacy with civil order; they have few qualities in common, but there may be a causal relationship between them, which is a question to be studied. Our answer to Eckstein's dilemma is to admit that politics has an infinite number of dimensions and to let the nature of the particular research determine the proper dimension to use.

Not wanting to repeat the mistakes of the writers on stable democracy and political development, we exclude from our concept of social cohesion all questions of who or how many govern, the process or effectiveness of policy-making, and the nature of economic policies. Some may object to this last exclusion, pointing out that the giving or withholding of access to vital material goods or services is as much coercion as shooting a person. Radicals in Latin America argue that death from starvation or malnutrition is just as violent as death from gunshots. Fear of losing a job is as likely to prevent the expression of discontent as fear of going to jail. We are sympathetic to these objections. But we have excluded economic controls from the phenomena we are considering for two reasons, one expedient and the other theoretical. The expedient reason is that the extent to which economic measures are used to control population is almost impossible to assess. The theoretical reason is that it is important to ask when a society has to go beyond the application of economic controls and resort to physical coercion.

We have decided, then, that the inclusion of phenomena relating to the use of physical coercion by either governments or the opposition is large enough for one dimension. We won't throw in more kinds of phenomena with these. But, isn't this conceptualization of social cohesion still too large? Isn't a general strike different from urban guerrilla warfare? Isn't repression by the authorities different from violence by the opposition? All have the element of coercion in common, but the

[7]Harry Eckstein, "A Theory of Stable Democracy," in *Research Monograph No. 10* (Princeton: Center of International Studies, Princeton University, 1961; *Division and Cohesion in Democracy: A Study of Norway* (Princeton: Princeton University Press, 1966); "Authority Relations and Governmental Performance," *Comparative Political Studies* 2 (October, 1969) pp. 269–325; *The Evaluation of Political Performance: Problems and Dimensions* (Beverly Hills: Sage Publications, 1971).

organization needed to carry out these different coercive activities is different, the participants are different, the motivations are likely to be different, and the consequences are different. Also, we notice that societies tending to have one kind of incident usually don't have as many of the other kinds of incidents. These are strong arguments for keeping the different kinds of incidents separate and working on less general concepts than social cohesion. But the theoretical and statistical arguments for combining incidents are as strong, so we kept the general concept.

In this book, we both combine and keep separate these different kinds of incidents, hoping to have the best of both worlds. We seek societal measures for political repression, unarmed violence, and armed violence. We study them together and we study them separately. In the correlation analysis, not reported here, we found that very little was lost in explanation by combining armed and unarmed violence. Furthermore, we noticed a tendency for expressions of discontent in countries to proceed from unarmed to armed measures. To maximize generality and simplicity, we combine both kinds of violence in most of our discussions. Repression and violence have certain causes in common and some that are not. We treat them as separate dimensions and as a combined dimension in order to understand both aspects.

The arguments used to show that the incidents cited at the beginning have, in some respects, similar meaning have gone a long way toward answering the next question: Do similar appearing incidents mean the same thing in one country as in another? This question takes us to the most basic issue of comparative analysis: Are there general concepts among societies that can be compared? This problem of comparability is the problem of conceptual equivalence.

Repression in one society may be used to preserve the status quo, but in another it may lead to a more equalitarian political culture. A strike in one country may express extreme discontent with living conditions; in another it may reflect only jurisdictional disputes between unions. These problems can never be completely resolved in a comparative study. We decided to exclude Cuba from our comparisons in the 1960s because repression and violence had very different social meanings in Castro's Cuba than in the other countries of Latin America, resulting from different causes and producing different consequences. We also decided to drop voter turnout as an explanatory variable because the meaning of the vote shifted from country to country. Aside from these cases, we concluded that the phenomena we were analyzing had sufficiently similar social meaning in the countries studied to make cross-national comparison legitimate and meaningful. Again, the final argument for our choice comes from the rest of the book. If we did not have equivalent phenomena to deal with, we would not be able to find any common explanation. And we must have identified phenomena that are at least partially equivalent because some explanations passed the statistical tests.

Why do some countries have more of one kind of incident and some have more of all kinds? In searching for explanations, we were eclectic, looking wherever a good argument offered an explanation. Our approach can be contrasted with that of Ted Robert Gurr's, who began with a single principle of social action: frustration-aggression.[8] Psychologists have found that animals and humans will strike out in aggressive action when frustrated. From this basic finding, Gurr deduced that circumstances in which civil violence is likely. We have no argument with the theory that frustration does, in most cases, produce aggression, but it seems rather narrow to suggest that only individual frustration will produce civil violence. People may resort to collective violence because they are frustrated, as Gurr suggests, but they may also resort to violence because they sympathize with oppressed groups, because they see violence as the optimum strategy to obtain political power, because they enjoy the excitement of violent action, and so on. When one accepts the multifaceted nature of human beings, one has difficulty working from one deductive model. We use deductions to examine the reasonableness of different explanations, but we base these on a number of different principles of human action.

The literature of social science is richer in explanations for oppositional violence than for government violence, though in many cases arguments made for the former can be extended to the latter. We have not felt constrained by the ideas of others on the subject of social violence, especially because most of the literature on it provides few well-reasoned causal interpretations. We have, therefore, refined the arguments of others and developed explanations of our own. We have limited ourselves, however, to explanatory concepts for which we found indicators to test the relationship between causal factors and violence and repression. One important possible explanation we were forced to omit is Eckstein's congruence theory because we were unable to measure the congruence of authority relations within the countries in our sample. Chapter 3 works out the arguments why certain socioeconomic concepts might help explain the levels of violence and repression, and tests the relationship with simple correlations of data from Latin America in the 1950s and 1960s. Chapter 4 does the same for

---

[8]Gurr first outlined his theory in "Psychological Factors in Civil Violence," *World Politics* 20 (January, 1968), pp. 245–278; he later elaborated the theory in *Why Men Rebel* (Princeton: Princeton University Press, 1970).

certain structural and political concepts. All these concepts are brought together in multiple variable analysis in Chapter 5 before being applied to separate countries in Part II.

We chose Latin America to test propositions about social cohesion, first because that was the area of our expertise, and because we could obtain data more readily from there than from any other part of the world. It was a choice of convenience. Our overall familiarity with Latin America gave us the tacit knowledge necessary to think about the applicability of the concepts and to question the reliability of measurements.[9] The limited number of cases which Latin America offered allowed us not only to treat each case separately but to compare cases as well. In addition to these convenient reasons, there were also some important analytic reasons.

We have already referred to the problem of conceptual equivalence. Making the comparisons in one cultural area limited the problem. For instance, we could use the invoking of a state of siege as an indicator of repression because all constitutions in Latin America make provision for the suspension of constitutional rights. The consumption of material goods has similar meanings because all countries have been widely exposed to Western material culture. The comparison of religious structures was made easier because of the prevalence of the Catholic Church in Central and South America.

Similarity of culture is helpful in establishing equivalency, but it could be very detrimental to comparative analysis if it meant there was little variation in the societal variables analyzed. Fortunately, in Latin America the variation on all the variables we used was nearly as great as the worldwide range.

In Gurr's systematic measurement of political violence for 127 countries of the world from 1961 to 1965, the Dominican Republic was second highest, and a number of Latin American countries were very near the bottom.[10] Half of the Latin American countries had more political violence than did the United States, and half had less. No one has made as systematic a measurement of repression in the world as Gurr has. Nevertheless, the Dominican Republic under Trujillo and Haiti under Papa Doc Duvalier became very nearly totalitarian, and Costa Rica in the 1960s and Uruguay in the 1950s were among the freest

[9]See Sheldon Wolin, "Political Theory as a Vocation," *American Political Science Review* 63 (December, 1969), pp. 1062–1082 for the importance of tacit political knowledge.

[10]Data is reproduced in Ivo K. Feierabend, Rosalind Feierabend, and Ted Robert Gurr, eds. *Anger, Violence and Politics* (Englewood Cliffs, N.J.: Prentice-Hall, 1973), pp. 213–215.

countries in the world. The rest of the countries are distributed fairly evenly between these extremes. The distribution of social cohesion in Latin America not only matches the range in most of the world, but is even normal, a convenience for statistical purposes.

The distribution of our explanatory concepts also worked out quite well. Latin America exhibits a large variation in economic development, and an even larger variety of forms of communication and urbanization. Furthermore, the differences in the presence of political parties and the church are also wide. The one variable on which the range was as little as half the worldwide variation was land equality (which does not take into account the recent developments in Cuba and Chile) where the vestiges of Iberian colonialism continue to leave their mark.

The incidents discussed in the first part of this chapter, a state of siege, the arrest of opposition leaders, a general strike and bombings, are examples of coercion used by one group against others in the same society, and we have concluded that such phenomena, when they are aggregated, tell us the extent to which a society lacks social cohesion—a concept that is unidimensional for some purposes but that for other purposes is better divided into two dimensions, repression and violence. Latin American countries vary a great deal in repression and violence, as they differ on other variables that may explain the differences in repression and violence.

2

MEASURING
THE DEPENDENT VARIABLES

The goal of our analysis is to further the understanding of the bonds that hold nation-states together and allow individuals to work together in society with a minimum of destructive conflict. The first step toward this desired objective is to ascertain what type of society has more conflict than others and what type has less—and how both types are changing. In this chapter we measure the degree of political repression and violence for each country in Latin America for each year between 1950 and 1970. We then combine these measures to provide a negative indication of the broader concept of social cohesion.

Repression

Repression is considered in this study to be the use of governmental coercion to control or eliminate actual or potential political opposition. Coercion may come in the form of arrests and imprisonment or exile of individuals who oppose or are suspected of wanting to oppose the government. It may also come in the form of denial of due process to these individuals. The government may prevent opponents from associating and organizing. It may deny them the right to communicate through public media. Repression, to put it another way, is a form of violence used by those in power against any opposition, violent or peaceful. It could be called "official violence." Because officials have the power to issue decrees and laws and have large and highly organized coercive forces at their disposal, the forms and means of official violence are quite different from those of oppositional violence and must be studied separately.

It should be made clear at the outset that this study does not intend to deal with the question of when or where official violence may be justifiable or legitimate and when or where it is not. We, personally, find most uses of repression reprehensible, though governments that resort to it are bound in every case to defend it. We are interested in identifying the social conditions under which repression tends to occur and under which it tends to be absent. Our interest in repression arises because it is an indication that the government feels threatened. It is an admission by the government that the population would like to express its dissatisfaction with the government or the social situation rather drastically and would express such discontent if it were allowed to do so. We assume that the more repression used, the greater the government's sense of threat. In other words, the use of repression tells us something about the government's evaluation of popular support for itself and for the political and social system it represents and defends.

Our concept of repression is limited to the use of physical coercion against political opponents. It is very close to but distinct from the concept of oppression that refers more to the way a social system maintains a portion of the population in positions of poverty and impotence. Some use the term "repression" to refer to both concepts. We wish to keep them separate. We recognize, however, that a government need not fear political opposition from those whose physical and mental capacities have been sapped by hunger and malnutrition. We recognize that when the economic system keeps individuals in position of economic insecurity, they become more compliant. People who are thoroughly oppressed do not need to be repressed. By keeping the concepts of oppression and repression distinct, the answer to the important question of under what conditions the oppressed rebel unless repressed can be determined more easily. As our study will show, several countries where living conditions are miserable and inequality is great score low on both violence and repression.

The dependent variable studied here, then, is political repression, not economic oppression. We constructed an overall index of repression from scores on four different but closely related indicators: suspension of constitutional guarantees; arrests, exiles, and executions; restrictions on the organization of political parties; and censorship of media. At least some information exists for each Latin American country on each of these four dimensions. Some periodicals consider these subjects to be newsworthy, and insofar as these magazines and newspapers report anything about Latin America, they have reported on these indicators. Together, these four factors cover the main aspects of repression. Developing the index was not without its problems, some of which are discussed below. Nonetheless, we feel that it represents a close approximation of the relative level of repression in each country during the twenty-year period between 1950 and 1970.

Our aim is to establish with as much precision as possible the level of political repression at each point of time in each Latin American country during these two decades. We want to be able to say which country had more repression and which less and whether a particular nation experienced more or less repression at one point of time than another. If possible, we would also like to know how great the differences were. Many obstacles block the achievement of this goal, however. Information is sometimes scanty; countries differ in their style of repression; and there are, in many cases, few incidents that can be recorded in order to obtain interval data. Despite these obstacles we chose to go ahead because the benefits of such an index seemed to far outweigh the costs in time and effort. The lack of precision and even distortion in the nonquantitative discussions on the subject of repression are often very great. Repression, like all social concepts, is a very relative matter. One can be upset about a very little bit of it, especially if it affects one's interests. But one still needs perspective. One needs to know what is a little bit and what is a lot insofar as relative amounts of repression can be ascertained. Only with some determination of quantity is it possible to say what independent variables are associated with the dependent variable, repression. Insofar as the repression index lacks exactness and precision, our conclusions about relationships will have to be considered tentative. In this study, the relationships that we find are sufficiently strong to override any small errors that may have arisen in developing the index.

The problem of information is serious because the quantity of it published about repression is uneven. Most of it comes from those countries with a long tradition of press criticism. Surprisingly, information is good about the most repressive regimes, because they have attracted the attention of the Organization of American States Human

Rights Commission, the International Commission of Jurists, and other such agencies. Information from exiles and from special investigations makes it possible to know a great deal about the most repressive countries even if the data are disputed by the regime. The greatest lack of information comes from the in-between societies, countries where the press has been tamed but where repression is not so flagrant as to attract the attention of international agencies. In the United States, of course, information is also distributed according to what is newsworthy. The larger countries, as a consequence, receive more publicity than the smaller. On the other hand, regional information is often scarce in the larger nations.

We had to make two adjustments to accommodate for the scarcity of information in the written record. First of all, we had to limit ourselves to scoring each country in each category for each year from zero to four. A scale with more points would have meant that in some cases the information available would not allow a determination. Secondly, on three of our scales the determination is made on the basis of assessing the situation rather than in counting repressive occurrences or events. Thus, evaluating the situation, it is possible to utilize more sources and conduct a more intensive search for primary material where information is lacking.

No two regimes use the same combination of means to repress their populations, which raises the question of conceptual equivalents and weighting of different categories of repression. The four measures of repression are highly correlated (as can be seen in the correlation matrices in Table 1), but they do not scale. In other words, regimes that are high on one dimension tend to be high on other dimensions, though some will be more advanced on one dimension and others more advanced on different dimensions. Regimes vary in their style of repression, and the differences appear over time not only within nations but between them. The regime of Juan Perón in Argentina, for instance, was particularly harsh on the press. Succeeding governments were relatively lenient with the media, but continued to arrest individuals in large numbers and treated the Peronist parties as ruthlessly as Perón had treated the opposition parties in his administration. Perhaps the problem can best be demonstrated by comparing two national repression scores. Brazil had a score of thirty-nine for the decade of the 1950s and Colombia had the same score for the decade of the 1960s (see Table 2). The basis of their scores, however, is quite different. Brazil seldom invoked emergency powers or states of siege, whereas Colombia was under practically a continuous state of siege. Arrests and treatment of political parties were similar, but Brazil often exercised control of the press and Colombia did not. Is the score achieved in the

Table 1. Correlations between Repression Indicators, 1950–1970

Indicators	1950s					1960s				
	1	2	3	4	5	1	2	3	4	5
1. Suspension of constitutional rights	1.00					1.00				
2. Arrests, exiles, and executions	.85	1.00				.86	1.00			
3. Restrictions on political parties	.84	.92	1.00			.87	.88	1.00		
4. Censorship of the media	.89	.89	.84	1.00		.82	.87	.94	1.00	
5. Combined	.96	.94	.92	.94	1.00	.94	.95	.97	.95	1.00
1950 Scores						.58	.51	.41	.38	.57

one manner equivalent to the score achieved in another? Should states of siege and treatment of the press be weighted equally or differently? We decided to weigh each form of repression equally. The high correlation between the separate forms of repression as shown in Table 1 indicated to us that the cases where different weighting would change the results were relatively rare. The most important reason for combining the various aspects of repression was that preliminary regression analysis suggested that the independent variables we used explained a larger amount of the variation in the combined index than in the separate indexes and that the relationship between the independent variables and each of the different repression indexes was very similar. These results proved to us that one kind of repression would substitute for another, and that if we wanted to analyze a nation's repression in its entirety we needed to look at all forms of it together.

In the case of Castro's Cuba, however, we decided that repression was not conceptually equivalent to that of other Latin American countries. We did not, therefore, include Cuba's scores in the analysis, though its 1960 scores are listed in parentheses on the tables.

Before deciding on the criteria for scoring countries on repression, we first collected information for the 1960s on all forms of repression, including some categories not later included. This information was examined for coherent patterns, and then the criteria for scoring were developed. The criteria were refined as the scores were given, one category and one year at a time to each country. The score for a ten-year period, then, was based on forty separate judgments (the four repression indicators times 10). These criteria were then used for the collection of information on the 1950s. Information collection and scoring were done by one author and then checked by the other.

SUSPENSION OF CONSTITUTIONAL GUARANTEES AND OTHER INTERFERENCES WITH JUDICIAL PROCESS

One of the ways in which governments in Latin America have repressed individuals is by threatening them with arbitrary arrest and detention. Latin American constitutions grant the individual the basic rights of due process. These assure him that if he is arrested he will know why and be able to defend himself. At the same time, however, these constitutions allow the suspension of these rights in time of foreign invasion or internal disorder. The most common term for the suspension of constitutional rights is "state of siege," but some constitutions make no formal reference to the term. A less severe form is "state of emergency" and a more severe form is "martial law." These conditions are formally decreed and publicly announced. In the twenty years between 1950 and 1970, all Latin American nations have had recourse to states of siege for situations of internal security. Paraguay has been under nearly a constant state of siege.

The wording of the constitutional provisions allowing for the suspension of guarantees, and even the term for such suspension, varies from country to country. Even so, the Organization of American States Commission of Human Rights has found that an underlying similarity exists between all Latin American states on this question. Its study deserves to be quoted at length:

> In general . . . the most significant aspect of the state of siege, the one on which virtually all American states are in accord, is that the right to freedom from arbitrary arrest and detention is incompatible with national security in times of emergency. The executive is accorded the right to arrest and detain citizens without adhering to the ordinary safeguards of immediate arraignment, right to counsel, right to be impartially judged, right to habeas corpus, and other rights usually accorded the accused. The gravity of this exception is underscored when we recall that the entire foundation for individual security, essential to the functioning of a democracy, is rooted in the individual citizen's knowledge that he cannot be arrested and detained at the whim of public authorities. When individual security is gone, the confidence to enjoy the other freedoms disappears with it.[1]

[1]Organization of American States, *Preliminary Study of the State of Siege and the Protection of Human Rights in the Americas*, OEA/Series 50/5/2.8 (Sept. 17, 1963), P. 27.

It might be added that when the state of siege is in effect it is also much more difficult to find out who has been arrested. Party leaders and publishers are also more guarded in their actions. It seems necessary, then, to include the suspension of constitutional guarantees in our operationalization of repression. The basic similarity between the constitutions in Latin America makes the concept of this form of repression roughly equivalent from country to country. There are, however, important differences between the countries in what rights are suspended and which organ has the authority to suspend them. These differences mean that the equivalence is only approximate, not exact. For the most part, these differences have not been taken into account in our scoring. In two cases, however, constitutional provisions give the head of state powers that go a long way toward nullifying the constitutional guarantees even when they have not been officially suspended. These flagrant variations were taken into account in the scoring. In other more extreme cases, the formal suspension of guarantees is meaningless because the regime simply ignores the constitution and this situation was also taken into account.

Nicaragua and El Salvador have made relatively little use of the state of siege powers in their constitutions because the constitutions grant the executive sufficient arbitrary power in normal situations. In El Salvador the constitution grants jurisdiction over civilians to military courts in cases of treason, espionage, rebellion, sedition, or "other offenses against the peace or independence of the State."[2] In Nicaragua, the constitution gives discretion to the president "to detain persons for a period of up to ten days, 'or to order their confinement' apparently without time limits if, in his opinion, such is necessary."[3] He does not need to declare a state of siege or state of emergency to invoke this provision; all that is necessary is for him to believe that "the public tranquility is threatened." In both El Salvador and Nicaragua, we need additional information in order to find out how repressive situations there compare with those in other countries. To our knowledge, no one has ever studied the use of these constitutional provisions in these two countries. Both still have found it useful to declare states of siege, indicating that the executive feels somewhat constrained by the constitutional guarantees. We have hedged on the side of underestimating their levels of repression and added only one point to their scores in this category.

As long as the judicial procedures still operate in a country and the government follows the constitutional provisions with its built-in

[2]Ibid., p. 64.
[3]Ibid., p. 74.

checks on the state of siege, arbitrariness has its limits. Once, however, the government goes outside the constitution entirely and destroys the judicial procedures by turning over the judicial function to secret police or to "unofficial" bands, the system becomes completely arbitrary. Rafael Trujillo was notorious for his arrangement of automobile accidents and the use of thugs to eliminate opposition. More recently, the government of Guatemala has allowed, or perhaps encouraged, the formation of right-wing gangs to assassinate numerous persons suspected of being associated with the guerrilla opposition. Duvalier's use of the Tontons Macoutes in Haiti followed a similar pattern. We consider these cases to be the most severe examples of the suspension of constitutional guarantees.

When the major exceptions mentioned above are taken into account, the two basic criteria for scoring in this category of repression are these: (1) how far, geographically, the suspension of constitutional guarantees applies within a country, and (2) how long it applies. The criteria for scoring this dimension for each year are as follows:

0– No report of any suspension of constitutional rights or intervention in the judiciary for internal purposes.

1– Constitutional rights are suspended only temporarily (less than thirty days for entire country or less than sixty days for one part of the country) and no reported intervention with judiciary.

2– Suspension of constitutional rights for more than thirty days but less than nine months for whole country or more than sixty days for part of country. No intervention with judiciary and legal procedures followed.

3– Suspension of constitutional rights for more than nine months for whole country, or intervention in the judiciary for the purpose of bypassing constitution, or both.

4– Legal procedures dispensed with entirely as military, secret police or "unofficial" gangs replace judicial decisions for determining punishment. Such a situation may exist with or without the formal suspension of constitutional guarantees.

In the twenty-year period covered by this study, Costa Rica used the suspension of constitutional guarantees less than any other country. It invoked the state of emergency only briefly in 1955 when threatened by an invasion of "exiles" from Nicaragua. Chile made considerable use of the state of siege and the less severe state of emergency during its periodic labor disputes. When public order broke down in Uruguay in the last half of the 1960s, it also resorted to the suspension of constitutional guarantees. Nevertheless, the suspensions were of such short duration in these countries that an individual could assume that if he should be detained, he soon would be able to appeal to the judiciary.

Colombia has consistently scored higher on states of siege than on other dimensions of repression. One reason for its high score has been that the executive used these special powers to decree certain emergency economic legislation that it could not get through the congress. In order to keep this legislation in effect, it had to continue the state of siege. Nevertheless, the government at the same time used these powers to deal with the continuous armed revolt of guerrilla bands. We, therefore, felt no modification should be made in the scoring. Brazil, after 1964, provided another case where the evaluation was difficult. The suspension of constitutional guarantees was never formally made; instead, the military government ruled by a set of Institutional Acts that had the same effect. Also, during this period military courts were set up around the country to deal with "security" cases.

One thing that strikes the observer throughout Latin America is that the governments of the countries usually proclaim the suspension of constitutional guarantees when they feel the need of special powers. In spite of the cliché that constitutions in Latin America are meaningless, on this very important matter the governments follow their constitutions and one does not have a great deal of difficulty in defining the situation.

Arrests, Exiles and Executions

This category represents the active element of repression. In the other categories we are dealing with the way in which the government uses its power to set the rules to control opposition. Here we are dealing with what the government does to back up its rules. Threats of repression would be idle if it were not for the power to arrest and sentence individuals. We are concerned here not with all arrests and sentences but only with those that affect the freedom of political opponents. We consider any arrest, imprisonment, exile, or assassination of a person known for his political opposition to the regime as fitting into this category.

The mildest form of repression under this category occurs when the authorities arrest a number of students, labor leaders, or other groups "disturbing the political order," and then release them within a day or two. The situation is more serious when larger numbers are involved or the arrests are for a longer period of time. At this next level, we consider one or two political leaders in jail or in exile to be equivalent to the temporary arrest of a fairly large number of individuals.

When more than an occasional political leader is imprisoned or in exile, the situation becomes still more serious. We consider exile, a common practice in Latin America, as being equivalent to imprisonment, even though it seems to be the more civilized measure. It is possible, and in fact quite common, for exiles to form opposition political parties abroad, but it is difficult for them to do so while in prison. Many of the important parties have had their period of formation abroad: the AD *(Acción Democrática)* in Venezuela, Juan Bosch's PRD (Partido Revolucionario Dominicano) in the Dominican Republic, and Victor Raúl Haya de la Torre's APRA *(Alianza Popular Revolucionaria Americana)* in Peru. Nevertheless, in every one of the mentioned cases, the leaders who formed the parties would have had to fear for their lives if they returned to their homes.

Most Latin American countries do not have the death penalty, and official executions of political leaders are virtually unknown. Constitutions, however, have not prevented some governments from organizing or encouraging unofficial groups or secret police to do this dirty work. Automobile accidents have been known to occur under highly suspicious circumstances.

At the more extreme level of repression, it is hard to make distinctions on the basis of numbers. We decided at this level, then, to include only those cases where all political opposition was either dead, in prison, or in exile. The criteria used for scoring on arrests, exiles, and official assassinations are as follows:

0– No political arrests, exiles, or assassinations.
1– Only small-scale (less than ten per million), temporary arrests of one segment of the population for violation of public order when acting for political purposes.
2– Large number of temporary arrests (ten to fifty per million), an occasional long-term arrest or exile of a political leader, or both.
3– Mass arrests (more than fifty per million) with some held for more than a few months or exiled, or simply numerous political leaders imprisoned or in exile, or any case of assassination by "unofficial" groups where not prosecuted by the government. Some opposition groups are not affected.
4– Large number of political prisoners held or political leaders exiled. Leadership of all opposition political groups either dead, in prison, or in exile.

Few countries have gone for even a year without resorting to some arrests of the opposition. Uruguay in the 1950s, and Costa Rica and Chile in the 1960s have been the only countries where arrests have not occurred for several years. Chile and Uruguay, however, resorted to arrests of labor leaders during disputes, and Costa Rica arrested twelve students in 1968 before President Johnson's visit in order to prevent disturbances. Mexico provides an example of the difference between a score of one and a score of two. In that country, the occasional arrest of a political leader is fairly common, In 1958, however, the government rounded up a large number of strikers and kept the Communist artist David Alfaro Siqueiros and another opposition leader in jail for a much longer period. Mexico received a score of two in that year. Nicaragua is not well reported, but it received a score of two for most years because some opposition political leaders continued to live abroad. In 1956, however, when President Anastasio Somoza was assassinated, many opposition leaders were arrested and some held for several months, which gave Nicaragua a score of three for that year.

In Venezuela no publicity was given to the arrests made in the early 1960s by the democratic regime of Rómulo Betancourt. When the prisoners were released later in the decade, official announcements were made. The prisoners numbered in the hundreds. Similarly, Mexico resorted to long-term mass arrests of hundreds of students in 1968. The same scale of arrests existed in Bolivia in the 1950s but they were of the right-wing opposition rather than the left-wing opposition. The military governments of the late 1960s in Brazil and Argentina also reached similar levels of arrests.

The scale of arrests and exiles cannot be precisely ascertained in Paraguay. Calculations of the number of exiles range between 100,000 and 600,000, but most of these, it is agreed, left the country because economic opportunities were better in neighboring Argentina and Brazil. The number of political prisoners in Paraguay has been reported to be around 300. What is significant, however, is that all political leaders, even the very moderate ones, found it best to live abroad until 1966, when repression under Stroessner abated and some of them returned. In Haiti confusion about why many exiles were abroad also existed under Duvalier. All opposition leaders, though, were outside the country. Those who were not were eliminated.

RESTRICTIONS ON POLITICAL PARTIES

Opposition political parties ordinarily have as their major goal the replacement of the current regime by their own, either in the short or long term. Parties, then, provide the most explicit threat to the monopoly of rule by the incumbent regime. Understandably enough, competing for power, the opposition political parties in Latin America criticize the policies and persons of the government in power, suggest alternative policies, and, to a lesser or greater degree, question the integrity of the current social order. The temptation is great, then, for the leaders in power to prevent the formation and activity of some or all opposing political parties.

Even the democratic regimes are faced with a serious problem when certain opposition parties come into existence with the intention of overthrowing them. Of course, whether they actually would toss out the democratic rules if they came to power is always open to question. The majority of Latin American governments, nonetheless, have used such a possibility to justify the outlawing of Fascist and Communist parties. Some governments outlaw all "international" parties, which also denies the Christian Democrats the right to form a political organization. Where "extremist" political parties have never attracted the support of a large part of the population, and where prohibition of them does not interfere greatly with the dynamics of opposition, the mildest form of party repression was considered to exist. Only Uruguay and Chile in Latin America have allowed all political parties, even the "extremist" parties, the right to organize. All others place at least some restrictions on what kind of political organizations can be formed.

When larger groups of political organizations are suppressed or simply harassed, the free play between opposition and government is no longer possible. The regime can then be seen to be using coercion not just to maintain the democratic system but to maintain itself in power. At this next level of restrictions on political parties, major opposition is harassed rather than outlawed. Political organization becomes difficult but still possible. The difference between harassment and control is, of course, small, and the distinction is always difficult to make. We classified the populist authoritarian regimes of Juan Perón in Argentina and Gustavo Rojas Pinilla in Colombia as harassing regimes. Similarly, El Salvador and Honduras have fit into this category for a number of years.

At a certain point, harassment becomes control. When that happens, it can be stated categorically that no opposition political party will be allowed to organize a majority. When Manuel Odría suppressed APRA in Peru after 1948, he effectively prevented majority opposition to his regime. After 1965 the Brazilian military government took away the political rights of the principal opposition leaders and provided sufficient continuous control over the official opposition party to effectively prevent the majority from organizing a party. When the congress became recalcitrant anyway, the regime simply dissolved it and took away more political rights. At this level, some opposition continues to exist to organize mild criticism of the regime. Opposition is effectively tamed but not eliminated.

The most authoritarian regimes do not allow any organized opposition at all. Their desire for complete domination or their fear that small groups of political adversaries might grow into major groups of political adversaries makes them consider even tamed opposition as intolerable.

When the outlawing of political parties is temporary and little is done to destroy previous political leaders, the situation is clearly less serious than when repressive action is taken to annihilate the old parties at their very roots. Such was the situation in Guatemala between 1963 and 1965 and in Argentina between 1966 and 1971. They have been given the most severe classification, however, because, if the condition had continued, the parties would have died. The point is that the duration of repression over the years is as important in the elimination of opposition as the severity of repression in any one year.

Mexico has provided us with the most difficult situation to classify in the twenty-year period. Mexico allows the Communist Party to operate; however, through limitations on which parties can participate in the elections, it has prevented it from campaigning in elections. Opposition groups can organize, but they fail to grow because of the occasional use of coercive power and the much more constant use of the economic and social controls available to the government. Control of the opposition in Mexico is more subtle than elsewhere in Latin America. Originally, we defined the situation as belonging to the category where majorities were harassed, but the lack of evidence with which to back up this classification forced us to revise it to the first category where only extremes are prevented from operating.

The criteria used for the classification of restrictions on political parties were:

0– No restriction on the organization of a political party, but there may be some minimum requirements for the running of candidates.
1– "Extremist" groups with less than 10 percent of adult population as a following are not allowed to run candidates and legally organize political parties.
2– All but small extremist groups allowed to form political parties, but groups with large followings are harassed by restrictions on meetings and acts against leaders.
3– Control prevents the organization of a majority party. Major party or parties outlawed, many political leaders exiled or denied political rights. But, tame opposition is permitted.
4– No opposition is allowed to organize a political party.

Censorship of the Press and Other Media

Communication is an indispensable part of the working of all social systems. Complex societies require mass communication, and it is nearly impossible to mobilize opposition without the use of public media. Governments wishing to restrict opposition in Latin America have repeatedly acted to deny the public media to the opposition. The mass media include radio, television, and the press, but in the period dealt with in our study, television was of only minor significance in most Latin American nations. Radio was the most important media source.[4] Unfortunately, very little information is available on governmental control of radio broadcasting in Latin America. On the other hand, the world newspaper network, especially the Inter-American Press Association and the International Press Institute, have given wide publicity to violations of freedom of the establishment press. It is not unreasonable to assume that the control of radio corresponds closely to that of the press.

The press and media repression index correlated rather highly with the overall repression index. It seems, then, that the lack of information on the radio—as well as on the radical press—did not greatly distort the results. The media index correlates highest with the party index, indicating the close relation between parties and the press in Latin America.

Costa Rica is the only country for which no violations of press or other media freedom were reported during the twenty-year period. Chile and Uruguay imposed temporary controls from time to time, usually during their periodic labor crises. Mexico was not classified as completely free because the importation of newsprint was controlled to keep newspapers in line.

Few cases fell in between the category of very limited control of the media and much more severe restrictions. The pressure of the international guild system for press freedom may be effective in preventing even moderate longer term interference with the press. El Salvador was classified in this intermediate stage throughout its history because of the almost total lack of criticism of the government in the national press—for reasons that are still unclear. Other countries received this intermediate classification for occasional years.

The populist authoritarian regimes of Perón and Rojas Pinilla, and more recently the reform military government of Peru, furnish the most typical cases of strong but not complete control of the press. Both Perón and Rojas shut down newspapers with well-established reputations. Brazil's military regime, although it has not closed down any major newspapers, has effectively censored the press. In these situations, negative censorship is nearly complete. The press knows that if it publishes material considered offensive by the regime, it will be punished. This situation differs from the more extreme cases, however, in

[4]One study of Colombian elections found that two-thirds of the respondents considered the radio to be their most important source of information. Judith Campos and John McCamant, *Cleavage Shift in Colombia* (Beverly Hills; Sage Publications, 1972).

that restrictions are only negative. The independent press still decides for itself what it will print. In the more extreme cases, the government tells the press what to publish.

The criteria used for classifying press and other media repression are as follows:

0– No restrictions on newspapers or other media besides libel and slander laws.
1– Minor restrictions, such as banning the publication of certain news for less than a week, use of import licenses to restrict the supply of newsprint.
2– Longer term restrictions on publication of some kinds of political information. Banning of Communist or other minority press.
3– Censorship of all political news, but decision on news selection remains in private hands. Closure of major newspapers.
4– Government directs what news shall be published. All other news excluded.

The press repression index turned out to have a lower average score than did the other repression indexes, and it was lower in the 1960s than in the 1950s. This finding could be the result of the way in which the index was constructed. Yet the index does seem to reflect some fairly specific differences in repression patterns. Argentina and Colombia, for instance, gave considerable freedom to the press after the populist authoritarian regimes were overthrown even while the new governments were restricting other freedoms. In these cases, the established press shared the governments' intense hatred of the leaders of the previous regimes. It may also be that the international guild system, which has no counterpart in the protection of other freedoms, has been successful in moderating press repression.[5]

PATTERNS OF REPRESSION

The results of our scoring of repression are given in Table 2, and they show one thing dramatically: the enormous variation between and within countries. Latin America has had some of the freest nations in the world and some of the most repressive. Such descriptions have only limited validity, however, because most of the states in Latin America have experienced considerable variation in repression over the twenty-year period. Descriptive stereotypes should not be imposed on either the area or on countries; rather, one should speak of patterns of variation.

[5]Mary A. Gardner claims as much in her *The Inter-American Press Association: Its Fight for Freedom of the Press, 1926-1960* (Austin: University of Texas Press, 1967).

Table 2. Annual Repression Scores, 1950–1969

Country	'50	'51	'52	'53	'54	'55	'56	'57	'58	'59	'60	'61	'62	'63	'64	'65	'66	'67	'68	'69	Total
Uruguay	0	2	0	0	2	0	1	2	0	0	0	2	0	0	0	5	1	1	6	7	29
Costa Rica	5	4	3	3	3	4	3	3	2	2	1	1	1	1	1	1	0	1	2	1	43
Chile	5	5	3	3	4	5	7	7	1	1	1	3	2	0	2	1	0	2	0	3	55
Mexico	3	3	4	3	4	3	3	4	4	3	3	4	3	3	3	3	3	4	6	4	70
Ecuador	4	1	3	7	3	4	5	1	0	3	1	4	1	7	7	7	6	2	3	3	72
Panama	3	6	4	4	4	6	4	3	6	5	1	3	1	1	2	2	4	1	6	11	77
Honduras	4	4	4	3	5	5	7	1	3	5	1	1	1	7	10	6	5	5	5	6	86
Peru	9	9	9	9	9	9	8	4	3	5	1	3	5	5	3	6	3	1	8	4	113
Brazil	4	4	3	3	3	6	6	3	4	3	2	4	2	4	9	11	11	11	11	14	118
Nicaragua	5	5	5	5	7	6	10	8	6	10	6	8	5	5	4	4	4	7	4	5	119
Colombia	10	10	11	9	8	8	9	9	5	4	4	4	3	4	3	4	4	5	3	5	122
El Salvador	6	6	8	6	6	6	7	7	6	8	8	10	6	5	5	5	5	5	5	5	123
Bolivia	9	10	10	12	11	11	9	8	8	8	2	6	5	1	7	8	4	6	5	5	145
Guatemala	9	7	5	7	11	9	10	6	4	6	6	4	6	11	8	6	8	8	11	11	151
Venezuela	10	12	12	12	12	12	12	12	7	4	6	5	8	6	3	4	6	5	3	2	153
Argentina	8	9	10	10	10	11	8	8	7	9	7	6	7	8	1	4	9	8	10	12	162
Cuba[a]	3	2	7	9	5	5	9	11	11	6	(12)	(14)	(16)	(15)	(15)	(14)	(14)	(14)	(14)	(14)	(210)
Dominican Republic	16	16	16	16	16	16	16	16	16	16	16	12	5	7	7	9	5	7	7	8	243
Haiti	11	5	5	5	8	8	9	12	13	15	15	16	15	16	16	16	16	16	16	16	249
Paraguay	14	15	15	15	16	16	16	16	16	16	16	15	16	16	16	14	13	13	13	13	300

aFigures in parentheses indicate repression not functionally equivalent between Cuba and other Latin American nations in the 1960s.

39

Only four countries have varied in their annual scores by as little as five points out of a possible sixteen. Paraguay has been the most constant with a variation of three points, followed by Mexico and Costa Rica with four, and El Salvador with five. On the other hand, eight countries have varied by ten or more points during the twenty-year period. Cuba and Brazil have varied the most with a variation of twelve points, followed by Argentina, Bolivia, the Dominican Republic and Haiti, which have varied by eleven points. Constancy in repression seems to require regime stability. Paraguay has had stable dictatorship, Mexico stable one-party government, Costa Rica stable competitive elections, and El Salvador has had continuous military governments. Large increases in repression do not always follow the institution of military government; in fact, the largest increase was made by a civilian, François "Papa Doc" Duvalier. This variation within individual countries is taken up in detail in analyses later in this book.

Between 1950 and 1964, Uruguay's record was as free as any nation in the world. The government tolerated all political parties, kept a free and independent judiciary, and maintained press criticism. In 1965 Uruguay fell into more troubled times. Chile and Costa Rica, after having moderate restrictions on the opposition in the 1950s, enjoyed wider freedom in the 1960s. Mexico, while keeping a somewhat shorter rein on political opposition, granted considerable freedom. These four states would rank high on freedom in any scoring of all the nations of the world in any time period.

Where the freer countries of Latin America are different from the free countries of the North Atlantic region is in the tenuousness of the freedom. Freedom can easily be lost, and one can point out recent historical instances where it was threatened. Ecuador, Panama, and Honduras demonstrate the possibility of sudden fluctuations. All three had periods when they were considerably freer than Mexico, but the abrupt imposition of authoritarian regimes wiped out freedom, making their average scores somewhat higher than Mexico's.

The rest of Latin America has experienced even more severe or extended periods of repression. The difference in the ranking of the next ten nations is accounted for by the shortness of the interim of freedom. Peru and Brazil had periods of freedom that lasted more than ten years. Argentines and Cubans experienced only a few years of liberty. Nicaragua, Colombia, El Salvador, Bolivia, Guatemala, and Venezuela fall in between.

The levels of repression in the Dominican Republic, Haiti, and Paraguay over the twenty-year period are among the highest in the world. Repression was most severe under Trujillo in the Dominican Republic and under Duvalier in Haiti, but it was the most constant in

Paraguay. The Trujillo and the Duvalier regimes certainly compared with any so-called totalitarian regime in the severity of their repression. All opposition was ruthlessly eliminated. Life was enormously insecure. Adulation of the dictators was required. In these respects, the situation was worse than in Castro's Cuba. The difference between the "traditional" dictatorships of Trujillo and Duvalier and the rule of Castro was in the treatment of the masses. Duvalier and Trujillo left them alone if they accepted their poverty without complaint. Castro's regime has tried to elicit their cooperation and support and, at the same time, tried to lift their economic status. When treatment of political opposition is considered, however, the differences between them are slight.

The range of variation in repression in Latin America is very much like the range in all countries of the world in the years between 1950 and 1970. Most of Latin America's states were neither completely free nor completely repressive but had moderate levels of repression or fluctuated between extremes.

Leaving aside for the moment the vast differences between countries in the degree of repression, we have summarized the historical situation in Latin America in Figure 2 by multiplying each country's repression score by its proportion of Latin America's population and adding the results. Figure 2 combines number of people under repres-

Figure 2. Weighted Average of Repression in Latin America, 1950–1970 (Cuba not included)

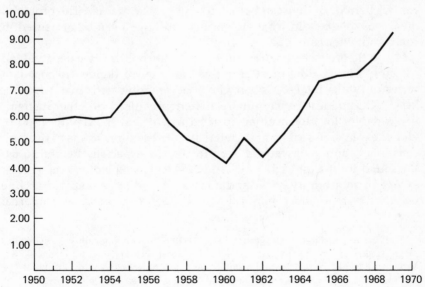

sion with the severity of that repression. The trend is not encouraging. By 1970, after eight years of the Alliance for Progress, more people were living under highly repressive regimes than at any other time in the twenty-year period. This expansion was not brought about by the situation in Cuba, which has few people and had fairly high levels of repression throughout, but by the right-wing regimes in Brazil and Argentina. The biggest impact was made by Brazil, which has one-third of the population of Latin America and went from a free situation to one of extreme repression.

The figure also shows that the period around 1960, when Tad Szulc wrote the *Twilight of the Tyrants*, proved to be only a temporary improvement. The optimism of that moment was not warranted. The extrapolation of the curve brought an erroneous prediction. One needed to know much more about the conditions that brought about repression in order to be able to predict its trend.

Violence

Violence, whether directed against the society at large, institutions of the society, or the government of the society, is a manifestation of social disintegration. But what does violence mean in empirical terms? To answer that question the variable of violence must be operational-ized so that: (a) it becomes a meaningful term, and (b) the relative degree of violence experienced by each Latin American country over various periods of time can be stated with some certainty. The problem, then, was to ascertain what violence is and how it can be measured in comparative terms?

The theoretical literature on violence in politics is extensive and growing. Perhaps the most ambitious attempt to define violence is a series of works by Ted Robert Gurr, culminating with his *Why Men Rebel*.[6] Gurr's ideas concerning relative deprivation and other instigat-ing variables for violence have proved useful, but his classification of violence (or "civil strife," as he terms it) into the three forms of turmoil, conspiracy, and civil war did not prove to be especially helpful to us. We found it difficult to distinguish between Gurr's various categories, except on an arbitrary basis, and there appeared to be no dividing line between turmoil and conspiracy, or between conspiracy and internal

[6]Princeton: Princeton University Press, 1970. Probably the other most explicit categorization of violence in Latin America has been accomplished by Douglas Bwy, particularly in his article "Political Instability in Latin America: The Cross-Cultural Test of a Causal Model," *Latin American Research Review* (Spring, 1968), pp. 17–66.

war. Further, we felt that the inclusion of coups as indicators of violence was, in the Latin American context, misleading. Most coups are accomplished without violence and may in fact be considered an institutionalized method for changing governments in countries such as Ecuador.

Faced with the difficulties inherent in previous attempts to measure the level of violence in Latin America, we decided to construct our own index of violence. It is an events-scoring index, that is, it measures actual occurrences within certain categories that took place in twenty Latin American countries from 1950 to 1970. A close examination of these particular events revealed two important things that were helpful in creating our measurement yardstick. First, violence appeared to be a logical manifestation of social disintegration—violence, that is, directed in opposition to the society or to parts of it. By considering only violence that indicated an opposition to something within the society we negated to some degree, of course, cultural differences in attitudes toward violence. Societies generally, and governments particularly, do not condone violence against the system, even though they might condone interpersonal violence. Thus, incongruities among societies are somewhat mitigated. Second, violent opposition appeared to be of two major types, armed and unarmed. People, in opposing a system, either armed themselves and embarked upon a course of guerrilla warfare or encountered the troops in the streets; or they relied more on mass demonstrations, strikes, and other means of causing pressure. Armed violence includes bombings and other terrorist acts, assassinations of public officials, riots in which the rioters are armed and fire on public authorities, urban and rural guerrilla warfare, and any other attacks on public officials or the public order. Unarmed violence consists of demonstrations, riots in which the rioters are essentially unarmed and in which gunfire comes primarily from public authorities, and strikes that have an overwhelming political content. In any case, there appears to be a logical dichotomy between the armed and unarmed opposition that can be operationalized. Because media reports almost invariably stated whether those opposing the system were armed or not, we were able to classify opposition as armed or unarmed; utilizing the criteria described above, we then placed events into one of these two classifications.

An annual armed opposition score was arrived at for each country. The number of days of armed opposition were counted, the number was then scaled with increasingly larger intervals, and the resultant index number was given a weight of two out of a total of four points (or fifty percent of the total armed opposition score of four). After going over the data, we found that we could come up with a fairly precise figure for the number of casualties (killed or wounded) for armed opposition, and that this number was a good representation of the intensity of the armed opposition. Casualties per ten million population for each country were included as part of the final score for armed opposition. This index was given a weight of one (or twenty-five percent of the final armed opposition score). The major reason for reducing the weight given to the casualties index vis-à-vis the days index was that, even with the information sources at our disposal, the casualty figure reported by the media were less reliable and more fragmentary than the reported number of days of opposition. As indicated, casualties per ten million population were used in order to adjust the figures for population differences among the various countries. Finally, we counted the number of participants per one million population in each act of armed violence, scaling them with increasing intervals, and gave the resultant index a weight of one in the final armed violence score (twenty-five percent of the total score). The number of people participating in armed violence in a country in a given year gives a good indication of precisely how widespread armed violence is throughout the population. Again, the major reason for the lower weight of this subindex was the relative absence of accurate media reports on number of participants in armed violence.

After each index was constructed, the three indexes described above were combined, given the weights indicated, and a total index of armed opposition was produced. The criteria for scoring each of the indexes for each year are given in Table 3.

UNARMED VIOLENCE

Unarmed violence consists of riots (in which the rioters were not armed, or at least did not use their armaments); demonstrations against the government or some other salient feature of the society; strikes which had as their main element a type of political protest; and various kinds of student demonstrations.

Reports on incidents of unarmed violence very rarely contained information on the number of casualties, so this part of the armed violence score was not included in the index of unarmed violence. Instead, a two-part index was constructed, using number of days of unarmed opposition per year, again using increasing intervals. This information was combined with the estimated number of participants (again controlling for population differences) in the unarmed violence. The number of days of reported unarmed opposition was given a weight of two (or two-thirds of the final score of three), whereas the number of participants was given a weight of one (or one-third of the

Table 3. Criteria for Armed Violence Measurement

1. *Number of Days of Reported Armed Opposition*
   (weight of 2)

0—No days	5—50 to 75 days
1—1 to 5 days	6—75 to 100 days
2—5 to 10 days	7—100 to 150 days
3—10 to 25 days	8—150 to 200 days
4—25 to 30 days	9—More than 200 days

2. *Casualties per 10,000,000 Population*
   (weight of 1)

0—None	5—20 to 30
1—1 to 5	6—30 to 50
2—5 to 10	7—50 to 100
3—10 to 15	8—100 to 200
4—15 to 20	9—More than 200

3. *Number of Participants per 1,000,000 Population*
   (weight of 1)

0—None	5—50 to 100
1—1 to 5	6—100 to 200
2—5 to 10	7—200 to 500
3—10 to 25	8—500 to 1,000
4—25 to 50	9—More than 1,000

final score). Again, the reporting on the number of days was more accurate than that on the number of participants. Finally, a total index of unarmed opposition was determined. Criteria, plus the scales used for conversion, are shown in Table 4.

As finally computed, the two indexes of violence are illustrative of trends, and can be compared internally on a national basis over time. They are not, as raw scores, strictly comparable with each other because the armed violence index contains four ingredients and the index for unarmed violence three. In other words, there is a weighting bias in favor of the armed violence index in the ratio of four to three.

The violence indexes yielded some interesting patterns, one bˆing that certain countries tend toward one type of violence. The population of some countries—Bolivia, Colombia, Cuba, Guatemala, Haiti, Honduras, Nicaragua, Paraguay, and Venezuela—tended more toward armed violence as a means of expressing its dissatisfaction. On the other hand, Chile alone had a much higher incidence of unarmed over armed opposition during the twenty-year period. Other countries—

Table 4. Criteria for Unarmed Violence Measurement

1. *Number of Days of Reported Unarmed Opposition (weight of 2)*

0—No days	5—20 to 25 days
1—1 to 5 days	6—25 to 30 days
2—5 to 10 days	7—30 to 40 days
3—10 to 15 days	8—40 to 50 days
4—15 to 20 days	9—More than 50 days

2. *Number of Participants per 1,000,000 Population (weight of 1)*

0—None	5—25,000 to 50,000
1—1 to 100	6—50,000 to 100,000
2—100 to 1,000	7—100,000 to 200,000
3—1,000 to 10,000	8—200,000 to 500,000
4—10,000 to 25,000	9—More than 500,000

Argentina, Brazil, Ecuador, Mexico, Panama, and Peru—presented a mixed picture, with armed and unarmed opposition about equal. Costa Rica, which experienced a moderate amount of violence during the 1950s, had practically none during the 1960s, with one minor demonstration in 1969 marring an otherwise perfect record of nonviolence.

A further analysis of violence totals indicates that certain countries exhibit certain norms regarding types of violence that are almost institutionalized. Argentines tend heavily toward strikes and mass unarmed demonstrations as a means of expressing discontent, as do the Uruguayans. In Bolivia and Colombia, on the other hand, rural guerrilla warfare seems to be the accepted means of opposition, although much of this violence can hardly be described as an organized guerrilla operation. Rather, disaffected peasants or workers, usually in some provincial city or rural area, take up arms against the authorities simply because they are unhappy over the local situation, because they feel slighted by government action or inaction, because violence has always been the modus operandi, or simply (as one author has suggested) because they are bored. Obviously, both anomie and alienation must exist to a high degree among Bolivians and Colombians. For both, armed violence and guerrilla warfare are undoubtedly facilitated by the terrain, which is conducive to local uprisings and which makes national control of the provinces difficult. The continuing weakness of the Bolivian government and the geographical limitation of its effectiveness to a few relatively urban areas on the *altiplano* also contributes to the continuing armed violence in Bolivia. In Colombia violence which began as a liberal-conservative "war" during the late 1940s and the 1950s degenerated, for the most part, into senseless killings by armed bands that roam the countryside. Perhaps Bolivian and Colombian societal norms favor the use of guns more than do Argentine and Uruguayan norms. We suspect that this is the case, and that a "gun culture" exists in Bolivia and Colombia much as it does in certain parts of the United States. In Guatemala and Venezuela, urban terrorism and guerrilla warfare prevail over other types of violence, although in both countries strong rural guerrilla movements have also existed. Most of Haiti's violence has emanated from the operations of exile groups landing on its shores; for this reason Haiti's violence has been even more erratic than that of most Latin American countries. In the neighboring Dominican Republic, almost all of the considerable violence that has occurred has been concentrated in and around the capital city, whereas in Mexico most of the violence has taken place in the outlying provinces. Other nations do not exhibit such sharp anomalies.

A comparison of trends in violence over time also yields some interesting intranational comparisons. One is the change in Argentina from a preponderance of armed violence during the 1950s and early part of the 1960s, to a preponderance of unarmed violence during the last five years of the sixties. Other countries have also revealed this tendency toward a relative increase in the amount of unarmed violence. Costa Rica, which had comparatively high totals of armed violence during the 1950s, had much more unarmed opposition during the last half of the 1960s; Ecuador witnessed a similar turnabout, although its global totals were much higher than those for Costa Rica. The relationship between armed and unarmed opposition underwent a corresponding change in Mexico much earlier, in the mid-1950s. Other nations— Brazil, Chile, El Salvador, and Peru—moved in an opposite direction, however: toward increased armed violence compared with unarmed opposition. Still others failed to exhibit any clear trends toward one type of violence.

We analyzed armed and unarmed violence separately, but for a number of reasons we have not reported the results separately. Conceptually, both forms represent a disruption of and a protest against political and social conditions. Empirically, the two forms were moderately associated (see Table 7) and, perhaps more importantly, the independent variables (discussed in Chapters 3 and 4) were associated in the same way with both and tended to explain the larger amount of the variation in the combined score than of the separate scores. For the sake of parsimony, then, analysis in the following chapters deals only with the measure of both forms of violence combined.

Table 5. Annual Armed and Unarmed Violence Scores, 1950–1969

Country		'50	'51	'52	'53	'54	'55	'56	'57	'58	'59	'60	'61	'62	'63	'64	'65	'66	'67	'68	'69	Total
Argentina	(A)	3	7	3	7	8	24	13	6	4	6	13	4	12	11	7	7	7	0	4	7	153
	(U)	3	4	3	3	4	10	4	6	6	6	3	8	8	4	7	9	18	6	5	19	136
Bolivia	(A)	17	10	20	10	10	5	8	6	15	18	22	12	4	10	21	17	2	29	8	9	253
	(U)	5	4	6	4	0	0	4	4	4	4	3	5	3	3	9	7	3	3	4	4	79
Brazil	(A)	4	3	0	3	5	0	4	3	4	3	4	0	6	3	11	5	3	5	7	4	77
	(U)	3	4	4	3	4	0	0	3	3	3	2	2	3	2	5	2	4	2	6	3	53
Chile	(A)	0	0	4	0	0	0	0	12	4	0	0	2	0	3	2	3	0	3	8	7	48
	(U)	5	4	2	0	3	7	4	3	2	0	1	3	4	3	0	4	2	2	1	4	60
Colombia	(A)	10	13	20	13	12	11	18	13	16	18	7	20	18	17	22	17	14	13	7	9	288
	(U)	3	2	2	0	3	0	4	4	3	0	2	0	0	3	0	5	4	2	2	4	43
Costa Rica	(A)	8	4	0	0	10	11	0	5	0	5	0	0	0	0	0	0	2	0	0	0	45
	(U)	3	0	0	0	3	0	0	0	0	0	0	0	0	0	0	0	0	0	0	4	10
Cuba[a]	(A)	3	6	9	13	7	8	22	29	33	19											149
	(U)	3	3	4	4	3	4	0	3	3	6											37
Dominican Republic	(A)	0	0	0	0	0	0	0	0	0	13	7	4	7	12	0	35	16	8	4	2	108
	(U)	0	0	0	0	0	0	0	0	0	0	2	7	5	5	5	6	6	2	2	3	43
Ecuador	(A)	3	4	6	10	2	5	10	0	0	17	5	13	6	11	4	7	5	0	0	4	110
	(U)	2	3	4	0	2	4	0	0	0	4	2	4	3	0	3	6	4	3	3	3	51
El Salvador	(A)	0	0	0	0	0	0	0	0	0	4	3	17	7	0	0	3	0	7	5	0	42
	(U)	0	0	0	0	0	0	0	0	0	2	3	4	5	2	0	0	0	0	3	0	23
Guatemala	(A)	13	10	3	10	23	10	11	6	0	8	16	7	20	15	15	16	18	19	27	9	256
	(U)	4	5	0	0	3	4	0	4	0	4	5	3	5	2	0	16	2	2	2	2	53
Haiti	(A)	0	0	0	0	3	0	4	16	11	20	6	13	5	21	0	4	12	14	15	13	174
	(U)	0	3	0	0	0	0	5	7	3	4	2	4	0	0	0	13	0	0	0	0	28
Honduras	(A)	3	0	0	0	9	0	17	10	0	21	14	0	13	21	4	3	0	0	5	0	130
	(U)	0	0	0	0	4	3	3	4	0	3	6	0	6	9	2	3	0	0	0	4	47

Mexico	(A)	0	4	10	6	6	0	0	4	5	3	6	4	4	0	5	5	5	5	2	75
	(U)	0	3	5	4	3	3	2	3	2	5	2	3	4	3	2	2	2	9	3	65
Nicaragua	(A)	0	0	0	10	0	6	3	0	11	17	15	12	0	0	0	0	22	0	0	96
	(U)	0	0	0	0	0	0	3	0	4	4	2	0	2	4	1	3	3	3	3	25
Panama	(A)	0	3	0	0	14	0	7	0	19	14	3	3	6	0	0	0	0	10	5	87
	(U)	0	5	4	0	0	3	0	0	5	5	2	3	2	4	4	0	0	5	0	43
Paraguay	(A)	0	0	0	19	6	0	0	0	6	14	18	0	0	4	0	0	0	0	0	89
	(U)	0	0	0	0	3	0	0	0	0	5	0	0	0	4	0	0	0	0	3	17
Peru	(A)	18	0	0	7	0	10	0	0	6	0	0	3	6	0	20	0	0	0	3	83
	(U)	4	0	0	0	4	0	6	2	5	0	0	6	6	0	0	4	2	3	3	46
Uruguay	(A)	0	0	0	0	0	0	0	0	0	0	0	5	3	0	5	2	3	3	2	42
	(U)	0	0	0	0	0	0	0	0	0	0	3	5	3	0	5	3	2	8	17	39
Venezuela	(A)	4	3	12	0	0	0	12	0	21	15	15	14	23	22	18	8	17	11	9	227
	(U)	3	0	0	0	0	3	5	3	9	4	9	4	4	3	2	2	0	2	3	57

[a]Violence data for Cuba for the 1960s were not available.

49

In combining the two forms, we had to make sure that the addition of the numbers would not lead to numerical distortions. The means and standard deviations of the two indexes were different because of the ways in which the two indexes were constructed. Combining them as they were would give armed violence a greater weight, with the weight varying from case to case. In order to combine them without distortion, it was necessary to put them in a form where both the means and the standard deviations were the same. Standard (or Z) scores all have the same mean of zero and the same standard deviation of one. Any index can be converted to standard scores by subtracting the mean from each score and dividing the result by the standard deviation. With both indexes in standardized form, they can then be added without distortion.

Standard scores solve the problem of unwanted distortion, but they do not solve the problem of weight. Does unarmed violence represent the same amount of social disintegration as armed violence? No mathematical procedure can answer that question. In our estimation, however, armed violence was the stronger indicator of social disintegration; furthermore, giving it extra weight increased the explanatory power of the analysis. We therefore assigned armed violence a weight of one and one-half against a weight of one for unarmed violence. To arrive at a total violence score, in other words, each standardized score of armed violence was multiplied by 1.5 and then added to the standardized score of unarmed violence. Standardized scores for violence in Latin America are shown in Table 6.

A ranking of the twenty nations of Latin America in terms of total violence for the decades of the 1950s and the 1960s reveals six countries that experienced considerably more violence than the rest of Latin America. Argentina, Bolivia, Colombia, Guatemala, and Venezuela all had extremely positive standard scores for the twenty-year period (as did Cuba for the fifties), whereas the rest of the Latin American nations were negative with the exception of Haiti, which was only slightly positive. Four countries—Paraguay, Uruguay, El Salvador, and Costa Rica—had substantially less violence than other Latin American nations.

The greatest increase in violence from the 1950s to the 1960s occurred in the Dominican Republic. Uruguay, Venezuela, and El Salvador also had substantial increases in violence between the decades. The greatest decreases were in Costa Rica, Panama, and Paraguay.

We have already alluded to the fact that a relationship exists between cultures and types of violence, whether it be the armed-unarmed differential in Argentina and Bolivia, or the guerrilla warfare-mass demonstration differential in Guatemala and Panama. A relation-

Table 6. Total Violence Scores

	1950s					1960s					Twenty-Year Total
	Armed		Unarmed		Total	Armed		Unarmed		Total	
	Raw	Z	Raw	Z	Z[a]	Raw	Z	Raw	Z	Z[a]	Z[a]
Cuba	149	2.15	37	1.31	2.01	72	.01	87	3.18	1.70	2.52
Argentina	81	.54	49	2.24	1.35	134	1.32	44	.82	1.50	2.45
Bolivia	119	1.44	35	1.16	1.47	144	1.53	22	−.39	1.04	1.99
Colombia	144	2.03	21	.07	1.38	152	1.70	25	−.22	1.26	1.72
Guatemala	94	.85	28	.61	.84	154	1.75	33	.22	1.53	1.55
Venezuela	73	.35	24	.30	.37	123	1.09	6	−1.27	.25	.12
Haiti	51	−.17	22	.15	−.05	70	−.03	30	.05	.07	−.05
Honduras	60	.04	17	−.24	−.08	55	−.35	32	.16	−.13	−.23
Ecuador	55	−.08	19	−.09	−.09	40	−.67	38	.49	−.20	−.32
Mexico	35	−.55	27	.54	−.13						
Dominican Republic	13	−1.07	0	−1.56	−1.40	94	.47	43	.76	.82	−.53
Brazil	29	−.69	23	.22	−.36	48	−.50	30	.05	−.30	−.60
Peru	41	−.41	21	.07	−.24	42	−.63	25	−.22	−.54	−.70
Panama	57	−.03	22	.15	.05	33	−.81	21	−.44	−.93	−.78
Chile	20	−.91	30	.77	−.26	28	−.92	26	−.17	−.73	−.87
Nicaragua	44	−.34	8	−.94	−.64	52	−.41	20	−.50	−.51	−1.00
Paraguay	56	−.05	11	−.71	−.35	33	−.81	6	−1.27	−1.22	−1.36
Uruguay	0	−1.38	0	−1.56	−1.60	42	−.63	39	.55	−.14	−1.50
El Salvador	0	−1.38	2	−1.40	−1.53	42	−.63	21	−.44	−.65	−1.87
Costa Rica	43	−.36	6	−1.09	−.72	2	−1.47	4	−1.37	−1.78	−2.14

[a] Added scores are always restandardized and hence are not the sum of the component scores.

ship also exists, however, between violence and repression levels. Haiti is perhaps the best example of the effect an extremely repressive regime can have on the type of violence within a country. Approximately 95 percent of Haiti's violence has been armed, almost all of it in the nature of guerrilla warfare. Unarmed opposition during the 1950s was not uncommon, but as the Duvalier regime became more oppressive, the opposition to it became increasingly clandestine. From 1965 to 1970 there were no published reports of unarmed opposition to the Duvalier regime. Extremely repressive regimes are not likely to allow open and peaceful opposition; they thereby create the nature of the opposition. Opposing forces must, perforce, express their opposition through covert means and use arms to protect themselves as best they can. This has been the case in Haiti, and to a slightly lesser degree in Guatemala, Paraguay, and Bolivia. In these nations, regimes exhibiting high degrees of repression have contributed substantially to the type, if not the amount, of opposition expressed within their borders.

Finally, in order to talk about trends in violence in Latin America, it was necessary to weight the national raw scores by population, as we did with repression. The weighted and aggregated Latin American scores for each kind of violence are shown in Figure 3. The higher

Figure 3.   Weighted Average of Armed and Unarmed Violence in Latin America, 1950–1970 (Cuba not included)

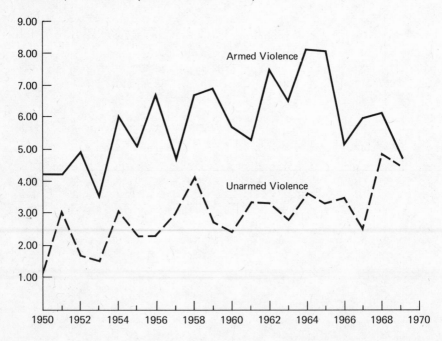

position of armed violence on the figure is due to the way in which the two violence indexes were constructed. The year 1950 was the twenty-year low for violence of both kinds, and both armed and unarmed violence totals were greater during the 1960s than in the 1950s. Armed violence peaked in 1964 and 1965 when Brazil, the largest country in Latin America, was experiencing considerable violence. Unarmed violence peaked a few years later, when totals in Argentina, Brazil, Mexico, and Uruguay had increased considerably over earlier figures. Both indexes ended the decade on the downswing, although yearly totals at the end of the 1960s were higher than at any time prior to 1966. These high levels, plus the rather erratic movements of the indexes, precluded making any optimistic predictions from what may be a short cyclical movement.

THE AGGREGATION OF INDEXES

The four types of repression and the two types of violence represent different forms or manifestations of political and social disintegration. They are negative indicators of social cohesion. More of any one of them suggests protest and thwarted protest against some aspect of the social and political condition. In a sense, then, they represent one concept. They also represent, however, different things. Some societies repress all forms of social protest—armed or unarmed—whereas others hesitate to curtail public liberties even though discontent is comparatively high. A basic question facing all empirical research is which concepts concerning the variables being considered should be combined and which should be separated. Where should the line be drawn between aggregation and disaggregation of concepts?

The goal of analysis is explanation. The criteria for determining when to aggregate, then, must arise out of the problem of explanation. If combining variables allows greater explanation, then one should aggregate. The first criterion for combining must be conceptual similarity. If two variables have nothing conceptually in common, it is nonsense to combine them. Our problem is that our variables have some things conceptually in common and some things distinct. We could justify either putting them together or leaving them separate.

Correlation analysis offered information that helped us to make a choice. On repression, we decided to aggregate the indexes of four different kinds partly because they were very highly correlated. Table 7 presents the intercorrelation between the two types of violence, a combined violence score, and a repression score for each decade. Unarmed violence and armed violence have a correlation coefficient of .62 in the 1950s and .16 in the 1960s. Unarmed violence in the 1960s is negatively correlated with repression, and armed violence is positively

Table 7. Correlations between Scores of Violence and Repression

	1950s and 1960s[a]							
	1	2	3	4	5	6	7	8
(1950s)								
1. Unarmed violence	1.00							
2. Armed violence	.62	1.00						
3. Combined violence	.85	.94	1.00					
4. Repression	.00	.21	.14	1.00				
(1960s)								
5. Unarmed violence	.48				1.00			
6. Armed violence		.69			.16	1.00		
7. Combined violence			.64		.64	.86	1.00	
8. Repression				.64	−.17	.30	.14	1.00

[a]Cuba's scores excluded.

correlated with repression; all correlations are quite low. The correlational analysis does not provide strong evidence in favor of combining indexes, but, at least in the case of the two violence scores, it would allow it.

The analyses in the following chapters provide evidence in favor of combining violence and repression into an index of social cohesion—and some evidence against doing so. In either event, of course, our interest is in determining which nations of Latin America have lower levels of violence and repression, and which have higher levels of a combined measure. We have operationalized the concept of social cohesion as being the relative absence of either violence or repression; a relatively high level of both reflects the opposite of social cohesion, social disintegration. Given the possibility of conceptual similarity between violence and repression, plus the fact that some independent variables have a higher correlation with the combined measure than with the separate measures, we decided to produce a combined measure of social cohesion in Latin America. To arrive at this combined measure, we simply added the Z, or standard, scores for violence and repression, calculated new Z scores for the combined measure, and changed signs from positive to negative (and vice versa) to indicate the positive aspect of social cohesion. Social cohesion scores for Latin America are shown in Table 8.

Two countries—Costa Rica and Uruguay—had substantially higher levels of social cohesion for the two decades than the rest of Latin America. Three countries—Argentina, Bolivia, and Haiti—experienced higher levels of social disintegration than other Latin American nations. These three together with Paraguay, Guatemala, Venezuela,

Table 8. Social Cohesion in Latin America

Country	1950s	1960s	Twenty-Year Score[a]
Costa Rica	1.11	2.02	1.47
Uruguay	2.11	.74	1.34
Chile	.65	1.27	.90
El Salvador	1.11	.45	.73
Panama	.38	1.09	.69
Mexico	.68	.54	.53
Ecuador	.70	.41	.52
Nicaragua	.47	.48	.45
Peru	.09	.72	.38
Honduras	.57	.18	.35
Brazil	.75	−.12	.30
Colombia	−1.14	−.33	−.69
Dominican Republic	−.58	−.93	−.71
Venezuela	−.83	−.80	−.77
Guatemala	−.60	−1.15	−.82
Paraguay	−1.19	−.61	−.85
Haiti	−.32	−1.84	−1.01
Bolivia	−1.41	−.80	−1.04
Argentina	−1.23	−1.32	−1.20
Cuba	−1.31	—	—

[a]All scores are standard.

the Dominican Republic, Colombia, and Cuba had substantially greater social disintegration than the rest of Latin America. As a geographical group, Mexico and the Central American countries (with the exception of Guatemala) had higher levels of social cohesion than the countries of South America. The Caribbean nations also fell into the group of countries experiencing high levels of social disintegration. Haiti and Uruguay experienced by far the greatest decrease in social cohesion from the 1950s to the 1960s; whereas Costa Rica, Colombia, Panama, Peru, Chile, Bolivia, and Paraguay all had higher levels of social cohesion in the second decade.

Figures 1 and 2, taken together, show that the level of social cohesion in Latin America was less in the 1960s than in the 1950s. Repression was still on the upswing at the end of the 1960s, though both armed and unarmed violence appeared to be diminishing, at least temporarily. The fascinating part of this analysis remains, however, the differences among the Latin American nations in social cohesion, rather than trends over time in the area.

CHAPTER 3

SOCIO-ECONOMIC EXPLANATIONS

Why do some Latin American countries have low levels of violence and repression while others have high levels? Why have some nations dropped from high to low levels as others have witnessed increases in the incidence of violence and repression? There is no simple answer. Any complete answer would need to take into account the simultaneous actions of several variables and the interactions between them. Even then, unpredictable and unmeasureable acts, chance events and conditions, or the leadership of individuals are likely to reduce the predictability of violence and repression. Nevertheless, one must begin to arrive at an answer with the consideration of single variables and their effects on violence and repression. Chapters 3 and 4 introduce a large number of independent variables that we suspect influence levels and changes in violence and repression.

In these two chapters we first consider why a theoretical relationship might exist between an independent variable and the dependent variables of violence and repression, and secondly we report the degree of association between variables measured by the correlation coefficient. The tentative acceptance of a relationship requires both logic and association.

One key issue that arises in such an analysis is what time periods should be used. Political violence and, to a lesser extent, repression have a sporadic quality to them. Discontent may seethe under the surface until some incident sparks a violent explosion, which may be followed by repression. Then, all is quiet again. Because we wanted to understand the underlying social conditions that lead to repression and violence rather than the incidents that ignite the explosions, we aggregated time into five-year and ten-year spans. After finding that the relationships were somewhat stronger for the ten-year periods, we decided, for the sake of simplicity, to report here on only ten-year time spans.

This chapter will discuss several socio-economic factors or variables: societal welfare and social mobilization and the differential between them; changes in welfare and mobilization; inequality and social stratification; and international economic dependency. These factors, which vary from society to society, may influence violence or repression or both directly through the satisfaction or discontent of individuals (and hence their disposition toward aggressive behavior) or indirectly through the provision of resources for political and social organizations and public policies.

Inasmuch as we are working for the most part with simple relationships between two variables in this and the next chapter, our conclusions depend on the assumption of *ceteris paribus*, or other things being equal. In a few cases we report partial correlations in order to check out the possibility of interactions with other variables. Most of the discussion of the interaction between independent variables is left to Chapter 5 where we combine variables in multiple regression analysis.

Societal welfare and social mobilization

The wealthy countries of the world do have, on the average, a lower level of violence and repression than do the poorer countries. This obvious association has led writers to conclude that economic development is one of the causes of "stable democracy."[1] Because our variable

[1]Seymour Martin Lipset, *Political Man, the Social Bases of Politics* (Garden City, N.Y.: Doubleday, 1959) especially chapter 2, "Economic Development and Democracy"; and Bruce M. Russett, *Trends in World Politics* (New York: Macmillan, 1965).

violence overlaps with what these writers mean by "stable" and our variable repression with their "democracy," this worldwide correlation between wealth and democracy applies also to violence and repression and their combination—social cohesion. Economic development refers both to the state of having a developed productive system and to the process of acquiring one. This section will concentrate on the first interpretation, levels of economic development; the next section will look at the dynamic variables of change in economic growth and social mobilization.

An elementary knowledge of the Latin American situation prompts one to question the relationship between levels of economic development and levels of violence and repression. Cuba was one of the wealthiest Latin American countries at the time of its revolution. Argentina, long the wealthiest country in the Southern Hemisphere, has alternated between repression and violence since 1930, and at times has experienced a high level of both. Venezuela, which now boasts the highest per capita gross national product in Latin America, went through an exceptional (exceptional in Latin America, not in Venezuela) period of repression under dictator Marcos Pérez Jiménez in the 1950s, and after his fall Venezuela had its share of wide-scale violence.

The proposition that economic development leads to lower levels of violence and repression rests on a very simple logic: people that have more market goods and services are more satisfied than those who have less; being more satisfied, they are not so inclined to violence; because the competition for resources is less intense, repression is not required. This logic is part of the conventional wisdom of Western culture. How can any of us who are complaining about our low wages say that people would not be more content with higher wages?

When we consider only the benefits received from economic development, or more broadly "modernization," we can think of no counter-argument to the above logic. However, some social conditions that tend to accompany higher levels of economic development have quite different effects than do higher levels of consumption. As greater production satisfies wants, greater exposure to the possibilities of consumption generates new wants. It is almost as if wants expand to meet the possibilities for their fulfillment. The processes that generate wants, although highly correlated with the welfare indexes, are conceptually distinct. Urbanization and increased personal travel make people more aware of what stores have to sell. Mass communication, at least in capitalist societies, also means mass advertising, which stimulates the desire to consume. We can separate out, then, those aspects of the "modernization syndrome" that tend to satisfy wants from those that tend to generate them. The term that measures the ability of a society to satisfy wants we call societal welfare and the term that measures the pressures that generate wants in a society we call social mobilization.

The concept of social mobilization was suggested by Karl W. Deutsch.[2] He says it "can be defined . . . as the process in which major clusters of old social, economic and psychological commitments are eroded or broken and people become available for new patterns of socialization and behavior.[3] Deutsch suggests that social mobilization brings with it pressures for changes in political practices and institutions and also places new demands for government services. We will examine these political implications later. Here we would like to stress the economic side of social mobilization, not treated by Deutsch. Social mobilization is what makes a population susceptible to what the economists call the "demonstration effect." It demonstrates the consumption possibilities in other classes and in other regions of the country as well as in other nations. The social, economic and psychological commitments that are most immediate and continuous are those that relate to the consumption of market goods and services. Citizens have always held their governments responsible for basic economic conditions, and in the present era of economic planning governments have come to acknowledge their responsibility. Economic satisfactions or dissatisfactions, thus, become political variables.

These considerations cause us to revise the simple proposition that economic developments lead to greater satisfaction and less violence to the following:

> When societal welfare is relatively higher than social mobilization, the population will be more satisfied and tend to be less violent than where societal welfare is relatively less than social mobilization.

The link between discontent and violence is, perhaps, not obvious. Certainly not all discontent results in violence. Withdrawal and apathy, with or without the aid of drugs and alcohol, is as likely as violence. On the other hand, violent people are apt to be discontented and frustrated. Discontent may be necessary but not sufficient to breed violence. Gurr's frustration-aggression theory is based on the necessity of frustration for violent action.[4] One can posit another kind of link that is less indivi-

---

[2]Karl W. Deutsch, "Social Mobilization and Political Development," *American Political Science Review* 55 (September, 1961), pp. 493–514.

[3]Ibid, p. 494.

[4]Ted Robert Gurr, "Psychological Factors in Civil Violence," *World Politics* 20 (January, 1968), pp. 245–278. Douglas Bwy uses the notion of "systemic satisfaction" in "Political Instability in Latin America," *Latin American Research Review* 2 (Spring, 1968) pp. 17–66, but he does not specify the individual or emergent qualities of this variable.

dualistic in its nature. People are social animals and tend to respond to the attitudes and feelings of others. Opposition political leaders will initiate violent political action against the political and social order when they consider it unjust because it does not provide the necessities for the masses and when, at the same time, they can generate a following around some principle of action to change the social order. Instead of relying on blind impulse and individualistic response, this link relies on normative judgment and leader-mass interactions. Higher levels of discontent are likely to lead to higher levels of violence in either case. Our aggregate data do not allow us to distinguish between these two alternative paths, which are not necessarily mutually exclusive, but what little knowledge we have of leadership in violent protest seems to support the second alternative.

The welfare-mobilization differential seems of immediate relevance to the concerns of the general population and its behavior, but the question remains whether it will have a similar effect on governmental behavior and the level of repression. Insofar as repression is the government's response to perceived dissatisfaction, the above proposition should hold equally for repression, that is, the greater the differential the less the repression. We found that it did not have the hypothesized effect, however, and had second thoughts about the matter. The effect may exist, but it is overwhelmed by certain counter-effects. Economic development not only increases satisfactions, it also changes the structures of human interactions. People become more interdependent, and organizations become more complex.[5] Interdependence raises the cost of repression of any particular group. When subsistence farmers are repressed, it is difficult for them to take countermeasures. When industrial workers are repressed, they can retaliate by striking and damaging the whole economy. Interdependence gives all groups greater leverage to influence the rest of society and the government. Whether organizational complexity, as such, makes repression more difficult depends on the autonomy of the organizations. Where the government controls complex organizations (the military for example) repression may be easier, but where the organization is independent of government, it may make resistance to governmental repression easier. Where a strong private economy exists, economic development makes repression more costly through the interdependence of groups and the organizational resources of nongovernmental

---

[5]Robert A. Dahl discusses this relationship in *Polyarchy, Participation and Opposition* (New Haven: Yale University Press, 1971), in Chapter 4, "The Socioeconomic Order: Concentration or Dispersion?"

groups. Where the government controls economic groups, only the interdependence effects are important.

Like changes in production, changes due to social mobilization have somewhat different effects on repression than they do on violence. The primary change caused by social mobilization, we have suggested, is to raise the demand for market goods and services. Moreover, social mobilization should raise the demand for participation in politics and for public goods and services. These additional demands raise the level of dissatisfaction and at the same time increase the resistance to repressive measures of the government. These attitudinal changes, like the structural ones caused by changes in production, raise the cost of repression. The resistance to repression in Venezuela in January, 1958, and in Argentina during the military dictatorship after 1966 is inconceivable in a place like Haiti or Paraguay.

These further considerations, then, motivate us to revise our original thoughts about the effects of the welfare-mobilization differential on repression. Both welfare and mobilization may have similar effects on repression instead of the different effects postulated for violence. If they do, both should be negatively associated with repression, and the differential between them should have a lower association with repression than with violence.

Data on economic and mobilization levels are inherently much more difficult to collect than are the data discussed in the previous chapter. Fortunately, however, large-scale governmental efforts have been made in recent years to collect data on economic production, communication, literacy, urbanization, and population. Furthermore, international technical assistance has standardized the procedures for data collection on these social and economic variables, making them relatively reliable and comparable.

We say "relatively reliable," not completely reliable. The data from Cuba and Haiti are not as good as from the other countries, and data from other countries are still far from perfect. In the early 1960s, Guatemala's reported per capita gross national product nearly doubled because of changes in procedures for compiling the data. Bolivia's per capita gross national product was revised downward from $160 in 1968 to $135 in 1969 because new census data showed that the nation had a larger population than was known before. In short, even though these data are "relatively reliable," one still needs to use them with a good deal of circumspection.

Of greater consequence is the question of whether these data are valid indicators for our concepts of want satisfaction and want generation. Our concepts relate to attitudes and behaviors of individuals; our data are demographic and economic. Does a person with a higher income have a greater satisfaction with life? Does a person who lives in a city have a greater awareness of consumption possibilities than someone who lives in the country? It is quite possible that a family that has a higher income because both the husband and wife work is less satisfied with its life than is a family with a lower income because only the husband or wife works. Some people who live in cities may be less aware of what is going on around them than others who live in rural areas and travel a lot.

To these problems of conceptualization at the individual level are added those that come from the aggregated nature of the data we use. Per capita gross national product says nothing about the distribution of the benefits of that product between regions or income groups. The number of people living in cities of more than 20,000 says nothing about regional differences. Our indicators, even where completely reliable, only imperfectly represent the theoretical concepts we have in mind when postulating societal relationships.

The indicators that we used to represent social welfare were per capita gross national product, literacy, caloric intake, and level of health services. For analysis of violence and repression in the 1950s and 1960s, we used data from the midpoint of each decade. Gross national product is the most comprehensive of the indexes available and presumably covers every item of consumption and investment except leisure. The principal problem with governmental reports on gross national production is that they are estimated in terms of national currency, and it is very difficult to translate these national currency estimates into a value common for all countries. International exchange rates are poor approximations of a currency's value in goods and services consumed within a country. Stanley N. Braithwaite has developed more equivalent standardizations by using purchasing power parities.[6] He used price information collected by the United Nations Economic Commission for Latin America on 374 items and weighted them according to the average consumption and investment pattern in Latin America. The final figures also took into account prices in the United States in order to achieve estimates that would have broader comparability. Braithwaite's GNP per capita data make up half of our index on societal welfare.

The rest of the index is comprised of items that relate more to minimum standards of living than to average levels of consumption. They therefore tell us something about the extent to which the masses share the basic requirements for a decent life. Literacy rates, based on

---

[6]Stanley N. Braithwaite, "Real Income Levels in Latin America," *Review of Income and Wealth* 14 (June, 1968), pp. 113–182.

data from the census, give an indication of the extent to which the masses have any chance for social advancement. Average calorie intakes, calculated from national sample surveys, give an indication of the absence of starvation. Health services, a combined index of medical doctors and hospital beds per 10,000, suggests the extent to which the population may receive medical attention. Each of these items made up one-sixth of the index.

Tables 9 and 10 present the standardized scores of each of the items composing the index as well as the total standardized scores of societal welfare. All the indexes were highly associated with a correlation coefficient of at least .60 in the 1950s and of at least .45 in the 1960s. Some of the deviations may be due to measurement error. For instance, Brazil's reported high calorie intake for a country at its level of GNP

Table 9. Societal Welfare, 1955 (Standardized scores)

Country	GNP	Literacy	Calories	Health	Total[a]
Argentina	2.07	1.67	2.39	1.66	2.18
Bolivia	−1.08	−1.10	−1.13	−.56	−1.08
Brazil	−.59	−.12	1.09	.24	−.08
Chile	1.10	1.24	.60	1.33	1.19
Colombia	−.28	−.03	−.31	.12	−.17
Costa Rica	.23	1.24	.48	.84	.61
Dominican Republic	−.70	−.18	−.97	−.49	−.66
Ecuador	−.44	.23	−1.00	−.44	−.44
El Salvador	−.56	−.72	−.91	−.80	−.73
Guatemala	−.60	−1.30	−.43	−.89	−.78
Haiti	−1.29	−2.24	−1.15	−2.62	−1.77
Honduras	−.86	−.82	−.39	−.92	−.84
Mexico	.30	.09	.88	−.34	.30
Nicaragua	−.53	−.74	−.88	−.06	−.58
Panama	.18	.81	.04	.42	.35
Paraguay	−.53	.58	.00	−.19	−.20
Peru	−.32	−.19	−.75	−.19	−.36
Uruguay	2.27	1.54	1.41	1.61	2.08
Venezuela	1.47	−.03	−.24	.61	.88
Cuba	.18	.99			.65

[a]The total score assigns half of the total weight to GNP per capita and one-sixth each to literacy, calorie consumption, and health care.

Sources: GNP from Stanley N. Braithwaite, "Real Income Levels in Latin America," *Review of Income and Wealth* 20 (June, 1968), p. 146–7. Literacy and health from Organization of American States, *America en Cifras 1961* (Washington: Pan American Union, 1961). Calories from *Statistical Abstract of Latin America* (Los Angeles: Center of Latin American Studies, University of California, 1963), p. 29.

Table 10. Societal Welfare, 1965 (Standardized scores)

Country	GNP	Literacy	Calories	Health	Total[a]
Argentina	1.89	1.50	1.09	2.55	2.00
Bolivia	−1.20	−1.24	−1.52	−.57	−1.28
Brazil	−.55	−.04	1.67	−.11	−.13
Chile	1.13	1.37	.20	.82	1.07
Colombia	−.30	.35	−.54	−.28	−.25
Costa Rica	.38	1.02	.47	.48	.57
Dominican Republic	−.91	.20	−.82	−.04	−.63
Ecuador	−.54	.11	−1.28	−.61	−.63
El Salvador	−.43	−.70	−.57	−.62	−.59
Guatemala	−.44	−1.41	−.45	−.67	−.71
Haiti	−1.47	−2.51	−1.33	−1.49	−1.80
Honduras	−.93	−.75	−.73	−.85	−.95
Mexico	.67	.07	1.03	−.63	.46
Nicaragua	−.59	−.64	.06	−.48	−.52
Panama	.69	.77	−.11	.24	.55
Paraguay	−.70	.53	.84	−.23	−.18
Peru	−.13	−.10	−.20	−.29	−.18
Uruguay	1.59	1.38	2.04	2.25	1.93
Venezuela	1.84	.33	.17	.53	1.21

[a]The total score gives half of the total weight to GNP and one-sixth each to literacy, calories, and health.

Sources: GNP from Stanley N. Braithwaite, "Real Income Levels in Latin America," *Review of Income and Wealth* 20 (June, 1968), p. 146. Literacy and health from OAS, *America en Cifras 1967* (Washington: Pan American Union, 1968). Calories from IDB, *Socio-Economic Progress in Latin America* (Washington: IDB, 1969).

may either reflect the abundance of land or the result of undersampling the more impoverished northeast Brazil. One also wonders about Paraguay's exceptional literacy rate. Costa Rica's literacy rate, however, can be explained by the attention given to primary school education over the past century. The addition of these alternate indicators of societal welfare to the GNP per capita data left the scores of most countries more or less the same. The principal change came in Venezuela's score, which dropped by more than .60 standardized scores in both measurements. Brazil, Costa Rica, and Paraguay, on the other hand, had their standard of living scores increased by the inclusion of these indexes for literacy, health, and calorie intake, to national production per capita.

The results of the correlations of these standardized scores with violence and repression indicated that the modifications we made on the GNP per capita data in order to arrive at the societal welfare index made very little difference in the association between variables. We also examined the associations of violence and repression with two other economic measures—agricultural product as percent of GNP and agricultural workers as percent of economically active population—and still found very similar correlations between these measures and violence and repression.

The social mobilization index combines communication and urbanization scores. The communication index is made up equally of newsprint consumption per capita, radio receivers per 1,000 and television receivers per 1,000. Newsprint consumption was used instead of newspapers per 1,000 in order to make use of information derived from different sources. Urbanization is the percentage of population living in cities of more than 20,000, a stricter view of urbanization than in official calculations. The total social mobilization score gives equal weight to communication and to urbanization.

Tables 11 and 12 present the standardized scores for the components of social mobilization. Using relative scores in each separate time period obscures the rather dramatic changes in social mobilization throughout Latin America between the 1950s and the 1960s. The next section will take up these changes, but here we are interested in comparing levels in the two decades. In the 1950s, the television industry was only in its infancy in Latin America (except for Cuba) and its index is not highly related to the other components of social mobilization. By the mid-1960s, however, television sets per 1,000 persons were more highly correlated with the other measures than were radios per 1,000. In the 1960s Bolivia, Mexico, and Peru underwent a transistor revolution that went way beyond the development of other means of communication or urbanization.

With standardized scores of both societal welfare and social mobilization, it is no problem to see whether any particular Latin American country is higher, in relation to others in the region, on societal welfare than on social mobilization. Bolivia, for instance, was 1.28 standard deviations below the mean on the societal welfare index in 1965, but only .45 standard deviations below the mean on social mobilization. It was relatively lower on welfare than mobilization by .83 standard deviations (see Figure 5). Neighboring Paraguay, on the contrary, had a score on societal welfare in 1965 of .18 standard deviations below the mean, but was .97 standard deviations below the mean on social mobilization. Paraguay, then, was .79 standard deviations higher on welfare than on mobilization. Whereas both Bolivia and Paraguay were relatively poor and unmobilized, Bolivia was much more mobilized and had less welfare whereas Paraguay had higher welfare and was much

Table 11. Social Mobilization, 1955 (Standardized scores)

Country	Newsprint per capita	Radios per 1,000	TVs per 1,000	Percent Urban[a]	Total[b]
Argentina	1.56	1.40	.78	1.94	1.78
Bolivia	−.79	−.25	−.65	−.33	−.50
Brazil	.34	−.20	.30	−.19	−.03
Chile	.74	.32	−.65	1.44	.88
Colombia	−.33	−.27	.16	.02	−.07
Costa Rica	.29	−.11	−.65	−.26	−.23
Dominican Republic	−.84	−.69	−.24	−.83	−.79
Ecuador	−.38	−.75	−.65	−.33	−.52
El Salvador	−.28	−.98	−.18	−.83	−.73
Guatemala	−.79	−1.06	−.24	−.97	−.93
Haiti	−1.09	−1.14	−.65	−1.43	−1.35
Honduras	−.94	−.95	−.65	−1.26	−1.18
Mexico	−.33	.17	.71	.02	.11
Nicaragua	−.68	−.82	−.45	−.61	−.70
Panama	.03	.86	−.65	.30	.21
Paraguay	−.94	−.22	−.65	−.76	−.76
Peru	−.33	−.27	−.45	−.12	−.28
Uruguay	2.94	2.98	−.24	2.36	2.37
Venezuela	.29	.74	1.73	.87	1.00
Cuba	1.51	1.22	3.43	.87	1.63

[a]Percent of population in cities of more than 20,000.

[b]Urbanization is given half the weight in the total score and each measure of communication is given one-sixth of the weight.

Sources: Newsprint, radios, TVs from United Nations *Statistical Yearbook, 1957* (New York: United Nations, 1958), pp. 632, 634, 640. Urban population from IDB, *Socio-Economic Progress in Latin America* (Washington: IDB, 1968), pp. 342–343.

less mobilized. Figures 4 and 5 portray the societal welfare and social mobilization variables together and give the difference between the two scores. The countries are presented in order of the size of the differential.

The figures illustrate, among other things, the extent to which welfare and mobilization are associated. Most countries differ on the two by less than .20 standard scores. At the extremes, however, considerable discrepancies exist. For both decades Costa Rica and Paraguay have relative welfare levels that far exceed their relative mobilization levels. Haiti and Bolivia represent the other extreme. Cuba, in the 1950s, had a differential that was far lower than any other country in Latin America.

Table 12. Social Mobilization, 1965 (Standardized scores)

Country	Newsprint per capita	Radios per 1,000	TVs per 1,000	Percent Urban	Total[a]
Argentina	2.76	1.93	1.90	1.80	2.11
Bolivia	−.90	.03	−.98	−.23	−.45
Brazil	−.35	−.56	.30	.02	−.10
Chile	.89	.59	−.75	1.74	1.05
Colombia	−.19	−.01	−.22	.39	.13
Costa Rica	.45	−.63	.02	−.48	−.28
Dominican Republic	−.78	−1.24	−.43	−.60	−.75
Ecuador	−.35	−.45	−.67	−.17	−.35
El Salvador	−.03	−.06	−.51	−.78	−.52
Guatemala	−.75	−.56	−.51	−.97	−.83
Haiti	−1.18	−1.58	−.95	−1.40	−1.39
Honduras	−.98	−.89	−.87	−1.15	−1.09
Mexico	−.11	.76	.18	.02	.16
Nicaragua	−.47	−.96	−.59	−.48	−.61
Panama	−.11	.72	1.26	.20	.44
Paraguay	−.94	−.67	−.98	−.97	−.97
Peru	.21	.57	−.27	.02	.10
Uruguay	1.92	2.38	1.98	1.85	2.08
Venezuela	.85	.63	2.02	1.19	1.24

[a]Urbanization is given half the weight in the total score and each of the measures of communication is given one sixth.

Sources: Newsprint, radios, TVs from United Nations *Statistical Yearbook, 1967* (New York: United Nations, 1968), pp. 512, 770, 772. Urban population from IDB, *Socio-Economic Progress in Latin America* (Washington: IDB, 1969), pp. 342–343.

DIGRESSION ON CORRELATION

Before reporting the results of our simple correlation analysis, we will digress for a moment on the question of the interpretation of these correlation coefficients. The correlation coefficient measures the degree of association between two variables. A correlation of +1.00 or −1.00 indicates perfect association where a nation with a particular value on one variable would always have a specified value on the other variable. A correlation coefficient of zero indicates no association. All the correlation coefficients found in our analyses are less than one, as was expected, and we needed some criteria to allow us to say what correlation coefficients are high enough to indicate an interesting association.

One criterion used by statisticians to interpret whether any particular correlation coefficient is high enough to be accepted is the test of

Figure 4.   Welfare-Mobilization Differential, 1955

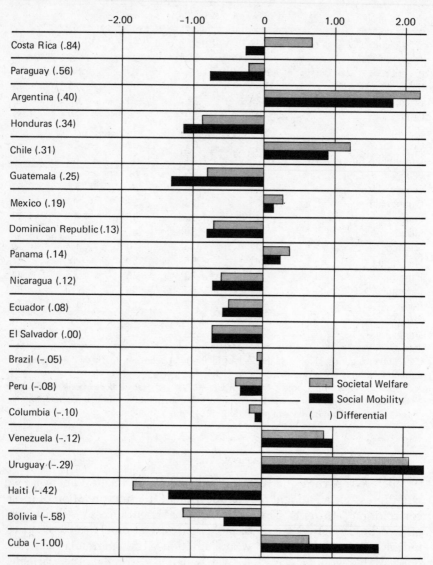

significance—significance in a statistical sense and not necessarily in a theoretical sense. The test of significance informs one of the probability that any particular correlation coefficient from a sample of nations, such as the Latin American nations in the 1950s, would hold for a larger population, such as all nations at all times. Application of a test of

Figure 5. Welfare-Mobilization Differential, 1965

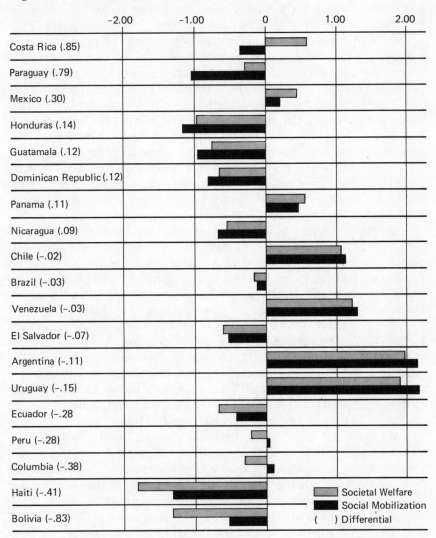

significance, however, requires that certain assumptions be met. The most important assumption violated in our analyses is that the sample be randomly chosen from the larger population. We have taken all Latin American countries in the 1950s and the 1960s, not a random sample of all countries at all times. Because of the violation of this assumption, it is not at all clear what the meaning of the test of significance is. Nevertheless, we do not want to consider correlation coefficients that might have resulted from chance, and the test of significance gives us some sense of how large a correlation coefficient needs to be in order that its difference from zero (no correlation) not be due to chance. With a sample of nineteen nations, a correlation coeffient of .45 has a 95 percent probability of being greater than zero, if chance were the determinant of the coefficient. With the same size sample, a correlation coefficient of .56 has a 99 percent probability of being greater than zero.

More important than the statistical significance of our correlations is their theoretical importance. Even if a correlation coefficient is accepted as a true description of a population, one still needs to know how important it is, that is, how much it explains? The square of the correlation coefficient gives the proportion of variation explained. A correlation coefficient of .33 is necessary to explain ten percent of the variation. Any variable that explains less than ten percent of the varia-tion is not of any particular consequence for a parsimonious theory.

We have samples from two different time periods, the 1950s and the 1960s. The dependent variables (violence and repression) in one period are related with the same variables in the other time period (violence between the two periods has a correlation coefficient of .63 and repression, .67), but they are sufficiently distinct to make consis-tency of relationships between the two periods an important criterion. It will be noticed that the correlations for the 1950s tend to be lower than for the 1960s. The data on violence and repression are not as good for that period with some apparent cases of underreporting of violence in particular. When we ran separate correlations for the late 1950s, they were considerably higher than in the early 1950s and much more similar to the results of the 1960s. Most of our data are better for the 1960s, and we will give greater credence to correlations of those years.

We also ran correlations between changes in the independent variables and changes in the dependent variables. If the size of the change in any independent variable is of consequence, consistency of this correlation with the correlations between levels in the different time periods is further indication that a true relationship exists.

Taking into account the above considerations, we make the follow-ing somewhat arbitrary criteria for the tentative acceptance of a rela-tionship between the two variables:

1. The simple correlation must be above .33 in at least one time period and above .20 in the other for the relationship to be given further considera-tion with the information available.
2. Simple correlations above .45 in one period and above .33 in the other period will be tentatively considered as significant and interesting.
3. If in addition to No. 2, the correlation between changes in the variables between time periods is above .45, we will consider that relationship

accepted for the purpose of this study unless it is shown to be the result of the interaction of a third variable.

Table 13 lists the correlation coefficients between the welfare and mobilization variables, the differential between them, and violence and repression in both time periods. Our original skepticism about the relationship between the social and economic development variables and violence is borne out by the correlation analysis. Both gross national product per capita and our combined measure of societal welfare show almost no correlation with violence. Measures of agricultural production and agricultural workers likewise show no relationship. The social mobilization variables have a small positive relationship with violence in both decades.

Table 13. Welfare and Mobilization Correlations

	Correlations with	
Independent Variables	*Violence*	*Repression*
1950s		
Societal welfare	.04	−.30[a]
GNP per capita	.00	−.28[a]
Agricultural production as percent of GNP	−.12	.12
Agricultural workers as percent of economically active population	−.05	.19
Social mobilization	.19	−.29[a]
Communications	.24	−.25[a]
Urbanization	.14	−.30[a]
Welfare minus mobilization	−.37[b]	.01
1960s		
Societal welfare	−.02	−.47[a]
GNP per capita	.08	−.50[a]
Agricultural production as percent of GNP	−.18	.58
Agricultural workers as percent of economically active population	−.05	.50
Social mobilization	.21	−.53[a]
Communications	.18	−.44[a]
Urbanization	.21	−.51[a]
Welfare minus mobilization	−.60[b]	.03

[a]Minimal criterion met.
[b]Second criterion met.

On the other hand, both the welfare and the mobilization variables have a consistent negative relationship with repression despite our citing of the exceptions of Cuba, Argentina and Venezuela. Both types of variables have almost identical coefficients, making it impossible to choose between them. Curiously, the variable with the highest correlation with repression, agricultural production as a percent of GNP, is also the most inconsistent between the two periods. The extreme position of Haiti on agricultural production and its shift from moderate repression to extremely high repression between the 1950s and the 1960s accounts for much of this inconsistency. The theory that more complex societies are more difficult and costly to repress than simple agricultural societies receives some support from these correlations.

The only relationship that meets our second and higher criterion for acceptance is that between the welfare-mobilization differential and violence. The differential explains fifteen percent of the variance in the 1950s and 35 percent in the 1960s. The proposition that situations where want generation is relatively higher than want satisfaction bring about violence is supported by this correlation.

The correlations between these socio-economic variables and violence and repression provide absolutely no support for the idea that violence and repression are different aspects of the same dimension, social cohesion. None of these independent variables has a similar correlation with the two dependent variables of violence and repression. In the 1960s, the spread is around .60 points between the two correlations for each independent variable. When violence and repression are combined and correlated with these independent variables, the result is, in every case, an averaging of the correlations. No premature conclusion should be drawn from these disparate correlations, however, because these socio-economic variables are exceptional and have the widest spread between the two correlations of any independent variables in our study.

Changes in welfare and mobilization

We deal with changes in welfare and mobilization in a separate section because the dynamics of change may differ in its effects from the static conditions of levels of welfare and mobilization. The arguments in the previous section still hold, and where changes in welfare and mobilization significantly affect the levels of these measures, the effects of changes and levels cannot be separated. Generally, however, changes in welfare and mobilization are rather small relative to the absolute levels, but we expect that they may still affect repression and violence.

James C. Davies, in one of the most explicit theories of revolution, bases his whole theory on long-run socio-economic changes. He postulates that the needs of people are primarily a function of long-term growth rates:

> Revolutions are most likely to occur when a prolonged period of objective economic and social development is followed by a short period of sharp reversal. The all-important effect on the minds of people in a particular society is to produce, during the former period, an expectation of continued ability to satisfy needs—which continue to rise—and, during the latter, a mental state of anxiety and frustration when manifest reality breaks away from anticipated reality. The actual state of socio-economic development is less significant than the expectation that past progress, now blocked, can and must continue in the future.[7]

He illustrated his thesis with the now famous J-Curve which is reproduced in Figure 6.[8] Davies' concept of revolution is a very broad one which includes unsuccessful rebellion as well as successful cases of government take-overs. It seems fair, then, to interpret his discussion to include cases of large-scale violence as well as the few cases where a new group takes over the government by force and makes radical policy changes.

Davies gives more evidence to support his theory than most writers on the subject. He has examined the growth trends prior to Dorr's Rebellion of 1842, the Russian Revolution of 1917, the Egyptian Revolution of 1952, the French Revolution of 1789, the American Civil War of 1861, the Nazi Revolution of 1933, and the U.S. black rebellion of the 1960s. He finds that in each of these cases there is a growth curve resembling his J-Curve. The evidence is far from conclusive because he did not specify with any precision how long or how rapid the socio-economic growth needed to be, nor how great the short-term drop in growth. Furthermore, he examined only cases of rebellion. He did not demonstrate that wherever his curve occurred, revolution occurred also. The gap between expectations and satisfaction illustrated by the J-

---

[7]James C. Davies, "Toward a Theory of Revolution," *American Sociological Review* 27 (February, 1962), p. 6.

[8]James C. Davies, "The J-Curve of Rising and Declining Satisfactions as a Cause of Some Great Revolutions and a Contained Rebellion," in *Violence in America*, Hugh Davis Graham and Ted Robert Gurr ed. (New York: Bantam Books, 1969).

Figure 6.   Need Satisfaction and Revolution

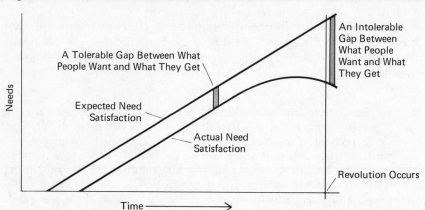

Source: James C. Davies, "The J-Curve of Rising and Declining Satisfactions as a Cause of Some Great Revolutions and a Contained Rebellion," in *Violence in America*, ed. Hugh Davis Graham and Ted Robert Gurr (New York: Bantam Books, 1969), p. 691.

Curve may be a necessary cause, but Davies gives us no evidence to judge whether it is sufficient.

Latin America provides a useful sample of countries with which to test Davies' theory somewhat more rigorously. The first question to pose is, What is a "prolonged period of objective economic and social development"? Does enclave development, as in the cases of banana plantations along the north coast of Honduras or tin mining in the Bolivian Andes, count as development? Only Haiti and Paraguay in Latin America have not had at least that kind of development; neither has experienced social revolutions, but each has known bloody civil wars.

Leaving aside the marginal cases of development, we can say that Argentina, Chile, Costa Rica, Cuba, Mexico, Panama, Uruguay, and Venezuela have all definitely had a prolonged period of economic and social development in this century. Of these, Costa Rica, Mexico, and Panama have not suffered any short-term reversals of economic growth since 1930, and Mexico and Panama have not experienced any large amount of violence in that period. Costa Rica, on the other hand, experienced a short but severe outbreak of violence in 1948. Argentina, Cuba, Chile, Uruguay, and Venezuela have all had periods when their economies were more or less stagnant. Cuba's economy grew rapidly until 1930, but it has been dormant ever since. Violence, however, increased in Cuba in the 1950s after the economy had resumed a slow rate of growth. The timing of the Cuban Revolution certainly presents a problem for the theory. Argentina's and Chile's growth rates have been more erratic. A few bad years are usually followed by some good years. Both were hit hard by the world depression in the 1930s, but both recovered fairly rapidly. Chile had a three-year slump in the mid-1950s which was followed by its worst urban riot. The extreme violence that accompanied the overthrow of Salvador Allende in 1973 came after a two-year economic slump. Argentina's outbreaks of violence, however, do not seem to follow any economic pattern.

Venezuela and Uruguay have had more pronounced economic downturns. After a period of rapid growth, Venezuela's per capita annual growth dropped to −.3 for the 1958–1961 period before it resumed a slower pace of growth. After 1961 Venezuela had its worst bout of violence in this century. Uruguay's economic downturn was less pronounced but more enduring. Its growth throughout the 1950s and the 1960s was very low. Its worst period was between 1965 and 1968 when it had a −1.6 percent annual per capita growth rate. Urban terrorism broke the relative harmony of Uruguay's social life at the end of this period.

Two other instances of social revolution in Latin America fit the J-Curve less well than even the above cases. Both Mexico and Bolivia experienced unambiguous social revolution before they enjoyed any long-term economic growth. Clark Reynolds reports that Mexico's per capita production at the end of the nineteenth century was about what it was at the start.[9] Bolivia's per capita GNP at the time of its revolution in 1952 could not have been much above 100 U.S. dollars, hardly the result of any prolonged economic growth. Nor is there any indication of a downturn in the economy of either country before its revolution. As Reynolds points out: "The 2.2 percent rise in per capita product during the last days of the administration of President Porfirio Diaz was higher than that of the period from 1925 to 1965."[10] As world tin prices went up in response to the Korean War, Bolivia had a good growth of five percent per capita in the year immediately preceding its revolution. The growth curves of both Mexico and Bolivia prior to their revolutions contradict the Davies J-Curve theory.

The Mexican and Bolivian cases illustrate the biggest problem in Davies' theory. Like so many of the writers on social development, he lumps together all kinds of social and economic development. Different kinds of development have different effects and need to be separated.

[9]Clark W. Reynolds, *The Mexican Economy* (New Haven: Yale University Press, 1970), pp. 16-17.
[10]Ibid., p. 2.

Mexico went through some profound social changes in the late nineteenth century without experiencing overall economic growth. Railroads were built, the cities grew, and the world capitalist market swamped the small-scale local markets. These changes took place without improving the per capita product. Mexicans became aware of the products of the industrial world without being able to buy them. Likewise, the development of Bolivian tin mining, accompanied by the unsettling experience of the Chaco War, mobilized much of the Bolivian population without improving its welfare. The revolutionary situation can be detected, then, only by disaggregating "economic and social development" into at least welfare change and mobilization change. The J-Curve theory can be superseded by a welfare change-mobilization change theory that will explain the same cases that the J-Curve explains and cover the cases the J-Curve does not explain at all.

Economic growth and changes in social mobilization tend to be correlated over long periods but not necessarily over short periods. The ten-year averages of economic growth and social mobilization change in Latin America in the 1950s and 1960s have a positive correlation of only about .2. Economic growth may generate changes in communication and urbanization, but mobilization changes can occur without economic growth. Furthermore, when economic growth slows down or stops, mobilization changes are likely to continue apace. Both Cuba and Uruguay underwent television revolutions despite their stagnant economies. Migration to the cities can occur because of stagnant agricultural economies as well as because of dynamic urban economies. When social mobilization takes place without economic growth, dissatisfactions are generated, moving people to violent acts.

New mobilization may have more unsettling effects than long-standing levels of mobilization. Moving to the city may generate more wants than does growing up in the city. Being exposed to commercials on a new media may stimulate more material desires than do advertisements on the familiar media.

At the same time, economic growth may be satisfying even though a person, or a country, is still poor. As Davies said, economic expansion arouses expectations of continued expansion, but what he did not say was that these expectations, as long as they remain credible, satisfy and make people more willing to wait for the future. Promises can often replace actuality. Economic growth has other favorable effects on society. It makes upward social mobility possible without any downward mobility to balance it. Governments find it possible to raise new revenues without making anyone worse off and to expand services and government positions as a consequence. All of these aspects of economic growth tend to increase satisfactions and lessen the likelihood of violence.

The effects of socio-economic conditions on repression, we argued in the previous section, depended more on structural conditions than on want satisfaction. Economic development decreased levels of repression by making repression more costly because of the greater interdependence of groups and the greater organizational resources of autonomous social units. The dynamic effects of want generation and satisfaction would be, then, less important for repression than for violence. The structural effects of growth in any one year, or even in a decade, may not be sufficient to make much difference in the level of repression, but it might show up in changes in the level of repression.

We measured changes in welfare only with GNP per capita growth rates because the data on calorie intake and health services are not sufficiently reliable to measure annual changes. Data on changes in communication are the same as those used for levels of communication. The change in urbanization is the growth in percent living in cities of more than 20,000 between the 1950s and 1960s censuses, adjusted to correspond to a ten-year period if the censuses were not exactly ten years apart. Table 14 reports the economic growth rates in average annual per capita percentages, which were then converted to standard scores before subtracting the change in social mobilization scores. The 1960s per capita growth rate was used to calculate two differentials, using both the 1960s social mobilization change and the 1950–1969 social mobilization change. Only the latter is shown here, and is the index used in the multiple regression analysis in Chapter 5.

High economic growth rates usually assure that the differential between welfare and mobilization changes is positive, but Venezuela, with the highest economic growth rate in the 1950s, still had a negative differential. Panama, on the other hand, with the highest growth rate in the 1960s, had a remarkably high differential. A low economic growth rate does not imply a negative differential. Honduras and Paraguay both had low economic growth rates, but they had even lower changes in social mobilization. Costa Rica and Nicaragua had economic growth rates that exceeded their mobilization rates in both decades with only moderate rates of economic growth.

The countries where mobilization relative to all Latin American countries most exceeded welfare were all wealthier countries, except Colombia. Argentina, Chile, Uruguay, and Venezuela, in addition to Colombia, had mobilization considerably above their economic growth rates. One can see how the welfare-mobilization change theory yields results similar to Davies' J-Curve theory. The countries that have had a

Table 14. Economic Growth and Social Mobilization Changes, 1950–1969

Country	1950s			1960s		
	Economic Growth	*SM Change*	*EG—SM Change*	*Economic Growth*	*SM Change*[a]	*EG—SM Change*[a]
Argentina	.7	1.15	−1.77	1.9	1.23	−.92
Bolivia	−1.3	−.23	−2.04	2.5	−.07	.48
Brazil	2.5	.39	.46	2.7	.29	.33
Chile	.8	.83	−1.36	2.2	1.44	−.89
Colombia	1.5	1.32	−1.27	1.7	1.00	−.87
Costa Rica	1.6	−1.08	1.17	2.4	−.86	1.04
Dominican Republic	2.2	−.06	.66	.9	.15	−.73
Ecuador	1.8	.01	.26	1.4	.27	−.49
El Salvador	1.1	−.17	−.13	2.2	−.46	.59
Guatemala	.8	−.70	.14	1.7	−.90	.62
Haiti	−.2	−1.24	−.14	−.6	−1.35	−.52
Honduras	.8	−.62	.06	1.3	−.91	.37
Mexico	2.7	−.05	1.05	2.9	.19	.55
Nicaragua	2.8	−.25	1.34	3.2	−.32	1.13
Panama	1.7	−.52	.70	4.6	.15	1.67
Paraguay	.4	−1.73	.83	1.0	−1.81	.88
Peru	2.4	.08	.68	2.4	.22	.20
Uruguay	.5	−.45	−.35	−.2	−.51	−.92
Venezuela	4.1	2.75	−.57	.7	2.25	−2.49
Cuba	1.0	.59	−.77			
Mean	1.4	.00	.00	1.8	.00	.00
S.D.	1.2	1.00	1.00	1.2	1.00	1.00

[a]Social mobilization change from 1950 to 1969.

Sources: Economic growth from Organization for Economic Cooperation and Development, *National Accounts of Less Developed Countries 1950–1966* (Paris, OECD, 1968); and IDB, *Socio-Economic Progress in Latin America* (Washington: IDB, 1970). Passim. Social mobilization same as Tables 11 and 12.

prolonged period of growth are the ones where mobilization continues, with or without economic growth. If the economic growth drops, the differential increases. However, the welfare-mobilization differential theory can account for some cases, as Bolivia and the Dominican Republic, which would not be picked up by the J-Curve theory.

The correlations on Table 15 give further evidence for evaluating Davies' theory. The theory implies that a drop in economic growth stimulates more violence than does a continuous low economic growth rate. If such were the case, then change in the economic growth rate should be more highly correlated with levels of violence than the rate of

Table 15. Correlations with Welfare and Mobilization Change, 1950–1970

Independent Variable	Violence	Change in Violence	Repression	Change in Repression
1950s				
Economic growth	−.24		−.06	
Mobilization change	.37[a]		.02	
Urbanization change	.18		.06	
Communication change	.45		−.03	
Economic growth minus social mobilization change	−.61[b]		−.08	
1960s				
Economic growth	−.28	−.52	−.46	−.20
Change in economic growth (1950s to 1960s)	−.15	−.55	−.15	.00
Mobilization change, 1960–1970	.30[a]			
Mobilization change, 1950–1970	.44[a]	.20	−.48	−.50
Urbanization change	.40	.21	−.34	−.46
Communications change, 1950–1970	.30	.10	−.50	−.34
Economic growth minus social mobilization change, 1960–1970	−.49[b]	−.42	.02	.32
Economic growth minus social mobilization change, 1950–1970	−.57[b]	−.57[c]	.00	.22

[a]Minimal criterion met.
[b]Second criterion met.
[c]Third criterion met.

growth. Growth rates have a negative correlation with levels of violence in the 1950s of −.24 and in the 1960s of −.28, not high enough to meet our first criterion. The correlation between changes in growth rate and the level of violence is even less, −.15. In short, those countries that had a drop in growth rate did not have appreciably higher levels of violence than did those with increases in growth rates. Changes in growth rates do correlate quite highly, −.55, with changes in level of violence. This correlation supports the idea that growth rate, regardless of previous rates of growth, affects violence, and when the growth rate changes, levels of violence adjust accordingly.

The correlations give moderate support to the hypothesis that changes in mobilization tend to generate violence. Longer run mobilization changes, from 1950 to 1970, have a stronger association with violence than do shorter run changes, 1960 to 1970. However, we have urbanization data for only the first ten-year period.

The differential between economic growth and change in social mobilization proves to have the most consistently high correlation with levels of violence that we have found in our study. It is the only variable that yields a correlation in the 1950s with violence that exceeds .50. This differential also correlates with changes in violence between the 1950s and the 1960s. This correlation means that changes in the level of the differential tend to be associated with changes in the level of violence, giving greater support for the argument made in the previous section that the difference between societal welfare and social mobilization will be associated with the level of violence.

The correlation with repression yields rather inconsistent results. Both economic growth and mobilization changes are negatively correlated with levels of repression in the 1960s, but not in the 1950s. We had not hypothesized that there would be such a relationship, because we felt that the attitudinal effects of socio-economic change, which are reinforced by short time changes, are less important than the structural changes, which are not greatly influenced by short-term change. The long-term mobilization change, from 1950 to 1970, does show a moderate association with changes in repression with a correlation of −.50, giving further support to the structural theory.

The measures of mobilization change continue to show quite different relationships with violence than they do with repression. Economic growth, on the other hand, shows similar, if somewhat low, relationships with violence and repression. Economic growth, then, is the first variable that we have found giving support for the idea that repression and violence are substitutable responses to the same condition.

Inequality and stratification

Ever since men have studied and discussed the nature of societies and politics, they have concluded that the way in which wealth and power are distributed in society helps determine the peace and harmony of that society. We developed several measures of equality in Latin America and found no association between them and our measures of violence and repression (although we did find a connection between racial characteristics and repression). The limited amount of variation in inequality, or equality, in Latin America, and the inadequacy of the measures, do not allow any definitive conclusions to be drawn from this lack of association, but the evidence does inject some doubt into one of the long-accepted hypotheses of social science.

The often-repeated logic of the inequality hypothesis seems to be simple common sense. The poor, who have nothing to lose but their chains, become envious of the wealthy and resort to violence to obtain their goods. The wealthy, in order to maintain their position, resort to repression. Therefore, when inequalities are great, high degrees of violence and repression can be expected. On the other hand, where there are proportionately more people of middling income with fewer poor or rich, people respect each other's freedom and property.

This simple logic overlooks a number of complications. For instance, it does not distinguish between situations where people have equal opportunities for themselves and their children to earn great wealth and those where they do not. It says nothing about how political power is organized and how it may affect the distribution of income. It lumps together situations where the distribution of wealth, power, or both may be becoming more equal with situations where it is becoming less equal. It pays no attention to the amount of wealth in the society, nor how it is changing, and, finally, it makes no mention of the degree of solidarity of the poor or the rich when solidarity would seem to be a prerequisite for class action. In short, it is quite possible that some kinds of inequality will have different results from others.

When we began our research on this problem, however, we expected that all kinds of inequality would correlate highly among themselves and that all would be positively associated with repression and violence. The measures that we could develop on inequality—the percentage of land in multifamily estates, the percentage of landless rural workers, gini indexes for land and income, the percentage of white and mestizo, and the combined size of the upper and middle classes—are shown in Table 16. We have no direct measure of equality of opportunity, but opportunity should be reflected both in these measures and in those of economic growth. These different measures of inequality are not associated as we had anticipated. Land inequality and income inequality measures have a correlation coefficient of $-.02$. The size of the upper and middle classes and income inequality have a correlation coefficient of .03. Only the percentage of white and mestizo population and the size of the upper and middle classes show a significant correlation of .74, both being highly associated with economic development variables.

Table 16. Measures of Inequality, 1960–1970

Country	Percent area in Multifamily Estates	Landless Rural Workers	Land Gini Index	Income Gini Index[a]	Percent White & Mestizo	Size of Upper and Middle Classes
Argentina	36.9	35.0	.857	.422 (.457)	96	36
Bolivia	—	—	—[b]	.485	43	8
Brazil	59.5	59.8	.796	.537 (.548)	59	15
Chile	81.3	47.6	.934	.439 (.431)	91	22
Colombia	49.5	23.2	.859	.619 (.467)	79	22
Costa Rica	—	—	.765	.501	95	22
Dominican Republic	—	—	.785	—	19	—
Ecuador	45.1	32.5	.867	.327 (.353)	39	10
El Salvador	—	—	.833	.516	60	10
Guatemala	40.8	24.6	.758	—	33	8
Haiti	—	—	—	—	0	3
Honduras	—	—	.721	—	60	4
Mexico	—	—	.947	.517 (.486)	70	—
Nicaragua	—	—	.787	—	86	—
Panama	—	—	.732	.478	58	15
Paraguay	—	—	—	—	35	14
Peru	82.4	26.7	.933	.612	50	—
Uruguay	—	—	.821	—	98	18
Venezuela	—	—	.928	.42 (.513)	80	—
Cuba	—	—	—[c]	—	50	10

[a]The numbers in parenthesis are alternative gini indexes derived from United Nations Economic Commission for Latin America data. A gini index is a measure of inequality. The index varies from 1.000 (perfect inequality) to .000 (perfect equality). The higher the number, the greater inequality.

[b]The land gini index for Bolivia in 1950 before the redistribution brought about by the revolution was .938.

[c]The land gini index for Cuba for 1945 was .792.

Sources: Columns 1 and 2, Solon L. Barraclough and Arthur L. Domike,'' Agrarian Structure in Seven Latin American Countries,'' *Land Economics* 42 (November, 1966), pp. 395, 397 from data developed by Inter-American Committee for Agricultural Development. Column 3 is derived from official land census data reprinted in *Statistical Abstract of Latin America, 1967* (Los Angeles: Center of Latin American Studies, 1968) pp. 132–133. Column 4 is derived from data published by Irma Adelman and Cynthia Taft Morris, "An Anatomy of Income Distribution, Patterns in Developing Nations,"*Development Digest* 9 (October, 1971), p. 27. Column 5 is from data developed by the Institute of Latin American Studies, University of Texas, and reprinted in Charles F. Denton and Preston Lee Lawrence, *Latin American Politics* (San Francisco: Chandler, 1973), p. 43. Column 6 is from Gino Germani and Kalman Silvert, "Politics, Social Structure and Military Intervention in Latin America," in *Government and Politics in Latin America*, ed. Peter Snow (New York: Holt, Rinehart, and Winston, 1967), p. 301.

Table 17. Correlations with Inequality and Stratification Measures, 1950–1970

Independent Variable	N	Violence	Repression
Percent of land in large multifamily farms	7	−.84[a]	−.64[a]
Percent of rural families without land	7	−.48[a]	.10
Land, gini index	16	.13	−.26
Income, gini index	12	−.15	.01
Upper and middle class	14	.05	−.34
Percent white, 1950s	19	.00	−.35[b]
Percent white, 1960s	19	.06	−.29[b]
Percent white and mestizo, 1950s	19	−.04	−.49[c]
Percent white and mestizo, 1960s	19	−.12	−.71[c]

[a]With an N of only seven, our criteria do not apply.
[b]Meets minimal criterion.
[c]Meets second criterion.

Moreover, none of our measures of inequality, with the exception of percent white and mestizo, had any significant association with either violence or repression, as is shown on Table 17.

The more reliable measures of land inequality, for which data were available on only seven countries, yielded a negative correlation coefficient with both violence and repression, the opposite of what we had anticipated. On the other hand, the most complete data on land distribution, the gini index, had a very small positive association. These results certainly throw some doubt on Bruce Russett's conclusions, based on worldwide data, that land equality is associated with higher levels of violence.[11] Similarly, the correlations with the size of the middle class are inconsistent with John J. Johnson's findings that the emergence of the "middle sectors" produced less violence in Latin America.[12]

There are at least two qualifications that should be made to the conclusion that there is *no* relationship between land inequality and

[11]Bruce M. Russett, "Inequality and Instability: the Relation of Land Tenure to Politics," *World Politics* 16 (April, 1964), pp. 442–454.

[12]John J. Johnson, *Political Change in Latin America* (Stanford: Stanford University Press, 1958).

repression or violence. First, there is not a very high range of variation in land inequality in Latin America. Russett found a worldwide range in gini indexes from .437 in Yugoslavia to .938 in Bolivia. The Latin American range is only about two-fifths of that range. Because productivity of the soil, ownership of more than one farm by one individual, and a host of other factors make land census data a very imprecise measure of true rural inequality, it may be that the small range of variation is overshadowed by the error of measurement of the true situation. Second, our measurement of repression is oriented toward the central government, not toward the *hacienda*. The *hacienda* can be a very repressive place on its own without help from the central government. Certainly the traditional large landholders have never allowed peasant organizations to form in the areas under their control. Furthermore, the violence that takes place on the *hacienda* often goes unreported. If we could develop more accurate measures of inequality and take into account all the rural violence and repression, it might still be possible to to find some kind of positive relationship between land inequality and social cohesion.

Even though most measures of inequality showed no significant relation with our dependent variables, the data relating to racial stratification did yield significant coefficients and deserve closer inspection. Racial divisions, with their accompanying cultural traits, provide the sharpest divisions in society in Latin America, even if they are somewhat more blurred than those in the United States. Latin Americans don't make the gross distinctions between black and white, or Indian and white, that are made in the United States and northern Europe.[13] Rather, they ask how black or how brown a man is, using these terms in both a racial and a cultural sense and making distinctions on the basis of all shades. The heritage of slavery and conquest has nevertheless left a strong imprint.

Wherever blacks or Indians live in Latin America, their conditions of life and their political power are much lower than either the whites or the mestizos. The division between white and mestizo is much less sharp and one sees persons of darker skin in power in a number of countries such as Mexico, Nicaragua, and Colombia. One can expect, then, that the larger the percentage of white and mestizo, the larger the middle class and the less inequality there will be in the society as a whole. Where the proportion of blacks and Indians is small, the situation of these groups still may be relatively bad, but it would have less

---

[13]Pierre L. van den Berghe, *Race and Racism, A Comparative Perspective* (New York: Wiley, 1967), and H. Hoetink, *The Two Variants in Caribbean Race Relations* (London: Oxford University Press, 1967).

effect on the society as a whole. In our analysis we used both the percentage of white population and the combined percentage of white and mestizo population, but both varied together and the latter proved to have the stronger relationships.

The proportion of white or mestizo, however, showed no correlation at all with our measures of land inequality or income inequality. The population data are more reliable statistics, and one suspects that in some cases they may better reflect basic inequalities. Guatemala, for instance, scored moderately low in our measures of land inequality, both from the gini index and in the proportion of agricultural area in large multifamily farms, but the most abject poverty of the Indians exists next to conspicuous consumption by the whites. All outward appearances would make Guatemala one of the most unequal of societies. Ecuador's equality also seems to be overrated. Its income equality is at variance with the obvious discrepancies in living conditions that one sees throughout the Sierra.

The presence of a large number of blacks or Indians seems to be accompanied by cultural traits in human relations that may be worse than the objective material and political inequalities. The dominant group develops an ideology that justifies its superior position, and the subjected group tends to accept the ideas that rationalize its lower position.[14] The result is a culture that brutalizes and dehumanizes the relationship between the two groups as the dominant group convinces itself that the subordinate group is something less than human. The subjected group has submissiveness beaten into it. These cultural traits that develop out of the relations between races are not restricted to that relationship, but seem to affect all relationships in society. The labor relations that developed as a result of the subjugation of Indian workers in Guatemala, for instance, have come to characterize labor relations with the *ladino* (mestizo) workers as well. Furthermore, when members of the subjected group reach positions of power, they seem to take on the same characteristics of their oppressors—witness Rafael Carrera, the illiterate Indian who was the first brutal dictator of Guatemala, the mulatto Fulgencio Batista of Cuba, and the black François Duvalier of Haiti.

Both the racial inequalities and the accompanying cultural characteristics could produce higher levels of both violence and repression. However, the brutality is more often exhibited by the dominant groups, and the subjected group is usually submissive in these societies. One could expect then that the size of the subjected racial group would be more highly associated with repression than with violence.

[14]Frank Parkin, *Class Inequality and Political Order* (New York: Praeger, 1971).

That, in fact, is what we found. Neither percentage white nor percentage white and mestizo showed any association with violence in either the 1950s or 1960s. The relationship with repression, however, was strong. The percentage white and mestizo was correlated with repression in the 1950s with a correlation coefficient of $-.49$ and in the 1960s with a coefficient of $-.71$.

These correlations are sufficiently high to make us reconsider the correlations between repression and the various economic development measures. Because the racial characteristics variables are associated with the economic development variables, it is possible that the negative correlation between economic development and repression is spurious, being due to the association between racial characteristics and economic development. Partial correlations between per capita GNP and repression, holding racial characteristics constant, did, in fact, come out slightly positive for both the 1950s and the 1960s (.01 and .06). Before entirely discounting the relationship of the economic development variables with repression, one needs to recall that change in urbanization had a $-.50$ correlation with change in repression, a result that could not be due to racial characteristics.

ECONOMIC DEPENDENCY

The variables discussed up to this point have referred to the internal conditions of the Latin American countries, but factors controlled from outside the boundaries of these twenty nations have also been a factor in their destinies. All Latin American countries lack the relative autonomy of the United States, the Soviet Union, and the People's Republic of China. They are all militarily and economically weak relative to the United States and all the other industrial powers, and they are therefore more easily intimidated by foreign military acts and more easily dominated by foreign economic forces. The relationship of these countries to the United States government, and, American business enterprises in particular, has been branded as colonial or dependent in nature. We want to consider in this section the possibility that these dependency relationships have an effect, either direct or indirect, on violence, repression, or both in Latin America.

Before going any further, it is important to clarify what is meant by "dependency."[15] Writers on this subject take as their basic premise that the dependency relationship is essentially economic. The economies of

---

[15]James D. Cockcroft, Andre Gunder Frank, and Dale L. Johnson, *Dependence and Underdevelopment* (Garden City, N.Y.: Doubleday, 1972); and Ronald H. Chilcote and Joel C. Edelstein, eds, *Latin America: The Struggle with Dependency and Beyond* (New York: Wiley, 1974), provide two basic summaries in English on the subject.

Latin America are economic satellites of the metropolitan countries, which exploit them for their cheap sources of labor and raw materials and as markets for surplus goods and capital. The satellites are left in a state of "underdevelopment" that prevents autonomous economic growth. The basic relationship, then, refers to trade and investment. Military intervention, Central Intelligence Agency manipulation, foreign aid, and military assistance, although important, are secondary to the economic relationship; they are tools for maintaining the dependent economic status.

The underlying assumption of the dependency writers is that men act in their own economic interest, and that interest is determined by one's position vis-à-vis the dependency relationship. On the one side are the foreign capitalists and their allies in Latin America, the national oligarchies, whose interest it is to preserve the system of dependency; on the other side are all who are exploited by the relationship, whose interest it is to break the system of dependency. Where dependency is greater, assuming that the relationship is subject to quantitative variation, more will be at stake between the opposing interests. The foreign capitalists and national oligarchies will, therefore, exert a greater amount of repression to maintain the system, and the oppressed will fight back harder. The dependency theory may be likened to Marx's theory of increasing class contradictions in higher stages of capitalism. It implies that the greater the dependency, the greater the violent opposition and the greater the repression.

The direct relationship between economic dependency and violence and repression is not the only possibility. Merle Kling has suggested an indirect relationship with the intervening variable being social mobility:

> Because of the colonial nature of the Latin American economies, an exceptional economic premium attaches to control of the apparatus of government as a dynamic base of power. Whereas the conventional bases of power effectively restrict mobility in economic status, control of government provides an unusually dynamic route to wealth and power. Thus the contrast between the stable character of the conventional economic bases of power and the shifting, unconventional position of government provokes intense and violent competition for control of government as a means of acquiring and expanding a base of wealth and power.[16]

Kling does not consider "the colonial nature of the Latin American economies" as a variable in Latin America, but from the way in which he uses the concept, it clearly is: It is the proportion of the nonagricul-

---

[16]Merle Kling, "Toward a Theory of Power and Political Instability in Latin America," *Western Political Quarterly* 9 (March, 1956), p. 34.

tural enterprises owned by foreigners. His dependent variable is somewhat ambiguous, but seems to refer to the numbers of coups d'etat, cases of *continuismo*, and the degree of violence used by both government and opposition in the competition for political power. Kling neither operationalized nor tested his proposition, but Manus Midlarsky and Raymond Tanter claim to have done so.[17] Their operationalization, however, of the "colonial nature of Latin American economies" is faulty and their results should be rejected. To derive the index they call "economic presence," they multiplied United States investment per capita by proportion of total trade with the United States. First of all, there is no reason to use only U.S. investment and trade because the logic applies equally to all foreign presence. Second, investment per capita does not relate the foreign presence to the size of the national economy, and what results is a combination of U.S. investment and the wealth of the economy, not the importance of the foreign presence. Third, by multiplying the two figures, the distribution of the combined index becomes highly skewed, invalidating any regression analysis used on that data.

A second indirect relationship between economic dependency and violence can be derived from both Andre Gunder Frank's discussion of the effects of dependency on economic growth[18] and the second section of this chapter. Frank argues that the long-run effect of trade and foreign investment in the international capitalist system is to destroy the possibilities of continued autonomous economic growth. What he does not discuss is that new trade and new investment does generate short-term economic growth. New trade and new foreign investment bring additional resources and employment, which definitely stimulate the economy in the short run. He concentrates his argument, however, on the long run, where trade has destined a country to specialize in production of primary products and where foreign investment siphons off profits from the principal productive sectors of the satellite and returns those resources to the world metropolis. Economic dependency, according to this theory, produces short-term growth and long-term stagnation. This pattern related to Davies' J-Curve and our modification of that theory. When a nation's economy, after growing, begins to stagnate, it will be much readier for revolution than if earlier growth had been slower but more autonomous. Whether the problem arises from the decline of the growth rate, as Davies hypothesized, or because social mobilization continues to climb after growth has slowed down,

[17]Manus Midlarsky and Raymond Tanter, "Toward a Theory of Political Instability in Latin America," *Journal of Peace Research* 4 No. 3, (1967), pp. 209–227.

[18]Andre Gunder Frank, *Latin America: Underdevelopment or Revolution* (New York: Monthly Review, 1969).

as we have hypothesized, the result is the same. A process is set in motion by the economic dependency relationship that stimulates wants that, in the long run, will not be satisfied.

We developed data on three kinds of international economic relationships: private foreign investment, foreign trade, and foreign aid. We consider the foreign investment variable the most important part of the dependency relationship. The private foreign investment data available for all Latin American nations in the 1950s refers only to U.S. direct investment in 1952. The Organization for Economic Cooperation and Development gathered data on total investment from OECD countries for 1967. The data on the other variables were easily obtainable. Table 18 lists trade data for all countries and aid from the United States and international organizations. Because our interest was in the extent to which foreign investment, trade, or aid dominated the economy of the Latin American country, we divided the national totals by each country's gross national product.

One of the striking points about the data shown in Table 18 is the extent to which the three kinds of dependency are not related. The only association of any consequence is between investment and trade in the 1950s, which has a correlation coefficient of .64. The notion that investment goes to exploit raw materials for export to the United States and that aid goes to support this relationship does not hold up. Investment, trade, and aid each seems to have its own rationale.

In the 1950s Cuba scored the highest on both investment and trade dependency. Venezuela was close behind in the 1950s and still very high in the 1960s. However, foreign investments flowed into Panama at a phenomenal rate during the fifties pushing that country far ahead of all other countries on investment. Honduras, Chile, and the Dominican Republic were also very high on investment. Honduras, El Salvador, and Peru were the highest on trade. Foreign aid was relatively low everywhere in the 1950s. In the 1960s, Bolivia, the Dominican Republic, and Nicaragua received the most foreign aid in proportion to the size of their economies.

The correlations between the three dependency variables and violence and repression in both the 1950s and the 1960s are shown in Table 19. They lead us to reject the proposition that any of the three forms of dependency has a direct relationship with either violence or repression. The situation in Cuba was misleading. True, Cuba was highest in dependency on investment and trade in the 1950s, and it did have an enormous amount of violence in the 1950s, but other countries with high amounts of investment and trade did not follow this pattern. Honduras, Chile, and Costa Rica were also relatively high on economic dependency but were relatively low on violence and repression.

Table 18. Economic Dependency Variables

Country	Foreign Investment		Foreign Trade		Foreign Aid	
	1950/GNP	1960/GNP	1955/GNP	1965/GNP	1950s/GNP	1960s/GNP
Argentina	2.3	9.4	7.3	7.9	.3	.5
Bolivia	1.9	21.0	13.7	18.2	3.0	6.8
Brazil	4.2	13.2	8.5	7.3	1.0	1.4
Chile	12.5	18.8	8.7	15.1	.8	3.2
Colombia	4.5	11.6	15.4	9.0	.7	2.8
Costa Rica	14.0	21.4	20.4	18.8	1.5	3.2
Dominican Republic	17.9	15.8	16.5	14.0	.1	5.9
Ecuador	1.3	7.0	8.6	16.1	1.1	2.1
El Salvador	3.0	9.2	16.4	23.8	.6	2.0
Guatemala	13.0	10.6	12.7	14.2	1.5	2.1
Haiti	3.6	9.5	10.8	9.4	1.9	1.6
Honduras	19.3	31.6	16.9	24.9	1.3	4.1
Mexico	3.0	8.2	5.7	5.9	.5	.7
Nicaragua	2.7	11.8	21.0	25.2	1.5	5.6
Panama	15.5	119.0	20.1	12.5	1.7	3.4
Paraguay	1.4	7.5	6.9	13.0	1.0	3.8
Peru	5.3	25.4	10.9	22.1	1.1	1.8
Uruguay	2.6	3.6	10.8	11.5	.5	1.1
Venezuela	23.2	46.0	20.6	36.1	.1	1.1
Cuba	24.8		21.2		.2	1.2

Sources: Foreign investment: United Nations, *External Financing in Latin America* (New York: United Nations, 1965), p. 32; OECD, *Stock of Private Direct Investments by DAC Countries in Developing Countries at the end of 1967* (Paris, OECD, 1972); foreign trade: United Nations, *Statistical Yearbook, 1957 and 1967* (New York: United Nations, 1958 and 1967); foreign aid: United States Agency for Independent Development, *U.S. Overseas Loans and Grants and Assistance from International Organizations* (Washington: AID, annual). Passim.

Table 19. Correlations with Dependency Variables

Independent Variables	Violence	Repression
1950s		
1952 U.S. direct investment/GNP	.18	.08
1955 Exports/GNP	.06	.04
Average aid/GNP	.15	−.09
1960s		
1960 Total foreign direct investment/GNP	−.11	−.25
1965 Exports/GNP	.02	−.24
Average aid/GNP	−.03	.00

The Kling theory that greater dependency leads to less social mobility and, therefore, to greater political violence likewise receives no confirmation from these correlations. The use of partial correlations, holding GNP or agricultural product constant, does not change the size of the correlations. Kling's theory refers more specifically to the proportion of the nonagricultural sectors controlled by foreign enterprise rather than to total foreign investment. Even so, it is unlikely that a good measure of that proportion would give different results.

The theory that dependence on foreign investment and trade in primary products leads to long-run economic stagnation where social mobilization outruns social welfare is harder to test because it distinguishes the effects of new investment from those of old investment. The data in Table 18 and the correlations in Table 19 do not make this distinction. Furthermore, the effects are important only where foreign investment is sizable. Cuba is the most extraordinary case of a boom being financed by foreign investment after which profits were withdrawn. U.S. investment moved toward Cuba very rapidly in the 1920s, but then came to a standstill or was withdrawn until the 1950s, when interest was renewed. Economic growth stopped with the drying up of foreign investment, in part because all the profits from the boom had been taken back to the United States instead of being reinvested in Cuba. Thus, Cuba's specialization in sugar production had no payoff for development of other kinds of production. Nevertheless, Cuba's social mobilization continued to climb. In 1955 Cuba's level of social mobilization was far higher than its welfare relative to all other Latin American countries, and mobilization continued to change faster than did welfare in the 1950s.

The second most striking case of disinvestment that led to economic stagnation came in Venezuela. Between 1961 and 1967, total U.S. investment in Venezuela dropped from $3,008,000,000 to $2,553,000,000 at current prices. At the same time, the earnings of U.S. companies averaged $500 million a year. In those seven years, then, roughly $4 billion dollars in capital and profits were taken out of Venezuela (equivalent to half of one year's gross domestic product) economic growth plummeted, but social mobilization continued to increase. For the 1960s, Venezuela's economic growth was one standard deviation below the Latin American mean, but its change in social mobilization was more than two standard deviations above the mean. The difference was much greater than any place else in Latin America during the 1960s.

The data for Guatemala and the Dominican Republic indicate that U.S. investment was high in 1950 in these countries and then tapered off. Economic growth was almost nonexistent in the same period, but our measures of social mobilization in these countries were not particularly high. Neither showed a low score on either the level of welfare/mobilization differential or the differentials of economic growth and change in social mobilization. Both countries, however, had a large increase in the level of violence during the period of foreign investment stagnation.

In short, all four nations—Cuba, Venezuela, Guatemala, and the Dominican Republic—where U.S. investment was high and then stagnated experienced high violence. Two of them—Cuba and Venezuela—showed exceptional scores on the welfare/mobilization differential. This more complex view of economic dependency indicates a relationship with violence, which may be indirect through the welfare/mobilization differential, or may possibly be direct.

Summary

The consideration of four categories of socio-economic variables has yielded one strong relationship with violence and one strong relationship with repression. The principal socio-economic explanation of violence in Latin America is the welfare/mobilization differential, both in its static and dynamic forms. The principal socio-economic explanation of repression is the proportion of white and mestizo persons in the population.

A number of hypotheses had to be rejected because of the lack of supporting evidence. Economic development has no relationship with violence in Latin America. Neither land nor income inequality has any relationship with either violence or repression. The amount of foreign investment and foreign trade and aid has no relationship with either violence or repression.

When a population is exposed to the higher possibilities of greater material welfare through urbanization and mass communication, and these wants cannot be met because the average welfare is relatively low, the population does become more violent. The change in mobilization and welfare makes an impact independent of the levels of development. The evidence strongly supports this hypothesis.

One of the explanations for the development of a situation in which social mobilization has and continues to outrun societal welfare is that economic dependency tends to stimulate short-run growth as it tends to retard long-run growth. When new foreign investment slows down, stops, or is withdrawn, economic growth also slows down, but social mobilization is likely to continue.

Higher levels of socio-economic development, whether measured by welfare or mobilization, are associated with lower levels of repression. A highly integrated society, however, measured by the proportion of the population which is white and mestizo, is even more highly associated with low levels of repression.

CHAPTER 4

POLITICAL AND STRUCTURAL EXPLANATIONS

How an individual responds to his socio-economic environment depends on two things: on his interactions with other people and on the kinds of organizations, including governments, that he and others are able to develop to structure their relationships. These relationships are both subtle and complex and, hence, exceedingly difficult to measure. This chapter not only presents ways in which structural and political variables might have a bearing on repression and violence, but attempts to measure these variables. The first half of the chapter discusses the extent and way in which social life is structured, and the last part deals with the degree to which governments have responded to public demands for goods and services. These concepts and their measurement are only suggestive of the patterns of social interactions that might affect repression and violence, but the strength of the associations found indicates that politics is definitely important.

94

The institutionalization of the structures of society

Societies are not composed of isolated individuals. They are made up of people, or roles, arranged in certain structural relationships. These structures affect an individual's values, his relations with other people, and how he works to achieve his goals. These structures will certainly influence the way in which the individual relates to his government and the way in which government relates to individuals. To say structures are important, however, is only to state the obvious, even if the obvious is too often ignored. The basic questions are what structures are crucial for what behavior, and how does variation in structures modify variation in behavior—in this case, violence and repression.

William Kornhauser has provided probably the best statement on the difference between a structured and an unstructured society in his *Politics of Mass Society*.[1] His concern is with the rise of those mass movements that become totalitarian. Mass society lacks structure except for primary groups and the state. Atomized individuals without inter-mediary structures between them and the state are susceptible to mobi-lization into mass movements, and at the same time, they are likely to engage in violent action. To Kornhauser they tend to focus their atten-tion on remote objects, such as "national and international issues or events, abstract symbols, and whatever else is known only through mass media,"[2] all of which decreases their sense of reality and responsi-bility. Yet the mode of response of atomized individuals tends to be direct, not "mediated by several intervening layers of social relations." "People act directly when they do not engage in discussion on the matter at hand, and when they do not act through groups in which they are capable of persuading and being persuaded by their fellows."[3] Direct action may be violent, and it may lead to mass movements, which Kornhauser believes are likely to become totalitarian. Totalitar-ian governments are, by definition, the most repressive political sys-tems.

Kornhauser applied the notion of mass society primarily to the process of policy formation in society. It could also be applied, how-ever, to the processes of the struggle for governmental positions and the propagating of community-wide standards and values that limit and harmonize the conflict of interests. His theory can also relate to the

[1]William Kornhauser, *Politics of Mass Society* (Glencoe, Ill.: Free Press, 1959).
[2]Ibid., p. 43.
[3]Ibid, p. 45.

pluralist idea that independent structures are necessary to resist the tyrannous acts of governments. All of these processes may affect the levels of repression and violence.

We can't go far in the discussion without referring to specific structures. The argument seems to apply to a number of structures: associations, interest groups, political parties, organized religion, and perhaps, to the legislative and the military segments of the government. All might be structures through which resistance to repression could be organized. All but the military are set up to facilitate discussion and negotiation about policy.

Information about legislatures is almost totally lacking in Latin America, and the consideration of interest groups also presented problems. Not only is it difficult, if not impossible, to collect the requisite information on interest groups, but the theoretical problem of balance between different groups must also be confronted. What might be the result of having well-institutionalized landowner organizations, but no peasant organization? What is the relative merit of having the labor movement divided as opposed to having it united? The problems of finding the data and sorting out such theoretical questions meant that interest groups could not be fitted into the confines of the present study. This study, then, deals only with the church, political parties, and the military as independent social structures.

Kornhauser discussed intermediate groups in terms of their existence or absence. In making a comparative study of Latin America, that distinction was not sufficient. Groups *exist* everywhere. We needed a more sophisticated way of distinguishing degrees of existence. Huntington's notion of institutionalization seemed most relevant. He says that "the level of institutionalization of any particular organization can be measured by its adaptability, complexity, autonomy, and coherence."[4] As will be discussed, these criteria are still one step short of measurement and had to be modified when applied to specific organizations. Nonetheless, they do provide a sense of an organization's strength. In a difficult environment, of course, organizations can exist that have no ability to accomplish their objectives. Other organizations can fight back and improve the environment. Only the latter are likely to have an impact on violence, whether official or unofficial.

After attempting to work with Huntington's criteria, we decided the most important aspects of institutionalization were two: independence from control by outside organizations (i.e., autonomy), and the

---

[4]Samuel P. Huntington, *Political Order in Changing Societies* (New Haven: Yale University Press, 1968), p. 12.

ability of the organization to guide and direct individuals within it rather than being manipulated by powerful individuals. In short, the question is: To what extent does the organization structure the roles of its individual members? An organization that is autonomous and orients the roles of members will have a life of its own greater than the sum of its parts; it will be institutionalized.

Church institutionalization

The Roman Catholic Church, the religious organization to which more than ninety percent of Latin Americans belong, is the most institutionalized organization in the world at the international level. It excels on Huntington's criteria. Huntington uses age as an indicator of adaptability, which puts the Catholic Church ahead of all national governments. The Catholic Church compares with or exceeds in complexity the largest organizations in the world, such as the U.S. Department of Defense, General Motors, or the Communist Party. Furthermore, it is autonomous and establishes clearly defined roles for its members. Despite the presence of this highly institutionalized organization in Latin America, the region seems to be neither higher nor lower on violence and repression than other parts of the world. The international Catholic Church, however, is not as monolithic as its antagonists have alleged, and in Latin America, the national churches, and even the dioceses and religious orders, vary greatly in character, strength, and relationship with the population and the government. For our purposes the national church is most important. And to us the question is: How do the national churches vary in ways that would help explain differences in violence and repression?

Ivan Vallier stimulated our interest in the relationship between churches and social cohesion in his book, *Catholicism, Social Control, and Modernization in Latin America.*[5] His primary thesis is that the weakness, not the strength, of the church in Latin America is responsible for "political instability" on the continent. He summarizes his reasoning:

> Political instability in Latin America is bred, in part, by the absence of a durable religio-moral foundation within which political processes can be stabilized. Such basic integrative principles as cooperation, compromise,

[5]Ivan Vallier, *Catholicism, Social Control, and Modernization in Latin America* (Englewood Cliffs, N.J.: Prentice-Hall, 1970).

and mutual trust, which make up the cultural bases of institutional life, are weak. Consequently, political conflicts, short-run contests, and changes in political leadership are only tenuously linked to collective meanings about social goals and national objectives.[6]

By extending his discussion, we can suggest a causal chain: A "developed church" brings about values in the society that improve the functioning of all other institutions, both associational and governmental, which in turn leads to lower levels of violence and repression. Vallier does not state it in quite this form because he is not concerned with an explicit test of the relationships but only with why the Catholic Church had not fulfilled this function. Although he does discuss a number of differences among national churches, he does not relate these differences to variations in political stability. We have no data on the distribution of values in the Latin American countries that would allow us to test the relationship between the church and values. If the relationships on all the links are strong, however, there would be a positive association between "church development," which we will attempt to measure, and party and military institutionalization, and violence and repression.

Vallier traces the roots of the failure of the Catholic Church to create a "religio-moral foundation" for society to its organizational weakness. The church, he says, "is ideologically divided, extensively segmented at the national and diocesan levels, and generally uncoordinated in its administrative and pastoral efforts."[7] He attributes its fragmentation to the way in which it was scattered "with great haste, throughout a territory of vast proportions." In the absence of overall coordination and organization, the local churches became dependent on the local status groups. Weakness and dependence led the church in Latin America to develop a political survival strategy that entailed "a maximization of short-run gains when conditions are favorable, an exercising of restraint in periods of uncertainty, and an every-ready willingness to be inconsistent if the situation demands it."[8] In its concern with political maneuvering, it failed to develop or teach autonomous religious goals.

The situation in some countries was a good deal worse than Vallier's description. The church not only failed to inculcate a religio-moral foundation, it stimulated dissensus and conflict through its fight to

---

[6]Ibid., p. 43.
[7]Ibid., p. 24.
[8]Ibid., pp. 25–26.

maintain its political prerogatives and material possessions. Most of the civil wars of the nineteenth century were between "liberal" and "conservative" parties over, among other things, the possessions of the church, the secularization of marriage and education, financial support for the church, and the involvement of the clergy in politics. The conflict was more intense in some countries than in others. Colombia probably suffered most from violence over clerical issues, as the two parties there were very similar in strength and neither side ever achieved a definitive victory. In other countries, for example, Guatemala, Honduras, and the Dominican Republic, the Catholic Church was completely defeated in the nineteenth century and greatly weakened. The Mexican Revolution brought the anticlericals to power, but the clericals were not routed completely until the Cristero Rebellion was put down around 1930. Even so, the church was not destroyed in Mexico as it was in Guatemala and Honduras; it was only disestablished. Chile and Costa Rica, on the other hand, never had violent conflict between clericals and anticlericals.

We can supplement Vallier further by citing some positive effects of the church in resisting oppression. This argument is a simple extension of the pluralist argument: organizations independent of the government will resist government attempts to expand its power. Because of its international standing, the Catholic Church is more difficult to suppress and control than many other kinds of organizations. In Brazil it has proved to be the most resistant organization in that country to the military government's dictatorial power. In the first years of the Brazilian military dictatorship (the mid-1960s), the church was divided and less effective, but in the early 1970s, it clearly exerted its influence to temper the excesses of the regime. The church also played a prominent role in the overthrow of three dictatorships in the 1950s: Juan Perón's in Argentina, Gustavo Rojas Pinilla's in Colombia, and Marcos Pérez Jiménez's in Venezuela. The relative autonomy and strength of a national church increases its effectiveness in resisting tyranny.

We can now spell out which qualities of the church are related to violence and repression in Latin America. The unity and resources of the Catholic Church are important for it to be able to affect the values of the population and resist the power of the government. They should also contribute to its autonomy. Also important is how political conflict over the separation of church and state was resolved. Autonomy is only possible where the conflict has been resolved so as to make the church independent of the government, and the government equally independent of the church. According to Vallier's line of reasoning, and our supplements to Vallier, the greater the strength and autonomy of the church, the lower the level of violence and repression.

Marx's suggestion that religion is "opium of the people" is an alternative theoretical relationship between religion and violence. To Marx, religion is a substitute for protest against inhumane conditions. If his theory were correct, the strength of the church would be negatively related with violence, as was the case in Vallier's theory, but the autonomy of the church, contrary to Vallier's theory, would be irrelevant. Furthermore, Marx's theory would imply either no relationship with repression or a positive one.

The factors that go into making a national church strong or weak are many and complex. One would want to consider its financial resources, both their quantity and sources, the numbers and training of clergy, the development of lay organizations, and the degree of unity and cooperation among different parts of the church. The determination of the strength or weakness of a national church is complicated because different national churches have received different degrees of support from foreign churches and the Vatican. Of these factors mentioned above, we have chosen the number of clergy as a proportion of the population serving the requirements of being both available and a valid indicator of church strength. The question of the recruitment of clergy has been one of the critical issues throughout Latin America. This nominally Catholic area has long been short of clergy and has had to depend on missionaries from North America and Europe. The number of national clergymen reflects past strength in terms of the church's earlier ability to obtain commitment from the population and its present strength in terms of the possibilities for contacting the people. We chose clergy per 100,000 population as of 1940 for the analysis of violence and repression in the 1950s, and as of 1950 for their analysis in the 1960s. The earlier period indicates the condition when the generation of adults were more susceptible to socialization and at the same time omits the large influx of missionaries after 1950.

The range of differences in church strength, as shown by the number of clergy per 100,000 population is wide in Latin America, as can be seen in Table 20. In 1950, the Dominican Republic had only 1.9 priests per 100,000, while Ecuador had 15.87. Even Ecuador had far fewer priests in the recent period than in 1912, when it had 33.3 per 100,000, and it also had fewer priests than all Western European countries in 1950, reflecting the acknowledged "crisis of vocations." The number of priests in Latin America ranges from a sufficient number to reach a good proportion of the population to not enough to reach any but the most privileged. In fact, the Dominican Republic, Guatemala, and Cuba have been close to being churchless nations. The absence of the Catholic Church has provided a vacuum in these nations that has not been filled by other religious institutions or by secular organiza-

Table 20. Church Institutionalization

Country	1940 Clergy per 100,000	1950 Clergy per 100,000	Civil Divorce	Separation of Church and State	1950s Church Score (Z)	1960s Church Score (Z)
Argentina	8.06	10.86	no	no	−1.28	−.54
Bolivia	9.90	7.69	yes	no	−.04	−.33
Brazil	7.19	6.28	no	yes	−.58	−.65
Chile	13.88	12.19	no	yes	.74	.66
Colombia	15.62	15.62	no	no	.20	.52
Costa Rica	14.70	12.50	yes	no	.90	.73
Dominican Republic	2.62	1.91	yes	no	−1.47	−1.62
Ecuador	18.51	15.87	yes	yes	2.54	2.40
El Salvador	6.94	5.98	yes	yes (1962)	−.62	.20
Guatemala	3.26	2.14	yes	yes	−.46	−.65
Haiti	5.49	7.04	yes	no	−.90	−.48
Honduras	5.46	3.84	yes	yes	−.03	−.28
Mexico	16.94	14.28	yes	yes	2.23	2.04
Nicaragua	10.20	9.61	yes	no	.02	.09
Panama	5.20	4.45	yes	yes	−.08	−.25
Paraguay	9.00	6.53	no	no	−1.10	−1.51
Peru	10.41	7.75	yes	no	.06	−.32
Uruguay	7.29	6.28	yes	yes	.34	.26
Venezuela	9.17	7.93	yes	no	−.19	−.28
Cuba	4.06	3.00	yes	yes	−.30	—
Mean	9.20	8.36			0	0
S.D.	4.50	4.10			1.00	1.00

Sources: Data on priests from Center of Intercultural Documentation, *Latin America in Maps, Charts, Tables: No. 2, Socio-Religious Data* (Mexico D.F.: CIDOC, 1964), p. 93. Qualitative data from J. Lloyd Mecham, *Church and State in Latin America* (Chapel Hill: University of North Carolina, 1966).

tions. On the other hand, the Catholic Church in Chile, Colombia, Costa Rica, and Mexico have had sufficient clergy to reach five to eight times more of the population than in the Dominican Republic.

Our theory postulates that the strength of the Roman Catholic Church will be important in reducing repression and violence only if its strength is accompanied by autonomy. Autonomy, is perhaps, a more nebulous concept than strength. A rather detailed sociological analysis would be needed to find out the extent to which each church has ceased to use the political order to preserve its privileges and has also managed to escape being dominated by the political authorities. In the absence of such a study, we felt we would best rely on the legal situation. The official separation of church and state has been an important and meaningful turning point in the position of the church. For the most part, separation has taken the Catholic Church out of politics and the government out of the church. Another important legal question has been the extent to which the church has maintained its influence in the regulation of marriage and divorce. The presence of legal divorce, we felt, indicated a further step in the autonomy of the church. Both are, of course, only crude indications of the more complex relationships involved.

In some countries, these two indicators seemed to reflect fairly well the situation described by other writers. Vallier points out that the Catholic Church is greatly involved in political affairs in Colombia, and that it is dominated by the government in Argentina. Neither country has official separation of church and state or civil divorce. At the other extreme are Mexico and Uruguay where the separation is complete, as reflected by both official separation of church and state and legal divorce. Vallier has suggested that in Brazil and Chile the church has a high degree of autonomy, but the church in both nations received only an intermediate score on our operationalization.[9] Because divorce is not allowed in either country, it may be that the government is not as free of church influence as it is in some other places.

We gave a score of one to countries with both separation of church and state and civil divorce, and minus one to those with neither. Those differing on the two items received a zero. These scores were then added to the standardized (or Z) scores on the clergy to obtain an overall church institutionalization score (Z). Ecuador and Mexico received the highest combined score in the two decades, and the Dominican Republic and Paraguay the lowest. Subjective views would probably dispute some of the high scores and commend most of the low scores. We felt that the inadequacies of these objective criteria were less than the inadequacies of more subjective criteria.

Because of our interest in the relationships between the church institutionalization scores and the other institutionalization scores, we will test these hypotheses later in this chapter after the other scores and relationships have been developed. Our basic proposition is that the church institutionalization score is positively related to the other institutionalization scores and negatively related to repression and violence. The alternative proposition, derived from Marx, predicts that only church strength is negatively related to violence, but autonomy does not affect the relationship. If church institutionalization has any association with repression, it would be positive.

---

[9]Ivan Vallier, "Church Development in Latin America: A Five-Country Comparison," *Journal of Developing Areas* 1 (July, 1967), p. 471.

Political party institutionalization

Political parties provide the organization for bringing together political leaders and political followers in the competition for personal power and policy formation. To the extent that parties exist, political participation of both leaders and followers becomes structured. Latin America provides an intriguing area to study the effects of these structures because the variation in political parties pretty well covers the range that exists in the world.

Political parties exist in all countries in Latin America, except for Haiti, but the extent to which they structure political activity varies enormously. One of the clearest distinctions among parties in Latin America is between those that organize and control the activities of political leaders, and those that are ad hoc arrangements for the pursuit of power by particular leaders. One of the clichés of studies on Latin America is that its culture of politics is characterized by *personalismo* and *caudillismo*, in which loyalties are to individual leaders as opposed to institutions. Allegiance to powerful personalities certainly exists in Latin America as it does elsewhere, but its prevalence varies with time and place. In some countries, political parties are extremely important. Where parties are strong, they control positions in the government and nominations for public office. They distribute the rewards and benefits available to them as parties or as holders of official positions. The parties work out and promote policies arrived at collectively. In short, neither personalities nor institutions are uniformly important throughout Latin America. Rather, the differences on this dimension form an important variable that distinguishes political systems and that may help explain the variation in violence and repression.

One of the ways in which political parties may have an impact on the degree of conflict is through the simplification and direction of the succession process, a result that may be as important where free elections do exist as where they do not. Where parties are strong, they establish a career pattern for would-be political leaders. Persons who want to get ahead in politics must work their way up through party positions and government service in a prescribed way; only after a period of apprenticeship and proven ability in party matters can they attain high positions in the party and be eligible for nomination for high public office. Where parties exist, politicians will tend to be professionals and persons from other spheres will tend to be excluded from political offices. Furthermore, the parties will narrow the choice for public office considerably. In a one-party system, they will try to keep it at one, and in competitive party systems, they will restrict the choice to a few, usually two or three. The situation that existed in Guatemala before the 1963 coup d'état, where sixteen persons had nominated themselves to the presidency, could not happen where political parties were firmly established. Without political parties, the succession process becomes something of a free-for-all, and chance circumstances determine the winner.

A chaotic free-for-all for public office may have no direct bearing on the level of violence in society. Where groups are not well enough organized to rally around a few candidates, it is unlikely that they are well enough organized to enter into violent conflict. However, such chaos may invite military intervention, as it did in Guatemala in 1963, and stimulate public support for more authoritarian solutions. Certainly, the lack of meaningful choice in a democratic election will tend to undermine the democratic processes.

At the same time that political parties are clarifying the choices in democratic elections, they are promoting a system of elections. Political parties stand to gain more in a direct sense from nonrepressive electoral systems than do any other organizations. As a result, when not in the government, they are the first to resist tyranny, and the strength of their organization will determine their ability to oppose repression. The overthrow of General Rojas Pinilla in Colombia in 1957 and that of General Pérez Jiménez in Venezuela in 1958 were organized by the political parties, which effectively led a general strike in each case.

Political parties may also make repressive controls less necessary by providing less coercive means of control. An alternative to repression is co-optation, and co-optation can be best used where power is organized by a political party. Anderson and Cockroft have taken the concept of co-optation from Philip Selznik and shown its importance as a control mechanism in the Mexican system:

> The process of absorbing new elements into the leadership or policy-determining strata of an organization as a means of averting threats to its existence or stability is called co-optation. In the Mexican case, the intent of the PRI is certainly to avert threats to the stability of the polity and the co-opted dissident groups certainly come to believe that they will get a measure of influence but the extent to which they get any real influence, that is get some parts of their programs enacted, is hard to determine. Co-optation is an exchange process, and can thus hardly be an enduring phenomenon unless the co-opted groups, led by rather astute politicians, received some concessions.[10]

Anderson and Cockroft have overemphasized the extent to which co-optation requires fulfillment of group demands as opposed to the

---

[10]Bo Anderson and James C. Cockroft, "Control and Co-Optation in Mexican Politics," in *Dependence and Underdevelopment,* James C. Cockroft, Andre Gunder Frank, and Dale L. Johnson, ed. (Garden City, N.Y.: Doubleday, 1972), p. 232.

particularistic demands of political leaders. The Mexican system provides privileges, possibilities for personal enrichment, and jobs and private benefits for the followers of political leaders as well as (sometimes instead of) group benefits. The Mexican system is a well-organized political machine that tends to substitute particularistic benefits for group benefits. By involving most political contenders in the system of spoils, they disarm the opposition, thereby avoiding violence and making repression unnecessary.

The most publicized work of political parties is their creation and dissemination of programs for potential public policies. The development of the party programs provides one of the best opportunities for political leaders to consider future policies and evaluate old ones; in the process, they learn what their followers are thinking and how they will respond to new ideas. Both the noncompetitive party campaigns in Mexico and the intensely competitive party campaigns in Chile bring political leaders and followers together in the exchange of ideas. Without a party organization, this kind of discussion is less prevalent and less well-structured. In this process, too, leaders and followers may take on values that they would not necessarily consider in the absence of organized public debates. Political policies, or platforms, should make party governments more responsible and responsive, but under certain conditions, they also serve to polarize society. Colombia in the late 1940s and Chile in the late 1960s and early 1970s were both polarized by the programmatic activities of political parties. Polarization can always stimulate repression or violence or both. On this point, then, one can never be sure what the effect of institutional political parties in Latin America will be.

Where a highly institutionalized political party governs, it should provide more effective government than would a less institutionalized political party. Governing requires the coordination of a large number of politicians and appointees in legislatures and in administrative positions. Without this coordination, policy will not be passed by the legislative body, where that is required, and, if passed, may not be implemented. Generally, it is necessary for a political party to assure this coordination. More effective government should lower the level of discontent and hence lower the level of both violence and repression.

All of these hypothesized effects of institutionalized political parties would tend to reduce both violence and repression—except, of course, for the additional hypothesized effect of an ideological polarization of society. The increasing effectiveness of government and the greater possibility of compromise and co-optation where a party or parties exist would reduce both violence and repression. The organization of succession should make democratic processes more stable and increase the possibility of continued freedom. The ability and willingness of parties to resist tyranny should also reduce repression. Adding these facts together leads us to hypothesize that institutionalized political parties will correlate negatively with violence and repression, and the correlation will be stronger with repression than with violence.

The institutionalization of political parties is conceptually independent of oppositional violence, but the question can be raised of whether it is a cause or a result of repression. The arguments presented above establish the plausibility that institutionalization of parties may prevent repression, but it does not exclude the possibility that repression may prevent the institutionalization of parties as well. Nevertheless, there are no cases in Latin America where a repressive regime has destroyed a highly institutionalized political party. The Pérez Jiménez regime in Venezuela made a concerted effort to destroy the fledgling party, *Acción Democrática*, but in the end it failed and was brought down by the AD acting in conjunction with other parties. For the most part, parties were nonexistent, weak, or badly divided when repressive regimes have been established in Latin America. Haiti had long periods when parties could have been organized but were not. Guatemala never managed to organize anything more than highly personalist parties. The parties in Cuba in 1952 and in Argentina in 1930 were divided and falling apart. Even though the relationship is clearly reciprocal, the causal direction from parties to repression seems the stronger. We will make some modifications on the measurement of party institutionalization to reduce the degree of association that results from the effect of repression on party institutionalization.

The important point distinguishing institutionalized political parties from noninstitutionalized political parties is the extent to which those ambitious for political power work within and through the party organization. It was not feasible to find information on all politically ambitious persons, but the most important are those who actively seek the presidency. We judged a political party to be more institutionalized if the presidential nominee of that party had worked within it, and if competition existed for the presidential nomination. Age of party also seemed important because long-term loyalties and the development of professional politicians required permanence of the party.

The scoring of each political party participating in elections in the last twenty years was made according to the following criteria:

- *One point* was given if presidential nominee had worked his way up through the party and served the party or was representative of the party.
- *One point* was given if competition existed for the party nomination whenever two or more candidates became eligible for that position in

party. Parties were considered to have competition if their leadership was composed of individuals of more or less equal influence.

- *Two points* were given if party was more than thirty years old; one and one-half points if between twenty and twenty-nine; *one point* if between ten and nineteen.

Our interest was not in parties as such, but in party systems. We had to aggregate the party scores into national scores. To do this, we weighted each party by the percentage of its total vote in the election. Parties that did not participate in any way in elections or in the government were not counted. Election years, then, were test years for party system scores. At these times, the presidential nomination and the vote distribution gave us key information. Table 21 presents the average party institutionalization scores by five-year periods.

Noncompetitive and rigged elections did not prove any liability for this scoring system. It just meant that all the weight was given to the ruling party. It was not necessary, for instance, to concern ourselves with the honesty or competitiveness of the vote in Mexico. Because the *Partido Revolucionario Institucional* took the major share of the votes,

Table 21. Political Party Institutionalization

Country	1950–1954	1955–1959	1960–1964	1965–1969
Argentina	1.45	1.91	2.10	.36 (2.10)
Bolivia	2.57	2.77	2.92	1.85
Brazil	1.51	2.36	1.52	.21 (1.52)
Chile	2.83	2.70	3.66	3.66
Colombia	3.18	3.31	3.06	3.07
Costa Rica	1.00	1.45	2.48	2.74
Dominican Republic	1.50	1.50	1.72	1.58
Ecuador	2.82	2.48	2.53	2.56
El Salvador	.88	.98	1.00	1.34
Guatemala	.64	.48	1.19	1.33
Haiti	0	0	0	0
Honduras	2.11	3.06	3.41	2.90
Mexico	3.18	3.78	3.88	3.94
Nicaragua	2.50	2.73	2.89	2.96
Panama	2.21	2.34	2.43	2.49
Paraguay	2.00	2.00	2.00	2.21
Peru	0	.80	1.40	1.68
Uruguay	3.86	3.94	3.92	3.90
Venezuela	1.03 (2.50)	1.00 (2.50)	1.90	2.52
Cuba	.73 (1.82)	.00 (1.82)		

PRI's institutionalization score mattered most. Similarly, the much more authoritarian regime in Paraguay reflected the institutionalization of the Colorado Party.

Generally, few cases were difficult to evaluate. The two largest problems came in Brazil after 1964 and in Argentina after 1966. In Brazil, parties were first outlawed and then reorganized. The old professional politicians flocked to the new official party, *Aliança Renovadora Nacional* (ARENA), and the official opposition, *Movimiento Democrático Brasiliero* (MDB). Parties, then, did exist under new names and with many of the old politicians, but they were more shadows than real parties, as they were unable to make policy in the national legislature nor to determine presidential candidates. In Argentina, parties were simply outlawed, though they continued to have more substance than those in Brazil. In these two cases, and in the similar circumstances in Cuba and Venezuela in the 1950s, we used the party institutionalization score obtained before the outlawing of parties in order to reduce the effects on the regression and correlation analysis of the reciprocal relationship. The scores in parentheses on Table 21 are the scores used in the statistical analysis.

As Table 21 illustrates, the general trend over the twenty-year period was toward an increase in party institutionalization. Costa Rica showed the greatest increase in institutionalization as the parties came into existence in the 1940s, continued in existence, and prospered. In addition to the loss of institutionalization in Brazil and Argentina, party institutionalization in Colombia and Bolivia fell for different reasons. In Colombia, the traditional parties lost much of their luster and gave way to the noninstitutionalized populist party organized by former dictator Rojas Pinilla, which came very close to winning a victory in 1970.[11] In Bolivia, the ruling party, *Movimiento Nacional Revolucionario* (MNR), broke apart because the government, with declining tin revenues and pressure from the United States government, could not satisfy its workers' section. With the MNR split, the military came to dominate the situation, though it continued to cooperate with political parties.

Military institutionalization

The degree of political party institutionalization should be considered in the light of military institutionalization because the integrity of the civilian processes in Latin America depends in part on the extent to

[11]Judith Talbot Campos and John F. McCâmant, *Cleavage Shift in Colombia* (Beverly Hills: Sage Publications, 1972).

which the military allows parties to operate and in part on the extent to which parties do not try to subvert the military for their own partisan ends. We are particularly concerned, then, with the boundary between the civilian and military spheres of government. We are also concerned with whether the military, if it does intervene in the political process, places a personalist military leader in power, rules as a collective military body, or nominates a civilian to rule. Other aspects of military institutionalization, such as complexity or professional training, would be important in the consideration of other relationships, but for its consequences on violence and repression, the important aspects of military institutionalization are institutional unity and nonintervention in the civilian processes.

The degree of military institutionalization is not solely a military question. The military may intervene despite a desire to avoid such action because of a breakdown in civilian processes or strong pressures from civilian groups. Military institutionalization, then, measures an aspect of the civilian processes as well as the integrity of the military forces.

The degree of military institutionalization may influence the level of violence and repression because, first of all, military officers possess skills and values different from those of civilians. Military men are trained to use coercion and their institutional experience is in using weapons, either in practice or in actual fighting. Further, the basic principle of organization in the military is hierarchical; military men are taught to value obedience above all else. Civilian politicians, on the other hand, are less accustomed to unquestioning obedience, and have far more experience in negotiation and compromise. In view of these different skills and values, we would expect military men in government to be much readier to resort to coercion than to try to work out compromises. Lack of military institutionalization, then, would lead to higher levels of repression.

A highly institutionalized military would never be divided so seriously as to war against itself. On the other hand, a military that contemplates intervention because of the personal ambitions of military leaders, or because of partisan divisions within the military, is likely to have internal power struggles. Lack of military institutionalization, then, would lead to greater violence between military units.

Lack of military institutionalization is also likely to lead to greater civilian violence. Because military intervention legitimizes the use of violence as a political method—military might makes right—guerrilla power then becomes an equally legitimate means to obtain power.

The control of the government by the military also prevents the politically minded, ambitious civilian from even hoping to be able to rise to power. Fidel Castro, for example, seemed willing to cooperate as a nonviolent politician within the Ortodoxo Party until Batista cut off the civilian route to power in 1952. One could point to many other examples of frustrated politicians turning to conspiracy when the civilian processes were closed down by the military.

These arguments all point to a strong negative association between military institutionalization and both violence and repression. We have already suggested additional arguments why noninstitutionalization of the military is more likely to lead to violence than to repression, and that may be the strongest relationship.

In operationalizing military institutionalization, or rather its opposite, the lack of military institutionalization, the first question was whether any military intervention existed. If no intervention had occurred, the military was considered completely institutionalized. If the military did intervene, however, we wanted to distinguish among the ways in which it used its power. The dates of intervention were also important, because the further away in time the intervention had occurred, the less it signified for the present military. Taking these questions into account, we scored successful coups d'état as follows:

- Coups where an individual personalist leader takes control were given a score of 1.00.
- Coups where a military junta or leader not involved in the plotting took over were given a score of .50.
- Coups wherein the military placed a civilian in charge of the government were given a score of .25.
- If the military merely ousted the president but did not take control, allowed the vice president to take over or called for elections, no score was given.
- The coup score was further reduced if it occurred in the previous decade by multiplying the above coup scores by .75, and if it occurred two decades earlier, by multiplying by .50. Coups that had taken place more than two decades earlier were not counted.

Figure 7 portrays all the coups in Latin America since 1930 and the original score assigned to each. Where several coups occurred in rapid succession, they were scored only once. The values were then reduced, according to how far in the past they had occurred, and summed. The numbers on the right-hand side of Figure 7 give the final military institutionalization scores in standard deviations, positive numbers meaning greater institutionalization.[12]

[12]We have been questioned on the independence between this measurement of military institutionalization and our violence score. It will be recalled that military coups per se were not considered to be violent events. Some coups, however, were accompanied by violence, and in these cases the measurement of the two variables would not be completely independent. However, more than ninety percent of the violence occurred on

Figure 7.   Coups and Military Institutionalization, 1930–1970

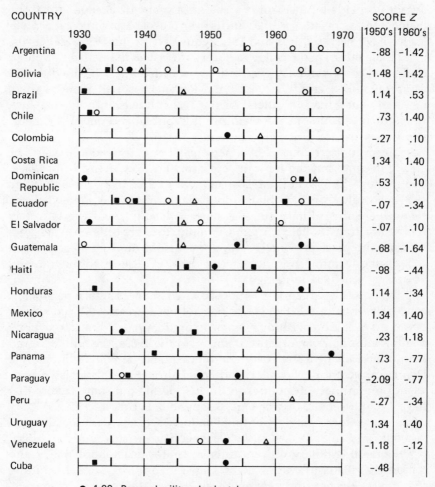

COUNTRY	1950's	1960's
Argentina	-.88	-1.42
Bolivia	-1.48	-1.42
Brazil	1.14	.53
Chile	.73	1.40
Colombia	-.27	.10
Costa Rica	1.34	1.40
Dominican Republic	.53	.10
Ecuador	-.07	-.34
El Salvador	-.07	.10
Guatemala	-.68	-1.64
Haiti	-.98	-.44
Honduras	1.14	-.34
Mexico	1.34	1.40
Nicaragua	.23	1.18
Panama	.73	-.77
Paraguay	-2.09	-.77
Peru	-.27	-.34
Uruguay	1.34	1.40
Venezuela	-1.18	-.12
Cuba	-.48	

KEY

● 1.00 Personal military leader takes over.
○ .50   Junta or officer who did not organize coup takes over.
■ .25   Military places nonelected civilian in power.
△ .00   Military intervenes, then supervises openly contested election.

occasions when there was no military coup. In only four countries, Argentina, Brazil, Panama, and Paraguay, was the level of violence appreciably higher during years in which military coups occurred. This fact also means that the problem of reciprocal causation was not important. Coups were not ordinarily the result of a high amount of civilian violence.

The coup pattern has changed considerably during the four decades considered in Figure 7. The most dramatic change is that the instances in which the military turns over power to an imposed civilian leader have occurred less and less frequently. In the 1930s and 1940s, more than a third of the coups in Latin America ended with an imposed civilian in the presidency. The military was much less inclined to rule as an organized group. Ecuador and Panama resorted more to these kinds of coups than to others. In the 1960s, however, only two such coups occurred, one in the Dominican Republic and one in Ecuador, and they provided only very temporary solutions.

The military coup used by a personalist military leader may also be on the decline, but the trend is less clear. Five occurred in the 1930s, two in the 1940s, six in the 1950s, and two in the 1960s. The two in the 1960s, however, in Honduras and Panama, resemble somewhat the kind where the military rules as an organization, and the two may represent a transitional position. Certainly, they are different in character from the great personalist military coups of the past—Trujillo's in 1930 in the Dominican Republic, Somoza's in 1936 in Nicaragua, and Stroessner's in 1954 in Paraguay.

Despite the reduction in imposed civilian and military personalist coups, the total number of coups has not been greatly reduced simply because a new kind of coup has come to predominate—the take-over by a military group as an organized entity. In the 1960s, the military as an institution took over the government in Argentina, Bolivia, Brazil, the Dominican Republic, Ecuador, and Peru. Alfred Stepan's incisive analysis of the military in politics in Brazil[13] points out some factors that have brought about this change throughout Latin America. Military officers have increasingly identified national security with social development, and military schools have begun to teach courses in social development. Military officers thus generate ideas about policy and national civilian structures, ideas that they are interested in putting into effect. Further, the new emphasis on counterinsurgency, encouraged by the United States military missions, has made the military more concerned with internal "subversion," which in turn has justified its intervention as preventing the coming to power of "radical" elements.

By our operationalization, Bolivia, Paraguay, and Venezuela had the least institutionalized military in the 1960s. Paraguay and Venezuela had militaries that still served as the vehicle for politically ambitious military leaders. Bolivia, Guatemala, and Argentina also had

---

[13]Alfred Stepan, *The Military in Politics; Changing Patterns in Brazil* (Princeton: Princeton University, 1971).

politically ambitious military officers, but the military was further undermined by political divisions and rather strong feelings about removing subversive elements in the society.

In the 1950s Costa Rica, Mexico, Uruguay, and Honduras had the most institutionalized military: in the 1960s the first three were still the leaders and Chile had replaced Honduras. These were the countries where civilians dominated the governing processes, and the military had a developed tradition of staying in the barracks. The changing nature of the military in Latin America has led to its greater involvement in Uruguay, and an outright take-over in Chile in the 1970s, leaving only Mexico and Costa Rica with highly institutionalized militaries.

Institutionalization versus mobilization

The previous arguments suggest that institutionalization of a society's structures will tend to lower the levels of violence and repression, whatever other factors are at work in the society. Kornhauser and Huntington, however, were both quite explicit in pointing out that the more society had departed from "traditional" conditions, the more it needed institutionalization. Kornhauser considered that communal society, where most relationships were within the small community, did not require the same kind of structures as an urbanized and industrial society. Huntington claimed that as social mobilization increased, institutionalization was necessary to channel the new demands and to tie individuals to the larger system.

In view of this relation between institutionalization and social mobilization we developed a measure of institutionalization relative to the degree of social mobilization. The three kinds of institutionalization—church, party, and military—were combined by adding their standardized scores, and the result was again standardized. Social mobilization was developed from a combined measure of communication and urbanization, as discussed in Chapter 3. We then took the difference between the standardized score on institutionalization and the standardized score on social mobilization. The result is shown in Table 22.

The extreme scores on the institutionalization-minus-social-mobilization measure reveal a certain plausibility to the hypothesis that higher mobilization levels require greater institutionalization. Argentina, Cuba, and Venezuela all scored very low on this measure. Mexico, Honduras, Ecuador, and Nicaragua all scored fairly high. Of the more mobilized countries, then, Mexico and Chile were the only ones with a level of institutionalization that exceeded the mobilization.

Table 22. Institutionalization Minus Social Mobilization

Country	1950s			1960s		
	Total Institutionalization	Social Mobilization	I Minus SM	Total Institutionalization	Social Mobilization	I Minus SM
Argentina	-1.00	1.78	-2.78	-1.25	2.17	-3.52
Bolivia	-.33	-.50	-.17	-.71	-.47	-.34
Brazil	.26	-.03	.29	-.61	-.11	-.50
Chile	.97	.88	.09	1.40	1.10	.30
Colombia	.51	-.07	.58	.55	.13	.42
Costa Rica	.68	-.23	.91	1.02	-.31	1.33
Dominican Republic	-.55	-.79	.24	-.87	-.78	-.09
Ecuador	1.35	-.52	1.87	.92	-.36	1.28
El Salvador	-.67	-.73	.06	.04	-.52	.56
Guatemala	-1.00	-.93	-.07	-1.37	-.88	-.49
Haiti	-1.53	-1.28	-.25	-1.29	-1.28	-.01
Honduras	.74	-1.18	1.92	.08	-1.15	1.23
Mexico	2.06	.11	1.95	2.06	.15	1.91
Nicaragua	.39	-.70	1.09	.70	-.64	1.42
Panama	.43	.21	.22	-.31	.43	-.74
Paraguay	-1.30	-.76	-.54	-1.01	-1.02	.01
Peru	-.67	-.28	-.39	-.57	.09	-.66
Uruguay	1.51	2.37	-.86	1.34	2.16	-.82
Venezuela	-.92	1.00	-1.92	-.20	1.28	-1.48
Cuba	-.90	1.63	-2.53			

Tests of the Institutionalization Hypotheses

The correlations among the three different kinds of institutionalization shown in Table 23 are not high, but they are consistently positive. The institutionalization of the Roman Catholic Church may promote values that facilitate the forming of other organizations, as Vallier has suggested. The correlations ranging between .41 and .56 suggest that the different kinds of institutionalization tend to go together and may represent a common dimension with common causes and common consequences.

The hypotheses suggesting negative relationship between church and party institutionalization and violence are not supported. The correlations, ranging from −.02 to −.21, are not sufficiently high to be of any consequence and may be spurious. It is unclear what Vallier means by "political instability," but if he means civil violence, we must conclude that the evidence does not support his contention that a developed church reduces political instability. Political parties don't seem to make much difference, either.

Table 23. Correlations with Institutionalization Measures, 1950–1970

1950s	*1*	*2*	*3*	*4*	*5*
1. Church institutionalization	1.00				
2. Party institutionalization	.47	1.00			
3. Military institutionalization	.43	.31	1.00		
4. Total institutionalization	.82	.76	.75	1.00	
5. Institutionalization minus social mobilization	.61	.25	.50	.58	1.00
6. Violence	−.04	−.02	−.49	−.22	−.35
7. Repression	−.66	−.33	−.70	−.73	−.35
8. Combined violence and repression	−.46	−.20	−.79	−.63	−.46
1960s					
1. Church institutionalization	1.00				
2. Party institutionalization	.52	1.00			
3. Military institutionalization	.45	.54	1.00		
4. Total institutionalization	.80	.84	.81	1.00	
5. Institutionalization minus social mobilization	.47	.30	.49	.52	1.00
6. Violence	−.21	−.16	−.54	−.37	−.56
7. Repression	−.57	−.70	−.46	−.71	−.07
8. Combined violence and repression	−.52	−.57	−.66	−.71	−.42

Marx's allegation about religion serving as the opium of the people does not seem to be borne out. The presence of numbers of Catholic priests does not provide sufficient "opium" to lessen violent expressions of discontent. On the other hand, the greater presence and autonomy of the church does have a highly significant effect on the level of repression, contrary to the implication of Marx's statement.

Military institutionalization has the highest negative associations of the three separate variables with violence, and it has a very similar effect on repression.

The thesis that institutionalization becomes more important as the population becomes more mobilized, implying that it is the relative degree to which institutionalization is ahead of social mobilization that matters, is confirmed for violence, but not for repression. Because the writers promoting this thesis were primarily concerned with violence, their arguments are supported by this evidence.

The two correlation matrices had one curious characteristic—a tendency toward higher correlations when the institutionalization measures are combined. Military institutionalization correlates more highly with the combined measures of violence and repression than it does with the separate measures. This pattern indicates that there may be some functional substitution between different kinds of institutionalization in preventing repression, and that violence and repression may be alternate means of expressing the problems that arise from lack of institutionalization.

Governmental output

In the previous chapter, we found that the degree of violence was highly associated with the difference between societal welfare and social mobilization. Populations appear to react collectively and politically to conditions, even when the conditions are beyond the control of the government. In addition, one would expect that large proportions of the population would be aware of the extent to which the government is responsible for social conditions and is attempting to alleviate problems, and that they would tend to support or protest against the government on the basis of their evaluation of its performance. At the same time, the government, if it did not want to give benefits to certain sectors of the population, might repress them instead.

From a system perspective, governmental output becomes a critical variable in discussing the level of support or opposition toward government. David Easton, in his system of inputs and outputs, considers outputs and their relation to the wants of the population as feedback, which in turn relates to the operation of the whole system:

> The success or failure of outputs in winning the supportive response of members will depend on the extent to which the outputs . . . are able to meet the current demands of the members or anticipate and abort possible future demands by preventing grievances from arising. Satisfaction derived from outputs that have met present or anticipated demands will serve as a major means of inducing the input of specific support.[14]

From Easton's discussion, one can see that it is not outputs by themselves that increase diffuse support, which lowers the intensity of opposition to a government, but rather the relation of outputs to the demands of the populace. It is very nearly impossible, however, to develop any precise measure of the extent to which current government output meets demands or anticipates future needs. The argument does make clear that we cannot simply take the number of roads built, sewers installed, or children educated, and expect a relationship with either violence or repression. The satisfaction derived from these investments and services depends on the level of demand.

In dealing with financial data on governmental expenditure, it is usual to convert it to a percentage of the budget or a percentage of GNP. That takes one step toward relating expenditure to demand because decision-makers see the problem as one of trade-offs between different expenditures or between government and private expenditures. Whereas demand for education, or any other governmental service, may vary from society to society, there is a much more constant expectation of what proportion of the available resources should be spent for a given service. A poor country does not expect to have the same level of schooling as does a rich country, but it might expect the same proportion of its gross national product to be spent on education. Some worldwide data suggest that demand for public services might go up faster than GNP, but the data in Latin America do not indicate that in this range of GNP the relationship is sufficiently strong to take into consideration. For financial data, then, we will use the percentage of GNP as our indicator of governmental output, realizing that it is only a rough approximation of the relationship of output to demand.

In one case, however, we were able to develop a different way of relating output to anticipated demand. One of the most reliable data on physical output is the number of children enrolled in school—data

---

[14]David Easton, *A Systems Analysis of Political Life* (New York: Wiley, 1967), p. 403.

collected by UNESCO. Schooling demand must first be adjusted to the number of school-age children in the population, and UNESCO makes this adjustment. The one factor that might determine demand for schooling more than any other variable is social mobilization. We ran a simple regression analysis of proportion of children in primary school against our measure of social mobilization, and found the correlation to be high (.59 in the 1950s and .68 in the 1960s). Figure 8 illustrates this relationship. It can be seen that the deviation from the regression line is much greater at lower levels of social mobilization. A mobilized population may have more effective means of making its demands felt. Our interest is in how far a country deviates from the line. If it is above the line, we consider it to be producing above the demand, relative to other Latin American countries, and if it is below the line, we consider it to be producing below the demand, relative to other countries. Our measure of the extent to which demand for schooling is met is simply that distance above or below the line.

Different kinds of government outputs benefit different groups of individuals, and different kinds of tax systems place different costs on them. Our basic hypothesis is that groups that feel they are benefited by the government, that the government is meeting their demands, will support the government and not resort to violence nor draw repression from the government. Unfortunately, the data do not allow us to

Figure 8.   School Enrollment Residual

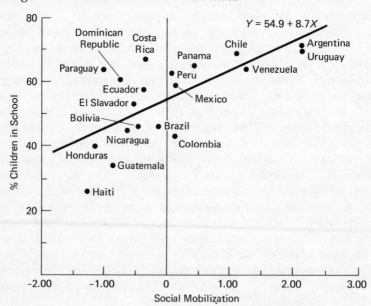

know with any precision who benefits and how they respond. We have chosen education to represent the extent to which the masses receive benefits from the government. It is the most general service provided by government, and in addition, data on it are among the most complete and reliable published. Public health services, another possibility, is administered by different levels of government in different countries, but the data are reported only for the central government level. Data on education are shown in Table 24.

We expect that countries providing more welfare benefits relative to the demand will have less violence and less repression, that the population will evaluate its government as more responsive if it provides more education, and that the people will be less likely to resort to violence against the government. The government, in turn, will not feel the need to resort to repression.

The population, however, feels much less direct benefit from defense expenditures, especially in Latin America, where external threats are minimal. International conflict has been pretty much brought under control by the mediation procedures of the Organization of American States, and by the overwhelming military superiority of the United States, which shields Latin American countries from other large powers and stops intracountry conflicts within Latin America. (The recent ambitions of the military government in Brazil, of course, may undermine the validity of this statement.) Defense expenditures, then, are not an indication of outside threats, but are rather a response to internal desires or pressures. Where defense expenditures are relatively high, we would expect the government to be less responsive to the population in general and more responsive to the military as an interest group and to the status quo distribution of goods in general. We would hypothesize, then, that high military expenditures would be positively related to violence and repression.

Another possibility exists, however, in the relationship between defense expenditure and violence. Several authors have postulated a curvilinear relationship between coercive potential and violence. They say that low coercive potential would be associated with low levels of violence, and that middling levels of coercive potential would be associated with high levels of violence, but when coercive potential is very high, violence would drop. Coercive potential is an elusive concept at the societal level. It could be measured by either repression or some measure of the size of security forces. At the end of Chapter 2, we indicated there was no such curvilinear relationship between repression and violence in Latin America, nor do we find that violence necessarily goes down at the highest levels of defense expenditures there. We plotted both military expenditure and military manpower

Table 24. Policy Output Variables

Country	Ed. Exp./ GNP 1955	Ed. Exp./ GNP 1965	School Enrol. resid.[e] 1955	School Enrol. resid.[e] 1965	Defense Exp./ GNP 1950s	Defense Exp./ GNP 1960s	Tax/GNP 1966–1968
Argentina	1.7%	2.9%	.61	-.30	2.8%	2.1%	19.5%
Bolivia	1.1[a]	3.3	-.76	-.51	.6	2.2	10.8
Brazil	1.8	2.5[b]	-1.20	-.84	2.7	2.7	24.6
Chile	1.9	3.5	.47	.49	2.7	2.1	26.2
Colombia	1.2	2.3	-.81	-1.39	1.6	1.6	11.5
Costa Rica	2.4	3.9	1.74	1.41	.6	.5	14.7
Dominican Republic	1.9[c]	2.3	1.79	1.39	6.0	3.6	15.6
Ecuador	1.4	2.9	.51	.67	2.2	2.1	15.8
El Salvador	1.9	2.8	-.32	.28	1.5	1.2	10.3
Guatemala	1.2	2.0	-1.17	-1.42	.9	1.1	8.7
Haiti	1.1	1.2	-.91	-1.91	1.8	2.5	8.0
Honduras	1.0	2.7	-.44	-.52	1.3	1.3	10.9
Mexico	1.8	2.5	-.22	.30	.7	.7	11.2
Nicaragua	1.0	2.1	-.44	-.46	2.5	1.5	10.1
Panama	3.3	3.7	.96	.69	.3	.2	14.0
Paraguay	1.0	1.7	2.03	1.94	2.1	1.6	11.7
Peru	1.6	3.4	.06	.79	1.6	2.8	16.7
Uruguay	3.0[c]	2.6	-.27	-.39	1.6	1.6	20.0
Venezuela	1.7	3.4	-.97	-.21	1.9	2.3	23.2
Cuba	2.8[d]	6.5	-.63	—	1.8	7.4	—

Footnotes to Table 24:

[a]Calculated from data in James W. Wilkie, *The Bolivian Revolution* (Los Angeles: Latin American Center, University of California, 1969), pp. 68–73.

[b]Estimated from noncomparable data.

[c]Estimated from recurrent expenditures.

[d]Calculated from educational expenditure data in *Cuba 1968, Supplement to the Statistical Abstract of Latin America* (Los Angeles: Latin American Center, University of California, 1970), and GNP data in *Latin American Research Review 4* (Summer, 1969), p. 52.

[e]School enrollment residuals are given in standardized scores.

Sources: Educational expenditures and school enrollment figures taken from United Nations Education, Scientific and Cultural Organization, *Statistical Yearbook 1968* (Louvain: UNESCO, 1969), pp. 69–91 and 197–333. Defense expenditures from Joseph E. Loftus, *Latin American Defense Expenditures, 1938–1965* (Santa Monica: Rand, 1968), and United States Arms Control and Disarmament Agency, *World Military Expenditures* (Washington: United States Arms Control and Disarmament Agency, annual). Taxation from IDB, *Socio-Economic Progress in Latin America, 1970* (Washington: IDB, 1971).

against violence and found no curvilinear relationship. It may be that coercive potential ordinarily does not reach the highest levels anywhere in Latin America. The Dominican Republic in the 1950s and Cuba in the 1960s were the only cases in recent years where defense expenditures were more than four percent, and they were 6.0 and 7.4 respectively. In those two cases, violence was low. We can say, then, that Latin America, with only two exceptions, has had coercive potentials in the middling range, where previous writers have postulated positive relationship, and that the limited evidence in Latin America with higher levels supports the hypothesis that violence declines at the highest levels.

Reliable tax data exist only for the 1960s. We have introduced it because it seems to be a good indicator of the capability of a government to respond to all demands, be they for services, employment, or investments. For instance, Chile, with an exceptionally high tax capability, is able to spend large amounts on both education and defense. In this light, one would expect a strong negative relationship between tax capability and both violence and repression. On the other hand, taxes are not viewed favorably by any taxpayer. Crane Brinton even found that revolutions are preceded by an attempt to raise taxes.[15] Nowhere in Latin America are tax rates high compared with Western Europe, and one could surmise that taxpayers do not feel too much burden. However, an equal percentage of tax may impose a higher burden in poorer countries. What may be most important is the efficiency and effectiveness with which tax revenues are used—and that no one has succeeded in measuring. Because of these problems, taxation may not be highly associated with violence and repression.

Table 25 shows the correlations we found between these governmental output measures and our measures of violence and repression. The relationship between education and violence and repression proved to be as expected, but with a twist. The expenditure data were very highly associated with repression, with a negative correlation, but not with violence. The school enrollment residual was highly associated with violence, with a negative correlation, but not with repression. There is a certain logic behind this difference as expenditure is the most relevant aspect of education for the authorities, who repress, and children in school are the most relevant aspect of education for the population, who choose to protest.

Defense expenditure had the positive relationship with violence, which we expected in the 1960s, but it had the opposite association in the 1950s. The relationship is not strong in any case. Defense expendi-

---

[15]Crane Brinton, *Anatomy of Revolution* (Englewood Cliffs, N.J.: Prentice-Hall, 1938).

Table 25. Correlations with Governmental Output, 1950–1970

	Violence	Repression
Educational expenditures, 1950s	−.16	−.40
Educational expenditures, 1960s	−.17	−.79
School enrollment residual, 1950s	−.38	.29
School enrollment residual, 1960s	−.56	−.18
Defense expenditure, 1950s	−.22	.55
Defense expenditure, 1960s	.38	.35
Taxes/GNP, 1960s	−.01	−.35

tures are correlated with repression, as was expected, highly in the 1950s and moderately in the 1960s.

The contrary aspects of taxation seem to have canceled each other out. Although taxation is negatively related to both violence and repression in the 1950s and 1960s, the relationship is quite small.

Summary

Violence has a high and consistent negative relationship with military institutionalization and with the extent to which primary school enrollment is above demand. Where the military leaves the regular processes of government to the civilians, and the government provides sufficient education, the population is less violent. We argued that military institutionalization would lead to greater negotiation and compromise, and that co-optation would make violent methods less legitimate and would give ambitious civilians an opportunity to express their ambitions in political activity. More education relative to demand would simply make people more satisfied.

Total institutionalization and education expenditures, expressed as a percentage of GNP, had strong negative associations with repression. The structuring of all the organizations we looked at seems to be important in lowering the incidence of repression. These structures make it easier to resist arbitrary governmental coercion and make negotiation and compromise possible as substitutes for repression. At the same time, governments that spend more on education and less on defense are less likely to be repressive, either from lack of need or inclination.

In the previous chapter, the correlations provided little evidence that violence and repression were a single dimension. In every case, the correlations with the combined variables were a compromise between the correlations with the separate variables. Military institutionalization, total institutionalization, and institutionalization minus mobilization, however, provide higher correlations with the combined violence and repression variable than with the separate indicators, or at least are more than a compromise between them. This result indicates that there may be something in the idea of social cohesion after all. Institutionalization seems to provide conditions under which neither violence nor repression is likely. The lack of institutionalization leads to either violence or repression or both, and the two manifestations may serve as functional substitutes in this situation.

CHAPTER 5

MULTIPLE
VARIABLE RELATIONS

The previous two chapters have dealt with one independent variable at a time, establishing causal interpretations and testing propositions with simple measures of association. That analysis allowed us to identify some tentative single-factor explanations of our dependent variables—repression, violence, and their combination—interpreted as the negative of social cohesion. Causes or explanations, however, do not come one at a time. The situation in any country is due to a large number of forces working together. We want to find the equations that combine the fewest variables to explain the largest amount of variation in our dependent variables.

This exercise allows us to test the importance of the independent variables in a different way. It also gives us information that we can use to determine which countries are well explained by our variables and which are not. We will give a brief discussion of the deviant cases in this chapter, but detailed discussion will have to wait for the historical case studies in Part 2.

To find these equations for violence, repression, and social cohesion, we used step wise multiple regression analysis.[1] This procedure first identifies the independent variable that has the highest correlation with the dependent variable and includes it in a linear equation. It then calculates the partial correlations and F-values (the distribution of the F-value or F-ratio is used to test whether any particular regression relationship is significantly different from zero) of the other variables, holding the variable in the equation constant, and includes the second variable with the highest F-value in the equation. It again holds the variables in the equation constant and searches for the variable with the next-best fit, and so on until some limit is reached. This procedure does not always find the best-fitting equation, but by manipulating the procedure, one can easily identify the alternative equations that work best. We simply report the final version.

The basic question in choosing the best equation is when to stop adding variables. By adding enough variables, one can explain nearly all the variance, but because parsimony is a virtue in theory construction, the fewer variables used, the better. Further, the fit of the later variables declines, so that at some point, the contribution made to explanation of the dependent variable may be due to chance rather than to a real relationship. We used the F statistic as our criterion for when to stop entering variables. When the F-value for any variable dropped below the .05 level of probability, we stopped adding variables. With only nineteen cases (countries), the cutoff point for the F-value was quite high, and we ended with no equations with more than three variables. The equations we report, then, are all statistically significant at the .05 level of probability, and each variable within the equation is also statistically significant. We should mention again, however, the reservations expressed in Chapter 3 concerning the ambiguity of the term "statistically significant," given the nature of our sample.

We developed equations from the 1960s data, which are more reliable and yielded higher correlations than the 1950s data. Stepwise regression produced somewhat different equations for the 1950s, which are not reported here. We forced the variables selected by the analysis of the 1960s data into a regression equation for the 1950s data, and used the results as a check on the 1960s equation. In many cases, the F-values were not significant in the 1950s, but we rejected only those variables that produced results inconsistent with those found in the 1960s. The degree of consistency—which is equally important to the F-value for estimating the generality of the theoretical relationship—is observable by comparing the regression coefficients from the two time periods.

---

[1]The program for running this analysis comes from Norman H. Nie, *Statistical Package for the Social Sciences* (New York: McGraw-Hill, 1970).

We will give an interpretation of the equations in verbal terms, but the statistics of the equation provide much greater precision in specifying the relationship. Of importance is the multiple correlation coefficient which, when squared, indicates the proportion of total variance explained. Each of the 1960s equations explains at least three-quarters of the variance in the dependent variable. The regression coefficients show how much change in the dependent variable is brought about by a corresponding change in the independent variable. As all the data used in the analyses were in standardized form, with a mean of zero and a standard deviation of one, the regression coefficients are the same as the beta coefficients. A large coefficient means that a variable is more important in explaining the variance of the dependent variable.

Violence

The equation that best predicts violence in Latin America follows.

$$\text{Viol}_{1960} = -.57\,(\text{EG–SMCh}) - .50\,\text{MilIn} - .34\,\text{SchR} \qquad F = 15.6\ R^2 = .76$$
$$\qquad\qquad (15.0)^a \qquad\qquad (14.9) \qquad\quad (6.6)$$

$$\text{Viol}_{1950} = -.42\,(\text{EG–SMCh}) - .31\,\text{MilIn} - .20\,\text{SchR} \qquad F = 4.9\ R^2 = .48$$
$$\qquad\qquad (4.0) \qquad\qquad\ (2.6) \qquad\quad (1.1)$$

More Violence Than Predicted				*Less Violence Than Predicted*			
1950s		*1960s*		*1950s*		*1960s*	
Cuba	1.32	Dominican Republic	.91	El Salvador	1.67	Haiti	.92
Panama	.77	Bolivia	.81	Uruguay	1.37	Paraguay	.58
Colombia	.60	Mexico	.81	Dominican Republic	.60		
				Haiti	.60		

[a]Numbers in parentheses are F = values for variables.

Violence increases when economic growth fails to keep up with the change in social mobilization, where the military is not institutionalized, and where primary education does not match the demand for it. The economic growth-change in social mobilization differential has the best fit, is the most consistent, and contributes most to the explanation of the variation in violence. Military institutionalization also holds up very well, but its F-value for the 1950s drops below the level of statistical significance. The school enrollment residual is not quite as powerful a variable. Together, these three variables explain 76 percent of the variance in violence in the 1960s in Latin America, and 48 percent in the 1950s. The variables have less explanatory power in the 1950s, but their behavior is quite consistent between the two periods.

The variable with the highest simple correlation with violence, the static measure of societal welfare minus social mobilization, drops out of the multiple regression equation when other variables are added. It is highly associated with both economic growth minus change in social mobilization and the school enrollment residual, and when these two variables are included, it does not explain any additional violence in the 1960s. We consider its failure to be included to be due to the problem of multicollinearity, which does not mean there is no relationship, but only that its influence cannot be separated out because of its interrelationship with other independent variables. It will be remembered that it was welfare minus mobilization that most distinguished prerevolutionary Cuba, and the failure to include this variable in the equation makes our prediction for Cuba less accurate than if it had been included. We sacrifice the prediction of one case for an overall better fit.

The major part of the variation in violence is explained by indicators of the degree of satisfaction of individuals. We considered that dissatisfaction would increase where urbanization and mass communication were increasing at a relatively more rapid rate than was the economy, and where the government's provision of primary education did not match the demand as reflected in social mobilization. The regression equation for violence bears out our hypotheses on these relationships.

The failure to institutionalize the military is the second most important cause of violence. Where the military interferes with the civilian processes, political accommodation is more difficult and the use of force tends to be legitimized. The opposition is, therefore, more likely to express its discontent through violence when the military moves out of its barracks.

With three-quarters of the variation in violence explained by this equation in the 1960s, the level of violence in most countries in Latin America is predicted quite closely. Bolivia, the Dominican Republic, and Mexico, however, had quite a bit more violence than predicted, and Haiti and Paraguay had less. Bolivia was expected to have considerable violence, but not as much as it did; the Dominican Republic was predicted to be about average, but turned out sixth, with its violence concentrated around the period of U.S. intervention in 1965. Mexico was predicted to have much less than average violence, but its disturbances around the time of the Olympic Games in 1968 pushed it slightly above the average. Paraguay was predicted to have little violence, but had even less—less than any country except Costa Rica. Haiti was expected to have a lot of violence, but experienced only a little more than average.

The equation for violence in the 1950s explains less variance than any of the other equations reported in this chapter, and hence there are more countries where actual scores were quite different from predicted scores. The largest deviants were El Salvador and Uruguay, with Cuba close behind. As was mentioned earlier, the situation in Cuba would have been predicted by a slightly different equation that used the variable, societal welfare minus social mobilization. El Salvador is something of an enigma. Its violence was probably somewhat underreported because of the absence of foreign correspondents and the subtle control of the local press. However, it would be deviant in any case. Uruguay experienced a favorable situation in the 1950s which degenerated in the mid-1960s.

Repression

The formula for predicting repression in Latin America follows.

$$Rep_{1960} = -.51 \text{ Inst} - .63 \text{ EdExp} \qquad F = 46.1 \ R^2 = .85$$
$$\qquad\quad (24.9)^a \qquad\quad (38.2)$$

$$Rep_{1950} = -.67 \text{ Inst} - .19 \text{ Ed Exp} \qquad F = 11.0 \ R^2 = .56$$
$$\qquad\quad (15.6) \qquad\quad\ (1.3)$$

More Repression Than Predicted				*Less Repression Than Predicted*			
1950s		*1960s*		*1950s*		*1960s*	
Dominican							
Republic	1.82	Paraguay	1.03	Honduras	1.03	Guatemala	.80
Paraguay	1.03	Haiti	.57	Guatemala	.81	Colombia	.59
Venezuela	.62			Brazil	.62		

[a]Numbers in parentheses are F = values for variables.

Repression was high where education expenditures as a percentage of GDP was low and where the combined institutionalization of the Roman Catholic Church, political parties, and the military was low. These two variables explain 85 percent of the variance in repression in Latin America in the 1960s, and 56 percent in the 1950s. The total institutionalization variable holds up particularly well, with a very high F-value in both time periods. The education expenditure variable was less consistent. It is extremely important in the 1960s, with a high regression coefficient, but both importance and fit drop considerably in the 1950s.[2]

[2]All education expenditures were much lower in the 1950s than in the 1960s, and hence the variable did not distinguish countries as well in the earlier period. Furthermore, the Dominican Republic under Trujillo was atypical, combining moderate education with high levels of repression, following more of a totalitarian pattern than is usual in Latin America.

It was noted in the previous chapter that the combined measure of institutionalization works better in explaining repression than do the separate measures of institutionalization. The church seems to be able to offset weaknesses of political parties, and the two can offset some of the weaknesses in the military. Where all three are high, they provide an institutionalized structure that makes the political system function smoothly and makes it possible to resist attempts at repression by any would-be tyrant.

The exceptional importance of institutionalization raises an important question: Why do some countries have greater institutionalization than others? We used our data to search for explanations of the three kinds of institutionalization. To understand the situation of the church would require going back into nineteenth-century conflicts, examining church leadership and outside resources, and determining why it was unable to recruit priests in most Latin American countries. Our data provided no explanations of church institutionalization.

The percentage of the population that is white and mestizo turned out to be an important explanation of both party and military institutionalization. The simple correlation between percentage white and mestizo and repression found in Chapter 3 may be best accounted for by a causal chain. Where the population is better integrated racially, and where racial domination has not destroyed the capacity of people to organize themselves, parties are able to form and the military is less likely to intervene in the political processes. With greater institutionalization, repression will be less necessary and more costly.

No other variables helped explain party institutionalization. Not even the repression of previous decades affected the level of party institutionalization. Sixty-two percent of the variation in party institutionalization remained unexplained. We would suggest that leadership may be a particularly important factor in the development of political parties. The strong parties that have developed in this century are all the result of able, dedicated leaders, usually a small group that originally came together in a university.

Two additional variables—the violence of previous decades, and communication—provided some explanation of military institutionalization. Both had negative effects. When violence increases, civilian groups quite often put pressure on the military to intervene, leading to its deinstitutionalization. Communication, to our surprise, also has a negative effect on military institutionalization when combined with the other two variables. The three variables—percentage white and mestizo, previous decades' violence, and communication—explain 71 percent of the variance in military institutionalization.

Education expenditures as a percentage of GNP are largely explained by economic factors. Expenditures go up as agricultural production declines relative to other kinds of production, and as economic growth and foreign trade increase. These three variables explained 61 percent of the variance in education expenditures in the 1960s, but had less explanatory power in the 1950s.

Because institutionalization and education expenditures explain so much of the variance in repression in the 1960s, almost all the countries were very close to their predictions. Colombia and Guatemala had less repression than expected; Haiti and Paraguay had more. Of these, only Colombia is a truly deviant case. Guatemala maintained some facade of democracy while assassinating all potential leftist opposition after 1965. Haiti and Paraguay's exceptionally high levels of repression were partly due to the way in which our tabulation exaggerated the repression scores of the traditional dictators. These two countries were predicted to have more repression than any others in Latin America. In the 1950s, Brazil had much less than expected, but this deviation was made up for after 1964. Brazil's repression was apparently latent and not manifested for a time. The Dominican Republic had much more repression than predicted in the 1950s, which may have been in part a measurement problem. Honduras had far less repression than predicted by this equation in the 1950s, but became a normal case in the 1960s.

Social Cohesion

Our third equation is on social cohesion:

$$SCoh_{1960} = .39\ (EG{-}SMCh) + .60\ Milln + .54\ EdExp \qquad F = 39.8\ R^2 = .89$$
$$\phantom{SCoh_{1960} = }(20.5) \qquad\qquad (48.2) \qquad\quad (39.1)$$

$$SCoh_{1950} = .18\ (EG{-}SMCh) + .70\ Milln + .03\ EdExp \qquad F = 10.2\ R^2 = .66$$
$$\phantom{SCoh_{1950} = }(1.3) \qquad\qquad (15.1) \qquad\quad (.03)$$

More Cohesion Than Predicted				Less Cohesion Than Predicted			
1950s		1960s		1950s		1960s	
Uruguay	1.19	Ecuador	.67	Cuba	.85	Bolivia	.58
El Salvador	1.04	Uruguay	.39	Colombia	.60	Dominican	
Ecuador	.68			Mexico	.44	Republic	.38

Social cohesion, operationalized as the absence of violence and repression, is high where institutionalization of the society's structures, particularly the military, is high, where educational expenditures are high, and where economic growth outpaces social mobilization. These variables explain 89 percent of the variance of social cohesion in the 1960s, and 66 percent of the variance in the 1950s. The educational expenditures variable, the most important in the 1960s, is the most inconsistent. The others are quite consistent, but military institutionalization is far the most important variable in the 1950s. The level of explanation for this combined variable is higher than for either violence or repression treated separately. The ability to obtain a higher level of explanation supports the combination of violence and repression to form a single dimension. Social cohesion, defined as the relative absence of coercion applied by either the opposition or the officials, is an explainable concept.

For a nation to be both peaceful and free, it must have a proper socio-economic environment, well-established institutions, and a governmental policy directed toward the welfare of the people. Each of these is important in about the same proportion. Where the socio-economic situation deteriorates more than institutionalization, oppositional violence will be more prevalent than official violence. Where institutionalization is low, but the socio-economic environment is relatively satisfactory, the lack of cohesion is more likely to be expressed in official violence.

Because the equation explains all but eleven percent of the variance in social cohesion in the 1960s, the predicted scores for individual countries and the actual scores are very close. Bolivia and Mexico demonstrate somewhat less cohesion than expected, and Ecuador and Uruguay show rather more, but none were off by very much. The deviations were greater in the 1950s.

PART 2

THE APPLICATION
OF THE THEORY
TO THE COUNTRIES
OF LATIN AMERICA

6

THE MORE
COHESIVE COUNTRIES

As we discovered in Chapter 2, certain Latin American countries between 1950 and 1970 exhibited less violence and repression than others. We have tentatively concluded that the absence of violence and repression is a manifestation of something we call "social cohesion." We have, therefore, labeled these countries—Costa Rica, El Salvador, Panama, Mexico, Ecuador, Nicaragua, Peru, and Honduras—"more cohesive." Uruguay and Chile scored higher than did most of these eight nations, but after 1970 suffered a considerable deterioration in their cohesion. They are, as a consequence, treated separately in the next chapter, along with Brazil, as cases illustrating a breakdown of cohesion.

Each of these eight countries, in addition to exhibiting low levels of violence and repression, places well on the various independent variables that, as we demonstrated in Chapters 3, 4, and 5, are associated with lower levels of violence and repression. This is not to say that all eight are the same. They are not. They all exhibit different patterns of violence and repression, and they all have different configurations of scores on the independent variables. Furthermore, each has had a unique national history that has influenced the level of social cohesion. Nevertheless, as a group they exhibit certain tendencies with regard to our dependent variables that allow us to write of them as societies with a relatively high degree of social cohesion. As Table 26 shows, the nations differed markedly in their level of cohesion, in the change in levels of violence and repression between the two decades, and in the amount of violence or repression in each society. Costa Rica for example, was by far the most cohesive society in Latin America during the

Table 26. More Cohesive Countries

Country	Variable	Dependent Variables[a]			
		1950s		1960s	
		Actual	*Predicted*	*Actual*	*Predicted*
Costa Rica	Violence	−.72	−1.27	−1.85	−1.71
	Repression	−.95	−.59	−1.22	−1.55
	Viol. & Rep.[b]	−1.11	−1.17	−2.02	−2.16
El Salvador	Violence	−1.53	.14	−.72	−.44
	Repression	−.14	.45	.02	.11
	Viol. & Rep.	−1.11	.07	−.45	−.35
Panama	Violence	.05	−.72	−.85	−.70
	Repression	−.62	−.78	−.67	−.69
	Viol. & Rep.	−.38	−.70	−1.09	−.94
Mexico	Violence	−.13	−.83	−.27	−1.08
	Repression	−.90	−1.37	−.57	−.85
	Viol. & Rep.	−.68	−1.12	−.54	−.90
Ecuador	Violence	−.09	−.19	−.19	.19
	Repression	−.97	−.78	−.44	−.62
	Viol. & Rep.	−.70	.02	−.41	.26
Nicaragua	Violence	−.64	−.55	−.58	−1.01
	Repression	−.07	.21	−.16	.17
	Viol. & Rep.	−.47	−.37	−.48	−.68
Peru	Violence	−.24	−.21	−.61	−.20
	Repression	.11	.55	−.49	−.30
	Viol. & Rep.	−.09	.07	−.72	−.39
Honduras	Violence	−.08	−.30	.01	.16
	Repression	−.77	.26	−.29	−.02
	Viol. & Rep.	−.57	−.77	−.18	.08

[a]All scores are standard.
[b]The combined scores for violence and repression are the obverse of social cohesion. That is, a minus score on this index represents a correspondingly high level of social cohesion.

1960s (with the lowest level of violence and repression); El Salvador, which was as cohesive (the same level of violence and repression) as Costa Rica in the 1950s, became less so in the second decade. Both Honduras and Nicaragua became more violent during the 1960s as the twentieth century finally began to impinge on these societies, whereas Panama exhibited much greater social cohesion in the 1960s than it had in the 1950s. Most of the scores predicted by the equations developed in Chapter 5 are very close to the actual scores.

The countries also differ in relation to the economic and political variables that are associated with low levels of violence and repression. Costa Rica ranks high on all of the variables; El Salvador's major weaknesses appear to be the lack of institutionalization previously discussed in Chapter 4; Panama does well on everything except institutionalized political parties. Mexico, as we shall show, owes much of its cohesion to the political machine that has controlled it since the late 1920s. Ecuador seems to be stitched together by the triple threads of a highly institutionalized Catholic Church, a low level of social mobilization, and an acceptable rate of economic growth. Nicaragua belies its image as a banana republic by demonstrating a reasonable political party system plus an excellent record of economic growth. Peru ranks low on many indexes, but has had a good record of economic growth. Honduras has a positive societal welfare-social mobilization differential, which is due almost entirely to the extremely low level of social mobilization in that country. Table 27 indicates the intercountry disparities in those independent variables that are most important to maintaining low levels of violence and repression.

Though Costa Rica is the most cohesive, Mexico offers the best example in Latin America, perhaps in the world, of the operation of an efficient political machine. Peru, though lower on cohesion, in recent years has demonstrated an interesting pattern of military leadership without high repression. For these reasons we have chosen to concentrate on these three countries in an attempt to flesh out the bare bones of our theory with some discrete examples of its operation. None of the three is "typical" of all eight nations in this group, but each does in a sense represent the others because they are all less violent and less repressive than other Latin American nations. Moreover, they all share, to a greater or lesser degree, certain economic, social, and political characteristics that tend to make them that way.

Costa Rica

A cohesive society doesn't make much news. It has no general strikes, no massive demonstrations, no bombings, no guerrilla attacks,

Table 27. More Cohesive Countries

| | Independent Variables[a] | | | | | | | | | | | | | | | |
| | 1950s | | | | | | | | 1960s | | | | | | | |
Variable	Costa Rica	El Salvador	Panama	Mexico	Ecuador	Nicaragua	Peru	Honduras	Costa Rica	El Salvador	Panama	Mexico	Ecuador	Nicaragua	Peru	Honduras
Welfare minus mobilization	1.96	–.09	.25	.37	.10	.20	–.29	.74	2.20	–.18	.28	.77	–.72	.23	–.72	.36
Economic growth minus social mobilization	1.17	–.13	.70	1.05	.26	1.34	.68	.06	1.04	.59	1.67	.55	–.49	1.13	.20	.37
Educational effort	1.74	–.32	.96	–.22	.51	–.44	.06	–.44	1.41	.28	.69	.30	.67	–.46	.79	–.52
Educational expenditure	.97	.23	2.29	.09	–.50	–1.08	–.21	–1.08	1.67	.11	1.38	–.31	.25	–.88	.96	–.03
Party institutionalization	–.79	–1.07	.24	1.22	.61	.57	–1.59	.54	.28	–1.15	.14	1.58	.21	.59	–.78	.82
Military institutionalization	1.34	–.07	.73	1.34	–.07	.23	–.27	1.14	1.40	.10	–.77	1.40	–.34	1.18	–.34	–.34
Church institutionalization	.90	–.62	–.08	2.23	2.54	.02	.06	–.03	.73	.20	–.25	2.04	2.40	.09	–.32	–.28
Total institutionalization	.60	–.74	.38	2.02	1.30	.34	–.76	.70	.98	–.35	–.36	2.05	.92	.76	–.59	.08
White + mestizo as a percent of population	1.28	–.01	–.08	.36	–.77	.95	–.37	–.01	1.23	–.02	–.10	.33	–.78	.91	–.38	–.02

[a] All scores are standard.

138

no political arrests, no exiles, no violations of individual liberty—in short, nothing to attract the attention of journalists. During the 1960s Costa Rica rated no more than an inch or two each year in the *New York Times Index* though it earned nearly a page in 1948 and again in 1954.

The only important incident of oppositional violence occurred in November, 1962, when the citizens of Cartago formed a Payments Strike Committee to protest the increase in electricity rates—an increase necessary to obtain a World Bank loan. When the government ordered the cessation of the protests, the citizens turned out in mass to defend their constitutional right of protest. They clashed violently with the Civil Guard, which had been directed to break up the demonstrations, leaving three dead and fifty injured. (This incident was reported in the *Hispanic American Report*, not in the *New York Times*.) The only other reported incident in the decade occurred when Nelson Rockefeller, then governor of New York, visited the country in May, 1969, as an official emissary of President Nixon. At that time, two thousand pro- and anti-Rockefeller demonstrators clashed in front of the presidential palace, but no casualties or arrests were reported.

Of more consequence was the continued ban on the Communist Party. The government did not persecute individual party members, but when they joined with other leftists to form the Popular Socialist Alliance to contest the 1966 elections, Congress outlawed all the groups as a Communist front. The Socialist Action Party, nevertheless, was able to run in the 1970 election, even though it included Communist Party supporters. The party had no large following in the country and posed no real threat to the government.

The limited number of violent and repressive incidents in the 1960s meant that Costa Rica scored much higher on social cohesion than did any other country in Latin America. Costa Rica also experienced conflict in the early 1950s, but still came out ahead for the twenty-year period studied. Unlike Uruguay, which scored high for most of the period, too, Costa Rica's score was predicted by our equations (see Table 26), indicating that it had the social conditions to sustain its exceptionally high level of social cohesion.

Positive manifestations of social cohesion are less newsworthy, but indications suggest its presence nonetheless. Travelers attest to the openness of Costa Rican society and the absence of tensions in its social life. Costa Rican citizens, especially when living in other Latin American states, boast vociferously of their country. The clearest manifestation of national cohesion is at election time. In Costa Rica elections have been fought vigorously but have been orderly; and in five successive elections the executive power has been transferred between political parties without incident.

The high cohesion demonstrated in the 1960s is not new. Costa Rica always has been different from its more violent and coercive neighbors. Dana Munro's summary of the political situation in 1918 could have been written in 1970:

> The president walks through the streets much like a private citizen, without fear of assassination or of being captured by his enemies, and the leaders of the opposition carry on their propaganda in San José without hindrance or persecution, and at times are even called in to consult with the president on matters of great importance. The press criticizes the administration fearlessly and at times scurrilously and animated political discussions may be heard every day on the principal corner of the main street of the capital.[1]

In the nineteenth century Costa Rica had free elections less frequently, but though the governments obtained power by conspiracy or imposition, they generally were not repressive, and the population did not engage in violent opposition. Munro pointed out that "the small landholders always have exerted a strong influence on the side of peace and stable government, for they have rarely joined in attempted revolution."[2]

The civil war that broke out in 1948, the "Revolution of 1948," deviated from this historical tradition and produced the minor disturbances that persisted into the early 1950s until they climaxed with a rebel invasion from neighboring Nicaragua in 1954. Inasmuch as this conflict is not well explained by our theory, our understanding of the events are dependent on the historical account.

As is usual in such instances, the victors are able to make their version of the events prevail. According to them, the dictatorships of Rafael Calderón Guardia (1940–1944) and Teodoro Picado (1944–1948) had failed to give the country needed reforms and were delivering it to the Communists. In order to maintain itself in power, the government annulled the elections of 1948. José Figueres rose up in rebellion from his farm, *Lucha sin Fin* ("Fight without End"), and led the country to a victory over the "tyrants."

The version of the carefully researched work of John Patrick Bell[3] differs considerably from what had been a widely accepted view. Calderón and Picado both had been freely elected and had made many

---

[1]Dana Munro, *The Five Republics of Central America* (New York: Oxford University Press, 1918), p. 148–149.

[2]Ibid., p. 143.

[3]John Patrick Bell, *Crisis in Costa Rica: The 1948 Revolution* (Austin: University of Texas Press, 1971).

reforms favorable to the workers that had caused considerable consternation among the upper classes. The small Communist Party did lend its support to their populist governments. The elections in 1948 were annulled by Congress, but there had been improprieties which it cited to justify its action. Several forces were attempting conciliation in the dispute that followed the elections, but before they could work things out, Figueres had gathered his small army, which had been preparing for a revolt for some time, and proceeded into battle.

Figueres had a personal pique with Calderón. In 1942 he had delivered a blistering attack on the Calderón government over the radio. The police prevented his finishing the speech, jailed him, and then sent him into exile. No one adequately has explained why the Calderón government took such excessive action against this one critic, but Figueres vowed his revenge. He obtained support from a reformist group of upper-class intellectuals, who were organized as the Center for the Study of National Problems. Figueres, the Center, and the Democratic Action Party joined together in 1946 to form a party for moderate reform, the Democratic Action Party. While preparing to fight a revolution, they supported the conservative candidate, Otilio Ulate, against the Calderonistas in the 1948 election.

The Picado government was prevented from an attempt to rig the 1948 election by the electoral tribunal, which was under the control of a Figueres supporter. But if there was any manipulation of the election, it had been done by the Figueres group. Congress's annulment of the election provided the excuse for which Figueres was waiting. After defeating the Calderón forces, Figueres remained in power for eighteen months before turning the government over to Ulate.

Calderón and his followers, including several Communist leaders, went into exile in neighboring Nicaragua and attempted to organize their return with some help from Nicaragua's President Anastasio Somoza. They made minor incursions into Costa Rica in 1950 and 1951 and managed a more serious attempt in 1954. The Costa Rican government, headed in 1954 by the properly elected Figueres, obtained the backing of the Organization of American States and put down the revolt with very little fighting. The Calderón followers made no more attempts to gain power through the force of arms.

Was the Revolution of 1948 the basis for the cohesion that followed after 1955, or was it merely a storm in a teapot temporarily disturbing an otherwise stable system? The personal nature of the feud between Calderón and Figueres argues for the second interpretation. Calderón's exile of Figueres in 1942, and Figueres exile of Calderón in 1948, had only limited repercussions on the political life of the nation, and reflected no deep or permanent division in the society. On the other hand, the Figueres revolt turned out to be popular, with Figueres gaining sixty-five percent of the vote in 1953, and the supporters of the 1948 Revolution organized a well-institutionalized political party. The National Liberation Party (*Partido de Liberación Nacional*—PLN) has gained a plurality in every congressional election since 1948 and has provided able leadership and loyal opposition.

Whatever the interpretation of the 1948 Revolution, it is clear that the country had sufficient cohesion to absorb the tensions generated by it. In 1962, Calderón again ran for the presidency without impediment, losing to the PLN candidate in a fair race. At no time was it necessary to impose harsh repression to control the outlawed parties, nor did the outlawed parties generate any great amount of disturbance in Costa Rican society, despite several years of attempted armed revolt. As Munro said in 1918, the small landholders have rarely joined in revolutionary efforts.

The 1948 Revolution does appear to be the exception that proves the rule—that is, our theory. It was not an indication of disintegration. It came in a burst of violence that lasted little more than a month and left no permanent divisions in the country. The ship quickly righted itself after the storm—a storm caused in large part by the personal feud between two men.

One of the basic causes of Costa Rica's cohesion developed from the manner in which it was settled. The Indians who originally inhabited that part of Central America fought the Spanish settlers and were killed, or died off quickly thereafter, leaving the colonizers without a subject race to do their work. Costa Rica began as a poor but frugal nation of small landholders. As coffee production increased in the nineteenth century, wealth and inequality increased, too, but a tradition of equality remained. The culture found its expression in the emphasis on universal primary education after 1885 and in the importance of the vote to the common man.

Costa Rica had the good fortune of being isolated from the turmoil of the rest of Central America, while at the same time its own population was concentrated and integrated into a small but fertile highland plain, the Meseta Central. Easy communication within the area of population concentration prevented regional differences and antagonisms from developing. When foreign investment came in the late nineteenth century to exploit banana plantations, it hardly affected the Meseta Central at all, as the plantations were operated on the coast with imported labor from the West Indies.

Before the development of commercial crops, Costa Rica had prospered under the labor of small landholders. The development of coffee exports increased prosperity without increasing urbanization. The country further gained, with no effort of its own, from taxation of the banana trade. One result of this kind of economic development was that the level of societal welfare far exceeded the level of social mobilization relative to other nations in Latin America (Table 27). During the 1950s and 1960s economic growth continued at a moderate pace with a relatively low level of social mobilization. These conditions, we hypothesized, led to relatively less demand for material goods and government services. The relative absence of strikes and the capability of achieving government savings without the suppression of popular demands indicate that the population was, in fact, more satisfied than people in other Latin American countries.

Costa Rica has long prided itself on having more teachers than soldiers. In the 1960s its education budget was eight times as large as its security budget. Up to 1940 it emphasized primary education and did not have even its own university. It has since established an outstanding one, but not to the detriment of primary or secondary education. As a result, educational opportunity is high for most of the population living in the Meseta Central.

The Roman Catholic Church has never been a divisive force in Costa Rican politics, and in recent years it has been a moderate voice in favor of reform. In the first half of the 1970s, it continued to have very close ties, under the leadership of Father Benjamin Nuñez, with the labor unions and provided a moderating influence in labor relations.

With the strengthening of the democratic system in the twentieth century, the army has been weakened and removed entirely from the political arena. Since 1948 the security role has been taken over by the Guardia Civil, which is primarily a police force. The post-1948 governments have not allowed it to become an independent force in any way.

The local and personalist nature of political competition in Costa Rica until recently worked against the development of institutionalized political parties. The increase and urbanization of the population has changed the nature of politics, and the country has responded with an increasing institutionalization of political parties. The emphasis on age of parties in our operationalization accounts for Costa Rica's relatively low score on this measure, but the activity of the parties in recent years suggests that they are well-institutionalized, despite their tender age.

Costa Rica, then, scored high on the variables that are associated with low levels of violence and repression. If anything, we have understated the institutionalization of the structures of Costa Rican society. The only danger that might conceivably arise in this otherwise very favorable situation would come from an excessive reliance on foreign investment for its economic growth. Recent governments, however, have sensed that danger and increasingly are trying to take control of the banana industry. In the meantime investment is fairly well diversified. Furthermore, Costa Rica has developed an entrepreneurial class that has the potential for taking charge of its economic development.

El Salvador

In the center of San Salvador during the rush hour, persons waiting for buses can be seen in long orderly lines. This unusual sight symbolizes the well-ordered nature of Salvadoran society, which sets it apart from its much more unruly neighbors. Whatever dissatisfactions exist underneath, they are kept under control by a succession of military governments and the "fourteen families" (the number is debated, but all observers attest to the dominance of a few families).

A moderate but well-organized political repression has kept oppositional violence to a minimum throughout the history of El Salvador with one bloody exception, the *matanza* of 1932.[4] Since that time, most of the mildly violent episodes have occurred during succession crises when one military generation has succeeded another. At other times a democratic facade has been maintained while the government manipulates the elections to yield the desired results. Moderate social reforms and an enterprising economic elite have given the country progress without yielding control to persons who would undermine the privileges of those in power.

During the 1950s El Salvador manifested more social cohesion than was predicted by our equations, but during the 1960s the actual situation was very close to what was expected from its score on our independent variables.

Military intervention and control has not had the negative results in El Salvador that they have had in other parts of Latin America. The military has been able to maintain a reformist image without unduly antagonizing the established wealthy families. It has worked in close cooperation with the well-educated and more progressive elite, has sought mass support through political parties, and has responded to the challenge of the Alliance for Progress without allowing its industries to be taken over by multinational firms. The Salvadoran military established an earlier and more moderate version of what the Peruvian military has made famous since 1968.

Through the last twenty years political liberties have slowly expanded, but they have never become complete. Labor unions have

---

[4]Thomas P. Anderson, *Matanza: El Salvador's Communist Revolt of 1932* (Lincoln: University of Nebraska Press, 1972). *Matanza* means "killing."

been encouraged. Oppositional political parties have been permitted and even encouraged by the adoption of proportional representation. The press has been free of any overt control. Nevertheless, when political unrest develops the government quickly asserts its control, resorting to its state of siege powers.

Panama

Politics in Panama has yet to develop any persisting social cleavages, leaving political conflict, at least until recently, to the maneuvering for personal power among a few elite cliques. Riots, street battles, invasion by exiles, arrests of opponents, and restrictions on mass communications occur without developing into permanent battle lines. The net result is a society that has manifested fewer incidents of repression and violence than most in Latin America, ranking fifth in total social cohesion for the twenty-year period under consideration.

The military take-over under the leadership of Colonel (now General) Omar Torrijos in October, 1968, did not mark any drastic departure from this tradition. Although political repression has been higher than in the past in Panama, relatively few people have been affected, and no unified opposition has formed. The election of local representatives in August, 1972, who in turn formally elected Torrijos to the presidency, was carried out with wide participation and little coercion or violence.

The 1968 military coup represented the third time that National Guard leaders had ousted the strongest personalist leader in Panamanian politics, Arnulfo Arias, from the presidency, having previously done so in 1941 and 1951. These three coups produced less violence than the passionate student demonstrations against the governing elite and its failure to promote national interests against the U.S. domination of the Canal Zone. Student agitation became pronounced in 1958 and again in 1964.[5] The overthrow of Arias in 1951 and the assassination of President José A. Remón in 1955 resulted in the short-term arrest of some political opponents but nothing more. The abortive armed invasion of 86 persons in 1959 reflected no basic unrest and was quickly brought under control.

Lower-class groups have never formed any organized opposition to Panamanian governments. Much of the rural population live a subsistence existence through a slash-and-burn culture of land obtained from squatting. Workers on the banana plantations, in the factories of the

[5]Daniel Goldrich, *Sons of the Establishment* (Chicago: Rand McNally, 1966).

multinational corporations, and in the Canal Zone belong to carefully controlled labor unions, and other urban workers are generally unorganized. It is yet to be seen whether Torrijos's support of workers will change this situation. In any case, rapid economic growth with moderate social mobilization has created a situation where the material goods are relatively adequate to cover the wants of the population. The government also expanded education quite rapidly in the 1960s.

Mexico

In many respects, recent Mexican history is the simplest to chronicle of any in Latin America. The official view as presented by the government is that Mexico had a social revolution between 1910 and 1919, and since that time has enjoyed increasing prosperity and political evolution. Both the Mexican peasantry and the proletariat participated in that revolution and are today sharing in the benefits it has brought to Mexico. Mexico, according to its officials, is one of the few Latin American nations to have freed itself from the domination of the United States. It has very little repression and most violence occurs in the rural areas, which have not yet quite caught up with the rest of the country in political and social development. At the same time, despite one-party rule, the nation is essentially democratic; conflicting interests are expressed within that ruling party and different groups have access to the political system through active participation in the PRI. Such is the official view of Mexico presented by the government, by most periodicals in this country and in Mexico, and by many scholars.

If only this view of Mexican history could be accepted in its entirety, we could end this section here, with perhaps a few words about some minor problems that the nation still faces in realizing the Western democratic ideal. Mexican history, however, is not so simple— and there is a darker side to it since the Revolution of 1910. For a long time this darker side was presented only by Mexican novelists, particularly Martín Guzmán and Mariano Azuela. The major thesis of these two commentators on the Mexican Revolution was that it had been a failure: men had shed blood and died for an ideal that had not been realized, was not being realized, and would not be realized unless another major change shook the nation. More recently, social scientists have increasingly arrived at much the same conclusions. Beginning with L. Vincent Padgett[6] and moving through Frank Brandenburg[7] and

---

[6]L. Vincent Padgett, *The Mexican Political System* (Boston: Houghton Mifflin, 1966).
[7]Frank Brandenburg, *The Making of Modern Mexico* (Englewood Cliffs, N.J.: Prentice-Hall, 1964).

Kenneth Johnson[8] to Pablo Gonzalez Casanova,[9] social scientists evaluating the Mexican political system became more and more critical of its
performance and its promise. Gonzalez, in fact, has concluded that the
Mexican political system functions poorly in many aspects. This evolution in writings on Mexico presents, then, not the clear picture first
outlined by the government, but a very confused one—perhaps the
most confused in all Latin America. We do not have a readily identifia-
ble dictator like Trujillo in the Dominican Republic, nor, it appears, do
we have a system such as in Chile in the 1960s where all political parties
competed rather openly for the vote. Mexico is not the paragon of
progress, peace, and an open society, but it obviously has much greater
social cohesion than do many of its dictator-prone neighbors. But what
is the status of Mexican society today? Is it the violent and repressive
society pictured by some, or is it the most socially cohesive society in
Latin America? Or is it somewhere in between these two extremes?

Obviously, a reading of the amount of violence and repression in
Mexico in the last twenty years will assist in determining how successful the Mexican Revolution has been in realizing the goals of its leaders
as embodied in the Mexican Consitution of 1917. Further, an examination of the data relating to societal welfare and social mobilization,
trends in economic development, the institutionalization of the various
groups in Mexican society that most affect the political system, as well
as a perusal of the outputs of the system itself, will help to form
some picture of Mexican society today. A few caveats are in order,
however. The authors believe, with some evidence to substantiate that
belief, that both the repression and the violence data on Mexico are
understated. The way in which the Mexican political system works
makes it highly likely that much rural violence, directed against the
government, goes unreported. The dual nature of the Mexican economy, with an extreme imbalance between the industrialized urban
areas and the poor rural sector, no doubt adds to the amount of rural
violence. Also, the Mexican government appears to utilize much more
sophisticated methods of repression than do most of its Latin American
counterparts. The press may be controlled through the rationing of
newsprint, and opposition political parties are probably controlled
through a type of co-optation process described by Kenneth Johnson:

> In Mexico those who live outside the public budget desperately seek access
> to it: those who are within the budget refuse to abandon their sinecures
> and are bitterly jealous of those in quest of entry. The public budget is the

[8]Kenneth F. Johnson, *Mexican Democracy: A Critical View* (Boston: Allyn and Bacon,
1971).

[9]Pablo Gonzalez Casanova, *Democracy in Mexico* (London: Oxford University Press,
1970).

PRI. In the event that a brilliant young challenger distinguishes himself as an opponent of the government, he is summoned to the seat of power, first to chat and to "break the ice," and later to offer him a public position within the budget and thereby to eliminate him as an enemy.[10]

Sometimes, naturally enough, this process does not work, and the *Partido Revolucionario Institucional* must resort to stronger methods, such as voiding elections where opposition candidates have won, or cutting off funds for localities that insist on electing officials from an opposition party. The PRI is the "official" party of the Mexican Revolution and has controlled Mexican politics since its founding—as the *Partido de la Revolución Mexicano* (PRM)—by President Plutarco Elías Calles in 1922. Probably the process described by Johnson covers the vast majority of cases involving opposition, but the process does not, of course, qualify as outright repression.

Violence data are also somewhat suspect in Mexico. Rural Mexico, especially, seems to have a culture of violence, probably dating from the extraordinary amount of violence that spread across Mexico during the revolutionary period and during the war of the *Cristeros* in the 1920s. It is quite possible that much of this violence, reported as simple homicides, was in reality antisystemic and in many cases organized. The guerrilla bands that have been operating in the State of Guerrero, at times within sight of the plush resort of Acapulco, were for years classed as simple bandits when in fact they had been organized into antigovernment units for some time.

In spite of these caveats, the picture that Mexico presents to the world, and to most social scientists, is that of a nation that has experienced large-scale repression and violence in the past but is now relatively peaceful and free and on its way to more peace and greater freedom. Certainly, our data on repression and violence in Mexico tend to substantiate this picture. Exact data on the level of violence and repression in Mexico from the time of the outbreak of the Revolution in 1910 through the 1930s is lacking, but contemporary, historical, and literary accounts all agree that violence during those years was widespread and almost continuous. They also agree that repression was used quite extensively in all regimes down to the Cárdenas administration beginning in 1934. During a time when the rest of Latin America remained relatively quiescent, Mexico experienced a profound revolution with the highest level of violence in Latin America. In contrast, during the twenty years from 1950 to 1970, Mexico had less repression

---

[10]Johnson, *op. cit.*, p. 185.

than did all other countries in Latin America with the exception of Chile, Costa Rica, and Uruguay. The Mexican government was able to surmount a rather serious threat to the stability of the system in 1968 with only a moderate increase in overall repression, even though the repression of the students who were posing the threat was rather severe. Mexico's violence totals for the two decades are exactly average for the Latin American nations. It had the tenth highest total in the hemisphere. Mexico had slightly more violence during the sixties than in the fifties, primarily because of the extraordinarily high (for Mexico) violence totals in 1968. Over the twenty years, Mexico had more unarmed than armed violence, an indication that the regime has not been heavy-handedly totalitarian.

At one time Mexico was hailed as the developmental example for the rest of Latin America, and various officials from the United States and international organizations were advising other Latin American nations to emulate the Mexican path toward development. Here was a nation, so the argument went, that had achieved a high rate of economic growth plus a relatively equal distribution of the rewards of that growth within at least a quasi-democratic framework. This talk of Mexico as the prototype for Latin American development has all but ceased, and with good reason. On many of our independent variables—societal welfare, land and income equality, and government outputs—Mexico lags well behind the leaders of the hemisphere; and on many of them, the nation ranks below the Latin American mean. In spite of decades of trumpeted agrarian reform programs, for example— one of the major aims of the Mexican Revolution—Mexico today has one of the most unequal land-tenure patterns in Latin America. Further, it also has, aside from Guatemala's, the most unequal distribution of income. The situation has improved in the last decade, but in 1960 Mexico was at the Latin American mean in level of economic development and in literacy, approximately at the mean in medical services, and well below the mean in percent of school-age population in school. By 1970 Mexico was above the mean in all of these indicators of societal welfare, but still far behind Argentina, Uruguay, and Venezuela. During the same decade Mexico's level of social mobilization also rose faster than the Latin American average, but by 1970 the country was little better off in terms of the differential between societal welfare and social mobilization than it had been at the beginning of the 1960s.

Mexico's rate of economic growth has been comparatively high by Latin American standards, but also quite volatile. In the first half of the 1950s, the Mexican economy advanced more rapidly than that of any other Latin American nation. From 1955 through 1959, however, Mexico's rate of economic growth was surpassed by eight Latin American

nations, and during the 1960s at least three Latin American nations—
Costa Rica, El Salvador, and Panama—had higher growth rates.

Even though Mexico's economic indicators do not demonstrate the
success of its revolution in bringing either economic development or an
equitable distribution of economic perquisites, the nation's indexes of
institutionalization demonstrate some of the strengths of the Mexican
system. Specifically, Mexico has a highly institutionalized Catholic
Church and the most highly institutionalized political party system in
Latin America. It appears that the Catholic Church has survived the
persecution of the 1920s and early 1930s admirably and may even have
profited from the experience. Not only does the Mexican church have
one of the lowest population-to-priest ratios in Latin America, it also
has extensive autonomy, which increases the degree of institutionalization. The institutionalized political party system refers, of course, to
one political party, the PRI, which has controlled Mexican politics since
its inception in the 1920s. Although the PRI is one of the most highly
institutionalized political parties in the world, the one major opposition
party, the Party of National Action (*Partido de Acción Nacional*—PAN),
is also highly institutionalized. It has existed in opposition for years,
and presents a coherent alternative to the PRI programs for Mexico. The
army also has become well institutionalized.

Any examination of repression and violence in Mexico would be
ignoring a major factor if it did not take into account the Mexican
Revolution of 1910. Not only did the revolution produce the PRI, but it
also produced the ideology of the PRI along with a generally positive
orientation toward the Mexican political system. Although this latter
phenomenon is not reflected in our data, it is probably a major source of
strength—if not *the* major source of strength—in the Mexican political
system. The orientation is described extensively in Gabriel Almond and
Sidney Verba's *The Civic Culture*. Their findings, which are based on
survey research that, unfortunately, has not been undertaken in the rest
of the Latin American nations, showed that "this revolution . . . is the
crucial event in the development of the Mexican political culture, for it
created a sense of national identity and a commitment to the political
system that permeates almost all strata of society."[11]

The book demonstrated further that Mexicans generally were aware
that their government was not performing in accord with the goals of
the revolution but that they still had faith that some day it would. It is,
of course, difficult to explain this apparent contradiction between the

[11]Gabriel Almond and Sidney Verba, *The Civic Culture* (Boston: Little, Brown,
1965), p. 372.

reality of Mexico for the past fifty years and the general satisfaction that Mexicans still feel toward their government. Obviously, the mystique of the revolution has been used effectively and pervades Mexican society. Mexican art, literature, music, and dance are suffused by it, and the media trumpet the achievements of the revolution at every turn (see *Hispano-Americano* over the course of a year or so). It boils down to the notion that Mexicans are proud of "their" revolution, that the revolution has been used effectively as a symbol, and that Mexicans are not going to allow the facts of poor performance by the Mexican political system to alter their basic view of their country—at least not for a while.

The Revolution of 1910 has possibly had another effect on recent Mexican politics—one not widely commented upon. Although the years of major violence are now receding into past history for most Mexicans, the realization that such events did take place within this century may be producing a sobering effect on those anxious for change within the nation. People, when they are aware of the tremendous carnage produced by a revolution, are usually more hesitant to embark upon a revolutionary course. This realization may still be present in Mexico, although it is certainly more attenuated than in Spain where memories of the Spanish Civil War undoubtedly inhibit those who would wish for the overthrow of the Franco dictatorship. Still, violence in Mexico was so extensive well into the 1920s that, instead of a tradition of violence producing more violence, as has been suggested by some authors, it may be inhibiting further violence by inhibiting the potential instigators of bloody antigovernment action.

By far the greatest violence occurred during the first stage of the Mexican Revolution, which lasted from the ouster of the Dictator Porfirio Díaz in 1911 until the consolidation of power by Venustiano Carranza in 1917. This seven-year period was one of extreme dislocation in Mexican society , in which various *caudillos*, all pretending to represent the true revolution, attempted to gain control of the political apparatus. Francisco Madero, Venustiano Carranza, Alvaro Obregón, Pancho Villa, and Emiliano Zapata all vied for leadership within the revolution, while Victoriano Huerta and Félix Díaz (nephew of the former dictator) attempted to establish a new dictatorship. The result was chaos and the most extreme violence in Latin American history. While there are no accurate compilations of the number of people killed during the years between 1910 and 1917, reliable estimates run as high as one million. The Mexican population, which had grown at a steady pace prior to the revolution, actually decreased during the seven-year period. The violence penetrated all areas of Mexico and reached into all strata of

Mexican society, although, as usual, the poorer classes suffered the most. And it was brutal as it was pervasive, as documents testify to mass tortures and killings of wounded soldiers and civilians.

The second stage of the Mexican Revolution, which lasted from 1920 to 1934, was one of initial attempts at institutionalization. The process in which the armed forces eventually became subservient to the civilian political leaders was begun during these years, culminating in the election in 1946 of Mexico's first civilian president, Manuel Ávila Camacho. Violence also occurred during this second stage, however, as the revolutionary governments began to implement the anticlerical provisions of the 1917 constitution. From 1926 until a final resolution in 1934, conflict continued between the church and its supporters and the supporters of the revolution. The War of the *Cristeros*, as it was called, was even more poorly reported than was the Revolution. The violence during this period was nowhere near as great as that during the first phase of the revolution, but lay priests did resort to armed rebellion against the government. They blew up trains, burned government schools, and stoned and killed teachers. The government retaliated with severe repression of anyone who supported the *cristero* cause. Most of the violence was limited to the western states of Michoacán, Jalisco, and Colima.

The third period of the Mexican Revolution lasted from 1934 to 1940 and was coterminous with the presidency of Lázaro Cárdenas. These years were characterized by an official reconciliation with the Catholic Church (in which the church tacitly agreed to drop its political role), by a strong element of anti-Americanism, by much greater emphasis on the original goals of the Mexican Revolution (particularly land reform), and by a full fruition of the sense of nationalism engendered by earlier events. The importance of Cárdenas, apart from his actual accomplishments (which were considerable), was in the symbolism of nationalism and control over the destinies of Mexico by the Mexican people.

The process of institutionalization begun during the 1920s continued under Cárdenas. The Confederation of Mexican Workers (*Confederación de Trabajadores Mexicanos*—CTM) was formed in 1936, and this organization has dominated the labor scene ever since. The revolutionary agrarian leadership formed leagues at the state level at about the same time and established the National Peasants Confederation (*Confederación Nacional de Campesinos*—CNC). Under a "four sectors" concept, Calles's PRM was divided into four sections representing the politically articulate members of the Mexican populace. These were the peasant, labor, military, and "popular" sectors, the last being a catchall for anyone who did not fall into one of the first three groups. The important point was that the Mexican Revolutionary Party, which by now had become almost synonymous with the government, was now organizing and preempting the areas of labor, military, and peasants for itself, thereby precluding the development of another political party with any significant base in these areas.

The final phase of the revolution began with the election of Manuel Ávila Camacho as president in 1940; it has been labeled the "consolidation" phase. This period has continued to the present and includes the twenty years with which we are most concerned. It has been characterized by relatively low levels of violence and repression; by a return to more conservative political, economic, and social policies; by the creation of the "new class" of Mexican industrialists; by increasingly friendly relations with the United States; and by continued successful efforts to maintain the hegemony of the PRI in Mexican politics. This phase has also been marked by increased alienation among those (largely rural) sectors of the Mexican population that have been left behind by the revolution and who have not benefited from it.

Camacho served until 1946 when he was succeeded by Miguel Alemán, and under their tenures Mexican politics took a sharp swing to the right. Alemán was the first civilian president of Mexico since the revolution, and his major achievements were the construction of the National University at Mexico City, the beginning of a modern road system, and the irrigation of large amounts of new farmland. Under Alemán, the pace of agrarian reform slowed markedly, and several major labor disputes broke out. The chief dispute occurred at the end of 1951, between coal miners in the State of Coahuila and the mining company. As a result of government inaction in the dispute, the miners organized the Caravan of Hunger, which marched to Mexico City, arriving there on March 10, 1952. Almost immediately the government appointed a board of arbitration; and by March 19 the board had announced its findings. They were partly in favor of the miners, and partly for the company, but the miners were induced to leave the city and return home. Major disturbances occurred in Yucatán in 1951 and 1952, in Colima in 1951, and in Oaxaca in 1952, all of them protests against actions by the national government. Throughout the Alemán regime, Communists were prohibited from taking part in elections, and various Communist leaders were jailed for short stretches of time. The biggest disturbance took place on May Day, 1952, in Mexico City when the Communist parade turned into a riot with several hundred wounded. The government had little trouble coping with the uproar, however, and used the occasion as a pretext for further arrests of leading members of the Communist Party.

By the end of 1952, and the end of the Alemán administration, the basic pattern of violence and repression in Mexico had been established. Violence was to continue in the provinces, usually in reaction to a government program, but in some instances, especially in Oaxaca, as a result of governmental inaction. The government, which more and more appeared to adopt a policy of concentrating its considerable largesse on the more densely populated plain between Mexico City and Guadalajara, would answer these protests with a combination of repression and concession, the amount of each depending to a great extent on the source and reason for the protest and on the person in charge of directing the governmental response. In the large population centers, where government control was better, there was much less violence, which is possibly why the widespread violence in Mexico City in 1968 was considered to be such a threat to the system. Violence in the capital city was regarded with much less tolerance than violence emanating from the provinces and was put down much more ruthlessly and quickly. The Communists continued to be persecuted, especially as long as one of their number—Vicente Lombardo Toledano—maintained an appreciable following. Only in 1968 did the Mexican government resort to any restriction of civil liberties, and even then it was limited both in degree and time.

Most of Mexico's repression score in the years between 1950 and 1970 resulted from restrictions on political parties, even though PAN gained most of its admittedly low strength during this period. Many observers have commented, however, that the growth of PAN was calculated by the leaders of the PRI in an attempt to legitimize their regime as a democracy. In a sense, if these observers are correct, PAN represents a gigantic effort at co-optation of opposition by allowing it some limited access to the public budget through the participation of PAN members in the National Congress and in certain provincial governments.

Most of the violence during the four-year presidency of Adolfo Ruiz Cortines came in 1953 and 1954 from the supporters of defeated presidential candidate Miguel Henríquez Guzmán. Henríquez, a member of the PRI, refused to accept the decision of the party naming Ruiz as the official candidate. Henríquez had run a well-organized campaign and had garnered 570,745 votes to Ruiz's 2,713,419 votes. In several instances after the election, the Henriquistas began desultory guerrilla operations and, at one point in 1954, succeeded in capturing, for a few hours, the town of Ticumán, near Cuernavaca. The movement was quickly suppressed, however, and Henríquez's political future, never very bright, vanished.

The Mexican Revolution entered a new stage with the election of Adolfo López Mateos as president in 1958. López, unlike his immediate predecessors, but in the tradition of Cárdenas, campaigned vigorously throughout the nation and was elected with no opposition other than the PAN, whose candidate received 705,000 votes, a jump of 500,000 over the 1952 totals. The six years from 1958 to 1964 were ones of renewed activity in agrarian reform and expropriation of foreign-owned utilities in Mexico. At the same time, the "Mexicanization" program was begun, under which all enterprises operating in Mexico were to be at least 50 percent owned by Mexicans.

Although López Mateos produced much more movement in government in the area of social reform, the level of repression and violence increased considerably. The Communists continued to receive the brunt of the government's repressive force, but various rightist groups, especially one under retired general Gasca Villaseñor, were also intimidated. Again, most of the violence came in the outlying provinces, the result of unpopular PRI candidates being forced on unwilling electorates. At least some of the stepped-up violence could be attributed to the unsettling effect of the increased political activity of ex-President Cárdenas. Cárdenas, now out of step with the new business leadership of the PRI, began to clash orally with PRI leadership over the degree of Mexico's approval of the Cuban Revolution. Cárdenas saw the Castro regime as a continuation of the Mexican model, whereas most of the current PRI leaders were much cooler in their approach to Castro and what they saw as essentially a Marxist-modeled revolution. López' troubles were additionally compounded by the return of the Catholic Church to political action, and a riot occurred in Puebla in June, 1961, after a demonstration supporting the church against "the Communists."

López Mateos's troubles were minor, however, compared with those of his successor, Gustavo Diaz Ordaz. As early as 1966 students in the provinces were demonstrating against unpopular candidates "elected" by the PRI; and in 1967, in the State of Sonora, a three-day riot by students and teachers protesting the nomination of an unpopular candidate for governor was put down by troops with at least eleven killed and thirty-five hurt. (The troops had received tear gas from the governor of Arizona, who defended his actions as part of "the good neighbor policy.") The first test of what came to be known as the Institutionalized Revolution began on July 26, 1968, when students celebrating the official holiday for Fidel Castro's movement were attacked by police. They responded by rampaging through Mexico City, and the police responded with even more force. From July until the end of the year, press reports from Mexico City read like those from Havana in 1958. Each student riot or demonstration was met with greater force by the government, which culminated in the killings of October 2. Approximately 3,000 students and others had gathered in a student housing project to protest prior actions by the police, when the federal troops opened fire on the demonstrators. Estimates of dead and wounded vary, but the best estimates seem to put the dead at approximately 50, and the wounded at 500. The mass movement disintegrated before this ferocious show of force, and from then on protests came from scattered small groups throughout the countryside and in Mexico City. The operations against the students were supervised by Minister of Interior Pedro Echeverria, who became Mexico's president in 1970.

Parallels with other threats to the stability in Latin American regimes are inexact at best, but it does appear that the ruling groups in Mexico were faced with a serious threat during the latter half of 1968. Why did the movement fail, and why did the government emerge relatively unscathed? There are three probable answers to the question. First, the revolution was institutionalized, as were the PRI, the CTM, the CNC, and all the subsidiary organizations built up over the years since 1917. When the test came, these institutions stood together and were strong enough to withstand the severe stress. Second, the economy had continued to outpace social mobilization. Third, although there were strikes, demonstrations, and other expressions of support for the students in Mexico City and elsewhere, the majority of Mexicans seemingly disapproved of the students' actions and supported the government, even in its more repressive moments. The equation developed for predicting the levels of violence and repression indicates that the level of violence and repression in 1968 were an aberration from what would be expected. The basic variables predicted a lower level of both than actually occurred. What is surprising, then, is the outbreak, not its failure. The outbreak, as well as the massive retaliation to it, were certainly stimulated at least in part by the excitement of the Olympic Games to be held within a few months in Mexico City, plus the fact that world attention would be focused on Mexico.

Violence in Mexico, however, is still higher than expected. The violence in the provinces continues, as the PRI continues to force its handpicked candidates down the throats of sometimes unwilling voters. Mexican students continue to protest what they consider to be the unfulfilled promises of more than sixty years of "revolution." In recent years, leftist terrorist groups have engineered several spectacular kidnappings, including that of the United States consul general in Guadalajara. For the most part, these kidnappings have gone unpunished by the Mexican government, and groups such as the Movement for Revolutionary Action appear to have succeeded in bringing violence to the cities. As Oscar Lewis's book, *The Children of Sanchez* (banned in Mexico for some time after publication), so searingly documents, alienation is not confined to the rural areas of Mexico, and urban guerrilla movements may find, if not outright support, at least some empathy among the urban proletariat.

On the positive side, the strength of Mexican political and social institutions must again be emphasized as well as their capacity for handling conflict "within the system," either through co-optation or repression. Lastly, and again repetitively, there is the mystique of the revolution itself. It has been documented by Almond and Verba, and written about by every commentator on Mexican politics, but what Mexicans have can be described best as a tradition to look back on and a faith in the future. When Mexicans—sometimes drunk and sometimes sober—shout "Viva Mexico, hijos de la chingada!" they are expressing an emotional attachment to a national ideal rarely found in other nations. This is part of the cement that holds the nation together.

Ecuador

Ecuador was much less repressive in the 1950s and much less violent in the 1960s than we had predicted. There are several features of Ecuadorian society that might account for its doing better than our theory indicates it would. First, Ecuador is a highly stratified society with a rigid class system, based in large part on a social-racial distinction related to the Indian characteristics of individuals. Quite probably, societies in which large numbers of individuals "know their place" simply do not need to repress as much as others, while at the same time a lack of any prospect of upward social mobility would tend to reduce the use of violence as a means to change. Second, Ecuador is a society of strong local elites. These elites are generally cohesive; they retain their confidence in their ability to govern without the aid of the national government. Their confidence is probably well-founded.

A congerie of other factors might also explain the lower levels of violence and repression: the most highly institutionalized Catholic Church in Latin America; political parties that, although they have taken their lumps recently from the military dictatorship, are fairly well institutionalized; and, finally, the promise of national riches from the extensive oil finds in the Oriente region. All have undoubtedly led to more social cohesion than was expected.

In spite of all the above factors, however, Ecuador is not a particularly cohesive society. Generally, Ecuador has been a society that has been unable to manage change, but which thus far has been able to avoid many of the effects of the twentieth century. In the past, the most serious violence has occurred in and around Guayaquil, which has become the center for the twenty-five to forty percent of the population classed as mestizo. It is this group, especially those who are now flocking to Guayaquil, and in the process making it Ecuador's largest city, that is the socially mobilized sector of Ecuador and that is most apt to protest against a continuation of the status quo society of the nineteenth century. It remains to be seen whether the military government, which has been noisily proclaiming itself as the leader of the Ecuadorian revolution, will successfully appeal to this group as it deals with the inevitable antagonisms of the more conservative elites that have controlled Ecuador for centuries.

Nicaragua

The Somoza dynasty in Nicaragua (Anastasio Somoza, 1937–1956; his eldest son, Luis Somoza, 1957–1963; and his younger son, Anastasio "Tachito" Somoza, 1968 to the present) has an undeservedly bad reputation for repression. Repression has been used in Nicaragua, but to a considerably less degree than under some traditional dictatorships or under rightist military rule. For the twenty-year period in Latin America, Nicaragua scored exactly at the median on repression and among the twenty-five percent least violent countries. The Nicaraguan political system reminds one more of the Mexican than of the Trujillo regime in the Dominican Republic, with which it has been more often compared. Political opposition is allowed to operate openly most of the time, but is subject to occasional suspensions of liberties and political arrest. Rewards of office are shared among a fairly wide circle of enterprising politicians, and support for the government is organized through a political party in alliance with the labor unions. The opposition complains of fraud at election time, but most observers concede that the Liberal Party of the Somozas would win in any case. Opposition is guaranteed a third of the seats in Congress.

Nicaragua always has been something of an anarchic state where violence in politics has been expected and accepted. The nineteenth century witnessed a perpetual battle between the Liberal Party elite located in León and the Conservative Party elite located in Granada. It was this battle which led to United States intervention in 1912, with a continued U.S. presence until 1933. One of Latin America's first guerrilla movements was organized by General Augusto César Sandino against the U.S. supported regime, fighting from 1928 to 1933.[12]

In more recent years, political violence and repression has centered around the question of whether the Somozas should remain in power or

[12]Neill Macauley, *The Sandino Affair* (Chicago: Quadrangle Press, 1967).

not. The principle occasions for repression in the 1950s came at the time of the attempted assassination of Anastasio Somoza in 1954 and the successful assassination in 1956, after which the government declared martial law and arrested hundreds of political opponents. From 1958 to 1962 a number of rebellions were organized outside the country, in Honduras, Cuba, and Costa Rica, to overthrow the regime headed by Luis Somoza. Conflict also broke out during the elections of 1963, in which René Schick represented the Somoza cause, and even more intensely in 1967, when Tachito Somoza, the head of the National Guard, sought and won the presidency.

Nicaragua has relatively low social mobilization, and for the last twenty years it has enjoyed an annual economic growth rate of around three percent per capita. As a result, conflict over the distribution of material goods has not become overly tense. The Somozas have been able to reward their followers abundantly, and the lower classes and the conservative opposition have also gained economically. Anastasio Somoza initiated a number of public investments in the 1950s, which helped to generate this economic growth, and the regime expanded social programs in the 1960s. Nevertheless, Nicaragua continued to score low on our educational measures, indicating a relatively narrow distribution of public benefits.

In the mid-1970s, the Nicaraguan government received a challenge from the guerrilla group, the *Frente Sandinista de Liberación Nacional*, which took advantage of the discontent over the graft and corruption in the distribution of relief funds following the disastrous earthquake of 1973. Even so, it is hard to see how this guerrilla force could make much headway against the populist machine politics of the Somoza clique.

Peru

For years political analysts predicted that Peru, the fourth-largest nation in Latin America, would experience violent social revolution in the twentieth century. An historical pattern of political violence, racial and social divisions, economic inequalities, and advanced ideological development made Peru one of the more unstable Latin American republics. Yet violent revolution in Peru has thus far been avoided, embarrassing political prognosticators and compelling explanations that revolution had been permanently thwarted or only temporarily postponed.[13] Central to these arguments and any contemporary under-

[13]David Chaplin, "Peru's Postponed Revolution," *World Politics* 20 (April, 1968), pp. 393–420.

standing of Peruvian politics is the role of the military institution. Under the aegis and impetus of the military, unprecedented economic, social, and structural changes are fast reorganizing present-day Peru within the concept of "revolution from above."

The military stands out not only as the most powerful social institution in current Peruvian politics but also in post-independence history. By 1841 when independence wars had culminated, a political tradition of military preeminence and *caudillismo* had been firmly established. Military strong men, heroized and legitimized by independence struggles, dominated the disorganized and weakened civilian elites. General Ramón Castilla, for example, ruled Peru between 1844 and 1862, a time of increasing economic development and national peace. Only in 1872 was the first civilian president, Manuel Pardo, elected amid civilian-military intrigues and growing civilian reaction against military rule. Pardo audaciously streamlined finances and cut the military budget, thus incurring partial blame for defeat in the War of the Pacific, 1879–1883, between Peru and Bolivia on one side and Chile, victorious, on the other. The consequences of the defeat for Peru were twofold. It discredited noninstitutional and political involvement in the long run, and more immediately, military dominance became more entrenched as antimilitary feeling was repressed.[14] In the face of the ever-present Chilean threat and burning hopes of Peruvian territorial revanchism, military budgets were kept high and generals kept a hold on the presidency from 1883 to 1894.

After the war three major political parties became prominent: the Democratic Party of Nicolás de Piérola, professing strong anti-militarism; the Constitutional Party of General Andrés Cáceres; and the Civil Party of Manuel Pardo. In 1895 a bloody civilian revolt in Lima, instigated by the Democratic and Civil parties against continued military rule, ended direct military involvement in politics and established the pattern of civilian personalist government until 1930. Between 1895 and 1919 the era of oligarchic civilian rule was broken by only one military interlude.[15] This "golden age" rested on Piérola's formalization of tacit military-civilian cooperation. The understanding was that the oligarchy, in exchange for guardianship of the status quo, would control political power but respect the military's independence and generous budgets. Piérola further strove to check military intervention by profes-

---

[14]Frederick B. Pike, *The Modern History of Peru* (New York: Praeger, 1967), p. 150; Robert E. McNicoll, "Peru's Institutional Revolution" (Latin American Studies, Interdisciplinary Occasional Papers, University of West Florida, Pensacola, October, 1973), pp. 1–4; Stephen L. Rozman, "The Evolution of the Political Role of the Peruvian Military," *Journal of Inter-American Studies* 12 (October, 1970), pp. 539–546.

[15]Robert Marett, *Peru* (New York: Praeger, 1969), p. 122.

sionalization, the assistance of a French military mission, the founding of the Military School of Chorrillos, and an obligatory military service law. However, these efforts did not fully succeed. Thus, despite lessened direct political involvement and a growing tendency toward military professionalization, oligarchic ambitions and the weakness of the political party system prevented a return to the barracks and inevitably brought on the historic confrontation of the military and the only broadly populist and reformist political party in Peru, the *Alianza Popular Revolucionaria Americana*, or APRA. APRA was the only political party to survive the eleven years of Augusto Leguía's dictatorship— from 1919 to 1930—with strong cohesiveness, discipline, and popular appeal. The party grew out of allied student-worker agitation in 1919 for university reform and the establishment of the eight-hour workday. Its founder, Victor Raúl Haya de la Torre, was deported as a student radical in 1923, and on May 7, 1924, established APRA in Mexico City. Originally linked in spirit with the indigenist and socialist philosopher José Carlos Mariátegui, the latter split with *aprismo* in 1928 and formed the Socialist Party of Peru, from which the Peruvian Communist Party emerged in 1930. In this decade APRA achieved the height of its political appeal. The Leguía dictatorship, despite political repression, had stimulated an era of economic growth. Extensive North American capital investments displaced British influence and provided plentiful national earnings, with which public works and beautification projects in Lima and the construction of roads and schools could be financed. By 1929, however, prosperity had dried up. With an economy so closely tied to the U.S. market that critics denounced it as subservient, with aid loans overextended, and with export earnings in petroleum, sugar, and cotton declining rapidly, Peru faced deep economic ruin when hit by the worldwide depression. Unemployment, an ever-ascending cost of living, and the devaluation of the *sol* generated dissatisfactions that directly contributed to working- and middle-class support of *aprismo*. Students and intellectuals, long alienated from the repressive Leguía regime, and radicalized by Marxist and indigenist philosophies, flocked to join APRA. Soon economic decline, political agitation, and mobilization established the climate for the army coup of Colonel Luis Sánchez Cerro on August 22, 1930.

The 1931 presidential election, which pitted APRA leader Haya de la Torre against the provisional military president, Sánchez Cerro, was the basis for the first crucial military-*aprista* clash. Both candidates could claim popular support: Sánchez Cerro urged national unity and the end to corruption and subservient economic policies of the dictatorship; Haya de la Torre preached violent revolution, death to Yankee imperialism, nationalization of land and industry, and Indo-American solidarity.[16] APRA lost, and, charging electoral fraud, instigated open warfare with the military. Violence and chaos culminated in the infamous July, 1932, APRA attack on the Trujillo military barracks, which left numerous dead and wounded on both sides. The assassination nine months later of Sánchez Cerro, blamed on the *apristas,* marked a violent and unforgettable period in Peruvian politics.

Government again fell to the military in the person of General Oscar Benavides, who in August, 1933, following a policy of conciliation, granted amnesty to APRA prisoners but prohibited legal political activity on the grounds that the party was internationalist. Continued agitation and terrorism finally provoked military repression and the outlawing of APRA in 1936. In a similar pattern the political fortunes of *aprismo* have been continued to the present: years of political amnesty, semi-legality, open organization and agitation have alternated with periods of exile, underground activity, and military repression. Although the zenith of political power and popularity of APRA has passed as increasing opportunism and ideological moderation reflected a changed party and electorate, *aprismo* has nonetheless irrevocably influenced and limited political alternatives in Peru.

By 1945 the party had attained a certain political respectability and bargaining power for the presidential elections, in which the reformist National Democratic Front candidate, José Luis Bustamante y Rivero, won. APRA secured 20 out of 49 senate seats and 50 out of 153 chamber seats,[17] and attempted to use this strength to push through reform measures. But disagreements with Bustamante and the boycott of the legislature by conservative congressmen defeated such tactics, and the APRA withdrew its support from the government.[18] Economic deterioration intensified by legislative collapse made rule by decree and the all-military cabinet of February, 1948, unavoidable. The failure of an APRA-instigated coup on October 3 was the prelude to the classic military response—the take-over, this one by General Manuel Odría in October, 1948. Once in control, Odría served as president until 1956 and persecuted APRA severely during his term.

By 1962 APRA was ready again to bid for supreme power. In return for the electoral support of Manuel Prado in 1956, the party was allowed to run Haya de la Torre legally in the presidential elections. The results attributed 32.96 percent of the votes to Haya de la Torre, 32.19 percent to Fernando Belaúnde Terry of *Acción Popular,* and 28.43 percent to

---

[16]Ibid., pp. 157–158.
[17]These figures are used by Rozman, *op. cit.,* p. 553.
[18]Marett, *op. cit.,* p. 172.

General Odría.[19] The percentages—indeed, the decimal points—are important because they show that no candidate had attained the one-third majority necessary for victory and that the Congress had to decide the outcome. The APRA, however, struck a deal with General Odría, an old enemy, and that triggered an institutionalized military intervention. New elections in 1963 resolved the succession controversy and declared Belaúnde president with 39.05 percent of the popular vote, versus 34.36 percent and 25.52 percent for Haya de la Torre and Odría respectively.[20]

The Belaúnde government—viewed by many as the last chance for a reformist-civilian process of development—failed. Despite a broad but conservative reform program and the momentum of electoral and personal popularity, Belaúnde was thwarted by economic and political factors within and beyond his control. The 1950s had brought the awakening and growth of *campesino* land hunger, the formation of rural syndicates and the militant occupations of some land, actions that culminated between 1961 and 1963 in wholesale land seizures under the leadership of Hugo Blanco in La Convención Valley.[21] Neither the mild agrarian reform proposals of the previous junta nor those of Belaúnde were radical enough to satisfy the campesinos. By early 1965 guerrilla centers had been organized in *sierra* Peru, and these tried to project *campesino* unrest into armed military encounters in order to radicalize the political situation and create the subjective conditions for social revolution. The guerrilla bands were eliminated by 1967, but their challenge and the ineffectiveness of the civilian leadership in dealing with them alarmed the military. It was increasingly clear that peasant unrest had progressed from a local problem to one that had national security implications.

Moreover, in Congress the APRA-Odría bloc impeded all executive reform measures, paralleling the legislative deadlock of 1948 that made military intervention necessary. Economically expensive reform and development projects stimulated inflationary spending and created acute governmental deficits. The consumer price index jumped from 100 in 1960 to 222 in 1968. Export earnings for fish products declined

[19]Marvin Alisky, *Peruvian Political Perspective* (Tempe: Arizona State University, 1973), p. 13; Jane S. Jaquette, *The Politics of Development in Peru*, Latin American Studies Program, Dissertation Series (Ithaca, N.Y.: Cornell University, 1971), no. 33. Jaquette attributes 32.98 percent of the vote to Haya de la Torre, p. 117.

[20]Jaquette, *op. cit.*, p. 130; Alisky, *op. cit.*, provides these figures: 39.06 percent, 34.35 percent, and 25.53 percent for each candidate respectively, p. 13.

[21]Vivian Trias, *Peru Fuerzas Armadas y Revolución* (Montevideo: Ediciones de la Banda Oriental, 1971), pp. 73–76; see also Marett, *op. cit.*, pp. 222–226.

sharply while import demands went up radically. By September, 1967, it was necessary to devalue the *sol*.[22] A contraband-corruption scandal, which broke in February, 1968, further discredited the civilian government. Nearly a month later the "eleventh page" scandal hit the media, which was charged with bowing to foreign interests.[23] The military, worried by economic deterioration, and wary of a possible APRA-*Alianza Popular* (AP) alliance for the upcoming electoral year, finally assumed executive leadership and launched Peru into radical development.

The military government formerly headed by General Juan Velasco Alvarado views rapid national growth and restructuring of the Peruvian system as tantamount to nonviolent revolution. "Revolution from above" has rejected the imperialist-capitalist dependency system, which has continually stymied Peruvian independence and industrial development and fostered acute social inequities. Point for point extensive reform laws have undermined the old system to bring the ultimate goals of a fully "participatory social democracy," and "moral order of solidarity," and a mixed, worker-managing economy closer to realization.

Reform began with the expropriation of the International Petroleum Corporation (owned by Standard Oil) in October, 1968, and the creation of Petroperu and Mineroperu. The June, 1969, Agrarian Reform Law guarantees a legal minimum holding for any Peruvian who works his land. It has since been instrumental in the extensive redistribution and cooperativization of coastal and *sierra* lands. The Mining Reform Law of April, 1970, places strict concessionary controls on foreign exploiters. The July Industrial Reform Law creates industrial communities with the ultimate goal of worker ownership and management, and compels foreign-owned companies to develop Peruvian majority ownership. The Fisheries Reform Law of March, 1971, "Peruanizes" holdings of this industry as well and firmly establishes government control over this vital resource. The March, 1973, Education Reform Law makes rural instruction in Indian languages and the teaching of history from an indigenist perspective compulsory; universities have been depoliticized. In finance, the government now directly controls the Central Bank and other key banking and credit sources,[24] and is implementing

---

[22]Jaquette, *op. cit.*, pp. 148–150, provides the foregoing economic data and interpretations.

[23]Jaquette, *op. cit.*, discusses details of the scandal, pp. 191–197.

[24]Alisky, *op. cit.*, presents these reform laws, pp. 23–27. See also *Area Handbook for Peru* (Washington, D.C.: U.S. Government Printing Office, 1972), which cites the expropriation of 8.15 million acres and the distribution of 3.2 million acres in mid-1971, p. 206.

progressive tax reform and thorough collection procedures. The government's struggle to control the communications media led to expropriations in 1970 of *Expreso, Extra,* and *La Crónica.* The broadcasting industry came under government control in 1971.[25] Junta disputes with the national press have been resolved by the expropriation of all newspapers with national circulation and their reorganization, under the Press Law of July, 1974, as mouthpieces of major functional social sectors.[26] To a great extent relative political and social peace in Peru has been a function of partial or asymetrical social mobilization.

Two Peruvian social philosophers, Gonzales Prada and José Carlos Mariátegui, have criticized the division of the nation into two distinct Perus—the *sierra* and the coast, the indigenous and the hispanic. Failure to integrate the country has been the most important impediment to national development and unity. Geography, in the form of the Andean Mountain chain, and poor communications have helped permit two subnations to develop, and racial and cultural cleavages have reinforced the geographic divisions. Nearly all of the Indian sector, from thirty-two to forty percent of the Peruvian population, is found in the *sierra* whereas roughly thirteen percent of the white population and possibly half of the fifty-four percent mestizo population live on the coast.[27]

Two parallel but distinct levels of social mobilization, then, have coexisted in Peru with minimal interdependence and have perpetuated extreme regional inequalities in the distribution of national economic benefits. For example, according to one writer, the coast has only thirty-three percent of the population but eighty percent of national industry and nearly three times the per capita income of the *sierra,* home for fifty-three percent of the population.[28] On the coast *barriada* dwellers and unionized agricultural workers boast an 80 percent literacy rate and turnover in electoral participation, whereas nearly the same percentage is illiterate and politically marginalized in the *sierra.*[29] The early agita-

[25]Alisky, *op. cit.,* pp. 28–30.
[26]"Gobierno militar del Peru exproprió 8 diarios limeños," *Presencia,* La Paz, Bolivia, July 28, 1974, p. 1.
[27]*Area Handbook for Peru,* p. vii.
[28]Marett, *op. cit.,* p. 199.
[29]Jaquette suggests 80 percent literacy for *barriada* dwellers, p. 98; otherwise our figures are based on our interpretation of percentages on urbanization of voting patterns presented in Rosendo A. Gomez, "Peru: The Politics of Military Guardianship," in *Political Systems of Latin America,* 2d ed., ed. Martin C. Needler (New York: Van Nostrand, 1970), p. 336. Because the right of franchise necessitates functional literacy, a voting pattern of thirty-five percent of registered voters in the Greater Lima area and twenty-five percent in the major coastal cities including Arequipa and Cuzco could

tion of agricultural and industrial labor on the coast ultimately paid off in welfare benefits and an improved standard of living. By the 1960s both the Communist General Confederation of Peruvian Workers (*Confederación General de Trabajadores Peruanos*—CGTP) and the APRA-affiliated Confederation of Peruvian Workers (*Confederación de Trabajadores Peruanos*—CTP), founded in 1944, functioned as successful labor pressure groups. Although peasant uprisings in the *sierra* have occurred with cyclical regularity and have been brutally repressed by local government and the military, the real land reform awakening and growth of syndical organizations began in the 1950s and reached a peak in the mid-1960s, coinciding with a deterioration in the coast-*sierra* dichotomy.

Geography, marginalization, and low social mobilization of highland Peru, therefore, have been significant reasons why the kind of social revolution that occurred in Mexico and Bolivia did not develop in Peru. In the early 1930s when APRA had a strong revolutionary following and the economic depression had created widespread urban misery, labor unrest, middle-class dissatisfactions, and civilian-military tensions, a coastal revolution was a viable possiblity. But because the *sierra* remained virtually unaffected and nationally isolated, a broad-based national movement was impossible. Levels of social mobilization on the coast were high (though not in the *sierra*). Most probably they were never as intense as in neighboring Bolivia, where the devastating Chaco War forced makeshift integration of two disparate national groups—the Indian and the white-mestizo upper and middle classes—and where geographic proximity ensured constant cultural confrontation and psychological recrimination.[30] Moreover, as coastal labor achieved more and more of its demands and improved its standard of living, it became de-radicalized—as did the APRA, its political spokesman. Middle sectors also attained sufficient economic mobility to undercut dissatisfactions. These reasons also explain why indicators of societal welfare and economic growth for the two decades, compared with social mobilization, are significantly better for Peru than for Bolivia (Figures 4 and 5; Table 14). Deterioration in social cohesion for Peru in the 1960s is also evident, nonetheless. Social mobilization in the

support our overall figures and interpretation. Also see David Scott Palmer, *"Revolution from Above": Military Government and Popular Participation in Peru, 1968–1972*, Latin American Studies Program, Dissertation Series (Ithaca, N.Y.: Cornell University, 1973), on literacy rates and general political mobilization of workers on selected coastal sugar plantations.

[30]See Marett, *op. cit.*, pp. 257–263, who makes similar observations on this point. He argues that the greatest peril for the oligarchy in Peru has been a coalition of poverty-line Indians, the urban proletariat, and radical middle-class sectors; such a combination of political forces almost became a reality between 1930 and 1933.

highland is increasing and continued marginalization of half of the nation is no longer politically acceptable nor institutionally possible.

Institutionalization indexes reflect improvement in party institutionalization from the 1950s to 1960s and a slight decrease in church and military institutionalization. On the whole, institutionalization has remained fairly stable. The relatively high level of military institutionalization in Peru—with the exception of counterinsurgency violence in 1965—has been the basis for low social violence and repression since the 1950s.

Military institutionalization in Peru, in view of the 1968 coup, necessitates singular analysis. A history of military guardianship of the status quo in Peru has provided the military's political role with a certain legitimacy, which has been unquestionably reinforced by the reformist outlook of the new military junta. Studies on the social-development orientation of the military attribute the change to progressive training in the Center of Advanced Military Studies (*Centro de Altos Estudios Militares*—CAEM), which has programmatically instilled a social consciousness about national problems. These studies also maintain that counterinsurgency duty in the highlands further sensitized troops and officers to the marginalization and poverty of the Indian. Another explanation suggests that the increasingly common lower- and middle-class social background of military officers has motivated a restructuring of the military in favor of Peru's dispossessed majority. The former junta president, Velasco Alvarado, exemplified the nonaristocratic military officer. Finally, CAEM training has strengthened military unity and discipline. Old-style militarism and personalistic leadership has been replaced by the institutionalized and technically prepared military of the present.

Church institutionalization may increase as a result of the new military orientation. Since the 1960s the church, a historically important social and conservative force, has spoken out for social justice. Currently the Catholic Church is one of the primary institutional supporters of military-initiated reforms. Thus changes within the military, which have brought reforms and new economic and social structures of participation, may contribute to greater national institutionalization and social cohesion, despite the danger of selective military repression in the immediate future.[31]

[31]An example of such selective repression, which may lead to violence, has been the Guardia Civil strike in February, 1975, for higher wages, in which armed forces and police clashed causing some thirty deaths. Similarly, severe labor strikes in mining centers of the Cerro de Pasco Corporation and other companies in 1970 and 1971 were repressed by the military. See, "Police Strike Sparks Peru Emergency," *Washington Post*, Feb. 6, 1975, p. A–12; and *Area Handbook for Peru*, p. 311, respectively.

High educational expenditures correlate with the absence of violence and repression. In Peru the educational effort and educational expenditures have increased dramatically within the two decades. Education as a percentage of the budget grew from thirteen percent in 1940 to 33.4 percent in the Belaúnde administration; between 1958 and 1968 students in public schools increased 113.7 percent.[32] (See also Table 24.) The Velasco administration attempted to equalize and energize national education, which may serve to improve social cohesion in Peru in the long run.

Reforms of the military government have progressed rapidly toward eradicating significant inequities in the Peruvian system, such as extreme land and financial inequality. Of usable lands, one-tenth of 1 percent of the landowners hold 60.9 percent.[33] An extremely unequal distribution and concentration of wealth has allowed an interlocking oligarchy to control banking, credit, and export-import interests. Only ten percent of the economically active population receives sixty percent of the disposable income, while the so-called forty families—approximately one-quarter of one percent of the economically active Peruvians—appropriate thirty-five percent of the national profits.[34] The existing government strongly condemns this unequal distribution and seeks to establish "a new order free and just for the men and women of this land; that is a society without economic exploitation, without political exploitation, without cultural alienation, and without foreign domination."[35]

[32]Jaquette, *op. cit.*, pp. 108–109.

[33]Trias, *op. cit.*, p. 44. Marett provides these figures of unequal land distribution: on the coast ten percent of the landowners hold eighty-nine percent of the land, and in the *sierra* and *selva* three percent of the landowners possess eighty-three percent and ninety-three percent of the land respectively. Marrett, *op. cit.*, p. 228.

[34]Jaquette, *op. cit.*, p. 56; she also gives the following statistics from Banco Popular del Peru, *Peru in Brief*, second quarter, 1965:

| | Distribution of Income | |
Group	Income Shares %	Economically Active Population %
Large landowner and investors	19.9	.1
Professionals, executives, and small private investors	6.3	.4
White-collar and skilled workers	46.7	20.0
Unionized urban and coastal rural workers	14.2	22.8
Nonunionized *sierra* and *selva* peasants	12.9	56.7

[35]Cited from Velasco speech by McNicoll, *op. cit.*, p. 9.

Because of a developmentalist priority, Peru's military "revolution from above" has been necessarily a centralized and controlled process, one that contains social mobilization while promising economic mobilization as a substitute.[36] Ostensibly missing in the reforms of the armed forces have been traditional measures to increase political participation, such as expansion of the franchise. In the past Peru has been a pseudo-democracy, a "formal democracy," as President Velasco expressed it, in which the partisan "interplay of political interests" overrode pressing national problems.[37] Few Peruvians were qualified to vote: out of a population of twelve million in 1963, there were only two million voters.[38] While military reformers have admitted the need for political participation, they have adamantly rejected the political party system. Instead the junta in June, 1971, established the National System for Support of Social Mobilization to develop, channel, and control popular participation. The question is, however, whether social mobilization can be contained by new and experimental institutional structures because radical reform measures will most surely intensify economic and political demands. Or will contradictions inherent in Peru's "third solution" impede realization of the avowed military goal—a "peaceful" process of revolutionary development?

Honduras

Honduras is *the* banana republic; and the stereotype, which has been so misapplied to other nations of Latin America, does fit this country moderately well. Government is weak with poorly developed public programs; succession processes are not well established; and competition for power is something of a free-for-all. The U.S.-owned banana companies dominate the coastal regions, operate many "public" services, and manipulate national political forces. Honduras, even so, has experienced a below-average amount of repression and only an average amount of violence. The violence, which is sporadic, comes primarily from individuals staging revolts in the hope of obtaining political power.

One of the characteristics that most distinguishes Honduras from its neighbors is the looseness with which its dictators have controlled

[36]Palmer, *op. cit.*, p. 180, mentions the concept of "political demobilization" versus economic mobilization.

[37]Palmer, *op. cit.*, p. 53 quoting from *Velasco: La Voz de la Revolucion: Discursos, 1968–1970* (Lima: Ediciones Peisa, 1970), pp. 114–115.

[38]Marett, *op. cit.*, p. 251.

the country during most of the last forty years. Tiburcio Carías Andino was the mildest of the dictators that took control during the depression years in Latin America. Actually, he was elected to the presidency in 1932 and took over complete power later; in 1948 he turned over power voluntarily to his chosen successor, Juan Manuel Galvez. Galvez respected the constitution and prepared for a free election in 1954. With the failure of any candidate to obtain an absolute majority in that election, three years of political maneuvering followed until the Liberal Party candidate, Ramón Villeda Morales, was elected president by the constitutional assembly. Air Force Colonel Osvaldo Lopez Arellano staged a coup shortly before the next scheduled elections in 1963 and consolidated his power through extensive repression. Once his control was assured, however, he moderated his rule.

Politics is the activity of a limited number of political and military elite of Honduras, though it is an elite that is not divided from the rest of the population along any strong racial or class lines. As the U.S. fruit companies operate the only really productive enterprises in the country, even the wealthiest Hondurans have only moderate means. Most of the population works small subsistence plots. The banana plantations suffered from labor unrest in the early 1950s, but the fruit companies, with the cooperation of the American Institute for Free Labor Development, have brought the labor movement under control. The electorate is divided into two fairly well-established political parties, but political competition lacks the intensity of feeling and the "inherited hatreds" that have led other countries into internal war.

The relative absence of political conflict seems to reflect fewer unsatisfied demands than average in Latin America, a circumstance caused by social welfare being relatively higher than mobilization. Nevertheless, the brief war with El Salvador in 1969 may have reflected a repressed national frustration. Whether the new reformist activity of Lopez Arellano had come in time remains to be seen.

In summary, the more cohesive countries of Latin America have, for varying reasons related primarily either to their economic performance or their political and social institutionalization, maintained low levels of both violence and repression throughout the two decades of our study. They have continued into the 1970s with minimal repression and violence, whereas other Latin American nations, once peaceful and nonrepressive, have become less cohesive.

7

COUNTRIES
DECLINING IN COHESION

Three Latin American nations had relatively low amounts of violence and repression through the 1950s and well into the 1960s. And then suddenly violence and repression came more and more to be a common experience. In a sense, these three countries—Brazil, Chile, and Uruguay—represent our "dynamic" cases because their societal situation changed markedly during the twenty years of our study. Brazil, which had been relatively peaceful and democratic during the 1950s, suffered a military coup in 1964 and was governed by a repressive military regime for the remainder of the decade. Uruguay, one of the freest and least violent countries in the world during the 1950s, began to experience great amounts of violence in 1967 and fell under the increasing control of the military in the 1970s. Finally, Chile, a country with a long tradition of civilian government and noninterference in politics by the military, went through a polarizing period of political confrontation in the early 1970s— one that culminated in a military coup in 1973 and the assassination of President Salvador Allende.

Some of the most important changes in these three countries can be seen in Table 29, which shows the rise in violence and repression during the latter years of the 1960s. (Most of the increase in repression in Chile and Uruguay, however, came in the early years of the 1970s). Table 28 presents the explanation for this disintegration in the form of our variables associated with repression and violence.

Brazil

This giant among Latin American nations—with a population of more than 100 million and a land area of 3.3 million square miles—has recently undergone two important changes—one political and one economic. Since 1964 the military has controlled Brazilian politics with an iron hand. Its dictatorship has become one of the most controversial and highly visible in Latin American history, with both opponents and defenders chronicling its deeds and misdeeds. At the same time, or more accurately since 1968, the Brazilian economy has entered upon a period of accelerated growth that has continued to the present. Brazil now has one of the fastest growing gross national products in the world—if not the fastest—and there are indications that the nation may

Table 28. Countries Declining in Cohesion

| | Independent Variables[a] | | | | | |
| | 1950s | | | 1960s | | |
Variable	Brazil	Chile	Uruguay	Brazil	Chile	Uruguay
Welfare minus mobilization	−.22	.66	−.81	−.08	.05	−.39
Economic growth minus social mobilization	.46	−1.36	−.35	.33	−.89	−.92
Educational effort	−1.20	.47	−.27	−.84	.49	−.39
Educational expenditure	.09	.23	1.85	−.31	1.10	−.17
Party institutionalization	−.09	.72	1.83	−.80	1.33	1.58
Military institutionalization	1.14	.73	1.34	.53	1.40	1.40
Church institutionalization	−.58	.74	.34	−.65	.66	.26
Total institutionalization	.20	.93	1.48	−.37	1.38	1.32
White + mestizo as a percent of population	−.04	1.13	1.39	−.06	1.08	1.33

[a]All scores are standard.

be entering an extended period of rapid increase in the national product. Again, there are both critics and defenders of this pheomenon, most of whom are concerned not about the growth rate but about the method through which it was achieved, and its implications for the Brazilian people. That military control and economic growth have been accompanied by extremely high levels of repression and moderate amounts of violence (at least by previous Brazilian standards) adds to the controversy surrounding events in Brazil since 1964.

The actual levels of violence and repression in Brazil for the 1950s and the 1960s, and those we predicted, are shown in Table 29. The table demonstrates the decided increase in repression between the two decades, as well as our major error in prediction, which was the level of repression during the 1950s. The political history of that decade, along with previous Brazilian experience, offers a substantial explanation of this differential.

The general history of Brazil, from its discovery to the present day, differs from the histories of other Latin American nations in several material aspects. First, Brazilian history has, in general, been less violent than that of most of its Spanish-American neighbors. The word "discovery" was used instead of "conquest" to describe the European colonization of that portion of the New World as there were no horrendous battles with the Indians as there were in other parts of the New World.

Independence came to Brazil without bloodshed, again in contrast with the situation in the Spanish colonies, and Brazil's entire nineteenth-century history was much more serene than that of its neigh-

Table 29. Countries Declining in Cohesion

| Country | Variable | Dependent Variables[a] | | | |
| | | 1950s | | 1960s | |
		Actual	Predicted	Actual	Predicted
Brazil	Violence	−.36	−.32	−.36	−.15
	Repression	−.77	−.15	.54	.38
	Viol. & Rep.	−.75	−.88	.12	−.28
Chile	Violence	−.26	.24	−.80	−.42
	Repression	−.72	−.67	−1.14	-1.40
	Viol. & Rep.	−.65	−.27	−1.27	−1.10
Uruguay	Violence	−1.60	−.23	−.21	−.10
	Repression	−1.58	−1.34	−.93	−.56
	Viol. & Rep.	−2.11	−.92	−.74	−.39

[a]All scores are standard.

bors, Brazil, which had an emperor for most of the century, was spared the ills of *caudillismo* and conflicting personalities that affected most of the rest of the continent.

Although possessed of great powers under the constitution, Dom Pedro II used the powers with restraint and attempted to rule through elected governments during most of his forty-nine year tenure. When in 1891, the handwriting was on the wall and the pressures for republican government had become too great, Dom Pedro contributed further to the Brazilian tradition of nonviolent political life by refusing to contest with those forces, especially the military, who wished to establish a republic.

The military as an institution, and as the leader of the coup against Dom Pedro, inherited some of his powers, which it has maintained until the present day and which helps to explain its role in Brazilian politics. The emperor's prime political weapon had been the *poder moderado*, or moderating power, which allowed him to annul acts of the legislature which he deemed to be against the best interests of the state. In a sense, the emperor was thought of as the guardian of the constitution, or as the moral conscience of the nation. The military, upon assuming political power in 1891, immediately assumed this power for itself and has maintained this power of guardianship over the Brazilian polity to the present. Under the military's interpretation of the power, it has the right and the duty to intervene whenever, in its opinion, the Brazilian polity is being mishandled by civilians. Prior to 1964, this modus operandi had always meant that the military would intervene to throw out the rascals whenever a civilian regime was guilty of abuses, and would then retire from the political arena as soon as a new civilian government more to its liking was installed.

The so-called republican era which lasted from the end of the military government in 1895 to the beginning of the Vargas era in 1930, was also a time of relative political calm. The unwritten agreement among the political elites of the states of São Paulo, Minas Gerais, and Rio Grande do Sul regarding alternation of the presidency resolved most crises before they began and provided a process for assuring some continuity in the national government. The only serious threat to the system was the *tenente* movement among some younger military officers, which began with a revolt in 1922. The *tenentes*—lieutenants— committed to a rather amorphous program of social change for the nation, found themselves isolated and leaderless after 1930, however, and the movement never attained political power in Brazil. The Revolution of 1930, although not very violent, may well be regarded as a major turning point in Brazilian political life. It came about primarily because the elites of the three states could not agree on a candidate for the presidency, so Getulio Vargas, the governor of Rio Grande do Sul, and several senior military officers seized the opportunity to establish what later became known as *O Estado Novo* (the New State). *O Estado Novo* amounted to a fifteen-year dictatorship by Vargas, with the acquiescence of the military.

During the Vargas era, many Brazilians began to believe that they had something to say about Brazilian politics, even if, in fact, they did not. The increase in urbanization, the birth of national labor unions under Vargas, plus the mobilization style of the Vargas government, all contributed to a greater awareness of and interest in politics by Brazilians, particularly those living in what has been termed "modern Brazil"—below the 30th parallel. Politics in northern Brazil continued to be largely dominated by the great land-owning families, as it still is to a great extent today.

A main effect of the Vargas years was to create a much greater sense of nationalism and personal identification with the nation than had previously existed in Brazil. Before Vargas, politics, especially in the more powerful states (and in the north) was conducted largely along state lines, and interference by the national government was minimal and quite sporadic. Vargas changed this conception of politics in favor of a drastically centralized government. In 1932 there was a direct challenge to this new type of Brazilian politics: the São Paulo revolt. It did not succeed, however.

Another feature of Vargas's rule was that repression of possible, rather than actual, sources of political opposition began to be accepted as a method of governmental operation. This policy was instituted after 1935, when an abortive Communist revolt in November played into Vargas's hands. Not only the Communists, but all movements on the left were quickly eliminated, and thousands of political suspects were imprisoned. Government was continually conducted under a state of siege decree granted by Congress until November, 1937. When Congress was closed a new corporativist constitution was promulgated, and Vargas became Brazil's first full-fledged dictator.

By 1938 every political group in Brazil had been outmaneuvered and decimated by Vargas, and his *Estado Novo*, while paying lip service to the more highly organized European Fascist regimes was, in fact, a highly personalist dictatorship. Although Vargas began in 1943 to lay the groundwork for a political movement which would guarantee him popular support in the postwar era, the two years remaining to him of his dictatorship were not enough to allow his plans to materialize. This was, however, the period of greatest labor union growth in Brazilian history, for Vargas had planned to make that sector his new base of support.

Vargas was finally deposed in October, 1945, after he had successively promised free elections for president and had then attempted to either sabotage them or to impose his own candidate through pre-electoral maneuvering. Once again, however, it was the army that deposed a president who was slow to move out when the time came (although when faced with the inevitable, Vargas, in true Brazilian fashion, departed peacefully). Vargas was removed from office not by civilian opposition, but by decision of the army high command. Once again, the military had asserted its powers as guardians of the constitution, just as it had on earlier occasions—in 1889, during the 1920s, in 1930, 1932, and in 1937. And once again the army's role had been accepted by the civilian opposition to the man in power.

In spite of the continuing repression of the left by Vargas's successor, Eurico Dutra, who remained in office for four years, the elections of October, 1950, were held in an atmosphere of relative calm and freedom. Much of the repression and violence were related directly to the elections, with a round-up of Communists just prior to the balloting and considerable violence immediately before and on election day. The election itself became primarily a contest among three candidates—one of them Getulio Vargas. Vargas had forged a political party for himself, really the only national political party in the country, the Brazilian Labor Party (*Partido Trabalhista Brasileira*—PTB), and had produced a neo-populist ideology calculated to appeal to the growing urban masses, including both the working class and the lower middle class. And he won with almost an absolute majority. On January 31, 1951, Vargas was inaugurated as the legally elected president of Brazil. He remained in office for almost four years, until his suicide on the morning of August 24, 1954. During his term repression was at a minimum, again with the exception of the Communists, and violence was limited almost entirely to states in the hinterland north. In 1952 there was no reported violence during the entire year. Vargas was rather successful in his appeals to Brazilian nationalism, which increased with each passing year, and in guiding the Brazilian economy, which, spurred on by higher coffee prices and still buoyed by the tremendous foreign credits earned during World War II, performed quite well.

As the Vargas administration advanced, however, the president's enemies, led by the newspaper publisher, Carlos Lacerda, became more articulate and better organized. Day by day Lacerda's papers blasted away at Vargas, while Vargas seemed older and more unsure of himself politically than ever before. Gradually, a group of the president's advisers became convinced that if Lacerda could be silenced the attacks on Vargas would cease. Accordingly, an assassination attempt was made against Lacerda, which failed miserably. The links to the administration were quickly exposed, and the army, which had been neutral for some time, stepped in to ask for Vargas's resignation. Faced with the threat of being ousted for the second time, Vargas committed suicide, leaving behind a note blaming his enemies, both domestic and foreign, for his death. Much has been made of the extent and depth of popular agitation at the news of Vargas's death, but actual violence was minimal. A mass demonstration erupted in Rio the day after his death, but aside from this one relatively peaceful manifestation of grief, there appeared to be little popular disposition to take to the streets to avenge the fallen president.

The period between 1954 and 1956 has been characterized as that of "caretaker" governments. With the military stepping in to supervise the governmental operation, repression increased rather substantially. The press was subjected to considerable censorship, and organized labor, which had been Vargas's fastest growing source of support, was subjected to severe new restrictions.[1] After several military coups in 1955 Juscelino Kubitschek was elected president the following year.

Under Kubitschek the Brazilian economy boomed, and from 1956 to 1961 violence and repression dropped to new lows. The economy was undoubtedly spurred by favorable economic circumstances, such as a relatively large domestic market, a sound climate for foreign investment, and the continued high price of coffee (at least until 1958). But the boom was also due to the dynamic nature of the Kubitschek government. Brazilians would have to pay for some of that dynamism with withering inflation in the early 1960s, but in the interim the rapid expansion of the economy, the charismatic nature of the president, and, above all, the building of the new capital of Brasilia in the interior, all contributed to the relative lack of violence and repression. Although the Kubitschek administration openly appealed to the private sector for additional investment, and especially to foreign private investors, the plan was presented to the Brazilians as a nationalist road to development. Kubitschek possessed a remarkable ability to please everyone, "to find something for everyone."[2] Kubitschek courted the military throughout his presidency, with a 1956 purchase of an aircraft carrier being the biggest payoff. Brazil's beleaguered Communists were about the only organized political group in the country that Kubitschek chose

[1] See John W. F. Dulles, *Unrest in Brazil: Political-Military Crises, 1955–1964* (Austin: University of Texas Press, 1970) for an excellent, if somewhat too exhaustive, account of the various intrigues between military and civilians and among the civilian contenders for power.

[2] Thomas E. Skidmore, *Politics in Brazil: 1930–1964* (New York: Oxford University Press, 1967).

to repress rather than charm. Several Communist-dominated labor unions were closed, but this act was perhaps balanced (ideologically at least) by the silencing of the right-wing newspaper controlled by Carlos Lacerda, who was then in exile.

Throughout his tenure, Kubitschek chose not to rely on the support of any one political party, and Vice President João Goulart was in too difficult a position with the military and the anti-Getulistas to risk an open alliance with the PTB. Accordingly, the degree of institutionalization of Brazil's political parties slipped badly during the late 1950s, with the result that Brazilian politics—now conducted on a national scale rather than on a state-by-state basis—continued into the 1960s with an even greater absence of institutionalized parties than before. Kubitschek's administration had been one largely of brilliant improvisation, probably unequaled in the annals of Brazilian democratic politics. Unfortunately, the extremely personal style of the president left Brazil's political institutions weaker than before, and at the same time there was no one on the Brazilian political scene capable of following the Kubitschek tour de force. Any euphoria concerning the bright future of democratic government in Brazil in 1960 was most certainly ill-founded. Moreover, the price of coffee had started to fall in 1958 as new low-cost African producers began entering the world markets. In the same year, inflation, which had been at relatively low levels in 1956 and 1957, once again surged ahead. In spite of the government's efforts, the rate of inflation increased rather rapidly during the last three years of the Kubitschek government, thus cutting heavily into Brazil's economic growth rate during these years.

In spite of these disquieting signs, optimism over the future of democratic government and the economy of Brazil had set in by 1960, and the presidential elections of that year were conducted in this atmosphere. The winner in those elections was Jânio Quadros, an unorthodox politician not identified with either the pro-Vargas or the anti-Vargas camps. Although Quadros was officially the candidate of the anti-Vargas Democratic National Union (*Union Democratica Nacional*—UDN) his relatively independent candidacy did nothing to further its fortunes. On the other side, Marshal Henrique Texeira Lott, the author of the 1955 coup that assured Kubitschek's inauguration, was finally chosen as the candidate of the PTB and the Brazilian Socialist Party (*Partido Socialista Brasileiro*—PSB). The election demonstrated once again the weakness of all three national political parties, and the continued dependence of the Brazilian political system on the charisma of a new leader every six years. Quadros won an overwhelming victory, winning forty-eight percent of the vote to Lott's twenty-three percent. The new vice president was again Goulart, the candidate of the PTB and PSB, who had won over the UDN candidate, Milton Campos.

It was at this point that both Brazilian politics and Brazilian economics began to come unhinged. Up to the early 1960s, the Brazilian political system had gone along in what seemed to be high gear, but in reality the charismatic qualities of two men—Getulio Vargas and Juscelino Kubitschek—had carried it through the period of the second republic. Neither of these leaders had seen the need to build ongoing political institutions (although Vargas had made some efforts in that direction) and the earlier development of the PTB as an institutionalized political party was cut short during the Kubitschek years. The loss of the 1960 election to the essentially independent Quadros was perhaps the final blow to the Brazilian Labor Party. On the other side of the political fence, the UDN, which represented the old anti-Getulista elite, probably was doomed from the end of World War II. The neo-populist appeals of Vargas, Kubitschek, and even its own candidate, Quadros, eroded any strength it might have had among the rapidly expanding urban middle class and proletariat. In addition to the charisma factor, the relatively calm nature of Brazilian politics through the 1950s had also been greatly aided by the outstanding performance of the Brazilian economy. The dynamic growth of the national product from 1950 to 1960 made it possible for at least some of the populist slogans to be realized. There really was more of everything for everybody, although it is doubtful that either Vargas or Kubitschek had much to do with this condition. Rather, it was the extremely high world price for coffee that produced the booming fifties. When the drop in prices came, it came suddenly. Coffee prices, which had reached a high of ninety cents a pound for Santos "B" in New York in 1956 and 1957, had dropped to forty cents a pound by 1962. The implications of this decline for the Brazilian economy were simply staggering. With almost all candidates committed to a program of more for everyone, however, and with an almost complete absence of institutions (other than the military) to help bring about the austerity called for by the situation, inflation began to spiral out of sight as the politicians continued to provide more goods and services despite a declining economy.

Quadros's term in office was illustrative of the problems Brazil faced. The declining economic situation began to precipitate strikes by transportation workers, police, and firemen. In certain towns martial law was declared to deal with riots by squatters who had taken over unused plots of land. Students at several Brazilian Universities rioted over such disparate grievances as rising prices and continued government interference with higher education. Faced with this deteriorating situation, frustrated by his inability to govern on a national scale as decisively as he had governed his home state of São Paulo, and plagued by personality problems, Quadros resigned the presidency in August, 1961. Surprisingly, in the light of his overwhelming electoral victory only ten months earlier, Quadros's resignation was immediately accepted by Congress, and there were no popular manifestations in favor of his return. The major question at that moment was whether Goulart, the vice president and constitutional successor, would be allowed to assume the presidency. Once again, the military provided the answer with the *legalista* arm of the army finally prevailing over those who were personally and ideologically opposed to Goulart and who believed that more Vargas-style populism should be stopped. Goulart assumed the presidency "on probation" under a parliamentary arrangement that severely limited presidential powers. It was an arrangement that lasted until January, 1963, when Brazilians voted five to one in a national plebiscite to return to the former presidential form of government.

Although Goulart was successful in regaining full presidential powers, he was confronted with an increasingly polarized and serious political and economic situation. Possibly because of his fear of army intervention, Goulart did not move quickly to implement programs that would have placated the left in Brazilian politics. Yet at the same time, the politics of compromise was becoming more and more difficult. On the right, the anti-Getulistas were implacably opposed to him, and such organizations as the Civil-Military Patriotic Front (*Frente Patriótica Civil-Militar*—FPCM) were energetically mobilizing popular support for their cause. Goulart's failure to move faster in the direction of nationalization brought about increasing dissatisfaction among many Brazilians and a gain for the left (who advanced nationalization) at the expense of the democratic center.

The first major outbreak against the Goulart government came from a rather unlikely source. On September 12, 1963, several hundred noncommissioned officers and enlisted men of the marines, air force, and navy staged a revolt in Brasilia. Quickly subdued, the uprising nonetheless made it obvious that the government was extremely weak and open to take-over from either left or right. This particular revolt was more or less leftist in nature—its organizers had been in contact with leftist leaders of the General Labor Confederation (*Confederacion General do Trabalho*—CGT) labor union before they acted—and this fact increased fears among the conservative army officers that Goulart might someday use this leftist feeling among the rank and file to his own advantage. In the face of mounting violence, Goulart first asked for and then withdrew a request for a thirty-day state of siege. By the end of 1963, Goulart's days were definitely numbered as inflation continued to soar (the cost of living in Guanabara State (Rio de Janeiro) had risen 81 per cent in 1963) and mobilization on both left and right continued.

Events in March, 1964, in which Goulart broke openly with the center and embraced the left and also intruded upon the military discipline of the services, convinced the *legalistas* within the military that they had to move. Chief among these was Army Chief of Staff Humberto Castelo Branco, who made known his changed views toward the Goulart administration in a memorandum on March 20. The United States government was also stating its opposition to the Goulart regime.

The revolt against Goulart, when it came, was quintessentially Brazilian, even if the results have thus far been decidedly un-Brazilian. It began among troops stationed in Minas Gerais, who then moved in the direction of Rio. Within two days, the troops in São Paulo had joined the revolutionaries, and the First Army, in Rio, reached an agreement with the revolutionaries that precluded an armed clash. By April 2, only six days after the uprising had started, the Third Army in Rio Grande do Sul had joined the revolutionaries as well. Fighting among the army units was minimal, but the situation both during and after the coup was tumultuous enough to produce Brazil's highest total of violence during the entire twenty-year period. Most of the violence occurred later in the year as opposition to the new military regime crystallized, largely around the realization that the military was going to deal with political dissidence harshly and that the generals meant to retain power for some time. Indeed, one of them—Castelo Branco himself—now headed the government. Most of the opposition came from the State of Goiaz where, in mid-November, Governor Mauro Borges defied Castelo Branco's regime. The opposition was quickly crushed by the military, and the dissident governor was as quickly evicted from office, on the grounds that he had connections with Communists.

Meanwhile, the new government had not been idle. On April 5, only three days after the military take-over, it moved against alleged Communists and their alleged sympathizers. By the middle of April more than seven thousand people had been arrested, and more than fifteen tons of "Communist" propaganda had been seized. On April 11 the first Institutional Act was promulgated. It was designed to permit the military to circumvent the provisions of the Brazilian constitution of 1946 while simultaneously legitimizing the new government by retaining the constitution. Briefly, the act declared democratic civilian government dead in Brazil for the time being, stripped the Congress of most of its authority, and gave ample new powers to the president. Under these new powers the Supreme Command could suspend the political rights of citizens for a period of up to ten years.[3] Almost immediately, most of the leading political figures of the country had

---

[3] A good analysis of this act and others that followed is contained in Ronald Schneider, *The Political System of Brazil* (New York: Columbia University Press, 1971), pp. 125–127.

their political privileges revoked, and a few days later the expected purge of the armed forces came. By April 15, when Castelo Branco was inaugurated president of Brazil, most incipient opposition had already been crushed, with only two groups—the students and the Catholic Church—yet to be dealt with.

By the end of 1964 violence had diminished, as it became more and more apparent that the military was in firm control. Rumors of torture of political prisoners made the rounds as the Castelo regime transformed itself into a full-fledged dictatorship. The military maintained tight control over the political process while allowing a civilian "technocracy" to bring rationality and order to the Brazilian economy. Three more Institutional Acts were approved; these provided for indirect election of the president and dissolved political parties, established a system whereby military candidates for governors could not lose, and proposed a new constitution for Brazil. Meanwhile, a government party, the National Renovating Alliance (*Alianza Renovadora Nacional*— ARENA) had been established, and the technocrats had succeeded in stabilizing the Brazilian economy (and bringing about the death of populism in the process).

Opposition to the military was fragmented, with most Brazilians accepting the new government. Armed rebels made their appearance in Rio Grande do Sul in March, 1965, and students at the University of Brasilia went on strike over the firing of a sociology professor in October. Important opposition, however, did not coalesce until mid-1968, when a student-military confrontation escalated into a major threat to the regime. By 1968, however, Brazil was a far different country from what it had been four years earlier under Quadros. The economy was growing at the rate of about nine per cent a year, and much of the population was either unconcerned with politics or excused the military's attacks on civil liberties as necessary concomitants of economic progress. Accordingly, the repressive action taken by the military against the student demonstrators in June and July, 1968, succeeded in stamping out that center of opposition. The threat posed by the demonstrations led, however, to a crisis within the government of Arthur Costa e Silva (who had replaced Castelo Branco as president in 1967), resulting in the victory of the hard-liners within the military and the promulgation in December of Institutional Act 5, which granted the president outright dictatorial powers.[4] The immediate results of Act 5 were an increase in the number of deprivations of political privileges, the recess of several state legislatures, and a new wave of police-military inquiries. By the middle of 1969, Brazilians were experiencing

[4]Schneider, p. 274.

the most thoroughgoing dictatorship of their history, and only the Catholic Church remained as a potentially viable opposition to the government.

At present, Brazil is still firmly under the military dictatorship begun with the 1964 military take-over and consummated with Institutional Act 5 in 1968. All political institutions except the army have been decimated. Organized resistance to the current government is almost nonexistent, with the Catholic Church providing the only consistent, coherent opposition. The political parties, which had begun to function only haltingly in the 1950s have disappeared. The Brazilian economy, which was in shambles in 1964, has for the past five years produced a rate of growth unparalleled in Brazilian history and Brazil has one of the highest (if not the highest) rates of economic growth in the world. Critics of this growth state that the benefits are not being felt by the mass of the population, who are no better off than before, but the fact of rapid growth cannot be denied. Divisions within the military— between the "hard line" and "soft line" elements—seem to have disappeared, at least temporarily. At the moment, the country continues to be governed by a relatively faceless group of generals (the current president is Ernesto Geisel), who seem determined to retain power for some time to come.

The country's high rate of economic growth in both decades, coupled with a relatively moderate increase in social mobilization, was a key factor in diminishing the amount of violence that occurred. The relatively high level of military institutionalization during the 1950s (the level was substantially less for the 1960s) also made for less violence in Brazil during the period. The most positive sign in Brazilian society today is the strong growth rate and the relatively moderate level of social mobilization. If this condition continues, the military government should be able to retain power with a moderate amount of repression. If, however, the economy falters, the extreme lack of institutionalization of political parties and the Catholic Church in Brazil may lead to increased violence, increased repression, or both.

Uruguay

From 1950 to 1967, Uruguay was one of the freest nations in the world. During most of these seventeen years, political parties of all persuasions were allowed to operate freely and to run candiates for public office. Press and other media were similarly unrestricted in what they wished to print or speak. Groups representing all causes were permitted to organize, with the exception of some restrictions on labor organizations during the mid-1960s. Political arrests and exiles were few and far between, and Uruguay was not once placed under a state of siege.

In the same seventeen-year period, Uruguay was also one of the most peaceful countries in the world, second only to Costa Rica in all of Latin America. During the decade of the 1950s, Uruguay experienced no anti-government violence at all, and though some violence did occur during the first seven years of the 1960s, the preponderance of it was unarmed and was of the type one would expect to encounter in the longest-lived and supposedly one of the firmest democracies in Latin America. "Despite the stresses," one analyst wrote in 1969, "Uruguay remains a democratic republic."[5] A year later two others observed that "in the areas of freedom, civil liberties, and democratic government, Uruguay ranks near the top in the Western Hemisphere."[6] Yet 1969 was, in many ways, a turning point. In that year the Uruguayan government had instituted repressive measures that ranked it higher than eleven other Latin American nations, including Bolivia and Nicaragua. At the same time the country experienced more antigovernment violence than any other in Latin America except Argentina. It also had the most armed violence. Both the amount of repression and violence have continued to increase during the 1970s.

Why this swift turnabout in Uruguayan politics? There have been any number of explanations, but perhaps the most common is the failure of the Uruguayan economy to generate an acceptable rate of economic growth during the 1950s and 1960s. It is undoubtedly true that the disappointing performance of the Uruguayan economy during this period created considerable discontent among large sectors of the population. Yet it is also true that Uruguay not only had a relatively high per capita gross national product to begin with, but that this product was more equally distributed among the population than in other Latin American nations. Also, all of the other indicators of societal welfare in Uruguay were considerably higher than the gross national product per capita. Without much question, Uruguay's faltering economy contributed to the nation's current malaise, but this factor alone cannot explain the increasing use of violence on the part of both the government and its opponents in recent years.

A second explanation is that the two traditional Uruguayan political parties—the *blancos* and the *colorados*—have, through a series of personalist schisms within their ranks, become de-institutionalized.

[5]Marvin Alisky, *Uruguay: A Contemporary Survey* (New York, Frederick A. Praeger, 1969), p. 49.

[6]Ben Burnett and Kenneth Johnson, *Political Forces in Latin America* (Belmont Calif.: Wadsworth Publishing, 1970), p. 555.

They have, in other words, lost their ability to socialize Uruguayans into the political system and simultaneously operate that system satisfactorily. If this explanation is correct, it is correct only in a relative sense. When compared with political party systems throughout Latin America, the Uruguayan system has shown a steady decline in institutionalization since the early 1950s; but in an absolute sense the Uruguayan political parties have demonstrated no loss of institutionalization over the twenty-year period. To put it another way, other Latin American political parties have become more institutionalized over the period, thus reducing Uruguay's comparative position, but the Uruguayan parties themselves show virtually no change during the fifties and sixties. Although it is true that the two major parties are fractionated (largely because Uruguayan election laws encouraged this), the *blancos* and *colorados* nevertheless have had a long history of meeting challenges to their political ascendancy with unity and intelligence. The presidential elections of November, 1971, were only the most recent example in which the two parties combined at the last moment to beat back a challenge by another force in Uruguayan politics. This time it was a coalition of parties—the Christian Democrats, Communists, and Socialists—united in a new political front called *El Frente Amplio*. The result, however, was the same as it had been previously: the *colorados* won with voter assistance from the *blancos*. So the old-line parties were not dead in Uruguay, though the new so-called ideological parties were perhaps becoming more institutionalized.

Yet a third explanation for the rapid increase in violence and repression, and the subsequent decrease of democratic government, not only places most of the blame on the nation's sluggish economy but pinpoints it on the type of welfare state system that has evolved in Uruguay during the twentieth century. It is certainly true that Uruguayan society has, since the two presidential terms of José Batlle y Ordóñez (1903–1907 and 1911–1915) been the most advanced welfare state in Latin America and one of the most thoroughgoing in the world. In fact, Batlle changed not only the social outlook of the nation, but its politics and economics as well, and until his death in 1929, continued to exert considerable influence on whatever action was taken in Uruguayan politics. Even today, both major political parties still claim the mantle of Batlle (he was a *colorado* and brought about the electoral ascendancy of the *colorados* from 1903 to 1958), arguing that their programs are in the tradition of Batllismo. And indeed, until quite recently Uruguay was in a sense the lengthened shadow of one man: José Batlle y Ordóñez.

What did Batlle do? Perhaps his foremost contribution to Uruguayan national life was his insistence on opposition to dictatorship and authoritarianism. In the social and economic arena, Batlle was a convinced champion of state ownership, welfare programs, and of protectionism. During the second Batlle regime, banking was nationalized, as were the electric company (1912), the national telegraph company (1914), and street cars and railways (1915). Ultimately, various production industries were also partially nationalized, including chemicals, fisheries, and the meat-packing plants. A complete social security system and various other welfare benefits for workers in both the private and public sectors were adopted. Protectionism meant that wherever possible, foreign private enterprise was replaced with Uruguayan state-owned enterprise. These actions had the effect of saving Uruguay from many of the depredations of foreign private capital to which the rest of Latin America was subjected during the rest of the twentieth century. They also meant, however, that the Uruguayan government became one of the largest and slowest-moving bureaucracies in Latin America. By 1969, in a population of about 2.6 million people, there were 332,000 pensioners, 230,000 to 240,000 public employees, and approximately 180,000 persons seeking employment.[7] The economically active population of Uruguay is estimated at 1.2 million people, which means that one-fifth of the economically active population works for the government, that approximately fifteen percent of the work force is unemployed, and that there is one pensioner for every four people actively working. The figures seem unreal, yet they are probably close to being correct—and for that reason indicate some of the magnitude of the problem caused by the dislocation of the Uruguayan economy. In spite of the problems caused by the imposition of the Batlle program, however, its benefits are imposing, and it is difficult to imagine violence and repression emanating from it.

A fourth explanation for the violence and repression in Uruguay has not received much attention either in the press or in the scholarly publications on Uruguay. The only English-language expression of this analysis of the Uruguayan situation is contained in the translation of a book by Maria Esther Gilio, entitled *The Tupamaros.*[8] There are, though, several works in Spanish that advance the same argument, namely, that Uruguay has been an oppressive state for some time, and that the current antigovernment violence is only a natural reaction to what has become a reactionary society. This analysis, which is sometimes Marxist and sometimes quasi-Marxist, states that though much of the Batlle program was good, he did not go far enough in creating the conditions for an egalitarian society. There is some truth in this criti-

---

[7]*Vision*, May 9, 1969, p. 22.

[8]Maria Esther Gilio, *The Tupamaros* trans. by Anne Edmondson (London: Secker and Warburg, 1972). The *Tupamaros* are an urban guerrilla group operating in Uruguay.

cism, as Batlle never suggested that the *latifundia* in rural Uruguay be abolished, or even ameliorated, nor did he suggest any real effort to bring about any real equalization of income. Uruguay had no income tax until 1961. Even today, the tax is not particularly progressive and is administered poorly.

According to this fourth analysis of Uruguay's problems, the Batlle program worked only so long as rather massive immigration continued to supply the necessary manpower for local industry, and only so long as the world economy, on which Uruguay was dependent, functioned well. However, beginning with the 1929 crash and continuing through the Second World War, both the international situation and Uruguay's domestic situation changed radically. Internationally, markets for Uruguay's beef and wool were much less secure than before, while domestically, several things began to happen at once. First, the waves of immigration slackened and then ended, and the new industries could no longer expand on the backs of the cheap labor provided by the aliens. Second, more and more of the working class came to realize that the Batlle welfare state provided no more than a rather wretched security for the proletariat while bringing about few basic changes in the distribution of the national wealth. Finally, the basically oligarchical government, when faced with a worsening crisis in the late 1960s, exerted considerable repressive force on those who were protesting the fraud they believed had been perpetrated on the Uruguayan working class.

Obviously, it is difficult if not impossible to determine the exactitude of any of the four above explanations. Each begins from a different ideological stance, and together they are all quite contradictory. Our explanation, which has less of an ideological bias than any of the others, tends to show other causes for the sudden increase in Uruguayan violence and repression during the late 1960s and the first half of the 1970s.

Our first explanation is that the Uruguayan economy, for whatever reason, has functioned disastrously since the mid-1950s, causing political unrest. Another explanation is that although Uruguay has had a high level of societal welfare during both decades of our study, the level of social mobilization in the country has been even higher, producing a negative differential. A third explanation pertains to Uruguay's political party structure. It is perhaps sounder than many recent critics have alleged, but the parties have not increased in institutionalization as rapidly as have parties in other Latin American countries.

The military, which had been highly institutionalized in support of the civilian-controlled governments, has also been a source of increased violence and repression. For some time it has been asking for a freer hand in dealing with the various terrorist groups, particularly the *tupamaros*. The *tupamaros*, organized in the mid-1960s, achieved considerable success against the various governments of the late 1960s with their urban guerrilla tactics of kidnappings, raids against banks, casinos, and arsenals, and seizures of public records to expose fraud. After several moves by President Pacheco Areco in 1967 failed to produce the expected military successes against the *tupamaros*, the generals began demanding more and more power in the government through a puppet civilian regime. The final step toward a military controlled government came on February 12, 1973, with an army and air force communiqué setting forth their politico-social program for Uruguay which, among other things, envisioned an important role for the military in labor and student affairs, plus the resignation of several officials of the current government.

There are other reasons for the violence and military reaction in Uruguay. For example, in spite of the early start on free public education for all, Uruguay in 1965 ranked below eleven other Latin American countries in expenditures on education (as percent of gross national product). Ten years earlier Uruguay had spent more on education than any other Latin American nation.

Additionally, Catholicism does not seem to enter into the daily life of the people as it does in most other Latin American countries, even though the Catholic Church in Uruguay is fairly highly institutionalized. Uruguayans generally attend mass less and participate to a lesser degree in the various sacraments of the church than do other Latin Americans. Further, the secular school system deprives the church of one of its prime socializing functions. Many writers, mostly Protestant, have seen this absence of church influence on Uruguayan national life as beneficial to the political peace of the nation, emphasizing the lack of authoritarianism in Uruguayan society as a possible result of the diminished influence of the church. If, however, our thesis regarding the Catholic Church as a mediator of social conflict in Latin America is correct, the absence of a strong church in times of stress represents a void that cannot easily be filled by other institutions.

Finally, there is probably some truth in the leftist critique that the Uruguayan welfare state is a facade for the continued exploitation of the powerless. The various social welfare schemes allow people who "benefit" from them to live in what can only be described as abject poverty. "Welfare" in a country with a per capita GNP of slightly more than five hundred dollars simply cannot provide the standard of living envisioned by Batlle when he visited Switzerland. One author has referred to the old-age pension schemes, for example, as "social perversion," and her descriptions of the living conditions of those receiving the pensions give the lie to some of the more glowing reports of Uruguayan welfare.[9]

Many of the stresses and strains in contemporary Uruguay can be traced to defects in the society that went largely unnoticed during the balmier days of the nation's more successful experiment in welfare democracy. After conditions had changed, the country continued to manifest less violence and repression than our analysis would predict, but finally, after 1967, the manifestations caught up with the underlying reality. The current military take-over behind a civilian puppet, then, is more than a reaction to the earlier successes of the *tupamaro* guerrillas; it is, rather, a reaction to a still deteriorating situation in which repression instead of violence, at least temporarily, is the telltale sign of societal breakdown.

Repression or violence, or both, will continue in Uruguay for some time to come. No real attempt is being made to correct the deficiencies that have caused the present situation; and in fact, any such attempts might well not succeed. The facts of economic and political life in the twentieth century may portend a bleak future for Uruguay: a declining economy beset by recurrent crises and a political structure marked by increased repression and violence with more and more interference from its two super-neighbors, Brazil and Argentina.

Chile

On September 11, 1973, the military took control of a Chile that was rapidly disintegrating into chaos. It took control with the enthusiastic support of the right, the acquiesence of the middle class, and the apathy of much of the lower classes. None, except perhaps the right, had suspected the brutality with which the military would act. It decided that it would have to eliminate a large number of leftist leaders to prevent armed resistance, and it rounded up hundreds of thousands of leftists, executing many on the spot, and filling the two huge stadiums in Santiago with detainees. No one knows the extent of the bloodshed, but educated guesses range from ten to thirty thousand dead. And among those assassinated was the president of Chile himself, Salvador Allende. The repression did not end with the elimination of potential opposition, however. The military continued its merciless suppression through 1975. In the process thousands of innocent people who never entertained an idea of armed resistance have suffered imprisonment, torture, and execution. Leftist political parties have been dissolved, and

[9]Ibid., p. 13.

other political parties are "in recess." No news or commentary critical of the regime has been allowed. All constitutional rights have been suspended. Arbitrary arrests and torture have continued at a very high level.

What had happened? What had happened in such a brief time to one of the most socially cohesive countries in Latin America? Indeed, during the period of our quantitative analysis, from 1950 to 1970, Chile scored just below Costa Rica and Uruguay on the social cohesion index. Yet in 1972 and 1973 Chilean society was transformed into one in which massive unarmed confrontations took place, in which leftist and rightist paramilitary forces were armed and trained, and in which savage military repression became the ultimate climax. In 1973 Chile manifested less cohesion than any other Latin American country. This unprecedented disintegration of a social system cries out for explanation and presents a challenge to the theory of repression and violence developed in Part I of this book.

The theory does help explain what happened in Chile, but the history of Chile also deepens the meaning of our concepts beyond the operationalizations presented in the first part of the book. Before embarking on a discussion of the contentious events of the 1970s, however, it is important to understand the country as it was before that time in order to appreciate the tragedy of Sept. 11, 1974.

In the 1950s Chile's actual score on both repression and violence was lower than was predicted by our equations (see Table 29). In the next decade, the actual and predicted scores were considerably better, and closer. The moderately high levels of repression and violence predicted for the 1950s were based on an extremely low economic growth relative to the change in social mobilization, a loss of support for the established political parties, and a low expenditure on education. To us Chile of the 1950s seemed to be living on borrowed time, which it had accumulated during its more prosperous and better institutionalized period. However, the system recovered as the Christian Democratic Party filled the void left by the demise of the Radical Party and led a strong program of reform, albeit with a good deal of borrowed money. Though the wave of optimism that accompanied the first years of Christian Democrat Eduardo Frei's administration began to dissipate toward the end of his term in 1970, people could still believe that Chile had the cohesion to pursue a democratic way to socialism.

Since achieving its independence in 1817 Chile has boasted of its superiority in things political. It avoided the chaos, arbitrary governments and coups d'etat that rent the society of many Latin American countries in the nineteenth century. It established a strong and effective government that ruled a law-abiding citizenry, and demonstrated its effectiveness by handily defeating its neighbors, Peru and Bolivia, in the War of the Pacific. Even so, Chile had two major blemishes on its "political stability": the civil war of 1891 and the bitter labor relations of the first two decades of the twentieth century.

When Chile's political consensus broke down in 1891, the country erupted into one of the hemisphere's most bloody internal conflicts. Some ten thousand people were killed in the war, a war that developed out of a conflict between President Manuel José Balmaceda and the aristocratic Congress over the authority of the president to declare the budget. Despite the destruction wrought by the civil war, its aftereffects on the Chilean political system were slight.

On the other hand, the labor conflicts that raged at the turn of the century bestowed political divisions on future generations. These divisions were the basis for the polarization of Chilean society, which finally broke it apart in 1973. The nitrate industry located in the northern deserts was the source of much of Chile's prosperity, but it also concentrated large numbers of workers and generated labor disorders with which the paternalistic society of the Central Valley was in no way ready to cope.[10] Inflation ate away at the real wages of the workers, and when they protested through spontaneous demonstrations, the state backed the companies, sometimes killing large numbers of them, as in the Iquique massacre of 1907. Out of this conflict came a radical labor movement organized by Luís Emilio Recabarren. It joined the Red International of Labor Unions after the Russian Revolution and became the base for the strongest Communist Party in Latin America. A strong Socialist Party competed with the Communists after the disastrous years of the world depression in which Chile suffered more than other Latin American countries.

The depression left Chile as highly polarized ideologically as any nation in the world. On the left were the Communist and Socialist parties, in the middle was the Radical Party, on the right were the Liberal and Conservative parties, and on the far right was a semi-Nazi group. Yet the system absorbed these differences with little strain. The only event of consequence that demonstrated a lack of cohesion was the abortive uprising of the Nazis in 1937, which was mercilessly put down with the execution of some 100 young participants in the attempted coup. Shortly afterward, the country elected a Popular Front government of Radicals and Socialists with no violent reaction from the

[10]James O. Morris, *Elites, Intellectuals, and Consensus* (Ithaca: Cornell University Press, 1966).

rightist groups. The apparent harmony in which Chile lived, in spite of this extreme polarization, was made possible by a very limited participation in the political process and by an agreement on the part of the Popular Front government to leave the rural areas alone, not even allowing rural workers and peasants to organize.

The *modus vivendi* of the Chilean political parties broke down with the intrusion of the cold war into domestic politics in 1947. After forming a government, which for the first time included Communist Party ministers, Radical President Gabriel González Videla completely reversed his cooperative stance in response to pressures from the United States. His anticommunism was nurtured, it seems, during his visit to Rio de Janeiro for the signing of the Inter-American Treaty of Reciprocal Assistance. When he returned, he denounced the Communists for disrupting those extractive industries essential for the defense of the United States. In October, 1947, he broke relations with Yugoslavia, Czechoslovakia, and the Soviet Union and mobilized the army to take over the coal mines being struck by Communist labor unions. He placed the northern provinces under military control, with close guard around the copper mines owned by the United States, and proceeded to arrest hundreds of Communist labor leaders, all the members of the Central Committee of the Communist Party, and the editor of the Communist daily, *El Siglo*. Military tribunals were hastily set up to try these political prisoners, who were then sent to concentration camps in remote parts of the country.

President González Videla continued his attacks against the Communists through 1948. He formalized the repression of communism in September, 1948, with an act called, "Law for the Defense of Democracy." The measure outlawed the Communist Party, closed all its offices, banned Communists from public office, and struck all Communist voters from the registry. The law remained in effect until 1958, but it was enforced much more loosely by González's successor, Carlos Ibáñez del Campo, who favored authoritarian measures in general but had nothing in particular against the Communists.

Both Presidents González Videla and Ibáñez took strong action against strikes, including the use of the military to continue production, the mobilization of strikers into the military, and the arrest of strikers and strike leaders. The repression of the Communist Party and labor union leaders did not reduce the number of strikes, however. It simply added political strikes to the large number of economic strikes brought on by worsening economic circumstances that were in turn brought on by the fall of copper prices after the Korean War.

Labor conflict intensified through the 1954–1957 period, when three general strikes were called. In May, 1954, a general strike was called to demand the abrogation of the Law for the Defense of Democracy, and amnesty to all social and political prisoners. Only the coal, copper, and transportation workers participated in the strike. In July, 1955, however, the whole country was brought to a standstill when a million workers participated in a general strike that, this time, emphasized opposition to the economic policies of the government. The Central Union of Workers decided to call another nationwide strike for January, 1956, to protest the freeze on wages, salaries, and prices, but the Ibáñez government broke the strike by declaring a state of siege, occupying Santiago with 30,000 troops, and arresting 250 to 300 labor leaders.

Though President Ibáñez managed to bring organized labor temporarily under control, in April, 1957, Santiago experienced the worst urban riot in its history. The outbreak was touched off by student demonstrators and ended with lower class *rateros* looting and pillaging. The government declared martial law and imposed curfew and censorship in order to bring the riot under control.[11] Hundreds were wounded and at least twenty, probably more, were killed. The episode does not compare with the violence of the Bogotazo of 1948 in Colombia, but it comes close to the urban riots in Mexico City in 1968 and Córdoba, Argentina, in 1969. The event which sparked the outbreak was an increase in bus fares, which symbolized the plight of the unorganized worker: rising costs without equivalent increases in wages, accompanied by widespread unemployment.

After 1957, the situation improved on all fronts. No more outbursts of urban violence occurred, students and unions were relatively quiescent, the Law for the Defense of Democracy was stricken from the books, and Chile elected a president, Jorge Alessandri, who scrupulously respected liberal political rights. Incidents of violence and repression were almost totally absent from Chile in 1959 and 1960.

The conflicts of the 1950s were primarily those over the distribution of the national product. Chile was a relatively prosperous country, rating third in the region, and in the early fifties it was not overly mobilized. Chile's score on the welfare-mobilization differential was well above the average for Latin America in 1955 (see Table 28). Under these conditions, clashes over wages were resolvable, but inflation meant that every group had to maintain continuous pressure to preserve its purchasing power. Friction was more intense when economic growth was less, as it was from 1954 through 1956. From 1960 to 1966, the

---

[11]For an excellent discussion of the riot, see Kalman Silvert *The Conflict Society: Reaction and Revolution in Latin America* (New Orleans: Hauser Press, 1961).

economy recovered considerably, growing at an annual per capita rate of 2.9 per cent.

While economic growth was erratic, social mobilization increased at one of the fastest rates in Latin America. Newspapers and radios increased at the average Latin American rate, but a stagnant agricultural economy forced a high rate of urbanization. Between the census years of 1952 and 1960, the population in cities of more than 20,000 expanded from forty-three to fifty-five per cent.

The political life of the country also took on new vigor after the 1958 elections as the coalition of leftist parties (the *Frente de Acción Popular—* FRAP) under the leadership of Salvador Allende and the Christian Democrats under the leadership of Eduardo Frei solicited popular support for their respective solutions to the nation's problems. The positive programs and self-confidence of these political parties renewed hope in institutional processes and change through governmental reform. Chile's party institutionalization score in the 1960s reflects this renewed interest in political parties, a major shift from 1952 when the majority voted for the antiparty candidacy of Carlos Ibáñez. This renewed political activity, plus a change in the voting laws, stimulated an extraordinary increase in voting between 1958 and 1964, from thirty-four to sixty-one percent of the adult population.

The dramatic rise in political participation had no disturbing effect in the early 1960s because it was channeled through the political parties. The majority supported the reforms of the Christian Democrats, the so-called Revolution in Liberty, and Frei became president in 1964 with the overwhelming support of the population. To a great extent, their hopes were fulfilled with large increases in educational expenditures, the strongest land reform ever enacted by a democratic government, and the Chileanization of the copper mines. The reforms also received the enthusiastic support of the most progressive Catholic Church in Latin America. The church helped organize the peasantry and redistributed its own lands, even before the official government program began. With a relatively large and well-trained priesthood, the church provided a stimulus for change without violence.

Compared with the reforms of other elected governments in Latin America, Chile's policy innovations under the Christian Democrats were quite remarkable. But they were still not fully satisfying to the poor of Chile. Agrarian reform was debated for three years before it was passed, was subjected to numerous legalistic and administrative delays, and when finally the land was redistributed, there was not enough to satisfy all the claimants. In the meantime, the peasants developed their organizational abilities, and at times, took over land by invading it rather than following the cumbersome bureaucratic procedures. The expectations aroused by the reform and the encouragement of rural organizations actually increased needs and demands more rapidly than the process of reform could fulfill them. Urban reforms were as frustrating as the agrarian reforms, and urban groups organized and invaded property for housing projects.

When the economy again stagnated after 1966, dropping to an annual rate of only .4 percent per capita for the last four years of the Frei administration, frustration mounted. More strikes were called. Clashes between the police and organized invaders of property intensified, and for the first time, a small group of radical youths considered the possibility of resorting to armed protest. They organized the Movement of the Revolutionary Left (*Movimiento de Izquierda Revolucionaria*—MIR), committed an occasional act of terrorism, and began training for armed conflict.

While the masses were disturbing the system in local and isolated attacks, the business elite of Chile regrouped and counterattacked with a united force that would have far greater consequence for the nation. After the complete defeat of the Conservative and Liberal parties in the 1965 elections, the large landowners and big businessmen woke up to the fact they were isolated, that they were unsupported by public opinion, and that they were even losing their inside access to government. At the same time, certain Christian Democratic businessmen wished to demonstrate that private enterprise could be enlightened, helping to develop a "communitarian" society. The reactionary and reformist tendencies came together to form the *gremio* ("guild") movement, which sought to promote a new business ideology and organize both small and large business men in order to protect their mutual interests.[12] During 1967 and 1968, the *gremio* movement waged a campaign comparable to a presidential election battle in organization and public-relations activity.

The renewed strength of the right wing in Chile was demonstrated in the congressional elections of 1969. The newly formed Nationalist Party, regrouping the forces of the now-defunct Conservative and Liberal parties, achieved a respectable twenty percent of the vote. That the right was interested in more than electoral politics was revealed in the blatant encouragement by some right-wing politicians of the abortive revolt in October, 1969, led by General Roberto Viaux. Ostensibly the revolt was in support of higher military wages and greater privi-

---

[12]David Cusack, *The Politics of Business Organization under Christian Democracy* (Ph.D. dissertation, University of Denver, 1969).

leges, but in actuality it was to have much more profound political implications.

The resurgence of the right was a fairly clear indication that in 1969 the political system of Chile had once again become polarized. The middle way of the Christian Democrats had shrunk considerably since 1965, and the electoral strength of the left had not improved, remaining nearly constant throughout the decade. The strength of the right, however, had now reached a point where it could seriously consider the possibility of winning the 1970 presidential election by supporting the familiar and respected Jorge Alessandri. During the previous decade, partisans of the right and the left had become much better organized in the business sector, local communal groups, and peasant unions, and for the first time in more than two decades, small groups of romantic revolutionaries and vitriolic anti-Communists were advocating the use of force to achieve their aims. The resurgence of the right, however, proved insufficient to give it the presidency. Instead, it helped assure the victory of the candidate of Popular Unity, Salvador Allende. In a three-way race, Allende won with a vote of only thirty-six percent, three percentage points less then he had received in 1964.

Could Chilean institutions and traditions now provide a new way to achieve socialism, the *Via Chilena?* Certainly no other country in the world had learned to live as peacefully under such intense political debate. The tradition, of course, was not uniformly peaceful, and conditions in 1970 were not all propitious.

Many will debate for generations to come whether the *Via Chilena* could have worked if a few different decisions had been made. We shall deal here with only part of that question, the part that pertains to the level of repression and violence, not with the possibility of achieving socialism. With the benefit of hindsight, it is possible to see the march of events that led almost inevitably to the tragic end of democracy in Chile. At the time, however, no one believed that the conclusion would turn out as it did. Though our variables help explain the increasing violence up to Sept. 11, 1973, and the repression that followed, they did not predict the extraordinary level of repression, and we will suggest an additional factor to account for one of the bloodiest and most ruthless repressions in the history of the world.

The assassination in October, 1970, of constitutionalist General René Schneider, the commander in chief of the armed forces, by a right-wing group shortly before the Allende election was certified in Congress indicated the lengths to which the anti-Marxists would go in order to destroy the *Via Chilena.* From the start, their hope was to provoke a military intervention, which they calculated would favor their point of view. For three years, they used every tactic in their arsenal to bring down the Allende regime: foul and vile slander of members of the government, strikes and economic disruption, and assassinations. There were radicals of the left who welcomed the prospects for an armed conflict, believing that they had the force to win and wanting an opportunity to impose a dictatorship of the proletariat. In the middle were the fragile Chilean institutions; it is now clear that the continuance of Chilean democracy depended on the viability of those institutions.

The institutionalization that had seen Chile through so many conflicts began to atrophy under the contradictions of the Allende period. The basic problem was that Congress remained in the hands of the opposition while the administration was in the hands of a loose coalition, of which at least half refused to make the compromises necessary to win over enough of the opposition to achieve a majority in Congress. The ruling Popular Unity coalition (*Unidad Popular*—UP), it should be emphasized, was not a unified and disciplined party but a very diverse and loose coalition of "bourgeois" and "revolutionary" parties. It was particularly divided over the question of the importance of the democratic institutions, with some giving high priority to their preservation as others worked actively to undermine them. With a stalemate between Congress and the executive, little could be done "legally." The only significant reform bill to pass Congress was the nationalization of the copper mines. Otherwise, Allende had to make a transition to socialism without any new laws. He found legal loopholes that allowed him to proceed, but his interpretation of the law was often contradicted by the Contraloría General and the Supreme Court, both independent agencies with the responsibility of interpreting the laws and the constitution.

During Allende's entire tenure, then, his administration was at the margin of the law—not flagrantly violating the constitution, but pushing his interpretation against that of the "bourgeois apparatus" of the state. At the same time, a number of his party colleagues were clearly on the other side of the law in taking over farms and industries without "due process." Only occasionally would the legal apparatus be used to dislodge these illegal occupants; more often the administration would use its powers to "legalize" their confiscations.

The economic situation reflected the institutional situation. The Allende regime tried to do more than its scarce financial and human resources would allow. In response to demands for an immediate improvement in the standard of living of the masses, the government decreed wage increases. The added purchasing power stimulated the

use of previously unused capacity and accumulated stocks, while inflationary pressure was controlled through the regulation of prices. This
policy worked well for the first year, but the Allende government had
no long-term policy for expanding production and had failed to prepare
for falling copper prices and the lack of cooperation on the part of the
"bourgeois" elements of society.

Even though the Allende government was almost completely successful in extending the "social sector" and in reforming agriculture, it
lacked the resources and the will to increase investment and the human
resources and discipline to engender efficiency. After production
expanded about four percent per capita in the first year, it stagnated in
the second year and fell in the third. The energies of the bourgeoisie, in
the meantime, turned to the development of a black market where the
talented and unscrupulous made immense fortunes. The socialized
sector, too, was corrupted by the black market as workers who were
paid in merchandise hastened to sell for the high prices of the black
market and an occasional socialist manager yielded to the temptation of
diverting some of the company's production into the more lucrative
trade.

The economic chaos reflected in inflation of 186 percent in 1972 and
more than 500 percent in 1973 did more to distort the economy than to
deprive any groups. Workers' and professionals' wages failed to keep
up with inflation in the last year, and commercial and business sectors
won back much of what they had lost in the first two years. The old
landowners were not well compensated for expropriated land, but
many business owners found the Marxist government quite generous
in working out deals for the government take-over of their businesses.
Nevertheless, the chaotic way in which socialism was developed, plus
the violent verbiage of the revolutionary left, aroused enormous fears in
the middle sectors.

August, 1972, marked the beginning of the all-out assault by the
right to bring down the Allende government. That it took thirteen
months for it to succeed against an ineffective government suffering an
economic collapse is a tribute to Chilean traditions. The resistance of
the right was encouraged and supported by the United States Central
Intelligence Agency, whose funds were particularly important in enabling the independent truckers to maintain lengthy strikes in October,
1972, and again in August, 1973.

Chile underwent a virtual unarmed civil war from August to October, 1972, with strikes by the right, take-overs of factories by the left,
and massive demonstrations by both. The crisis was resolved by the
entry of the military into the government, which along with preparations for the congressional elections of March, 1973, produced a tempo-

rary truce. After the inconclusive elections, the situation deteriorated again. The military refused to continue its participation in the government. The labor union at the El Teniente copper mine went out on strike in April, 1973. An attempted military coup on June 29 demonstrated how weak Allende's support in the military had become. Then in August the truckers went out on strike again and were joined by other groups who opposed the Allende government. The right stepped up political assassinations, often with the cooperation of Chile's military intelligence (Servicio de Inteligencia Militar—SIM). Congress and the judicial institutions were totally without power to affect the course of events, and even Allende seemed to have lost control. Obviously, the situation could not continue indefinitely, and when the last efforts at peaceful resolution between the Christian Democrats and President Allende failed, a showdown was inevitable. In the early hours of September 11, the military moved to take control.

The two basic concepts developed in Part I of this book for the explanation of a breakdown in social cohesion are the increase in wants above the possibility for their fulfillment and the disinstitutionalization of the structures of society. To understand how these concepts worked in the Chilean case, it is necessary to consider many aspects that did not appear in our simple operationalizations of the concepts. The level of satisfaction in society was greatly complicated by the change in the distribution of income and the fear of further loss by the middle sectors. Desires were created, not only by social mobilization, but also by the intense politicalization of society and the expectations that came by having a Marxist president elected after decades of being in opposition.

Likewise, the institutionalization that was important in Chile was only partly reflected by the structures we chose to operationalize, the church, the parties, and the military. Whereas parties and the military were clearly damaged by the developments of the period, it was the formal government structures that suffered the most important disinstitutionalization, as the Congress and the courts were totally ineffective in expressing a majority view and the executive could not (or would not) control the militants of the ruling coalition.

Even the successful measurement of these complex concepts would not have allowed us to predict the massive repression that followed September 11, 1973. Clearly some other factors were at work. We would suggest that the Chilean military had been extraordinarily influenced by the counterinsurgency ideas developed in other countries through its close alliance with the United States military. The Chilean military received more military aid from the United States government than any other military establishment in Latin America. It had been made fully aware of the Brazilian and Uruguayan cases where moderate methods were ineffective and higher levels of repression eliminated the insurgents. The bloody elimination of Communists in Indonesia was also an example that was known and commented on in Chile before the military take-over. The Chilean military was among the most professional and best trained in Latin America and was determined to carry out its military mission successfully. That was basically the problem: it carried out a military mission instead of seeking a political solution. It thought all who opposed its take-over, and later its continuation in power, were foreign enemies. The enemy—political or nonpolitical—it had been taught, was to be defeated, and any measures that contributed to his defeat were justified.

Thus, the Chilean experiment in socialism ended with a Chilean experiment in counterinsurgency.

CHAPTER **8**

THE LESS
COHESIVE COUNTRIES

Seven Latin American countries have exhibited significantly greater degrees of repression and violence than other nations in the Southern Hemisphere. The difference in social cohesion between these nations and those in either of the first two societal categories that we have considered is great enough to warrant their being placed into a separate group—the less cohesive countries. Colombia, the Dominican Republic, Venezuela, Guatemala, Paraguay, Haiti and Argentina have all manifested social disintegration, and in ways that are vastly different. Paraguay, for example, was one of the least violent nations in Latin America during the fifties and sixties—but it was also the most repressive. Colombia, among the least repressive, was one of the most violent countries in all of Latin America between 1950 and 1970. Other nations in the group are less cohesive because of certain combinations of repression and violence. Table 30 shows both violence and repression

Table 30. Less Cohesive Countries

		Dependent Variables[a]			
		1950s		1960s	
Country	Variable	Actual	Predicted	Actual	Predicted
Colombia	Violence	1.38	.78	.99	.86
	Repression	.34	−.16	−.49	.10
	Viol. & Rep.	1.14	.44	.33	.61
Dominican	Violence	−1.40	−.80	.76	−.15
Republic	Repression	2.28	.36	.65	.83
	Viol. & Rep.	.58	−.49	.93	.55
Venezuela	Violence	.37	.81	1.47	1.40
	Repression	.89	.27	−.26	−.49
	Viol. & Rep.	.83	.92	.80	.52
Guatemala	Violence	.84	.39	1.20	.99
	Repression	.06	.87	.54	1.34
	Viol. & Rep.	.60	.47	1.15	1.30
Paraguay	Violence	−.35	−.08	−1.29	−.71
	Repression	2.15	1.12	2.20	1.43
	Viol. & Rep.	1.19	1.33	.61	.90
Haiti	Violence	−.05	.55	.19	1.11
	Repression	.54	.91	2.59	2.02
	Viol. & Rep.	.32	.73	1.84	1.64
Argentina	Violence	1.35	.90	1.65	1.28
	Repression	.51	.71	.36	.30
	Viol. & Rep.	1.23	.93	1.32	1.08

[a]All scores are standard.

scores for the seven nations during the two decades, and Table 31 demonstrates some of the reasons why they lacked cohesion.

Cuba and Bolivia, which have been even less cohesive than these seven, are considered in Chapter 9 as revolutionary societies.

Colombia

Colombia is a divided nation, both geographically and politically. Unfortunately, its divisions have contributed to the high incidence of violence that the country has experienced over the past two decades. The geographical division, caused by the split in the Andes Mountains in southern Colombia into three distinct ranges that head northeastward through the country, has hindered communications, isolated villages, and created conditions in which local guerrilla bands and

Table 31. Less Cohesive Countries

| | Independent Variables[a] | | | | | | | | | | | | | |
| | 1950s | | | | | | | 1960s | | | | | | |
Variable	Colombia	Dominican Republic	Venezuela	Guatemala	Paraguay	Haiti	Argentina	Colombia	Dominican Republic	Venezuela	Guatemala	Paraguay	Haiti	Argentina
Welfare minus mobilization	-.34	.22	.39	.51	1.28	-1.13	.88	-.98	.31	-.08	.31	2.04	-1.06	-.28
Economic growth minus social mobilization	-1.27	.66	-.57	.14	.83	-.14	-1.77	-.87	-.73	-2.49	.62	.88	-.52	-.92
Educational effort	-.81	1.79	-.97	-1.17	2.03	-.91	.61	-1.39	-1.39	-.21	-1.42	1.94	-1.84	-.30
Educational expenditure	-.79	.23	-.06	-.79	-1.08	-.94	-.06	-.60	-.60	.96	-1.02	-1.44	-2.15	.25
Party institutionalization	1.19	-.51	.46	-1.42	-.02	-1.95	-.33	.73	-.67	-.11	-1.06	-.22	-2.30	-.22
Military institutionalization	-.27	.53	-1.18	-.68	-2.09	-.98	-.88	.10	.10	-.12	-1.64	-.77	-.44	-1.42
Church institutionalization	.20	-1.47	-.19	-.46	-1.10	-.90	-1.28	-.52	-1.62	-.28	-.65	-1.51	-.48	-.54
Total institutionalization	.47	-.61	-.38	-1.08	-1.36	-1.62	-1.05	.55	-.89	-.21	-1.36	-1.02	-1.31	-.89
White + mestizo as percent of population	.69	-1.51	.73	-.99	-.92	-2.20	1.39	.65	-1.49	.69	-.99	-.92	-2.17	1.33

[a] All scores are standard.

bandit gangs can operate with relative impunity. The political division—between the two powerful parties that have dominated Colombian politics since the mid-nineteenth century—has been responsible for both the initiation of much of the violence and the "hereditary hatreds" that have sensitized the populace to the call of militant leaders.

In Colombia, the word "violence," used officially and unofficially, has become almost synonymous with the daily existence of much of the rural peasantry. Colombians and their governments have hacked away at each other with machetes, shot each other with assorted firearms, and, in general, killed each other with reckless abandon since the 1850s. Most of the violence in the past has been perpetrated by adherents of the two major political parties. A major civil war was fought in Colombia in 1876–1877 when the Conservatives in the Department of Tolima and Antióquia revolted against a national Liberal administration. Another—and bloodier—conflict erupted in 1899 and lasted until June, 1903. This time, the Liberals were revolting against a Conservative administration. In the "War of a Thousand Days," the Liberals were defeated and the Conservative government retained control of Colombian politics until the 1930s. Again in 1930, when the Liberals returned to power in a relatively peaceful election, an incipient civil war—in which the Liberals seemed to be trying to even old scores—was averted only by a Peruvian invasion of the Amazonian provinces. The subsequent surge of national solidarity was occasioned by that war.

Several things must be said about these outbreaks of violence in Colombia. First, although estimates of the numbers of people killed and wounded in the encounters are necessarily vague, it is generally agreed that vast numbers of Colombians were involved in the actions and that casualties ran into the thousands. Second, these large uprisings represent only those occasions when the normally high level of rural violence in Colombia reached such a degree that "civil war" was the only term for it. This does not mean that other years were times of peace in the Colombian countryside. Third, the past violence in Colombia was overwhelmingly political. Most of it was directly due to the deadly antipathy between the two political parties, which used government machinery, both local and national, to decimate the oppostion whenever they could.

Both parties have appealed to elements across class divisions, and both have strong roots in the rural societies of Colombia. Allegiance to either party is passed down through generations, so that villages and entire regions eventually are known as Liberal or Conservative. Many different analyses of these previous instances of violence, as well as those concerning the more recent era—known as "La Violencia"—have concentrated on various economic or psychological reasons for the extraordinary waves of killing that have swept Colombia. In their genesis, however, and in their resultant development, these waves of violence have been due, in large measure, to the determination of national and local leaders of both parties to "get" the opposition. It may be that the parties have capitalized on the existing conditions in Colombia—frustration, poverty, boredom, even the geography—to perpetrate violence, but the catalyst has always been their leaders.

The most recent wave of violence, which began in earnest in 1948 after the assassination of a popular leader, is obviously nothing new. It does appear, however, that this latest outbreak of official and unofficial violence has been bloodier than any of the previous ones, and that the complicity of the parties is, if anything, more pronounced than ever before. As Table 30 indicates, the level of violence in Colombia during the decades of the 1950s and 1960s was among the highest in Latin America, and that in both decades the actual violence was somewhat higher than that predicted by our indicators.

Table 30 shows that repression—as opposed to violence—was less than predicted in Colombia during the same decades. Although Colombian governments have not been as repressive as we predicted, it is difficult, in the context of the situation in both rural and urban Colombia, to determine what is repression and what is violence. For example, there is the well-documented case in which a major guerrilla leader in the eastern *llanos* region was supported for years by party politicians in Bogotá for their own political purposes.[1] While he was alive, Dumar Aljure's depredations of the countryside were reported as violence— that is, antigovernment activity—whereas a strong case could be made that Aljure's activities represented official violence—repression—condoned, at the very least, by some members of the party elite in Bogotá.

Most violence in Colombia has been local and rural, and therefore, has not been adequately reported in the international press. It is possible, even probable, that our violence data (high as they are) underestimate the amount of violence that took place in Colombia during the 1950s in particular, and, to some extent, in the 1960s. One serious attempt to estimate the deaths from violence brought forth a figure of 179,820 people killed between 1949 and 1958.[2] The same source quotes a study by the Colombian National Police which estimates that an average of 3,000 Colombians were killed annually as a result of the violence

[1]Richard L. Maullin, *The Fall of Dumar Aljure, A Colombian Guerrilla Bandit* (Santa Monica: Rand Corp., 1968).

[2]Germán Guzmán, *La Violencia en Colombia* (Cali: Ediciones Progreso, 1968).

between the years 1958 and 1962. Both estimates are considerably higher than our figures derived from the international press for the same periods.

The most recent period of violence in Colombia, while begun by the political parties as early as 1946 and carried on largely under their urging through June, 1953, roared beyond the control of any traditional Colombian institutions as early as the 1948 riot, known as the *Bogotazo*, which took place in the capital. Until the military coup of June, 1953, both Liberals and Conservatives had continued to orchestrate the violence for their own ends, though much of the rural violence was increasingly anomic. Still, old habits die hard, and even after the Liberals and Conservatives had agreed to the novel compromise of the National Front in 1958, there is hard evidence that many local politicians and some national figures continued to use violence for their own ends, rather than join in the effort to end it. Political checks on army operations against bandits and guerrilla bands, judicial leniency, and continued efforts by one group or another to utilize local bandit leaders in elections or nonvoting campaigns were manifold.

Violence in Colombia has been divided into four distinct phases: the Hatfield-McCoy Era, from August, 1946, until June, 1948; the First Guerrilla War, from April, 1948, to June, 1953; the Second Guerrilla War, from July, 1953, to May, 1957; and the Institutionalized Violence, from May, 1957, until July, 1965.[3] To these four periods, we would add a fifth: the ideological guerrilla warfare, from July, 1965, to the present.

In 1950, Colombia was in the midst of the First Guerrilla War. The Hatfield-McCoy Era, which had been an intensification of normal Liberal-Conservative feuding in the rural areas, had been limited geographically to a few Departments. However, most of the violence seems to have been started by the Conservatives, who won control of the government in 1946 with the election of Mariano Ospina Pérez as president, and the Liberals began responding in kind in the rural areas of the Departments of Boyacá, Nariño, and Tolima. The Conservatives, who had won the election only because of a split between the followers of Gabriel Turbay Ayala, a moderate Liberal, and those of Jorge Eliécer Gaitán, a Liberal with more radical ideas, apparently decided to maintain their power through force of arms, in spite of Ospina's calls for a government of national union.

After the death of Turbay in 1947, the Liberals subsequently united under the leadership of Gaitán, and the Conservatives became even more convinced that violence was the only way they could retain

---

[3]Russell W. Ramsey, "The Modern Violence in Colombia," (Ph.D. diss. University of Florida, 1967).

power. Still, the violence was shared fairly equally by the two political parties and was fairly well under control until, on April 9, 1948, Gaitán was assassinated on the streets of Bogotá. The wave of rioting, looting, burning, and killing that swept the capital in the next week spread rapidly to the rest of the country. The Liberals were convinced that Gaitán had been assassinated at the direction of the Conservatives. Some moderates in both parties pleaded for national unity in the face of impending chaos, but extremists on both sides prepared for open warfare. Vigilantes and small-town thugs from the preceding era of violence now began organizing guerrilla bands who attacked Conservative villages. The Conservatives responded, of course, and the National Police, controlled by the Conservative government, was used as a potent weapon against Liberals, especially in urban areas. In addition, criminal organizations, such as the *Pájaros* (Bluebirds) were given a free hand in attacking Liberal rallies and meetings. The situation worsened when, in the uncontested presidential election of 1950, the neo-Fascist Laureano Gómez gained the presidency. The power behind the throne in the Ospina administration, Gomez now took the reins openly. Government persecution of Liberals increased markedly, as now no holds were barred for the Bluebirds, the National Police, and other anti-Liberal groups. In June, 1953, the army finally acted to stop the violence. Gomez was ousted from office and a military government under the direction of Lieutenant-General Gustavo Rojas Pinilla took over with the avowed intention of ending the violence, which by then had spread to all parts of the nation.

Though the political events of the late 1940s and early 1950s provided the catalyst for the violence, underlying societal causes were in abundant evidence in Colombia. In Chapter 1, we stated that any theory of social action must begin with basic social conditions which stimulate the behavior that produces global and aggregate social phenomena, such as the Colombian violence. Table 31 demonstrates the efficacy of the theory. Colombia in the 1950s was obviously ready for large-scale violence and repression. Economic growth had failed to keep up with social mobilization as Colombians began streaming to the cities. In a strange case of intermingled cause and effect, the violence in the countryside, which was largely responsible for at least the first wave of urbanization, created social conditions—increased social mobilization—that would produce more violence. Though below average on societal welfare, Colombians were near the Latin American mean on social mobilization. Traditionally, newspapers have kept the Colombians in touch with the conditions and events of the world, but beginning in the 1950s radio became more and more important as the means of communication. The press and the radio stations were (and are) extremely partisan politically, so that the participants in the violence were subjected to a barrage of ideological reinforcement and justification from both sides. Economic growth, which depended largely on coffee production, was nominal during the period, but after a drop in world coffee prices in 1958, it failed to keep up with the rise in social mobilization. Colombia also neglected the schoolchildren during this period, which is made more poignant by the fact that the average age of the participants in the violence was between eighteen and twenty-five.[4]

The Catholic Church, the military, and the Colombian political parties were all rather well institutionalized during the 1950s, with the party score quite high, but of course it was precisely these parties that instigated the violence. In the Colombian case, therefore, the existence of two strong political parties did not have the same mitigating effect on repression that strong parties did elsewhere in Latin America. The party in control of the government in Colombia was initially interested in promoting overt repression of the opposition, rather than diminishing it, and the opposition party, resorting to violence as its primary means, also promoted repression as a reactive measure. The Colombian church was also strong, but highly partisan toward the Conservatives in the early period of violence. With little institutional autonomy, it was more concerned with the maintenance of its perquisites than with the values of society. A strange phenomenon of the violence was the outward religiosity of many of the participants. People wore religious medals in the midst of savage butchery. Many times, bandit gangs asked for the blessing of the local priest for their upcoming assault. If part of the mission of the Colombian church was to promote respect for human life, it clearly failed.

The Colombian Army was quite supportive of the civilian government until the 1953 coup, but another official armed force, the National Police, was in the thick of the violence from the beginning. Here, too, the complexity of the Colombian situation was not entirely captured by our indicators.

The initial efforts of the army to end the violence in the 1953–1957 Second Guerrilla War period failed. And they failed precisely because the army was using violent tactics to end the violence. Students were killed, *campesino* villages suspected of harboring *antisociales* were assaulted and burned, and, in general, the army behaved with the degree of political insensitivity and abandon characteristic of many military governments. The violence, which had abated slightly during

---

[4]Victor A. Delgado Mallarino, "El Delito Sexual y la Violencia," *Revista de las Fuerzas Armadas*, 1 (August, 1960), p. 609; cited in Ramsey, "Modern Violence in Colombia," p. 393.

the first two years of the Rojas regime, rose again in 1955, and it became obvious that Rojas was not going to fulfill his promise to end it. It was during this second period, too, that the violence became even more anarchic, as a second generation of participants in the bloodshed came to adulthood. These were people who had witnessed the atrocities of the earlier period, who now hated all Conservatives (or Liberals) for the simple, apolitical reason that they had seen their fathers cut open, their mothers raped, and their villages burned by the other side.

The reasons suggested for the coup that overthrew Rojas in 1957 vary. Perhaps the most basic charge is that Rojas was both venal and inefficient, and that a dictator cannot be both and remain long in power. Certainly Rojas had not terminated violence, and the political parties and the military came to agree that they could do the job more effectively. The Declaration of Benidorn, in which the Liberals and Conservatives agreed to a twelve-year political truce (later extended to sixteen years) and to share the responsibilities of government as the best means of ending the violence, was signed in Spain by leaders of both parties in July, 1956. Formalized in the Pact of Sitges, the agreement resulted in the National Front arrangement in July, 1957. The National Front came into existence with a plebiscite in December, 1957, and Alberto Lleras Camargo, a Liberal, became the first president under the National Front in 1958. Within the terms of the agreement, the presidency was to alternate between a Liberal and a Conservative every four years, and all other elective and appointive posts in the country were to be divided equally between the two parties.

The National Front coalition was at least partially successful in depoliticizing the violence. The National Police and other government agencies were used less and less as agents of official violence, and, at the national level at least, the political leaders were much more unified in their calls for an end to the killing. By this time, however, violence had become a way of life in the countryside (and increasingly in the cities), so that the moderate social reform measures of Lleras Camargo failed to reach the growing number of hoodlums who were perpetrating much of the killing. A sharp drop in violence after the ouster of Rojas was more than matched by an upswing beginning in 1960. By 1964, armed violence had again risen to an extremely high level. Unarmed violence and repression were generally lower than they had been, but it was painfully apparent that Lleras Camargo had failed, at least in the short run, to stop the violence.

Perhaps the main reason for the continuing violence was the desolation of the Colombian economy caused by the abrupt decline in world coffee prices after 1958. Economic growth, which had been negligible during the last half of the fifties, now slowed to practically nothing as

Colombia experienced a severe shortage of badly needed foreign exchange. Without it, Colombia was unable to buy manufactured goods and intermediary goods to keep its own factories working. At the same time, Colombian cities became even more swollen by the torrent of *campesinos* moving in from the devastated countryside to escape the violence.

Guillermo León Valencia, a Conservative, took office as president under the National Front in July, 1962. Although the Colombian Army, particularly during 1962, had conducted more and more operations against bandit gangs, their sorties were now formalized under a plan— Plan Lazo. The plan embodied the basic assumption that mere physical eradication of existing guerrillas and bandits would not solve the problem of violence in the Colombian countryside, and that the underlying causes of the violence—political, social, and economic—had to be eliminated. The military was the chosen instrument for this task. During the roughly four years that Plan Lazo was in effect (the years of the Valencia administration), armed violence in Colombia reached new heights before beginning a slow decline. Unarmed violence, on the other hand, increased as the economy declined, and Valencia provided no leadership in resolving the proliferating social problems. Where Lleras Camargo had at least operated on one front—social reform— Valencia chose to ignore both social reform and military repression of the violence.

Plan Lazo was probably founded on a fallacious premise: that the army was capable of the palliative social action that would reduce the likelihood of rural violence. After the departure in 1965 of the plan's principal architect, General Ruíz Novoa, and Valencia's departure from office in 1966, the armed forces adopted the different tactic of aiming at the physical elimination of the bandits and guerrillas. The new president, Carlos Lleras Restrepo, a Liberal, was much more active in the presidency than either of his predecessors, and one consequence was an improvement, after 1967, in the performance of the Colombian economy.

By the mid-1960s, however, rural violence had changed once again. In place of—or in addition to—the apolitical bandits and gangs of the early sixties, there now appeared three ideological groups that can be classed as openly revolutionary for they proclaimed themselves against the existing Colombian social order. The violence, therefore, that had heretofore been surprisingly free of the cold war ideology that might be expected in such a situation, at last became a minor insurgency factor in Colombia. Although the three groups had some early successes and have scored some propaganda triumphs, they have been pretty well contained by the army, even though all three are apparently still operating in Colombia.

More important, perhaps, the army after 1966 began to go after the rural bands with new élan. It pursued bandits to their mountain lairs and, apparently, adopted a new policy of killing them on the spot rather than submitting them to the vagaries of a trial in Bogotá. Probably a combination of circumstances produced the substantial decline in violence in the late 1960s which has continued to the present.

The National Front, then, has managed to depoliticize much of the violence in Colombia. Plan Lazo and similar efforts have also helped reduce the degree of violence by changing some of the conditions of life in the countryside. The Colombian economy began to grow at eminently acceptable rates after 1967, and the army has had greater success in suppressing violence, killing some of the more notorious bandit leaders. Armed violence decreased drastically after 1965, and by 1968, was at the lowest point in the two-decade period. While it would be difficult to mark 1965 as the year the violence ended in Colombia—for some still goes on, perpetrated mainly by the ideological groups—the early 1970s have seen Colombia a much more peaceful nation than at any time since 1946. It does appear that the National Front experiment, for all its shortcomings of immobilism, of failure to introduce meaningful social reforms, of refusal to allow new coalitions to enter the political system, has been successful in its major aim: to end the violence in Colombia. Our predictors, especially the economic ones, are on the upgrade. The rush to the cities, while not ending, is at least slowing down, and the vertiginous increase in social mobilization has also slowed. Most significantly, the two political parties appear to have learned how to cooperate in order to control the political system without resorting to violence. Colombian politics is still rent by factionalism within the two parties, but their leaders seem determined to operate at a new political level. Given the importance of the two parties to the future of Colombian politics—a good example of their strength is the way in which they turned aside a determined challenge from the neo-populist party of Rojas Pinilla—this cooperation and control will be the most vital determinant of Colombia's future. Deep social and economic problems remain, nonetheless, and these will require determined and cooperative party leadership to resolve.

Dominican Republic

Mid-century politics in the Dominican Republic has been characterized by high and low levels of repression and violence. Under the Trujillo dictatorship in the 1950s, the level of repression was relatively high and that of violence relatively low. In the following decade, the level of repression was lower, but the level of violence was a good deal higher after the assassination of the dictator. Actually, of course, the decade of the 1950s was merely the last full ten-year period of one of the longest personal dictatorships in Latin American history. General Rafael Leonidas Trujillo y Molina came to power in the Dominican Republic in 1930, and remained the only political force in the nation until his death in 1960. During that thirty-year period, Trujillo established his own personal rule, but in another sense, he was merely the most recent figure in what had become a long-established cycle in Dominican Republic politics: dictatorship followed by chaos, followed by a new dictatorship.

Dominican politics have always been marked by a cyclical pattern. The reasons for it are rooted in the history of the nation—particularly in the lack of developed societal institutions that might have provided the stability necessary for social cohesion. Many historical factors were responsible for this lack of development—the bitter personalist rivalries of the nineteenth century, the Haitian occupation of the mid-nineteenth century, the virtual destruction of the Catholic Church during the Haitian occupation, the destabilizing effects of U.S. policies—most particularly the U.S. intervention from 1914 to 1930—and the absence of an institutionalized military. Perhaps the chief factor, however—and most certainly the most crucial one of the recent times— was the thirty-year rule of Rafael Trujillo. In those three decades, Dominican institutions and normal political life were stultified, for until his very last years, Trujillo *was* the Dominican Republic, and he ruled it as his own fiefdom for the benefit of himself and his family.

Trujillo's rule was one of the most complete and all-encompassing in Latin American history. He relied extensively on army support as the principal prop for his regime, and under him it achieved a new status in the country. He gave it modern weapons and training, and vastly increased its size. Military officers were allowed to supplement their income by illegal business activities and protection rackets. Trujillo did not, however, simply allow the military to go its own way: he realized that while the army was the final source of his power, it was also the greatest potential threat to his regime. Accordingly, he maintained absolute control over the armed forces. His relatives were assigned to the highest posts and officers were moved up and down the military hierarchy, and frequently transferred, so that none could build up any independent base of power and support.

Trujillo also created an extensive intelligence apparatus to supplement the regular army. The Dominican *Servicio Inteligencia Militar* (SIM) became the model for similar organizations in Cuba, Venezuela, and other Latin American dictatorships. Under Trujillo, spies were omnipresent, and opponents either were jailed and never heard from again or mysteriously disappeared. Trujillo's terror at times reached outside the Dominican Republic to silence foes in Puerto Rico, New York, and Havana.

In a sense, Trujillo had more in common with Joseph Stalin than he did with most of his contemporaries in Latin America. Like Stalin, he was a hard worker and was willing to spend longer hours than his opponents at the job of maintaining power. Further, Trujillo was an excellent administrator, not unlike Stalin in his role as secretary-general of the Communist Party. Trujillo managed to dominate the government completely from 1930 until his death, and few details escaped his perusal. Bureaucrats, whose numbers grew, were subject to the same game of musical chairs, and for the same reasons, as the military. Trujillo not only controlled the military and the government, he also ruled the one political party in the country, the *Partido Dominicano*. Though it now appears that the party has outlived its creator, during Trujillo's lifetime he was complete master of the party machinery, and all party functionaries were at his command. Finally, Trujillo maintained complete control over all interest groups or incipient interest groups in the country. Labor was completely subservient, and even the traditional oligarchy was ground under by Trujillo and replaced by a new rich who owed their position to the dictator.

Perhaps the most overlooked or understated fact about Trujillo was that he was genuinely popular with many of the Dominican people. First, he provided stability, and this increased his popularity among members of the new commercial middle class in and around Santo Domingo—or Ciudad Trujillo, as it was called in those days. Second, Trujillo represented a triumph of the middle class over the oligarchy, especially the landed gentry around Santiago de los Caballeros in the north. Trujillo himself was of distinctly middle-class origins, and his decimation of the power of the landed oligarchs was welcomed by many as long overdue. Third, Trujillo created a sense of nationalism and managed to equate himself with that nationalism; as Dominicans began to identify with and be proud of their nation-state, they also began to identify with and be proud of Trujillo. Trujillo also remained on friendly terms with the United States, which retained the ultimate veto power over the direction of Dominican politics through the threat of or actual armed intervention. Relations with the State Department and Central Intelligence Agency deteriorated seriously toward the end of his regime, but even then Trujillo maintained close contacts with influential congressmen and both the State Department and the CIA were constrained in their attempts to oppose a continuation of the Trujillo era. Such disparate members of Congress as Senators George Smathers and James Eastland, and Representatives Wayne Hays and

Sam Cooley were wined and dined at the expense of the Dominican government, and Franklin Roosevelt's famous dictum, "He may be an S.O.B., but he's our S.O.B." was operative until the end.

Trujillo should not, of course, be treated as a joke. He was a genuine tyrant. Not only were there strict controls on press, political parties, the Catholic Church, and other organizations, but individual opponents of the regime never had a chance. The judgment of a Dominican historian probably sums it up best:

> Trujillo's cruelty was primitive, rudimentary, savage. There never has existed a despot, outside of the worst Roman Caesars, for whom human life represented so little value. Trujillo ordered an assassination as something automatic. No condition of the victim, or of circumstances could slow him down or make him indecisive. . . . To kill—it made no difference as to the identity of the dead person or his crime—was in sum, the principal theme of the regime.[5]

Under Trujillo's rule, unrest, or violence, did not come to the Dominican Republic until 1959. Until that year there was absolutely no overt opposition to the Trujillo regime within the Dominican Republic. When opposition did come, it was perhaps inevitable that it would come armed from outside the country. In June, 1959, an invasion by Dominican exiles, mounted from Cuba and with assistance from the Castro regime, was crushed almost immediately by the Trujillo troops.

The invasion failed but it nevertheless did signal a turning point for Trujillo. After that he became isolated diplomatically and the United States government (or at least the executive branch) began to work against him. Internal opposition also took shape, and during 1960 and early 1961 there were several open student demonstrations against Trujillo. They were quickly quelled, but they were the first outward signs in thirty years of public discontent.

The assassination of Rafael Trujillo on May 30, 1961, marked the end of an era in the life of the Dominican Republic. It was as if the nation had been born again, in the middle of the twentieth century, with no real political institutions, few social institutions, no civic culture to permit the orderly functioning of politics, and no real comprehension among any groups (except, perhaps, the Communists) as to how a political system should operate. The result was, predictably, chaos, although not immediate chaos. The Trujillo regime had been so strong that the slain dictator's family managed to hold on to the reins of

---

[5]Pedro Andrés Pérez Cabral, *La Comunidad Mulata* (Caracas: Grafica Americana, 1967), pp. 187–188.

government until November, when the last of the Trujillos left the Dominican Republic. Prior to their departure riots and antigovernment demonstrations had been gathering momentum, and from July through October clashes between the police and demonstrators in Santo Domingo became more frequent. After the final exodus of the Trujillo family, however, mobs surged through the city demonstrating against Joaquín Balaguer, the nominal president after Trujillo's death. The mobs forced Balaguer to accept the creation of a seven-man Council of State, which took office on January 1, 1962. After an abortive coup by the air force chief later in the month, the Council of State was reinstated and governed until the inauguration of a new president in February, 1963. In the interim, disorders continued. Much of the rioting took place in Santo Domingo, but the unrest spread also to other parts of the country. The riots were directed not only against Balaguer, who remained as head of the ruling Council of State, but the United States consulate was also attacked by a mob on December 13, and a demonstration took place in front of the American embassy on July 8, 1962. Balaguer was finally sent into exile, and from then on the violence abated somewhat. The period from the exile of Balaguer to the installation of Juan Bosch in December, 1962, as the new president was the freest in the history of the Dominican Republic. Political parties were formed; the media were free; and independent labor organizations were formed.

The nine months between Bosch's inauguration and his overthrow were also the most orderly since Trujillo's assassination. Where before mobs had roamed the streets, there were no reported incidents of violence in the country during Bosch's term in office, which ended rather abruptly on September 25, 1963, with a military coup. The coup had been in the making almost from the moment Bosch took office, and was a result of fears among the military, the oligarchy, and some United States officials that Bosch's frankly reformist policies would lead to a take-over of the government by Communists. Whatever else he may have been, Bosch was extremely popular among the urban proletariat and the students in and around Santo Domingo. Although the armed forces immediately turned power over to a civilian triumvirate, demonstrations against the new government broke out immediately and continued until the end of the year. The new junta, under the leadership of Donald Reid Cabral, embarked upon a much more moderate course of reform than had Bosch. It was a program, however, that did not set well with the more conservative elements in the Dominican military. At the same time, the new junta constricted liberties in the country to a greater degree than had Bosch. Specifically, the Communists, who had been operating openly under the Bosch government, were now proscribed, and Bosch's political party, the Dominican Revolutionary Party (*Partido*

Revolucionario Dominicano—PRD) was harassed. This moderate level of repression continued through 1964 and into 1965, and violence declined considerably. Once again it appeared that perhaps the Dominican Republic was making progress toward some form of orderly constitutional government.

A series of factors, however—some institutional and some political—were producing a climate for a major outbreak of violence. Our indicators showed a definite drop in the differential between economic growth and change in social mobilization during the 1960s, but they probably did not adequately demonstrate the rapidity with which social mobilization was taking place (see Table 31). The pent-up demands of the previous thirty years were now being unleashed upon a government ill-prepared to meet them. The Dominican economy, which had performed at about the same level during the 1960–1964 period as during the latter years of the Trujillo regime, began to experience problems in early 1965. The principal economic problem revolved around world sugar prices, which plummeted in 1965. Sugar normally accounts for more than fifty percent of the Dominican Republic's foreign exchange earnings. The *zafra*, or sugar harvest, began in December, 1964, and the realization that sugar sales in 1965 would probably be poor no doubt contributed to the general feeling of frustration that led to the outbreak of violence later in that year.

The extensive war which began in the Dominican Republic on April 24, 1965, and which resulted in Reid's ouster and the armed intervention of the United States, was touched off by the supporters of Bosch who tried to oust the junta and return him to power. They came close to succeeding before a countereffort by the military, led by Colonel Elias Wessín y Wessín, reinstated military dictatorship. It is difficult to say what would have happened had the United States not intervened, but American policy-makers were evidently quite convinced that the success of the coup would mean the triumph of communism in the Dominican Republic—a prospect they were not prepared to accept. So United States marines landed in a Latin American country for the first time in some forty years. The initial contingent of 405 men eventually grew to more than 20,000. The United States troops were joined by small contingents from Brazil, Nicaragua, Honduras, Paraguay, and Costa Rica. The fighting in the Dominican Republic quickly took on the aspect of a war between the people of the Dominican Republic and the United States military. The fighting, which was concentrated in and around Santo Domingo, went on through August, with serious incidents between U.S. forces and Bosch supporters continuing through the rest of the year. By late August, however, a provisional civilian government under Hector García Godoy had been established, and some semblance of normalcy had returned to the country.

Some circumstantial evidence supports the thesis that the intervention of the United States greatly increased the amount of violence that took place during 1965. This is the type of discrete event we cannot predict, but it does appear that foreign intervention in a violent situation will increase the level of violence considerably, not lessen it. In the Dominican Republic, for example, there were approximately twenty times as many reported instances of violence in the same time span after the United States intervention as there were before it. It is difficult (and not too productive) to say which of the two Dominican factions would have won had there been no intervention. Nevertheless, it seems safe to say that the intervention, while assuring the triumph of "our" side, greatly increased the amount of violence by converting an internecine battle into a national war against the invaders from the north. Except for this tremendous outburst of violence in the mid-1960s, our predictions would have been almost the same as the actual violence in the Dominican Republic for the decade.

New elections were scheduled for June, 1966, and the two leading contenders were Balaguer and Bosch. Under the supervision of the Organization of American States, the campaign was open, if at times marred by gangsterism on both sides. Balaguer won a surprisingly easy victory, and has remained in power ever since. He was reelected in 1970, and won again in 1974. Repression has continued at a medium level throughout these years, although the use of terror by the government shot up as the 1974 elections drew closer. Violence against the regime decreased sharply after 1965 and 1966, and a recent landing by Colonel Francisco Camaaño, the leader of the pro-Bosch 1965 uprising, was easily crushed by the government and Camaaño was killed. Balaguer's current slogan is "Balaguer—President 1973–1980," and he might well achieve his goal.

Balaguer has not discontinued the use of repression in the Dominican Republic. His principal instrument of terror is an organization known as *La Banda*, which has publicly stated that its purpose is to protect the country from communism. By 1971 *La Banda's* victims were averaging fifteen or twenty a month; and there were indications that Balaguer used the organization to bring about his reelection in 1974 by creating a climate in which the opposition could not organize. In the mid-1970s after two interventions by the United States to "defend democracy," plus massive infusions of U.S. economic aid since 1965," political life in the Dominican Republic remains both violent and repressive.

Venezuela

For nearly six years, Marcos Pérez Jiménez was dictator of Venezuela—from 1953 to 1958. Pérez Jiménez succeeded a military junta that had been in power since 1948. Not surprisingly, then, for Venezuelans the 1950s were characterized by repression. After Jiménez's ouster, repression declined—though violence increased drastically; by the end of the 1960s and early 1970s, Venezuela had become one of the least repressive states in Latin America.

Ironically, this nation, which had perhaps the strongest tradition of dictatorship in all of Latin America, has emerged as one of the few remaining democracies in Latin America. The violence, which had been the highest in Latin America during the early 1960s, diminished somewhat by the early 1970s, but the fourth successive constitutional government—headed by Carlos Andrés Pérez of the *Acción Democrática* party—still faced severe pressures from the violence and from the conditions in Venezuela that created it.

As Table 30 demonstrates, most of the violence in Venezuela is explained by our conditioning variables. In the 1950s only the growth of the Venezuelan economy, resulting from profits in mineral exploitation by foreign corporations, was working for reduced amounts of violence. In spite of this rapid growth, Venezuela's rate of social mobilization was outstripping the economy. Venezuela was one of the first nations of Latin America to be hit by the television revolution. People began streaming into the cities in increasing numbers. An economic downturn at the end of the 1950s further exacerbated the deteriorating situation. Both violence and repression were well predicted in the 1960s. As the Venezuelan economy faltered in the early years of the decade, the change in social mobilization swept ahead. Political parties continued to develop during the decade, but total institutionalization remained low. Violence in the fifties was not well predicted; the military dictatorship was able to keep the lid on until its downfall in 1958. Once the dictatorship disappeared, however, Venezuela erupted into a frenzy of violence that lasted well into the 1960s before diminishing toward the end of that decade.

The 1958 revolt which toppled Pérez Jiménez was brought about by the leaders of the political parties acting in conjunction with disgruntled military men. Led by students, opponents of the dictator rioted in Caracas for some twenty-two days prior to his ouster. A general strike organized by the political leaders of the opposition began the day before Pérez fled the country, and was extraordinarily effective. Once he had gone, the Caracas mobs reacted much as had the mobs some twenty-three years earlier, when the dictator Juan Vicente Gómez died.

Known members of the secret police were killed, and crowds roamed the streets of the capital for three days, destroying everything associated with the old regime. A provisional government under Rear Admiral Wolfgang Larrazábal, one of the leaders of the revolt, was set up, and a modicum of order was established. The visit to Caracas in May, 1958, of the then Vice President Nixon, however, provided the spark for new riots, this time directed against the United States and its representative. The United States was associated in the popular mind with the Pérez Jiménez regime, and the reaction to the Nixon visit was riotous. In the process, Nixon was nearly killed by the mob, and the United States ordered several regiments of paratroopers to be ready for a drop into Caracas if the necessity arose.

After almost a year of provisional government under Larrazábal, elections were held in 1958 and Rómulo Betancourt, of the *Acción Democrática* (AD), became president of Venezuela. He was inaugurated in February, 1959, a year that proved to be calmer than the previous one, though violence continued at a high level. Repression decreased sharply from the high levels of the previous regime, however. A key factor in the violence was the lack of support for *Acción Democrática* in Caracas itself. AD had garnered most of its votes from the rural areas. The capital was split into warring factions of left and right, with the Betancourt government caught in the middle. On the left were two major groups, the Leftist Revolutionary Movement (*Movimiento Izquierdista Revolucionaria*—MIR) and the Armed Forces for National Liberation (*Fuerzas Armadas de Liberación Nacional*—FALN). The MIR was composed of AD dissidents who had broken with the party in 1960 over the gradualist approach to the solution of Venezuela's problems and the continued control of the party by its elder statesmen. (This rupture was the first of many schisms within the AD that eventually reduced it from one of the more highly institutionalized political parties in Latin America to a minority political group.) The FALN was a 1962 amalgam of the Venezuelan Communist Party, which had been outlawed by Betancourt (as was the MIR for the 1963 elections), and Venezuelan supporters of Fidel Castro. The FALN was, perhaps, the originator of the concept of urban guerrilla warfare in Latin America, and because of the weakness of the ruling party in Caracas, its choice of guerrilla tactics was a particularly effective mode of resistance.

Violence also emanated from the right during this period. The Venezuelan military, which had enjoyed many of the perquisites of power during the dictatorship, suddenly found itself occupying a secondary role in government. The military was far from ineffective as an interest group, however, for everyone, Betancourt included, knew that the civilian government could continue only if a majority of the military were induced to allow it to do so. Nevertheless, several groups within the military tried to topple the civilian government, and even though none succeeded the resulting violence was considerable. A 1960 revolt in Táchira, a 1961 army revolt at Barcelona, and a marine revolt at Puerto Cabello in 1962 were the major attempts by sectors of the military to reassert control over the Venezuelan government. In addition, evidence exists that prior to his assassination, Trujillo moved to have Betancourt assassinated and on one occasion very nearly succeeded.

To counter the violence from both left and right—the leftist violence was more substantial—Betancourt resorted to various repressive tactics. Political arrests were made, and opposition leaders were jailed, usually for a short time, during periods of stress. The conditions of detention, however, were not nearly as severe as they had been under Pérez Jiménez. Beginning in 1962, restrictions were placed on the activities of the MIR and the Communists, and some press censorship was instituted. Civil liberties were also partially suspended under the recently enacted constitution, but here again the regime never resorted to the extreme measures of its predecessor, and constitutional rights were continually restored soon after the threat to the government seemed to be over.

The election of Raul Leoní as president in 1963 and his subsequent inauguration the following February demonstrated several things. First, it was the first time in Venezuelan history that a freely elected president had turned his office over to a freely elected successor. Venezuelan democracy had taken tenuous root, even though Leoní was from the same party as Betancourt. Second, most Venezuelans repudiated both left and right, even though terrorism in Caracas reached new heights during the month preceding the election. On election day, calm reigned throughout the nation, and more than ninety-one percent of the electorate went to the polls to vote for president and congressional candidates. Third, though AD won the election, it had lost considerable popular support; Leoní won the three-way race with only thirty-three percent of the vote as compared with Betancourt's forty-nine percent in 1958. The Christian Democratic Party (COPEI) was the big gainer in the election, becoming the nation's second largest political party.

Violence, still mostly a combination of leftist terrorism and military uprisings, decreased slightly in 1964 and 1965, dropped sharply in 1966, rose again in 1967, and then declined even further in 1968 and 1969 as yet another civilian government took power. Even though the Venezuelan economy of the 1960s was growing at a slower rate than in the late 1950s, the government was making progress toward ameliorating the worst excesses of one of the most unequal distributions of income in Latin America. In 1967, Venezuela actually instituted an income tax for the first time in its history, and in the face of great opposition from the wealthier industrial groups in Caracas. Early in the Betancourt administration, the government had embarked upon an extensive agrarian reform program, based primarily on the relatively costly method of colonizing new land (as opposed to the less expensive method of expropriating existing underutilized farmland). Fortunately, because of its oil reserves, Venezuela was rich enough to be able to choose the more costly but politically less abrasive colonization method; by 1964 the program was already producing results. Finally, the tremendous disparities between Venezuela's high GNP per capita (the highest in Latin America) and the rest of her societal welfare indicators have been somewhat dissipated. Literacy, food consumption, and health services have started to catch up with Venezuela's national wealth. At the same time the nation's tremendous rate of social mobilization during the late 1950s has slowed down, at least in comparison with the rest of Latin America. The differential between societal welfare and social mobilization had once more become positive by 1965.

Another major change which affected Venezuelan politics in the latter half of the 1960s was the increased institutionalization of COPEI. As AD, one of the most institutionalized left-of-center parties in Latin America, became more and more rent by schisms, COPEI continued to gain strength under Rafael Caldera, its founder and leader. Founded by Caldera in 1934, COPEI is one of the oldest Christian Democratic parties in Latin America; as such, it perhaps has had access to a more unifying ideology than has AD. By 1968, COPEI had participated in two coalition governments controlled by AD, but in the process had broadened its recruitment base to include students (the only democratic party to score heavily with students), labor, and many members of the middle class. As a result of COPEI's rise to prominence, plus the continued vitality of AD despite the splits that plagued it during the 1960s, Venezuela's political party system was much more highly institutionalized in the late 1960s than at any time in the nation's history.

A combination of factors, then, led to a lessening of tensions in Venezuela beginning with the election of Leoní in 1964 and continuing with the election of Caldera to the presidency in 1968. The transmission of power from AD to an opposition political party in 1969 also convinced many skeptics that Venezuelan democracy had a firm foothold. From 1967 on, there were no restrictions on the press, and the number of political prisoners had greatly dwindled. The Communists were still outlawed, and probably will remain so for some time to come, and the MIR appears to have been discredited and has all but disappeared from the political arena. Violence in Venezuela in the early seventies was at the lowest ebb since 1957, the last full year of the Pérez Jiménez dictatorship. The FALN was still operating, but had switched its tactics from urban guerrilla warfare back to the more "conventional" rural action. A student uprising in early November, 1969, was put down by the Caldera government after it declared an end to university autonomy and troops moved in and occupied it. Published reports and photographs of armaments collected by the occupying troops might explain the remarkable diminution in violence that followed the army action. As Table 30 shows, both violence and repression were well predicted by our independent variables in the 1960s.

Presidential elections were held in Venezuela again in December, 1973, and for the first time none of the leading candidates was a member of the "Generation of 1928"—the group of men who had graduated from the National University in that year and who had formed the principal Venezuelan political parties during the 1930s. The winner, Carlos Andrés Pérez of *Acción Democrática,* was minister of interior in the Leoní administration. His election was an indication that one more step had been taken in the continued institutionalization of Venezuelan political parties, and, further, that Venezuelan democracy was more firmly established than ever. The last reported attempt at a military coup came in 1966; it was easily crushed by the government with no bloodshed. Circumstances, of course, may change in Venezuela, but the armed forces seem to be adjusting to their new role as supporters of the civilian government.

Guatemala

In 1971, Victor Perera, reported the following concerning Guatemala:

> Everywhere I looked—on the overpasses, outside banks, government buildings, foreign embassies—were angel-faced young soldiers and policemen with submachine guns on their hips. Radio patrol cars with wire cages—called perreras, or dog-catchers—cruised up and down the city in pairs, as did army trucks crammed with olive-clad soldiers armed to the teeth. Guatemala has been under a "state of siege" and virtually martial law since last November 13, four months after President Carlos Arana Osorio took office. Until mid-February, a 9 p.m. curfew (later 11 to 5) was in force, and it could be restored at any time. In the first 12 weeks after November 13, at least 1,600 persons were arrested without formal charges or arraignments, and 700 to 1000 more—among them a dozen prominent Guatemalans—were assassinated by vigilante groups of the

military and the police. Urban guerrillas with Castroite or Maoist sympathies have accounted for 25 or 30 more assassinations, mostly of army and police officers and government informers.[6]

This situation represented the high point of violence and repression that had begun in earnest in 1966—and still continues. Guatemala, third lowest in Latin America on social cohesion for the 1960s, had the most successful guerrilla movement in the hemisphere and the most brutal repression. The repression had an unusual quality. Extraordinarily harsh in some ways and rather lax in others, it was necessitated by efforts to maintain a facade of democracy while simultaneously eliminating everyone with leftist leanings. Some freedom of speech and organization was allowed, therefore, as judicial rights were blatantly disregarded and death sentences were meted out by vigilante groups acting in behalf of the security organs of the state.

For both the 1950s and the 1960s, our equations predicted considerably more repression than was detected by our method of scoring the concept. Even the limited civil liberties existing in these decades were not characteristic of countries resembling Guatemala in other ways. At the same time, Guatemala exhibited somewhat more violence than our equations foretold. Overall, then, the low social cohesion was to be expected.

The low cohesion of the 1960s was only the more recent episode of a troubled history of dictatorship and anarchy imposed upon a system of harsh exploitation of the Indian majority. From 1838 to 1865, the illiterate Rafael Carrera supported the conservative and clerical cause with his ruthless use of power. The Liberals who replaced him, while destroying the Catholic Church, were easier on the political classes but not on the Indians, until Manuel Estrada Cabrera came to power in 1898. Estrada Cabrera's ferocity and arbitrariness along with his craving for fawning adulation are well-captured by Nobel Prize-winning novelist Miguel Asturias in *El Señor Presidente*. The last dictator of the line, Jorge Ubico, took power in 1931 and ruled until overthrown by the uprising of the middle class in 1944.

The domination and exploitation of the Indian in Guatemala followed less of a paternalistic pattern and more of a South African pattern than in other parts of Latin America. Most of the Indians, who make up two-thirds of the Guatemalan population, live separated in the highland area, where they have maintained their language and culture. A system of debt peonage and vagrancy laws were developed to coerce

---

[6]Victor Perera, "Guatemala: Always la Violencia," *New York Times Magazine* (June 13, 1971).

them to work on the coffee plantations in the piedmont area. This solution provided labor at extremely low cost and absolved the landowner of responsibility for the care and nurture of the Indian family.

Following the overthrow of Ubico in 1944, a decade of rapid reform was carried out under Presidents Juan José Arévalo and Jacobo Arbenz with strikingly little violence or repression. For a moment, Guatemala seemed to enter a new era—until its land reform hit the United Fruit Company. The company was keeping ninety percent of its land uncultivated in reserves, and it had no intention of allowing it to be distributed among small landholders. The Fruit Company and the United States Central Intelligence Agency armed and trained a small force under Colonel Castillo Armas in neighboring Honduras. The military decided not to fight and the recently organized labor and peasant groups put up no resistance as Castillo Armas's band took over the government and reversed the land and labor reforms. The leaders of the incipient workers movements were jailed, killed, or fled into exile.

They could not, of course, stamp out discontent, and in the early 1960s opposition came from a surprising quarter: the military. A group of officers, among them two young lieutenants trained in counterinsurgency in the United States government programs, Marco Yon Soza and Luis Turcios Lima, revolted against the ineffective, corrupt, and pro-U.S. government of Miguel Ydígoras Fuentes in November, 1960. The revolt was quickly squelched, but the two officers took to the hills to organize and train others for guerrilla warfare. They found no lack of rural support for their movement in the *ladino* (non-Indian) areas of recent settlement. They built their organizations slowly before making any major engagements, so that it was not until 1965 that guerrilla warfare became serious. How serious, however, is uncertain because the government has suppressed all news relating to the movement, and it is difficult to assess the degree of its activity in those first years.

In the meantime, politics went on in Guatemala City as usual. The chaotic preparations for the 1963 elections, in which sixteen candidates had themselves nominated for the presidency, were cut short by the intervention of the military under Colonel Enrique Peralta Azurdia. Peralta claimed no desire to stay in power, only that he wanted to clean up the government. In any case, he gave in to pressures by the United States and allowed free elections in 1966, in which a moderate reform candidate, Julio César Mendez Montenegro, was elected president. The military allowed him to rule as long as he did not interfere with their counterinsurgency program and did nothing to offend the upper classes.

This narrowly circumscribed arena of democratic politics seemed unreal in the midst of the conflict raging outside of its control. By 1966, the guerrilla movement was operating with impunity, assassinating unjust landlords and kidnapping business executives in downtown Guatemala City. The military, with the cooperation of the United States special forces, napalmed the jungle and tortured *campesinos* without seriously weakening the movement. Without the overt consent of the government, the military and police organized, or allowed to be organized, unofficial bands of vigilantes—called *Mano* and *Ojo por Ojo*—to employ more ruthless methods. These bands indiscriminately killed anyone they suspected of any association with the guerrillas.

The military's most successful counterinsurgency operation was run by Colonel Carlos Arana Osorio, the commander of the Zacapa Brigade. In 1967 he conducted a search-and-destroy operation, assisted by vigilantes and the United States Green Berets, killing all suspects in the region and accounting for at least 2,000 deaths in the campaign. Weakened in the countryside, the guerrilla forces turned toward urban terrorism. Their most notable victim, the United States ambassador, was killed in 1968.

The right-wing vigilante groups had the audacity to kidnap the archbishop of Guatemala, Mário Casariego—who had admitted that some social problems existed in Guatemala—in the middle of Guatemala City. That move, however, was one step too far, and the army officers and police with the closest ties to the vigilantes and to Colonel Arana Osorio's military terrorists were dismissed from their posts. The dismissal was a futile gesture, however, for the right-wing groups associated with the official and unofficial terror were in full command of the situation. Indeed, they were able to intimidate the population in 1970 into electing Arana Osorio president.

In the mid-1970s the brutal killings of the right have continued with the stated purpose of exterminating all leftists in the country. However, the guerrilla movements have not been eliminated and continue to make selective raids and assassinations. No one knows how many have been killed because the fighting has gone on everywhere, and no reports come from the rural areas where the population has been decimated and people disappear and are never heard from again. One estimate is that 13,000 people had been killed between 1967 and 1972. In that period and since, the number killed by the vigilante groups has outnumbered those killed by the leftist guerrillas by a ratio of approximately ten to one.

Our equations predicted high levels of violence and repression for Guatemala, but not because of economic problems. Table 31 shows that Guatemala has quite satisfactory scores on welfare minus social mobilization, economic growth, and economic growth minus mobilization. Unlike the troubled societies of Haiti and Bolivia, Guatemala has the resources to provide a better living for its poor and still have plenty left over for investment. During the 1950s and 1960s, with the development of cotton production on the Pacific Coast and foreign investment in industries for the Central American Common Market trade, Guatemala's economy grew at about the Latin American average. By 1970 Guatemala's per capita domestic product, at $350, was almost double that of Bolivia and more than triple that of Haiti.

Guatemala's trouble stems mainly from its government's failure to provide for the general welfare. From the nineteenth century on, its governments have been accustomed to exploiting the lower classes for the benefit of the wealthy and exploiting the wealthy for the benefit of the governors. The revolutionary government from 1944 to 1954 made some brave attempts to change this tradition, but the reactionary elite, with the full support of the United States, subverted and effectively halted these efforts. The educational measures in our study picked up the lack of social benefits. Only Haiti had a worse record. The Guatemalan government has never provided any education whatever for its Indian majority, and the military rulers have always hated the national university, where students read foreign books and pick up foreign ideals. The failure of the government to care for the basic needs of the population is demonstrated in many other segments of the society as well.

Given the nature of its economy, Guatemala's tax effort is ranked fifty-one in a list of fifty-two developing countries.[7] The upper classes refuse to pay more taxes. The tax system is a regressive one in which the poor pay a larger percentage of their income than do the rich. In the 1920s and 1930s, the United Fruit Company paid lower taxes on its banana production in Guatemala than anywhere else in Central America.[8] The railway company, wholly owned until recently by the United Fruit Company, paid no taxes at all. Neither did the United States-owned electric utility company, which furthermore was one of the few utilities in the world whose rates were not regulated by the government.

The exploitive nature of the government in Guatemala emerges most dramatically in the history of labor relations and land reform. The government has used its power to assure coffee and cotton planters of the cheapest possible labor by its exploitation of the Indian. The treatment of the *ladino* worker has been only slightly better. No labor unions

    [7]Jorgen R. Lotz and Elliott R. Morss, "Measuring 'Tax Effort' in Developing Countries," *International Monetary Fund Staff Papers* 14 (1967), p. 495.
    [8]Charles David Kepner, *Social Aspects of the Banana Industry* (New York: AMS Press, 1967).

were allowed until after the 1944 revolution, and most were destroyed after the 1954 counterrevolution. Exactly the same pattern was followed in land legislation: no help for the small rural farmer, then a positive program, followed by a complete reversal.

It is not surprising that a society that treats its lower classes in this fashion has been served by one of the weakest and most reactionary Catholic Churches in Latin America. The conservative church of the first years of independence, which lent its support to the destruction of the liberal reformists, was greatly weakened by the anticlerical policy of Carrera's successor, Justo Rufino Barrios, who expropriated church lands and, in some areas, persecuted the clergy. After 1871, the weakened church provided rituals for the wealthy and government, ran a few schools for the sons of the elite, but made no stand on social issues and provided no social programs, such as *Acción Católica*, for the lower classes. In 1954 Monseñor Mariano Rosell y Arellano, the archbishop of Guatemala, used all his influence to bring down the Arbenz government, organizing a flamboyant procession carrying the venerated image of the "Black Christ of Esquipulas" through the remote villages, and publishing a Pastoral Letter denouncing communism. Our method of scoring the institutionalization of the church undoubtedly understates the total lack of any kind of constructive religious influence stemming from the Catholic Church in Guatemala.

When Jorge Ubico fell from power, no political parties existed in Guatemala. The supporters of reform constituted a loose movement rather than a party. The Communists developed the best organized political party during the revolutionary period. The counterrevolution wholly destroyed all incipient parties. The attempt to choose governments through free elections since 1958 has led to much frenetic political party activity, but little coherence. The peasant, confronted with threats of violence from all sides, "developed the practice of signing up in a number of parties since membership in one or the other would serve to appease the various outside demands."[9] The right-wing managed to manipulate the Indian vote, the urban groups supported several moderate factions, and the leftist parties were outlawed.

The military is still the primary source of political power as it has been since Rafael Carrara used it to bring himself to the presidency in 1842. Colonels Arbenz, Castillo Armas, Ydígoras Fuentes, and Peralta Azurdia headed the government from 1950 to 1966. After the interim of Mendez Montenegro from 1966 to 1970, the military again took over under Arana Osorio. In the 1974 elections, the military decided that

[9]Richard N. Adams, *Crucifixion by Power*, (Austin: University of Texas Press, 1970) p. 203.

only officers could run for the presidency, and civilian groups nominated three of differing degrees of reaction. Even so, when the government candidate lost, the government recounted the ballots and imposed its candidate.

Guatemala in the mid-1970s is rotten, and no immediate solution for making it healthy seems likely. The brutality of official violence has destroyed what humanity existed in the country. The government cannot totally destroy its opposition, and the opposition can make little headway against the ruthlessness of the repression. The Indian majority has no voice, and its passivity has been used to the advantage of the reactionary power group. Will its passivity endure? If the Indians, once partly awakened by the reforms of the revolutionary government and now by the efforts of a church conscious of social problems, should shake off their apathy and resist their exploitation, the reactionary elite would soon topple from power.

Paraguay

Paraguay is an enigma: its level of repression far exceeds that of violence. Paraguay ranks with Haiti and the Dominican Republic as one of the most politically repressive societies in Latin America. Yet its level of violence in the 1950s ranked seventh lowest, and in the 1960s it had decreased to such an extent that it was the second lowest after Costa Rica. In terms of our overall index of violence and repression, Paraguay ranked fourth in the fifties, after Bolivia, Cuba, and Argentina, but improved its position by dropping to seventh in the 1960s. What then can be said of social cohesion in Paraguay? Can constancy in repression and a considerable decline in violence indicate political stability?

Significant developments in Paraguayan history have contributed to the creation of a nation that is tenaciously proud of its national identity and possesses a racially, culturally, and socially homogeneous population. Paraguay is a *mestizo* nation. Approximately ninety-five percent of the population is a mixture of Indians and Caucasians; the remaining five percent is of pure Indian, German, Japanese, and Negro extraction. Because intermarriage of races was an acceptable and promoted policy from the earliest Spanish settlement, by 1600 some 400 original colonizers in Paraguay were far outnumbered by individuals of mixed blood. The small number of Negroes brought to Paraguay as slaves by the Spanish were completely assimilated and no trace of them as a distinct ethnic unit remains.[10] Race, unless it involves the immigra-

---

[10]See *Area Handbook for Paraguay* (Washington, D.C., U.S. Government Printing Office, 1972), pp. vii, 10, 29, 30, and 33.

tion of Brazilian Negroes, has little divisive significance in the modern context.

Despite the predominantly Tupí-Guaraní Indian strains in the population, Paraguay is not an Indian nation as are Bolivia, Peru, Mexico, and Guatemala. Unlike these countries, the problem presented by the Indian as a majority of the population (and his cultural, political, social, and economic integration into the nation) has been resolved in Paraguay. Integration of the Chaco Indians and 40,000 forest Indians in the Paraná, who are not only isolated but make up a fraction of the population, is a marginal social issue. Consequently, thorough and long-lived racial homogeneity has been one significant factor contributing to a low level of violence and relative social cohesion in Paraguay. Given the high percentage of white and *mestizo* in the population, one would expect the repression scores for the 1950s and 1960s to have been lower.

Culturally, Paraguayan society is the product of complete fusion of the original Guaraní Indian culture and the hispanic one of the early European settlers. The cultural pervasiveness of the Guaraní language, understood by ninety percent of the population and preferred as the intimate language of the nation, is an example of how cultural duality has been superseded by a national culture. Indeed, in Paraguay we have the unique Latin American example of the conquerors adopting the language of the conquered.[11] On the whole, the Indian heritage has promoted strong cultural and social cohesion. In part, this positive cultural blending is the result of the benevolent Spanish colonization in Paraguay in contrast to the rapacious domination imposed upon primitive Indian societies in Andean countries. Because Paraguay totally lacked exploitable mineral wealth, Spaniards came to colonize. Agricultural fertility, a benevolent climate, and a pattern of extensive communication and cooperation between the indigenous and colonizing peoples founded the prosperous and relatively nonexploitative *encomienda* system.

Racial mobility contributed to social mobility and an open class structure. The repressive policies of Dr. José Gaspar Rodríguez de Francia in the nineteenth century against the peninsular and creole aristocracy, and the decimation and impoverishment of first families in the Triple Alliance War, precluded the development of an exclusive upper class based on heredity. Class distinctions were weak and derived from status sources such as new wealth, education, professional position, and, especially, political and military power. Moreover,

---

[11]See Efraim Cardozo, *Breve Historia del Paraguay* (Buenos Aires: Editorial Universitaria de Buenos Aires, 1965) p. 38.

wealth differences were never extreme between the classes, and the feudal peasant-lord distinction of some societies did not exist.[12]

Participation in two Latin American wars, which halved the population and devastated the territory, forged the firm Paraguayan nationalism. After twenty-six years of isolation imposed by Francia's controversial dictatorship, Paraguay was politically unified, independent, and economically sound and self-sufficient. Citizens could boast of scrupulously honest government as well as a high literacy rate and universal primary education—and mourn the virtual elimination of the original aristocratic and intellectual classes. From 1841 to 1862 international trade and relations were normally resumed by the government of Carlos Antonio López. His son, Francisco Solano López, who followed in the authoritarian tradition, enmeshed Paraguay in the War of the Triple Alliance—against Argentina, Brazil, and Uruguay—from 1864 until 1870. The war nearly destroyed Paraguay as a people and as a political entity. Nevertheless, the steadfastness with which the war was fought against insuperable odds left a dual and contradictory heritage—the first, an unshakable nationalism and self-determination; the second, a political tradition of division and war recriminations between the nascent political parties, the *Colorados* and the *Liberals*.

The Colorado Party controlled the government from 1880 to 1904, when it was overthrown by the Liberals who remained in power until 1940. Both political groups delved into ruinous economic policies that ostensibly sought to improve deteriorated finances but that resulted in high-level corruption. Disadvantageous loans were contracted and squandered as the national debt mounted alarmingly. Extensive sales of public lands shortly after the war created numerous foreign-owned *latifundios*, a forced peonage system, and the extremely unequal distribution of land.[13] The political party system during this period was characterized by its elitism and personalism, its disruptive and divisive influence in politics and society, and its purposeful neglect of suffrage, education, social welfare, and agricultural reform. Engineered political crises, plots, and petty partisan disputes created political unrest and compromised national security and unity to the eve of the Chaco War.

In 1932 decades of disputing over the Chaco territory with Bolivia culminated in a war often termed senseless. For Paraguay, however, the retention of the Chaco was a matter of national economic and political

[12]This view is supported by Frederick Hicks, "Interpersonal Relationships and Caudillismo in Paraguay," *Journal of Inter-American Studies* 13 (January, 1971), pp. 89–111; also see Paul H. Lewis, *The Politics of Exile: Paraguay's Febrerista Party* (Chapel Hill: University of North Carolina Press, 1965) pp. xix–xx, and Joan Rubin, *National Bilingualism in Paraguay* (The Hague: Mouton, 1968) pp. 40–43.

[13]Lewis, *Politics of Exile*, p. 26.

existence; for Bolivia it was predominantly an issue of national pride. Although troubled politically, the Paraguayan people relied on their heritage of cultural unity, which they pitched against the divided Bolivian foe. The repercussions of the Chaco War on society were historic for Paraguay. Its people experienced unprecedented physical displacement, social mobilization and organization, and the most effective affirmation of national pride—defeat of a numerically and economically superior enemy. Out of the unity forged in the Chaco campaign idealism surged as parties and people pledged to maintain solidarity to eradicate problems of development. But the war also unleashed political discontents and forces that had been fermenting in Paraguay since the 1920s. Ideas of socialism, Marxism, fascism, populism, social reform, and the rejection of the traditional political parties and their system were the bases for unprecedented political turmoil that culminated in the short-lived Febrerista Revolution of 1936. Between 1940 and 1947 political peace was imposed under the personalist military dictatorship of General Higinio Morinigo until the six-month civil war of 1947. Political stabilization in 1954 under the government of General Alfredo Stroessner ended fighting between and within the Colorado Party and the military.

The economic growth-social mobilization differential proved in our study to be the most significant indicator of social violence. Paraguay ranks fourth on this dimension for the twenty years with a differential unfavorable to social violence. Although economic growth is slow in Paraguay, it nevertheless exceeds social mobilization because of the rural life-style of the people and because of low urbanization. Paraguayan social welfare is not up to the higher continental standards, but for the 1960s Paraguay ranks just below Costa Rica on the welfare-mobilization differential and first in Latin America on the school enrollment residual. Given a relatively simple agricultural and communally oriented society with low mobilization, need satisfactions in Paraguay are met by the political, social, and economic system in excess of wants generation. Thus Paraguay shared with Costa Rica—one of the more stable and socially cohesive Latin American nations—a relative welfare level in excess of social mobilization for the two decades.

The failure to institutionalize the military is an important cause of violence in Paraguay. The Chaco conflict propelled the military into the forefront of national life. With the postwar breakup of the weakly institutionalized Liberal and Colorado parties, and the Febrerista Revolution in 1936, the military by necessity became the arbiter and force behind government, and often the government itself. Thus the recent wartime pattern of civilian-military collaboration was linked with the historic tradition of extralegal changes of government. Military institutionalization reached its lowest point between 1936 and 1940, when the military's political influence became greatest. As might be expected, violence was high from 1936 to 1940. The military was divided into revolutionary and counterrevolutionary forces, and national finances and economy were beset with postwar belt-tightening and agricultural and manpower shortages. Military institutionalization from 1940 to 1949 remained low, and Paraguay for the 1950s registered the lowest military institutionalization score in all Latin America. By the next decade its score improved considerably and it ranked fourth lowest— indicating a decrease in violence during the 1960s. Improved military institutionalization should have influenced a decrease in the 1960s repression score but it did not, partly because total institutionalization did not substantially improve.

The repression score is highly influenced by the level of education expenditures as a percentage of GNP and the combined institutionalization score. Paraguay, along with Honduras and Nicaragua, had the lowest educational expenditures in the 1950s, and the second lowest after Haiti in the 1960s, thus explaining its high repression index. A large portion of education in Paraguay at all levels is carried on by private institutions considered more prestigious (ten percent on the primary level and fifty percent on the secondary). [14] In part this situation explains why the overall educational expenditures for Paraguay were low in both decades, −1.08 and −1.44 respectively, while the educational effort or percentage of school enrollment was considerably higher: 2.03 in the 1950s and 1.94 in the 1960s. Moreover, educational expenditure as a percentage of GNP is second only to defense spending and has fluctuated from 16.2 percent in 1955 to an all-time high of 19 percent in 1965. [15] Although these levels are not among the highest for Latin America, the impression of educational neglect is tempered by the realization of Paraguay's high national literacy rate, estimated at seventy-five percent for 1971. [16]

Paraguay is clearly a country with low overall institutionalization, particularly political. The Liberal and Febrerista parties were exiled after 1947, and the Stroessner faction of the Colorado Party has controlled the government since 1954. A tradition of political repression and the employment of involuntary exile as a political weapon have facilitated Colorado Party control. George Pendle has estimated that in 1956 some 500,000 to 600,000 Paraguayans lived outside the country in Argentina and Brazil—roughly one third of the then national popula-

---

[14] *Area Handbook for Paraguay*, p. vii.
[15] *Ibid.*, p. 97.
[16] *Ibid.*, p. vii, and p. 7.

tion.[17] An important impetus for Paraguayan migration has been political, but migration to Argentina has also been for economic reasons. In fact, Paraguay's cultural and geographic affinity with Argentina has been a significant demographic factor since the nineteenth century, causing Eligio Ayala to isolate it as an important national problem.[18] Exiled political groups have contradictorily contributed to both internal stability and instability. They have limited outspoken internal political dissent and informally contained official repression by their absence from the system. Yet when sustained by substantial foreign backing, they have been able to harass and threaten established regimes. Since 1962, however, the Liberal Renovation Movement has been allowed limited political freedom and criticism as the "loyal opposition" to the government. The Febrerista Party was also offered legality in 1965, and from that same year the Christian Democratic Party has bluntly criticized the regime.

The church institutionalization index has been consistently low, ranking Paraguay as the second lowest country for the two decades. The Catholic religion pervades all aspects of Paraguayan society, but severe state persecution in the nineteenth century weakened its influence and led to the church's being either neutral or progovernment in politics. Since 1968, however, sharp political criticism of regime curtailment of civil liberties has come from the hierarchy and clergy. In part outspoken criticism of the Stroessner government stems from official relaxation of repression in the late 1960s. *La Tribuna*, the leading independent daily newspaper of Asuncíon printed only international and noncontroversial national news between 1945 and 1965, but within the last seven years it has increasingly censured the government in its editorials. Indeed, between 1972 and 1974, the paper made no opinions in favor of the government.[19]

Politics is primary in Paraguay—a source of riches and advancement, a prize to be zealously attained, cherished and defended. Partly as a consequence, the two-party struggle to control the government—the nation's largest employer—has been the most divisive element in Paraguayan society. The formal and informal organization of the population into two major political parties has resulted in strong grass-root

[17]George Pendle, *Paraguay: A Riverside Nation* (London: Royal Institute of International Affairs, 1954), p. 48; see also Lewis, p. xxiii.

[18]Juan F. Pérez Acosta, "Migraciones Históricas del Paraguay a la Argentina," *Boletín de la Cámara de Comercio Argentino-Paraguaya* 13 (Buenos Aires, September, 1952), pp. 4–14.

[19]Personal interview with Luis Zacur, administrative director of *La Tribuna*, on May 1, 1974; see also Victor E. Carugati and Reinaldo Montefilpo Carvallo, *Diario "La Tribuna"* (Asuncíon: no publisher or date).

ties and binding political loyalties. The system of interpersonal partisan relationship has sustained the cultural pattern of clientelism, political patronage, and caudillistic politics. As Frederick Hicks points out, political stability continues on the grass-roots level despite limited socio-economic improvements for the lower classes by the Stroessner government.[20] Political rule founded on personal loyalty, rather than organizational, has been the basis for low party institutionalization, the proliferation of factions, and a history of interparty violence. The franchise has had little relevance within a context of elections controlled by the party in government; instead, periodic leadership "revolutions" decide which party should control the government. Moreover, shorn by Francia of its intellectual class, Paraguay has been deprived of a source of political leadership. "El Supremo" immortalized for Paraguay the mystique of the benevolent dictator as the personification and expression of the general will of the people. Although he single-mindedly sought liberty for the nation-state, he prohibited personal and civil liberty. Thus an authoritarian governing pattern, which gave newly independent Paraguay repressive peace and stability, was established and continues to influence the political future.

Despite apparent national peace, political disquiet exists in Paraguay. The outstanding issues of political and intellectual constraint, and the social ones of land inequality, and foreign control (largely Argentinian and Brazilian) of national industries and resources still fester. Exile and political and economic emigration are poor escape valves for an extremely nationalistic people. Although social mobilization is low in Paraguay, the people are politically aware and active. So far, the division of scarce political and economic spoils among members of the party in power, while the "out" party endures hardship, has been an accepted cultural practice. Ruling Colorados and their affiliates enjoy a sense of relative advancement and prosperity, and although Liberals complain of specific deprivations, they have not questioned this exclusivist spoils distribution system. Mutual aid and patronage roles of both parties and the unifying force that political rivalry stimulates have diverted criticism from the political system *per se,* and undercut the development of lower-class discontent over slow social and economic progress.[21] Nevertheless, repressive stability generates its own ironic contradictions. First, it harasses the development of strong national institutions and interest groups that oppose the established order. Second, it controls and slows social mobilization and welfare because their successes can speed the downfall of the regime.

[20]Hicks, "Interpersonal Relationships."
[21]*Ibid.*

Third, repressive stability tends to deteriorate into political chaos when the repression is lifted—clearly the lesson of the Paraguayan political past and the danger in its future.

Haiti

Haiti has always been one of the most repressive countries in the world. More recently, the dictatorships of François ("Papa Doc") Duvalier (1957–1971) and his son Jean Claude (or "Bebe Doc") have killed all internal opposition and have successfully crushed all invasion attempts by exiles. We have fairly successfully predicted these high levels of repression for both decades, but we have consistently overpredicted the level of violence in Haiti.

What, then, are the major factors which explain violence and repression in Haiti? The lack of institutionalization of political parties (there are none), the Catholic Church (Duvalier wrecked the minimal hold it might have had on the Haitian people), and the military (the *Garde Haitien* was decimated by Duvalier and replaced by the *Tontons Macoutes*, a band of thugs) was a prime factor explaining the high levels of repression in Haiti. The economic decay and plummeting education expenditures of the 1960s also contributed to the repression and to the significantly higher levels of violence in the 1960s.

Still, we are faced with the perplexing question of why there has not been the overwhelming surge of violence predicted, not only by us, but by other scholars as well. Part of the answer lies in the fact that certain conditions commonly thought to be instigators of violence, such as inequality and poverty, simply do not produce violence in the real world. Also much of the error in predicting violence in Haiti stems from the extremely low level of social mobilization of the Haitian peasantry—and from Haitian history. It is probable that the degree of parochialism, resistance to change, and utter disengagement from politics are so complete that they differ in kind rather than in degree from the rest of Latin America. Decades of tyranny have taught the peasants that all Haitian governments will act in a ruthless, grasping manner, so that it does not really matter who is in the palace in Port-Au-Prince. Disengagement is the policy of prudence.[22]

When the extraordinary repression and extremely effective use of terror by the Duvalier regime is considered, the wonder is that anyone was willing to risk his life in an attempt to overthrow the dictatorship.

[22]Robert I. Rotberg, *Haiti: The Politics of Squalor* (Boston: Houghton Mifflin, 1971), pp. 20–24.

"Modern" Haiti is very much a prisoner of its past, and there is little indication of any real changes in the national life of the unhappy republic.

Argentina

Argentina is the most modern nation in all of Latin America. Walt W. Rostow estimated that Argentina was the first Latin American nation to pass his mythical "take-off" point in economic growth, and that this event occurred some time in the 1930s. Argentina consistently ranks highest in societal welfare of all the Latin American republics— considerably higher than either Uruguay or Venezuela, its nearest competitors. Subjective impressions confirm the data. The visitor to Buenos Aires is impressed, above all, by the fact that it has been a great city for a number of years and has a certain permanence about it that is lacking, in, say, Bogotá or Caracas. (The story is told of the Bogotano who went to Paris, looked around in amazement, and exclaimed, "It's finished!" He would probably have the same reaction if he went to Buenos Aires.)

Argentina also rivals many of the "developed" nations of the world in communications, with more newspapers, radio, and television per capita than any other Latin American nation. The northernmost section of the country might be classed as tropical or semitropical, but most of the populated land area lies within the temperate zone. Argentina's population is almost entirely European. Indians and blacks are rare, and a higher proportion of the Argentine population is non-Spanish (primarily Italian) than in any other Latin American country. Finally, Argentina is one of the most highly urbanized nations in the world; almost eighty percent of its people live in urban centers—most of them in the Buenos Aires megalopolis.

Argentina, however, has not only experienced violence and repression like other Latin American nations in recent years, it has practically bathed in both. From 1950 to 1970 Argentina had more violence than any other country in Latin America except Bolivia, Colombia, and Guatemala. In the same years, the nation was the fifth most repressive in Latin America, behind Paraguay, Haiti, the Dominican Republic, and Cuba. The country's violence totals for the 1960s were considerably higher than in the 1950s, whereas repression declined somewhat in the sixties due mainly to a relaxation of tensions during the Frondizi regime in 1964 and 1965. (see Table 30).

In Latin America those nations which enjoy more or less coherent politics appear to have gone through a political evolution that has led to the current state of affairs. Moreover, they seem to have certain economic and social conditions that further social cohesion. In the case of Argentina, the crucial historical factor that hindered the development of a political consensus, brought the military into politics, and probably fostered the rise of the Peronist movement as well, was the failure of the middle-class political party—the Radicals—to meet the challenges of institutionalization and national leadership during the 1920s. More personally, the state of present-day Argentine politics can be attributed to the failure of the leader of the *Unión Cívica Radical* (UCR), Hipólito Irigoyen, to seize the opportunities offered him between the years of 1916 and 1930 to forge a new middle-class political philosophy and ruling coalition capable of governing Argentina in the future. Irigoyen, who occupied the presidency from 1916 to 1920 and again from 1928 until his overthrow by the military in 1930, dominated the politics of the entire period, but was remiss in producing any viable political institutions. The "middle sectors" emerged during these fourteen years, but they failed to organize politically and to provide political leadership and consensus to the Argentine nation.

Perhaps another basically historical reason for the current Argentine malaise relates to the great European immigration between 1880 and 1930. As early as 1890, estimates placed the number of foreign-born Argentines at one million out of a total population of four million. The immigrants who came to Argentina came almost exclusively from Spain and Italy. Unlike the Irish (and Italian) immigrants in the United States, the Italians generally did not participate in the politics of Argentina in the crucial decades of the twenties and thirties, and even today many of the sons and daughters of the former immigrants are interested in politics only insofar as it affects the Argentine economy. The reasons for this lack of civic culture on the part of the immigrants are unclear. Perhaps part of the explanation lies in the overwhelmingly economic motive for most of the immigration, while part of it may be attributed to the antagonistic attitude toward the immigrants held by many of the old elite. John Gunther quotes one member of the elite as saying that immigration "wrecked the tradition" of the country, and that the immigrants "mongrelized" Argentina.[23]

By 1930 Irigoyen and the Radicals were, because of their failure to produce any meaningful reforms, thoroughly discredited, and the military take-over that year met no opposition. Within two years the military had returned control of the country to the Conservatives, who ruled until the military coup in 1943. The army-Conservative coalition remained in power for thirteen years, from 1930 to 1943, returning

[23]John Gunther, *Inside South America* (New York: Harper & Row, 1967), p. 176.

again and again, simply because it had the physical power to do so. By the 1940s, however, the Conservative ruling philosophy was thoroughly discredited among the middle class and among the rapidly growing urban proletariat, the *descamisados*, or shirtless ones, to whom Juan Perón later directed his appeal. Argentina in the 1930s and 1940s, then, was characterized by political drift, alienation, and disillusionment.

The coup of 1943 eventually brought to power—in the elections of 1946, which by all accounts were quite honest—Juan Domingo Perón. Perón was the new leader of the disillusioned proletariat and for much of the Argentine middle class. Although his regime became increasingly dictatorial, he acquired and retained the support of between one third and one half of the country's voters simply by providing them with a vague political ideology and with real material benefits that gave some meaning to their political actions. *Justicialismo* (the official name for the Peronist ideology) never really amounted to more than Argentine populism, with its promises to the forgotten Argentine sounding like a forerunner of George Wallace and his "forgotten American." Yet, alienation was so much greater in Argentina, and the abasement of the old-line parties so much more advanced than in the United States, that the populist programs of Perón gained widespread acceptance. As popular as Perón was, however, he managed during his nine years in office to offend substantial interests in the nation, most especially an appreciable sector of the Argentine military and the hierarchy of the Catholic Church. Even so, Perón and his ideology continued to exert a pull on the sympathies of many Argentines, and after his exile in 1955 the bifurcated nature of Argentine politics became ever more evident. Various political groups during the nineteenth and twentieth centuries had been able to create a unified nation from what were formerly warring provinces, but a positive sense of national will had not been engendered. In the 1950s and 1960s—and, indeed, to the mid-1970s—Argentines were sharply divided between two views of the nature of the state. On the one side were the conservative oligarchy and substantial portions of the military (the *quedantistas*, or *colorados*) who saw the Peronists as an unmitigated evil, and who wanted a return to some sort of society controlled by the landed elite and in which labor was kept in its place. On the other side were the Peronists, now awakened into political consciousness by Perón—and his wife Eva—who wanted to eradicate the last vestiges of the landed elite, who saw the army as their sworn enemies, and who wanted an Argentine state run more or less on the populist lines put forth by the official doctrine of Peronism. In between were the Radicals who, after one last gasp during the Frondizi adminstration from 1958 to 1962, subsided into impotence.

In spite of the decadence of Argentine politics from the late 1920s, serious violence did not erupt until the removal of Perón by the military. It was "relatively simple for the military to remove Perón,"[24] but the violence that surrounded the coup demonstrated both the deep divisions in the Argentine polity and the tremendous popularity of Perón among the urban proletariat, many of whom were willing to put their lives on the line for Perón and Peronism. Many contemporary accounts of the 1955 coup tend to gloss over the extensive bloodshed that engulfed Argentina before, during, and after Perón's removal in September. From June through November the entire country was wracked by violence, first from a series of unsuccessful coup attempts against the Perón regime, and later from resistance by the pro-Peronist forces to the successful revolt.

Much of recent Argentine political history, and the rather extensive violence that has been a part of that history, has been tied one way or another to the continuing deep divisions between the *peronistas* and their opponents. The Argentine military has been split in its attitudes toward the Peronists, with the *azul* (blue) faction generally advocating a soft line, and the *colorado* (red) faction (or *gorilas*, as they are called) proposing a much harder attitude. General Eduardo Lonardi, who was the original leader of the September coup against Perón, lasted only fifty days in office because of his unwillingness to take repressive measures against the Peronists. General Pedro Aramburu, who replaced him, was a *colorado*, and he dedicated his two-year provisional government to an attempt—unsuccessful—at eradicating the last vestiges of Peronism. In 1956 the Aramburu regime had to contend with a *peronista* revolt, which was put down after an air bombardment of rebel Peronist positions in Buenos Aires. A year later, on the fifth anniversary of Eva Perón's death, a demonstration of thousands of workers in support of Peronism in the streets of Buenos Aires and La Plata was finally quelled through the use of tear gas.

Elections in 1958 brought in the civilian government of Arturo Frondizi, in what was probably the last hurrah of the old-line political parties in Argentina. In that year, the UCR, which had managed to retain some political coherency through the Peronist years, split into two factions over the question of the party's attitude toward the Peronists. Frondizi headed the younger leaders within the party who favored cooperation with the Peronists, and who constituted themselves as the *Unión Cívica Radical Intransigente* (UCRI), whereas the older leaders took the title of *Unión Cívica Radical Popular* (UCRP). The real significance of the schism was not ideological but political, as it meant the

---

[24]Peter G. Snow, *Political Forces in Argentina* (Boston: Allyn and Bacon, 1971), p. 15.

serious weakening of the UCR as an institutionalized political party, and it paved the way for the increased military repression of the 1960s.

The civilian Frondizi government, while easing the repressive policies of the former military regimes, attracted more violence. It emanated from both the Peronists, who did not accept Frondizi's olive branch, and from the *gorilas*, who felt Frondizi was being too soft on them. In 1960 the government put down an attempted coup by a rural military garrison, and later an attempted revolution by Peronists in the port of Rosario. Both efforts failed, but the pro-Peronist General Confederation of Workers (*Confederación General de Trabajadores*—CGT) began calling general strikes with more frequency and with more effect. These successes, coupled with that of the Peronists in the 1962 congressional and provincial elections (in which Frondizi allowed them to participate) prompted Frondizi's removal by the military in March, 1962. The president of the Senate, José Maria Guido, then became president, and served until 1964 as a puppet of the *azul* faction in the military. Guido's tenure was threatened by an attempted *colorado* coup in September, 1962, but the crisis was resolved in favor of the *azules*, after some fighting in Buenos Aires. The *azules* permitted national elections in July, 1963, without participation by the *peronistas*; the result was another "civilian" administration, this one under an aged country doctor, Arturo Illia. Illia immediately adopted a stance designed to keep the military out of politics, but pressure from the Peronists, as well as strife within the military, resulted in yet another military coup in June, 1966. The *azules*, headed by General Juan Carlos Onganía, took over the government, and Argentina remained under military rule for the remaining years of the decade. Repression, which had dropped substantially under Illia, increased as mass arrests of Peronists and Communists occurred. Labor leaders were also harassed, political parties were dissolved, and the National University was invaded by troops. These tactics caused an initial decrease in violence during 1967 and 1968, but by 1969, bombings, demonstrations, strikes, and assorted terrorist acts were again on the upswing.

The nation recently returned to civilian rule—this time with the chief Peronist himself in charge once more, Juan Perón. Upon Perón's death in 1974 his third wife, Isabel, became president. She is the first woman president in the Western Hemisphere, and she faces some formidable problems, including urban terrorism by the People's Revolutionary Army (*Ejército Revolucionario del Pueblo*—ERP), opposition by certain sectors of the military, and inflation coupled with a sluggish economy. Repression decreased noticeably since the inauguration of Perón, but violence—especially armed violence—has become more and more prevalent. Table 30 indicates that our predictors of both violence and repression were quite accurate in Argentina during both decades.

The Argentine picture is one of a relatively rich and modern nation, but of a nation that has failed to develop the political and social institutions necessary to resolve conflicts. Further, the Argentine economy has not kept pace with greater social mobilization; and the result has been an increase in demands that Argentine society has not been able to meet. In addition to these basic problems, Argentina has been beset since the early 1950s by a continual dispute over the basic rules of the political game. All these problems erupted in a massive outburst of violence in the mid-1950s, in high levels of repression whenever the frequent military regimes have been in control, and in a recent escalation in urban terrorism, much of which seems to be directed against the Peronists as well as against the military and the old elite. As Table 30 indicates, both the predicted and the actual levels of violence and repression in Argentina were high for both decades.

Our indicators slightly under-predicted violence for the 1950s, which is at least partially explained by two factors: the accession of the *gorilas* to power from 1956 to 1958, and the almost total breakup of the UCR in 1958. We slightly overpredicted repression for the same period, and this can be explained by the temporary peace pact between the military and the Frondizi government beginning in 1958. In the 1960s we overpredicted violence, but were accurate in our prediction of repression. The violence differential can best be explained by the fact that in the last years of the decade the Argentine economy began to perform more efficiently and the gap between the increase in social mobilization and economic growth was narrowed somewhat. The basic facts of Argentine political life in the 1970s remain much as they were during the two previous decades. A lack of institutionalized means of resolving conflicts, an economy that has not kept pace with increased social mobilization, a government that does not perform as well as might be expected, and continuing divisions among the politically active parts of the Argentine population over the basic purpose of the nation, all conspire to prevent Argentina from achieving social cohesion.

CHAPTER 9

REVOLUTIONARY COUNTRIES

What differentiates a social revolution from other radical changes within a society, changes that might be called revolutions but are not? This definitional problem has long plagued political scientists interested in the phenomena of revolutions. As far as we know, there is no definitive answer to the question. We do know, however, that one aspect of all past social revolutions has been extensive violence, so that there is good empirical evidence to support the idea that societies which have experienced violence substantially greater than other societies may have experienced a social revolution. Other conditions—a change in social relations, changes affecting the daily life of members of the society, and new political and economic rules—are also viewed as necessary but not fulfilling criteria for social revolution.

From our concern with violence and repression in Latin America, plus our knowledge of Latin American history, we can identify two societies in which social revolutions took place during the two decades of our study. The 1952 revolution in Bolivia and the 1959 revolution in Cuba are two of only three such revolutions in all of Latin American history, the third being the Mexican. Social revolutions, then, are rare and deserve extended treatment. From our vantage point, the revolutions in Cuba and Bolivia can be defined operationally as situations in which violence, for varying time spans, became much more intense than in the other nations of Latin America. Further, the violence in both societies led to changes in the status quo ante, a result markedly dissimilar from that following upheavals and coups in the other nations of Latin America. Table 32 shows the extent of violence in Bolivia and Cuba during the 1950s and 1960s as well as our predicted levels of violence and repression for the same periods. Table 33 demonstrates, in part, why Bolivia and Cuba were such violent societies. The extended treatments of these two countries in this chapter include descriptions of the social and political processes that led to the violence and that have resulted in vastly dissimilar social resolutions.

Cuba

Cuba's history during the past two decades has been more frenetic in terms of repression and violence, than that of any other Latin American nation. Cuba had the highest five-year total of violence in Latin America, and its ten-year total during the 1950s was the highest in the hemisphere. Cuba's repression totals were also high. In the 1960s, while violence in Cuban society apparently abated considerably, repression totals climbed. It was a new type of repression for Latin America. It was repression used not to maintain the status quo but to change it and create a new order. Moreover, class relationships have

Table 32. Revolutionary Countries

| | | Dependent Variables[a] | | | |
| | | 1950s | | 1960s | |
Country	Variable	Actual	Predicted	Actual	Predicted
Bolivia	Violence	1.47	1.48	1.45	.64
	Repression	.66	.43	−.23	−.16
	Viol. & Rep.	1.41	1.42	.80	.22
Cuba	Violence	2.01	.69	n.a.	n.a.
	Repression	−.04	−.02	n.a.	n.a.
	Viol. & Rep.	1.31	.46	n.a.	n.a.

[a]All scores are standard.

Table 33. Revolutionary Countries

| | Independent Variables[a] | | | |
| | 1950s | | 1960s | |
Variable	Cuba	Bolivia	Cuba	Bolivia
Welfare minus mobilization	−2.55	−1.52	n.a.	−2.14
Economic growth minus social mobilization	−.97	−2.04	n.a.	.48
Educational effort	−.63	−.76	n.a.	−.51
Educational expenditure	1.55	−.94	n.a.	.82
Party institutionalization	−.22	.63	n.a.	.06
Military institutionalization	−.48	−1.48	n.a.	−1.42
Church institutionalization	−.30	−.04	n.a.	−.33
Total institutionalization	−.41	−.38	n.a.	−.69
White + mestizo as percent of population	−.37	−.63	n.a.	−.63

[a]All scores are standard.

been reordered and a new societal order has been established. In other words, Cuba has undergone a true social revolution.

Cuba, then, is a special case in any study of Latin American nations, and some reasons for its radically different history from the 1950s to the 1970s must be advanced. As Fidel Castro tightened his grip on the nation and became ever more stridently anti-U.S., many North Americans were asking, "Why Cuba?" This is the question we hope to answer. Our explanatory variables predicted much of the violence that was to ensue in Cuba during the latter half of the 1950s, though the actual violence was greater than our variables had indicated. Even though we closely predicted the actual level of repression, we foresaw less social disintegration in Cuba during the fifties than actually took place. Therefore, while our independent variables go far toward explaining why Cuba experienced the tremendous violence from 1957 onward, additional explanations are also in order.

First of all, the tremendous violence in Cuba in the 1950s, the concomitant social revolution, and the subsequent consolidation of that revolution on a nationalist, socialist, anti-United States model cannot be understood if the history of Cuba prior to the 1950s is ignored. Some have drawn parallels between Cuba of 1959 and Mexico of 1910, and even Bolivia in 1952; others have treated Cuba as if its history began with the second *Batistato* in 1952. Both these approaches, however, overlook two factors basic to an understanding of the Cuban situation.

First, Cuba in 1959 was not the premobilized Mexico of Porfirio Díaz or the remote Bolivia of the tin barons. The fact is that Cuba in the 1920s and early 1930s had already entered a revolutionary period: a popular revolutionary party had been formed, a constitution emphasizing social legislation had been adopted, and a new sense of nationalism prevailed. Probably the most important element in understanding subsequent Cuban history was the new nationalism which, because of the geographical, economic, and political situation of the island, would inevitably have to become anti-United States in its direction. Adding to the potential explosiveness of the Cuban situation in the 1950s were several other factors. First, Cubans had become rather highly politicized as a result of the massive popular participation in the overthrow of Gerardo Machado in 1933, and this politicalization process had continued through the 1930s and 1940s. Second, the overthrow in 1934 of the revolutionary and genuinely popular government of Ramón Grau San Martín produced a sense of frustration among many members of what was then the Cuban left. This frustration over the inability to effect meaningful reforms of Cuban society was compounded among many members of the *Auténticos* and the *Partido Socialista Popular* by subsequent events in Cuba up to the 1950s. The ten-year period from 1934 to 1944 was one of a return to the status quo ante under Fulgencio Batista, with a diminished United States political presence being counterbalanced by increased United States economic investment in the developing industrial sector of the Cuban economy. The years from 1944 to 1952 provided even greater frustration and disappointment for those who had believed in the ideals of the revolution of 1933 as the leaders of that revolution—Grau San Martín and Carlos Prío Socarrás— were each elected to the presidency and each responded by largely betraying (or at least ignoring) the ideals of the revolutionary movement they had created some years earlier.

A third factor that influenced the course of events in Cuba, if not the levels of violence and repression, was the complicity of the United States in the destruction of the 1933 revolution and in the subsequent reigns of Batista. This complicity meant that the Cubans interested in an overthrow of the status quo in Cuba would become convinced that the United States was their natural enemy, and that any subsequent revolutionary movement would have to contend with not only Cuban antirevolutionary forces, but the force of the United States government as well.

Thus, Cuba in the 1950s had a history of continued and widespread frustration at the inability of the "progressive" groups in Cuban society to produce basic reforms. As Orlando Fals-Borda has suggested in his book, *Subversion in Colombia*, such frustration can become a catalyst for extensive violence. Cuba in the early 1950s exhibited other lesions that contributed to subsequent events. Foremost among these was the inequality of development between Havana and the rest of the country. By the 1950s Havana had become a great, modern city, whereas the rest of the country was left far behind. Cuba's industrialization based on the sugar economy that had persisted for so long, was concentrated almost exclusively in and around Havana, while the Provinces of Las Villas, Camagüey, and Oriente remained virtually stagnant. Even within rapidly modernizing Havana there were obvious inequalities of income and social status that rankled the growing Cuban petite bourgeoisie. Additionally, this group, whose aspirations had been raised by some early economic success, now found further advancement blocked not only by a coalition of the Cuban sugar aristocracy and the expanding number of United States entrepreneurs who were involved in much of the industrial and commercial growth in and around Havana, but by a relatively stagnant economy. Early in the 1950s, then, one of Crane Brinton's key preconditions for revolution—a middle class with frustrated economic aspirations—had already been fulfilled. Revlon had captured the Cuban cosmetic market, the Hedges family was producing textile fabrics, Powe Machinery was supplying the needs of Cuban agriculture, Coca-Cola was there, the Las Vegas mob had taken over the thriving prostitution and gambling markets, and on and on. Small wonder that the Cuban middle class supported the revolutionary efforts against Batista, who was identified in the popular mind with these new North American interests.

Several other phenomena also contributed to the preconditions for revolution. A strong Roman Catholic Church did not exist. Mass on Sunday mornings was a social event attended by women, and the clergy exerted little or no moral authority over the mass of the Cuban people. Coupled with this lack of institutionalization on the part of the church was a widespread sense of both public and private immorality, especially in metropolitan Havana. Both gambling and prostitution were controlled by Las Vegas interests, and both pastimes depended upon the North American tourist for much of their income. Public morality, which had surfaced fitfully during previous Cuban history, was largely a dead letter by the 1950s. The corruption and venality of the Grau and Prío administrations had destroyed any faith in popular government that might have been kindled in the early 1930s, and once Batista returned to power, the issue was hardly ever raised. The most sought-after public office under Batista was director of customs for the Port of Havana, precisely because it offered the greatest opportunity for graft. The vice president of the republic supplemented his income by exerting pressure on the American Embassy to grant visas to those who were willing to pay for his services. One senator, Rolando Masferrer, kept his own army of private thugs who functioned alternately as a Mafia operation and as a terrorist group to silence Batista's critics. Another senator built "the world's largest theater" for his first wife and, after divorce and remarriage, proceeded to build an hotel-apartment complex overshadowing the theater for his second wife.

Cuba in the 1950s was also a racially discriminatory society. Blacks were concentrated in the poorer eastern provinces of the island, while those in the Havana area became domestic servants or filled some other low-status employment. Persons with Negro blood (suspected or proven) were not allowed into the many clubs which preempted the beaches in and around Havana, and Batista himself was reputed to have been denied membership in the prestigious Havana Country Club because of suspected Negro blood. Blacks emigrating to the United States often gave as the reason the milder forms of discrimination in the United States. Miscegenation involving the elite was virtually unknown, at least in the Havana area.

Perhaps most importantly, by the 1950s the institutions that had given direction (or had at least had the promise of giving direction) to Cuban life in earlier times had largely ceased to have any directive influence on the Cuban people. In short, Cuba's daily life had become unhinged, and a sense of anomie pervaded its daily existence. We have already alluded to the inefficacy of the Catholic Church, but the same was true of the nascent political parties of the early 1930s. The ABC Party had been seriously compromised by their opposition to the revolution of 1933, and their subsequent complicity with Batista. The *Auténticos,* who were the heirs of the revolution, had been discredited by the excesses of the Grau and Prío administrations. No new political institutions had risen to take their place, and the only institutionalized political party in Cuba in the early 1950s was the *Partido Socialista Popular* (PSP—the Cuban Communist Party) a party dedicated to the overthrow of the whole system. The Cuban military, which had become accustomed to participating in coups through the years, participated in yet another in 1952, thus further decreasing its support for any civilian system of government. In such a situation, it was not surprising that Cubans exhibited a startling lack of regard for others in their daily relations.

Cuba in the 1950s then, was a country characterized by an extraordinary amount of political alienation and frustration. Its institutions were weak, and its economy was deficient. It was a country in which nationalist anti-United States sentiments were widespread, and it was a country that had experienced an abortive social revolution—one that, nonetheless, prepared the way for a later, more successful revolutionary movement.

At the beginning of the decade, Prío Socarrás, one of the youthful leaders of the revolution of 1933, was midway through his term of office as president of the republic. He had been preceded by the hero of the 1933 revolution, Grau San Martín, who had been elected president in 1944, and had served his full term until 1948. Grau, as indicated above, had completely changed from the reformist of 1933, and his four years in office had been years of graft and corruption high even by Cuban standards. A $40 million indictment had been brought against Grau for fraud while in office, and though he was never convicted, an indictment of a key government official was unheard of in the relatively relaxed atmosphere of Cuban politics.

Prío had come to power in the elections of 1948—the last contested elections Cuba has experienced—as the candidate of the *Auténticos* and Grau's political heir. He had been opposed by Ricardo Nuñez Portuondo, representing a coalition of the old Liberal, Democratic, and Republican parties (and also of Batista's interests); Juan Marinello of the PSP; and Eduardo Chibás representing a reformist wing of the *Auténticos*, later to be called *Ortodoxos*. Chibás's influence on Cuban politics at this time and later is hard to fathom. He was a truly charismatic personality who made excellent use of radio to arouse popular enthusiasm, and undoubtedly raised the hopes of many that the goals of the 1933 revolution might yet be realized within the framework of the constitutional government. At the same time, Chibás was mercurial to the point of irrationality, and he thus sparked hopes and inflamed passions without any real hope of dealing with Cuba's problems. Chibás probably contributed further to the frustration and alienation of the masses. Certainly his suicide in August, 1952, after a highly unsuccessful debate with Minister of Education Sanchez Arango, further exacerbated an unstable situation. Chibás, "accomplished in his own death the destruction of Cuban political life—even ruining his own party, for they never recovered from his death, finding a worthy successor impossible to decide on."[1]

Prío's term in office was in most respects a continuation of the Grau administration. Graft and venality continued apace, as did political intrigue. Perhaps Prío's major achievement, aside from stealing money, was the harassment of the PSP through arrests of its members, attempted assassinations of its leaders, and a continuous campaign

---

[1]Hugh Thomas, *Cuba: The Pursuit of Freedom* (New York: Harper & Row, 1971), p. 438.

aimed at closing the Communist daily newspaper, *Hoy*. Except for the badgering of Communists, however, repression and violence for the last two years of the Prío administration were low. What violence there was pertained to the 1950 municipal elections, though early 1952 saw an increase in armed violence as the Prío administration drew to a close and political groups jockeyed for position in the May presidential elections.

The elections were never held, however. In the early morning hours of March 10, 1952, Fulgencio Batista struck with a well-organized coup d'etat. By the afternoon of the same day, all contemplated resistance (there was no actual resistance) had collapsed and Batista was once more in command of Cuba.

The year 1952 marked a definite change in Cuban history in many ways. Obviously, from then on Cuban political life was characterized not by democratic governments, corrupt as they were, but by a grinding personal dictatorship. The basic political issues became not honesty in government, but even more essential ones—a return to legal and constitutional government, torture by a secret police, the duration of Batista's tyrany. From 1952 to 1959 both government and opposition utilized increasing amounts of violence to further their causes. The two violences fed on each other in a spiral unequaled in the rest of Latin America. Opposition violence brought government repression, often of the most senseless and barbaric kind, while government repression engendered more strident opposition from ever-widening groups of Cubans. By 1957 and 1958, when Cuban violence and repression were both at their peak, daily life in Cuba had become extremely insecure, even for the ordinary citizen. Bombs were being smuggled into movie theaters and exploded randomly, while the Batista secret police—the dreaded *Servicio Inteligencia Militar*—responded to escalating terrorist acts by taking hostages and torturing and killing innocent bystanders. Entire blocks around some police stations from which the SIM operated were uninhabited because of the screams in the night of the torture victims. As the Batista regime became more beleaguered, the use of terror by the SIM became more and more bizarre and beyond the control of anyone, including Batista himself. No one was safe. It was as if Cuba had a secret government, answerable to no one and unaccountable to itself.

Batista's actions during the first days of his new regime were intended to obliterate any opposition to him from the middle-class *Auténticos*. Initially, the guarantees under the 1940 constitution were suspended, as well as the right to strike. In April, 1952, Batista proclaimed a new constitution which provided for much greater leeway in the suspension of speech, assembly, and press. New elections were slated for November, 1953, but until then all political parties were suspended. The old Congress was thrown out, and a new hand-picked Consultative Council replaced it. Batista also quickly rallied to his side Cuba's leading exponent of political gangsterism, Rolando Masferrer. Masferrer, a senator from Oriente, lived in the upper-class Havana suburb of Miramar, and maintained a battery of henchmen at his Miramar residence as well as in Oriente. Masferrer remained one of Batista's most faithful and effective supporters from then until 1959. In the last months of 1958, when the Cuban army was disintegrating, Masferrer's army quite literally became Batista's major fighting arm against the revolutionary forces. A final prop for the new Batista regime proved to be the national Cuban labor confederation, the CTC. Led by Eusebio Mujal, its secretary-general, former *Auténtico* labor leaders quickly swung over to the new government in return for unspecified favors, which undoubtedly included money and power.

Opposition to the *Batistato* was at first disorganized and ineffective. Even though violence increased rather markedly during 1952 and 1953, most of it was a spontaneous reaction on the part of individuals to specific acts of the regime. The only early organized opposition came from the students at the University of Havana, and in the press from the editorial pages of *Bohemia,* the great Cuban weekly news magazine.

It was a former student at the University of Havana, Fidel Castro Ruz, who led the first serious armed opposition to the Batista regime. On July 26, 1953, two forces of armed men attacked the Moncada military barracks in Santiago and in Bayamo. Although the revolutionists were outnumbered by about ten to one, they counted on surprise (the attack came at 5:30 A.M.) and the fact that the date coincided with carnival time in Santiago. Unfortunately for the Castro group, the surprise element was lost in the early moments of the attack, and perhaps eighty of the original one hundred and sixty revolutionaries were captured and put to death, most after torture. Those who escaped (Castro among them) were subsequently captured and brought to trial. The initial brutal reaction of the Batista army, however, caused a wave of revulsion throughout the hitherto apathetic middle class, and created additional opponents to the *Batistato* and additional sympathy for the nascent *26 de Julio* movement. Castro was tried in September and October and was sentenced to fifteen years' imprisonment. But the memory of the episode could not so easily be dispatched:

> The consquences on public opinion of Moncada and its aftermath were considerable. Had it not been for the repression, the Moncada attack would doubtless have been dismissed as one more wild and semi-gangster

incident in the life of Fidel Castro. The repression and the trial made Castro appear henceforth something of a hero. Professional, catholic, liberal, or middle class opinion was outraged.[2]

For some time after the Moncada episode, Cuban life veered toward normalcy. Harassment of the Communists increased, but restrictions on other political parties diminished, and Batista announced that general elections would be held in November, 1954. Press censorship was soon lifted, and the ninety-day suspension of civil rights came to an end in late October, 1953. The promise of elections, plus the jailing of Castro, took the wind out of the sails of those who wanted to overthrow Batista by force. The year 1954, while marred by various incidents of violence on the part of both government and opposition, was one of the most peaceful in recent Cuban history. The Cuban middle class seemed to believe that political gangsterism had been curbed, if not ended, and that government corruption was not as great as it had been under the *Auténticos*. The University was still in constant turmoil, and terrorist bombings were still commonplace, but Batista seemed to be steering a more moderate course.

Batista's position was made more secure by two additional factors: a booming economy and the support of the United States. The economy, based on sugar, was expanding at an irregular but significant pace. The year 1952 had been an excellent one for sugar production in Cuba and the harvest, coupled with rising world prices for sugar and the assured United States price, helped spur the Cuban economy. Although 1953 and 1954 were not as good years as 1952, both prices and production remained at relatively high levels. Massive new United States investments were also being made in what was now a most favorable climate for foreign private investment. New laws granting favorable tax treatment for private investment from abroad were put into effect, thus increasing the flow of foreign capital into Cuba. Meanwhile, the United States government expressed its most favorable attitude toward the regime. The new United States Ambassador to Cuba, Arthur Gardner, was an unashamed admirer of Batista and his government, while the career foreign service officers, beset by McCarthyism and its aftereffects went along with policies they may not have agreed with. In February, 1955, Vice President Nixon went to Havana to give the regime his blessing, and in April Allen Dulles, the new director of the Central Intelligence Agency, paid a visit. In mid-April of 1955, Batista relaxed and declared a general amnesty for all political prisoners,

[2]Ibid., p. 843.

and on May 15, Castro, his brother Raúl, and eighteen followers, left their prison home on the Isle of Pines. A short time later Castro left to take up residence in Mexico, and to plan his return to Cuba.

Between May, 1955, and March, 1956, several events occurred that portended more violence. First, the so-called *diálogo cívico,* which had been going on between Batista and a group of opposition leaders, led nowhere, and in March, after Batista had publicly ridiculed the demands of the group, the dialogue was ended. Second, the University students, who were more and more isolated from the feeling of the general population, finally gave up on their tactics of opposing from within the University and formed the new revolutionary organization known as the *Directorio Revolucionario,* whose aims were to gather together all who were interested in fighting Batista. Third, from Mexico Castro issued a pronouncement separating himself from all party alliances in Cuba and issuing a call to all those opposing Batista to take up arms under the banner of the July 26 Movement.

The early months of 1956 were marked by several plots and attacks on the Batista regime by elements within the Cuban Army, from both the right and left. Through the spring and summer antigovernment violence from these groups and from the *Directorio Revolucionario* was met with increasing repression by the Batista regime. All plots against Batista were overcome. By the end of November, 1956, when Castro finally sailed from Mexico for Cuba, the forces for future peace in Cuba were quiescent while those for violence were in the ascendent. On December 2, 1956, after a diversionary uprising by *26 de Julio* forces in Santiago nearly captured the city, Castro and his followers disembarked on the Cuban shore. From that time on the Batista government was faced with a disciplined and growing guerilla war.

The last few days of 1956 and the first of 1957 were marked by a rapid increase in both antigovernment violence and government repression. Bombings were met with torture by the Batista police, who now seemed more and more out of control. On January 15, constitutional guarantees, already suspended in Oriente, were dropped throughout the island. Two days later Castro's force, now about twenty strong, attacked the La Plata army barracks in rural Oriente in their first armed assault against the Batista government.

Much of the violence in Havana was not, however, the work of the Castro forces, but rather of the *Directorio Revolucionario.* On March 13, shortly after lunch, about eighty members of the DR conducted a frontal attack on the presidential palace, with the avowed purpose of killing Batista. The attack failed rather disastrously; thirty-five of the rebels were killed, and Batista remained safe in an upper floor of the palace. The attack, however, produced two effects. First, public opinion, at least temporarily, became more pro-Batista because the attack was viewed as a resurgence of gangsterism and not as a patriotic sacrifice. Second, the attack increased the level of repression. The Batista police proceeded to hunt down and kill any students who were suspected of complicity in the attack, and the hunt obviously extended to many whose involvement was only peripheral, at most. From that moment to the end of 1958, Cuba was in a virtual state of civil war. Arrayed on one side was the dictator Fulgencio Batista, the Cuban Army, the secret police, most of the American and Cuban business community in Havana, and at least the higher officials of the United States government. On the other side were increasing numbers of Cuban intellectuals and others from the Cuban middle class, the remnants of the *Directorio Revolucionario,* the *26 de Julio* movement, and the *New York Times,* whose editor, Herbert Matthews, had first brought Castro's guerrilla war to the attention of the American people.

The remaining months of 1957 and all of 1958 followed a similar pattern. Bombings, kidnappings, and assassinations of Batistianos in the urban centers of Havana and Santiago increased, while retaliation by the police in the form of summary executions, torture, and imprisonment also mounted. It is impossible to say what was in reaction to what. Both sides seem to have entered an insensate stage of violence in which one violent act bore no relation to any previous actions. Opposition violence was predominantly of two kinds: guerilla warfare in the Sierra Maestra mountains of Oriente Province, and urban terrorism in Havana. In addition, the *Directorio Revolucionario* now established a second guerrilla warfare front in the Escambray mountains in Central Cuba, and began attacking the Batista troops in that area. The July 26 Movement was clearly, at this time, the major guerrilla movement opposing Batista, and more and more middle-class Cubans were being won over to its side. Castro was viewed by many Cubans as a sort of modern-day Robin Hood, fighting the combined forces of the evil dictator and the patron to the north—the United States. Many of the sons of the middle class were slipping away to the mountains to join the Castro movement, which was still operating in phase one of guerrilla warfare; small group actions against numerically superior government forces. The urban proletariat were largely quiescent, although Castro began receiving more support from the *guajiros* of Oriente Province and from the proletariat in Santiago. Still, the July 26 Movement was, and remained until the ultimate overthrow of Batista, a predominantly middle-class movement. Although the indiscriminant bomb-throwing in the urban areas somewhat cooled the ardor of many in the middle class for Castro, their misgivings were largely overcome by two factors: the image of Castro as the brave *guerrillero* in the mountains and the random, overwhelmingly brutal use of counterterror by the Batista forces. No historian of the era has yet been able to determine just how much control Batista had over the secret police at this stage. Our own estimate is that he had very little, and that the SIM (under Esteban Ventura) operated in an autonomous manner. The point is, however, that this gang of sadists was all part of the Batista apparatus. It is equally difficult to say how many prisoners were tortured by the SIM during this period. Enough people, however, enough innocent people, were rounded up by the police, tortured, and then killed, to produce a general revulsion among middle-class Cubans. Batista, in effect, became persona non grata among a large sector of the Cuban population, and they turned, quite naturally, to the most "responsible" revolutionary movement, the *26 de Julio*. The DR was tainted by its association with the extremism of student factions at the University and with the abortive attack on the presidential palace.

As the rebel movements gained strength through the latter half of 1957, and as the Batista forces became ever more repressive and unpopular, a third movement against the dictator took form. This one evolved among members of the armed forces who wanted to replace Batista while at the same time denying the government to either Castro or the DR. In September, 1957, a section of the navy in Cienfuegos made a serious attempt to overthrow the regime. The attack, which was made with the cooperation of the *26 de Julio* movement in the area, came on September 5, and achieved initial success. Batista responded, however, by using B-26 bombers and tanks, all recently supplied by the United States, to quell the revolt. At the time, it was the largest action of the civil war; only the Santa Clara engagement in the waning days of 1958 occupied more troops on both sides. Approximately 400 rebels took part in the Cienfuegos uprising, of which approximately 300 were killed, either during the battle or afterward by the Batista troops who swept through the town killing anyone who looked suspicious. The navy revolt was the last overt move on the part of "progressive" officers in the armed forces to supplant both Batista and Castro. Several intrigues developed after the Cienfuegos affair, and some last-ditch efforts, supported by the United States Central Intelligence Agency, to bring Major Ramón Barquín to power were made, but with little or no success. From September, 1957, to January 8, 1959, the two contenders for Batista's power were the *Movimiento 26 de Julio* and the *Directorio Revolucionario*.

Difficulties mounted for Batista in the early months of 1958. In March, the U.S. State Department declared an embargo on further shipments of arms to Cuba, much to the consternation and disgust of Ambassador Earl. E. T. Smith, who remained committed to Batista. To further compound Batista's troubles, the Communists were slowly going over to the side of the revolution, and actually participated in the abortive general strike of April 9, called by the Castro forces. Moreover, the Catholic Church, long dormant in Cuban political life, was taking a critical line toward the Batista regime.

Batista's final offensive against the rebels began in May, 1958. Known as the *ofensiva del verano* (summer offensive), it was a complete disaster. The army literally fell apart in the mountains, and morale, which had been low, sank even lower. The rebels were now clearly in control of much of the eastern half of Cuba, and Batista's downfall seemed ever more imminent. The war ground on, however, for another seven months until, on January 1, 1959, Batista fled the island, accompanied by his wife and forty close associates. He had been defeated more by the alienation of the Cuban people and by the demoralization of his army than by Castro's rebels, who were always numerically inferior to the Batista forces.

The violence that had been anticipated with the overthrow of Batista did not occur. In fact, Havana was a much safer city on January 1, 1959, than it had been on December 31, 1958. There was some looting of former Batistiano residences, and some sporadic shooting, but generally the population remained calm and order was maintained by representatives of both the Castro organization and the *Directorio Revolucionario*, who suddenly appeared on the scene. For a while it appeared that serious fighting might break out between the DR and the *Movimiento 26 de Julio*, but it soon became obvious that Castro's forces were clearly in the ascendant. On January 8 Castro entered Havana after a triumphal march from Santiago, and Cuba's future political course was sealed. Violence in the rural areas continued well into 1959, but Havana was largely at peace, and even rural violence dropped sharply during the second half of 1959. Repression also dropped sharply in 1959, as the Castro regime for the first nine months of the year enjoyed almost universal support.

Castro's widespread support did not last long, however. Beginning in September, with the take-over of the Cuban labor organization by Castro's hand-picked Communist candidates, repression built up once again. Newspaper censorship became heavier, finally resulting in the destruction of all but the government newspaper. Summary court procedures, which had initially been instituted against only former Batistiano officers like the notorious Captain Sosa Blanco, were now used against all who were "enemies of the revolution." Leagues for the Defense of the Fatherland were formed, with the purpose of reporting all counterrevolutionary activities to the authorities. By 1960 Castro was well on the way to creating a "new order" in Cuba, and as his popularity declined, especially with the Cuban middle class, his control apparatus increased.

Castro's apologists have, while admitting the repression, excused it on the ground that it is necessary in order to create the new Cuban society and the new Cuban man. His detractors have emphasized the repression, and have used it as evidence that Castro is no better and probably worse than the dictators who preceded him in Havana. Whatever the viewpoint, the fact remains that Castro's repression is different from the repressions that preceded him: it is being used not to maintain the status quo but to create a new system. Whether this effort has been or will be successful is still being debated, and the answer often depends on what data are used and what interpretations are made of the data. What is indisputable, however, is that constitutional guarantees were abrogated, political arrests and exiles were made, political parties were abolished, and press freedom in Cuba was suspended during the 1960s.

While we do not have data on violence in Cuba during the 1960s, all commentators seem agreed that, after the Bay of Pigs invasion in 1961, which resulted not only in the disaster at the landing site, but also in the decimation of Castro's internal opposition, there has been very little opposition to the Castro regime. Certainly the high level of repression has made it extremely unwise to oppose Castro from within Cuba. Estimates of the general level of support for Castro among the Cuban population vary, but many Cuban youth support the revolution wholeheartedly. Castro has now had sixteen years in which to indoctrinate them, and he appears to have accomplished a much more extensive educational program than any of his predecessors.[3] Contributing to the lack of violence in opposition to Castro has certainly been the continuing exile of many Cubans to other countries, primarily the United States. During the decade of the 1960s, an estimated 400,000 Cubans left the island. Undoubtedly many of these people were potential opponents of the Castro regime, and they have now been effectively removed from the Cuban scene. Further, exiles appear to have become even more disorganized in their opposition to Castro since the Bay of Pigs fiasco, and many now seem resigned to the fact that they will live out their lives in their new countries.

The two major questions that inevitably arise out of any attempt to explain Cuban history of the 1950s and 1960s are: What were the causes of the 1959 revolution? and, What success has Castro had in trying to create the first Communist state in the Western Hemisphere?

---

[3]Richard Fagen, *The Transformation of Political Culture in Cuba* (Stanford: Stanford University Press, 1969).

The causes of the 1959 revolution are as varied as the theories of revolution advanced by writers over the years and, in fact, the Cuban revolution seems to "fit" several of these theories. If inequalities cause revolutions, then inequalities abounded in pre-1959 Cuba. If, as suggested by Alexis de Tocqueville and others, revolutions are caused by rising expectations, the rapidly expanding Cuban middle class had these in abundance. Some authors have suggested that the Cuban revolution was a revolt against continued domination by the United States. Certainly, after 1933, this domination was in the minds of many of the middle-class supporters of the revolutionary movements of the 1950s. Orlando Fals-Borda has suggested that violence is caused by a massive national sense of frustration brought about by abortive attempts at social change within existing structures. Both the Cuban independence movement of the last half of the nineteenth century and the revolution of 1933 would qualify as such abortive attempts. All of Brinton's preconditions for revolution were met in varying degrees by pre-1959 Cuba, among them a frustrated middle class. Cuban intellectuals, who never really had been for Batista, had most definitely deserted the governing system by the late 1950s. There was a definite crisis in self-confidence within the Cuban ruling class as some of its members, especially junior officers in the Cuban Army, came to question the rightness of what they were doing. The Cuban government was a poor government (in terms of government expenditures as percent of gross national product) in a rich country. Finally, as in all prerevolutionary societies studied by Brinton, there was "the Eternal Figaro," or an act of defiance against the regime that went essentially unpunished. In Cuba this act was, of course, the attack on the Moncada barracks, plus the subsequent amnesty for the engineer of the attack—Fidel Castro.

Our theory does not purport to explain revolution, but rather violence and repression, both of which are usually associated with revolution. As shown in Table 33, in terms of our indicators, Cuba was definitely in a previolence situation as early as 1950. Cuba ranked extremely low on all institutional variables. The Catholic Church was one of the weakest in Latin America; political parties, where they existed, were so feeble and so discredited that they had no effect on the governance of the country; and the Cuban Army was so venal and corrupt, particularly at the higher levels, that its support for any system of government could only be minimal. Quite possibly our index of military institutionalization underestimated the venality and alienation that existed among the members of the army and the National Police in the early 1950s, and this miscalculation may be a key element in our failure to predict even higher levels of violence. By the late 1950s, at any rate, the Cuban Army and the police really amounted to nothing more than bands of armed thugs, roaming the streets of Havana and other cities in search of someone to brutalize.

Cuba's level of societal welfare in the 1950s was high (bouyed mainly by a comparatively high gross national product per capita), but it was more than offset by an extremely high level of social mobilization. Thus, in the fifties Cubans were making more demands on the system than the system could meet. The nation's economic growth, which was rapid during the early half of the decade, trailed off rather abruptly in the late years of the 1950s. In 1958 the Cuban economy probably experienced an actual downturn in per capita product. The level of communications in Cuba was the highest in Latin America during the 1950s, as Cuba was the first Latin American nation to experience the "transistor radio revolution" and the first to utilize television. The plethora of daily newspapers and weekly periodicals, especially in Havana, further increased the level of communications. Further, although not reflected in the independent variables used to predict violence, it was evident to even the most casual observer that gross inequities in wealth existed in Cuba; both in geographical terms (Havana versus Oriente) and in class terms (the opulent life-style of the Cuban sugar elite versus the multitude of beggars along El Paseo).

Finally, Cuba's output variables were also conducive to violence and repression. The Batista government spent comparatively large amounts on education, yet Cuba ranked extremely low in terms of number of school-age children in school. This apparent paradox can be explained by the type and concentration of these expenditures. Generally, school expenditures were concentrated in and around Havana, in show projects such as the building of a luxurious new high school in the upper-class Vedado section of Havana, whereas expenditures in the rural areas were minimal. It is also a safe assumption that, given the standard of public morality throughout the island, much of the money earmarked for education found its way instead into the pockets of either the minister of education or the minister of public works, or of several of their cronies.

It should be emphasized also that the expenditures of the Batista government were a smaller slice of a smaller pie; that is, the government had less to spend as percent of the wealth of the nation, because it was unable to extract money from the populace. Expenditures on the military, which were substantially higher than those on education, were largely wasted because they were for costly but unsuitable equipment from the United States and because of the lack of discipline in the Cuban Army.

Our measures, then, indicate that Cuba was ripe for extensive violence and repression by the 1950s. The strange thing is not that violence and repression came, but that the signals indicating they would were ignored for so long by people who should have known better and who might have been able to change the course of Cuban history by doing something to avoid them.

The second major question emanating from Cuban history in the two decades of our analysis pertains to the success or failure of Fidel Castro in constructing a new society. Essentially, of course, the question is really not within the purview of our work. Still, it is an interesting one and one that deserves some attempt to answer. Much of the controversy over the answer revolves around the definition of success. If success is defined in terms of economic development (in terms of gross national product per capita) then Castro has not been successful. Cuba's national income per capita was about the same at the beginning of the 1970s as it was in 1958. Indeed, between 1962 and 1966, it actually declined, from $497 to $478. Tales of meatless days, of mismanagement of the collective farms, and of other economic failures abound. Yet several factors should be considered when evaluating the economics of Castro's Cuba, one being that within a short period of time the direction of the economy, hitherto almost totally dependent upon the United States, has been completely changed. The spare parts problem in Cuba alone has been enormous. In order to keep machinery and transportation running—all of which was "made in U.S.A." prior to 1959—Castro and his Communist allies have had to create spare parts supplies where none existed before, or else Castro has had to hunt for them in European markets. Further, the Cuban sugar crop, which formerly went almost wholly to the United States market, has had to be sold or bartered in both Communist and non-Communist markets throughout Europe and Asia. These factors must be taken into account when judging the economic success of the Castro regime.

More importantly, however, the Castro government has laid the groundwork for what should be substantial and, for the first time in Cuban history, balanced economic growth during the late 1970s. Much government effort in the 1960s went into the creation of a new Cuban infrastructure, which would be both more responsive to the needs of the Cuban people and also create sustained growth in the national economy. Expenditures for education, the primary prop for this new infrastructure, rose from 79 million pesos in 1958 to more than 350 million pesos in 1966; purportedly, they have continued to rise ever since then, though not at such a rapid rate. The number of students enrolled in and graduated from all levels of education rose sharply during the sixties. At the same time the type of education gained by Cuban students has changed. In 1958 more than 10,000 students were enrolled in the humanities and social sciences in Cuban institutions of higher education, while approximately a like number were studying all other disciplines, including the life and physical sciences, engineering, medical sciences, and agricultural sciences. By 1969 only slightly more than 2,000 students were studying the humanities and social sciences, while some 18,000 were enrolled in the other disciplines listed above. Further, more than 7,000 were enrolled in peasant-worker education, some in preparation for eventually entering higher education. Additional strides have been made in reducing illiteracy and in providing free public education for practically everyone within the society. The statement that "the quantitative gains claimed for Cuban education during the past decade are truly impressive regardless of how one views Castro and his revolution" is most accurate.[4]

While similar advances have been made in other areas, such as public health, it must be stated that the Cuban economy is still largely dependent upon Soviet aid. It must also be pointed out that as Castro's charismatic appeal to the Cuban people has declined, and as the Cuban economy has failed to produce many desired goods, the apparatus of control consisting of the armed forces and the Communist Party has grown in importance. The level of repression in Cuba has been high since the early days of the revolution, and it continues to be among the highest in Latin America. Given the existing control apparatus, plus the continued willingness of the Soviet Union to underwrite the Castro regime's economic deficits, large-scale violence appears unlikely in Cuba for some time. The Cuban Army is well-disciplined and under the effective control of the political command. It is far more institutionalized than was Batista's army. Fidel Castro himself, of course, is the prime factor in that control. Despite his somewhat lowered profile, he remains the symbol of the revolution in the minds of most Cubans. If he were to disappear from the Cuban scene, it is doubtful that anyone else could hold the Cuban system together in its present form. Certainly disaffected elements both inside and outside Cuba would be encouraged in their efforts to promote opposition to the Castro revolution, and violence would very likely be the result.

Bolivia

Bolivia, one of three Latin American nations that have undergone a violent social revolution, continues to be a violent and repressive

---

[4]Rolland Paulston, *Revolutionary Change in Cuba*, ed. by Carmelo Mesa Lago, Pittsburgh, University of Pittsburgh Press, 1971, p. 386.

society. The 1952 revolution, although succeeding in restructuring social and racial inequality, political elitism, and economic imperialism, has failed to maintain momentum. The historical and political forces that brought on the revolution are also partly responsible for the present deterioration.

The Bolivian social system struggles with the more difficult geographic, racial, and economic problems in South America. Regionalism remains a powerful divisive force, despite transportation improvements and more egalitarian governmental development programs. Three radically different climatic zones, the *altiplano* or highlands, the *valle* or valleys, and the *llano* or tropical lowlands, correspond to three distinct peoples and social customs, and nearly opposed mental and physical characteristics. Loyalties are first local and regional and then national.[5] Although a unitary state, the spark of federalism continues to smolder, especially in Santa Cruz, which has become a virtual urban oasis and commercial center in the eastern lowlands within the last twenty years.[6] Once an isolated economic and political backwater, it has translated its present economic strength based on increasing petroleum exploitation, into political influence, enabling it to rival the traditional supremacy of La Paz. In contrast, the northeastern department of Pando can only be reached from the capital by irregular air flights and remains virgin territory—the last in national development priorities. The existing Banzer government expends much propaganda energy to deflate regional tendencies but economic and geographic limitations still defy progressive measures.

The ethnic composition of Bolivia ranges from fifty to seventy percent Indian, twenty-five to thirty percent mestizo, and five to ten percent European-Spanish.[7] These percentages are based on the 1950 census, which underestimates an Indian population that may actually be as high as seventy percent.[8] Prior to the 1952 revolution, race was the most divisive force in a society fraught with deep cleavages. The Indians—most of whom belong to the Quechua and Aymara linguistic groups with a minority made up of numerous but distinct forest tribes

[5]Federico Avila, *El Problema de la Unidad Nacional* (La Paz; Editorial "Universo", 1939).

[6]See Hugo Farfan Alarcon, "Sistema de gobierno federal," *Presencia* (La Paz), Sept. 20, 1973, p. 3, which reports on a conference held in Santa Cruz with representation from Pando and Beni asking government and citizens for the "Implantation of the Federal System" and the division of the country into three zones: north, central, and south.

[7]*Area Handbook for Bolivia* (Washington, D.C., U.S. Government Printing Office, 1974), p. vii; Andrew Marshall, ed., *The South American Handbook, 1970* (London: Trade and Travel Publications, 1970), p. 108.

[8]Fausto Reinaga, *Tierra y Libertad, La Revolución Nacional y El Indio* (La Paz; Ediciones "Rumbo Sindical," 1952), p. 17.

in the lowlands—suffered ruthless exploitation in mining, agriculture, and rubber industries through the 1940s. With the revolution, the Indian became, technically, no longer the second-class citizen of the past because all Bolivians over twenty-one were given the right of franchise by law. Yet the Indian remains enormously disadvantaged in this society where his educational, economic, and social progress continue to be sharply limited. There have been national advances in education and health services, but figures reflect improvements in the large urban centers and only to a lesser degree any improvements in the countryside. In short, the Indian majorities still do not enjoy the benefits of effective citizenship.

Despite electoral influence because of their numbers, the Indians' political power is controlled and manipulated by shrewd local agrarian and union leaders. Under the existing Military-Peasant Pact, *campesino* leaders extend pro forma support to governmental actions. Labor union opposition is ineffectual against the combined peasant-military alliance, which constitutes the grass-roots political strength of the National Popular Front policies. Moreover, the armed worker militias created by the revolution to protect labor rights and to offset military power, have been curtailed by post-revolutionary governments. The present people's militia, which has been numbered at 16,000 (although figures vary greatly), is largely controlled by the government and the military.[9]

Indians in the mines have probably progressed the most with the revolution, especially during the early Paz Estenssoro government in the early 1950s when mining was first nationalized and numerous benefits and improvements extended to the miners. Continued mining unrest under the Siles Suazo government, however, and the second Paz term has been one explanation for the military takeover by René Barrientos in November, 1964.[10] The present government of Hugo Banzer propagandizes over national television the numerous regime-sponsored improvements in housing, education, and communications for the mining centers, which are relatively inaccessible from urban centers. And although there has been no open mining unrest within the last several years, the ever-increasing cost of living has disillusioned the lower classes of ever achieving the improved life-style they had envisioned after the 1952 revolution.

Bolivia continues to depend heavily on the uneconomic tin mining industry, now state-owned and organized, for fifty percent of its national exports and foreign currency earnings. The earning value of

---

[9]*Area Handbook for Bolivia*, p. ix.

[10]Fernando Diez de Medina, *El General del Pueblo* (La Paz; Ediciones "Los Amigos del Libro," 1972), pp. 80–81, 91, and 243.

the tin exports, however, has been further depreciated by miner demands for improved work conditions, by welfare and health services, and by an inefficient government management tainted with corrupt practices. Thus the Bolivian economy remains enmeshed in problems stemming from monoproduction. In the distant and recent past greater capital investments in industry and the mechanization of agriculture were proposed as solutions for diversifying the economy. Agricultural development does deserve primary attention, but it has often been neglected by governments. Bolivia has the potential for complete agricultural self-sufficiency, yet it continues to import wheat, and at times even rice and sugar are scarce. Only cotton and coffee have figured as major agricultural exports. Unscrupulous business practices permit, for example, the export of sugar for higher profits, stimulating artificial domestic shortages and price speculation. Agricultural autonomy has been the ideal and the policy proposal of Bolivian intellectuals since the nineteenth century, but successive governments have been unable to develop this sector fully, and sizable dislocations of population have been blamed for the continued impasse.

Most of the Indian population and most of the urban and mining centers are concentrated in the arid highland. Agricultural productivity on the *altiplano* is low because of poor soil and climate and primitive methods of cultivation. The 1952 revolution imposed sweeping land reform measures to improve agriculture. Prior to the revolution, land inequality was staggering. Based on the 1950 census,

> there were only 82,600 landowners in the country, of which 6.3 percent possessed almost 93 percent of all 80.9 million acres of privately owned land. Large estates of more than 2,500 acres were common, those of 25,000 acres were not unusual, and several had 50,000 acres or more. The two largest estates comprised five million acres and four million acres, respectively. Eight persons with the largest properties possessed one-tenth of Bolivia, yet cultivated less than one-tenth of one percent of their landholdings.[11]

The implementation of land reforms, however, proved extremely difficult, and the National Agrarian Reform Service is still bogged down with disputed cases; as of 1972, only about 320,000 peasant families possessed clear-cut titles to their property. Inefficiency and corruption in the Agrarian Reform Service is widespread with some rural officers and judges using their positions to accept considerations from claim disputants, and to be generally feted at local expense. The increased

---

[11]*Area Handbook for Bolivia*, p. 296.

mobilization and organization of the Indian community as a result of the revolution remains the single most effective guarantor of peasant rights.

Historically, Bolivia has been a violent and repressive society. Frequent Indian uprisings—one of the more recent in 1921—and mining disputes and strikes—such as the memorable Catavi Massacre of 1942—involved wholesale butchery by army troops. After the Chaco War, repression and governmental violence, either centralized or local, were the only means of maintaining the social and political status quo. The nineteenth century witnessed few periods of political peace. From independence from Spain in 1825 until 1842, the republic waged the battles that were to determine whether it would remain a single nation or part of greater Colombia, or, later, the Peruvian Confederation. The rest of the century was equally violent with the repressions of dictatorial governments and the humiliating defeat in the War of the Pacific. Postwar political reconstruction gave rise to the elitist Liberal and Republican parties, which stabilized politics somewhat though dubious legal processes and "democratic" elections from which the majority of the population were automatically barred by literacy statutes. Both the Liberals and Republicans were dominated by the tin interests, which achieved international earnings and vast profits at the turn of the century. The tin triumvirate of Patiño, Aramayo, and Hochschild—in descending order of production and profits—controlled politics, society, and the economy until the 1952 revolution. The landowners, tin barons, and personalist political factions—euphemistically called "parties"—composed the *rosca*, the most hated complex of interests in post-Chaco Bolivia.

The Chaco War had more unprecedented repercussions in Bolivia than in Paraguay. In Paraguay it led only to extreme political turmoil, but in Bolivia it directly contributed to the social revolution. President Daniel Salamanca, who bears much of the blame for the outbreak of war in 1932, once argued in the national legislature that Bolivian victory over Paraguay was inevitable and that the consequent elevation in national pride and confidence was vital to cement flagging national unity. Bolivia had strong claims to the Chaco, as did Paraguay. Paraguay, however, supplemented military efforts with vigorous colonization, whereas Bolivia sought to maintain the territory militarily without the population and infrastructure to support its policies. The result was the greast crime in Bolivian history—the mass slaughter of ignorant unacclimated highland Indians. Thousands died of disease and went insane from thirst, confused to the end as to the reason why they fought for that distant and inhospitable wasteland. The concept of Bolivian nationalism was alien to their experience of racial oppression, and their narrow communal mentalities. Thus the Chaco War, which ended in 1935, served as the greatest single factor in mobilizing the Indian masses against the old political and social order. Likewise shaken and activated from their past lethargy, the elite officer corps and upper-class intellectuals were physically disgusted by the corruption and incompetence of the army general command, and by the sterile military-political intrigues that had undermined strategic and tactical responsibility and leadership during the long campaign.

After 1935 political parties in opposition to the traditional Liberals and Republicans proliferated amid national disillusionment and ideological ferment. The Bolivian Socialist Falange (*Falange Socialista Boliviana*—FSB) was founded in 1937; the Nationalist Revolutionary Movement (*Movimiento Revolucionario Nacional*—MNR) in 1941; the Revolutionary Workers Party (*Partido de Obrero Revolucionario*—POR) in 1934; and the Party of the Revolutionary Left (*Partido de la Izquierda Revolucionario*—PIR) in 1940.[12] Under the ideological rubric of "national socialism," but with a distinctively Bolivian interpretation and application of that term, widely disparate ideological movements of right, left, and center temporarily allied themselves to achieve national reform. The Legion of Ex-Combatants, which organized Chaco War veterans in 1935, and the Syndicated Confederation of Workers of Bolivia, nationally organized in 1936, plus the new Socialist Party, a forerunner of the MNR, formed the backbone of the reformist, nationalistic, military governments of Colonel David Toro and Lieutenant Colonel Germán Busch.

The "state socialism" of the Toro government, in spite of a proliferation of reform proposals, achieved few changes other than improved pensions and governmental preference for war veterans. Presenting itself as forcefully anti-imperialistic, it was instead moderated and controlled by the conservative tin interests and enmeshed in sterile partisan debating. The Socialist Party was a politically confused and divided conglomerate of leftist forces, labor organizations, and war veterans. Factional and ideological squabbling prevented the government from either legislating or enacting vital reforms, and attempts to organize a corporativist state met opposition within and without the ruling circle. The more radical and impatient military sectors, under the leadership of Busch, pressured for results and for a firm hand with the tin interests. In a desperate effort to save his government, Toro

---

[12]Mario Anaya Rolón, *Politica y Partidos en Bolivia* (La Paz; Ediciones "Juventud," 1966).

confiscated Standard Oil holdings in March, 1937. But political dissension was so extreme, that in July Lieutenant Colonel Busch assumed the executive office.

The new government was initially devoid of political direction, although it affirmed the Standard Oil nationalization. Finally, in a move to speed reform programs through the legislative and party system, a constituent assembly was called to amend the constitution and legitimize the government. Vested interests, however, proved too strong to permit peaceful radical reform. The convention bogged down in political factionalism while reform proposals and the new constitution were attacked in the conservative press. Repressive measures increased with repeated press censorship, until Busch at last declared himself dictator in a memorable April, 1939, speech wherein he charged subversion of reforms by civilian political groups. Thereafter, reform decrees were issued at what the vested interests considered an alarming rate. The economic power of tin and business entrepreneurs was curbed by government taxes and regulations, such as nationalization of the Mining Bank and placement of complete control of foreign currency earnings with the Bolivian Central Bank. Fifty percent of tin earnings were pledged to public service and administration. No longer would the government and the people be dependent on the whims of financial barons for foreign exhange with which vital primary goods were imported and government budgets maintained. Busch elevated as his political slogan and goal "the economic emancipation" of Bolivia, and the employment of national wealth for the collective benefit. Moreover, the Código Busch, as his progressive social and labor welfare legislation came to be known, legalized unionization and made worker compensation programs mandatory in the mines. In the end, the significant social advances were short-lived, for with the suicide of the president in August, 1939, only four months after he had assumed dictatorial powers, status quo government under General Enrique Peñaranda was reinstated in 1940.[13]

Failure of the political experiment of the Socialist Party prompted the MNR to reorganize and split with ideologically opposed groups. Employing an extremely nationalistic ideology with Marxian dimensions, it proposed a Bolivian state socialism, government involvement in economics and social legislation, economic independence from foreign and tin-controlled influences, and a truly national culture incorporating the Indian as a citizen and projecting land redistribution. Politi-

---

[13]For the Toro and Busch governments, see *El Diario*, La Paz, March, 1937–August, 1939, and Herbert S. Klein, *Origenes de la Revolucion Nacional Boliviana: La Crisis de la Generacion del Chaco* (La Paz: Empresa Editora "Urquizo Ltda," 1968).

cal revolt in 1943 brought to power an MNR-army coalition government under President Gualberto Villarroel. This reformist government was stigmatized from the beginning by the political opposition as a Fascist dictatorship, and duly denied United States recognition. Following greater U.S. reductions in the acquisitions of strategic materials, such as tin, the Villarroel government faced a grave economic crisis with a fall in tin prices and stagnation in exports. The imposing conservative bloc of traditional parties, old-guard military, and rabidly anti-MNR leftist groups—formally termed the *Frente Democrático Antifascista* (FDA)—disrupted the National Convention of 1944–1945 and impeded the passage of such reform legislation as women's franchise, an agrarian labor law, and the right of the *campesinos* to unionize and strike. Nevertheless, the first Congress of Indians was proclaimed and met in 1945, resulting in abolition of *pongaje*, or involuntary personal labor of the Indian for the landlord, and enactment of programs to increase indigenous education. Again reforms were temporary. The FDA fostered a split between the civilian MNR leadership and the reformist military leadership to isolate and destroy both. Thus, in 1946 student unrest and a teacher strike were manipulated by the conservative politicians to spark a bloody coup that left Villarroel hanging from a lampost and reimposed conservative rule until 1951. Presidential elections of that year would have made exiled Víctor Paz Estenssoro the first MNR president were it not for another military take-over and abrogation of the elections. This action served as the final delegitimization of Bolivia's collapsing political system and as the immediate instigator of the plot that history now records as the Bolivian National Revolution of April 9, 1952.

In terms of the indicators developed by our study, Bolivia was not a socially cohesive society prior to the revolution. The foregoing historical sketch delineates a situation in which welfare was exceedingly low for at least seventy percent of the population in relation to high mobilization stimulated by the Chaco War. Economic growth had been favorable until 1929, when tin earnings started skidding toward the record lows of 1932, unprecedented labor and agricultural shortages developed, import costs rose due to the effects of the worldwide depression, and financial bankruptcy and inflation became rampant at the close of hostilities with Paraguay.[14] Between 1930 and 1941 prices in flour had increased 900 percent; in rice, 1,200 percent; in potatoes, 2,000 percent; and in rents, 2,500 percent. Worker salaries, however, had increased but slightly. Mining and labor strikes erupted constantly in protest of

---

[14]Augustin Barcelli S., *Medio Siglo de Luchas Sindicales Revolucionarias en Bolivia* (La Paz: Editorial del Estado, 1956), pp. 129–130 and 135.

economic hardships. The discrepancy between economic growth and the high levels of postwar mobilization, therefore, was extreme enough to promote civil violence.

Racial tensions were more intense because of the bitter experience of racial inequality throughout the war. The 1960 educational effort and expenditures were even lower than the 1950 score; indeed, newspapers and intellectual criticism of government output emphasized the pronounced neglect of education in the 1950s. Only under the short-lived reformist governments of Toro, Busch, and Villarroel were meager educational funds channeled to the countryside and peasant communities where the need was acute. Church institutionalization in Bolivia has not been strong. Although without much political influence, the Catholic Church has solidly and consistently reinforced conservative politics and the exploitation of oppressed classes.

Political institutionalization of Liberal and Republican parties after the Chaco War declined precipitously. Both groups succumbed to personalist feuding before and after the Chaco campaign. Without the support of the tin and landholding interests and conservative military men, neither could have achieved electoral advantage, nor retained legislative seats sharply contested by the newer more idealistic and institutionalized parties. The MNR was one of the more popular, disciplined and well-organized of these newcomers.

Military institutionalization also waned after the Chaco fiasco. The younger officers, alienated from the corrupted senior leadership, were convinced that partisan intrigues and dissensions were the root of national decay. If political parties could not rule then the military would have to do so. The great majority of the military who fought in the Chaco War, therefore, abandoned the ideal of nonintervention in politics. They argued that in the existing political vacuum only the military with its organization, discipline, and unselfish national loyalty could govern honestly and peacefully. Moreover, they felt that the prevailing intellectual position of civilians favored authoritarian rule over the discredited pseudo-democratic practices of the traditional political parties. If indexes for the 1930s and 1940s were to be constructed, they would surely reflect extremely low social cohesion for prerevolutionary Bolivia.

In the data for the 1950s and 1960s, improvements and slippages are notable. Overall, the fifties saw a greater degree of violence and repression as the result of the revolutionary take-over and political consolidation. As might be expected, armed violence greatly exceeded unarmed violence in this decade. Between 1958 and 1960, Bolivia experienced extreme economic deterioration such as inflation and labor and mining unrest. The slight improvement in the 1960s was attributable to the decrease in political repression. Nevertheless, violence, especially armed violence, exceeded that of the previous decade. Mining and labor strikes and armed clashes with the military, as well as counterinsurgency measures by the military against Che Guevara and his guerrilla forces in 1967, make the late sixties the highest in armed violence.

The economic growth-social mobilization differential improved from −2.04 to .60 in the two decades largely as a result of the revoluttionary reforms. Indeed, Bolivia in 1950 had the greatest negative differential in Latin America between economic growth and social mobilization. This indicator has best fit an overall explanation of violence and would thus suggest very low social cohesion prior to the revolution. The welfare-mobilization differential produced the strongest single socio-economic explanatory factor of violence. For 1955 and 1965 Bolivia ranked as the second lowest Latin American country after Haiti on societal welfare. Even today, illiteracy figures approximate sixty percent and caloric intake measures are extremely low. On the other hand, in both decades Bolivia was only the eighth lowest Latin American country in mobilization. Thus for the 1950s, Bolivia ranked second only to Cuba with a strongly negative differential. For 1960, despite the revolution, Bolivia ranked lowest in Latin America on the welfare-mobilization differential. The extremely unequal and negative difference between low welfare and high mobilization accounts for the high violence score and suggests future instability.

Though military institutionalization varied little between the two decades, from 1952 to 1964, the military remained politically inactive. A policy of the Paz Estenssoro and subsequent MNR governments was military reorganization, a return to the barracks, and the creation of people's militias to equalize the political power of the armed forces. Undoubtedly, the prerevolutionary data decreased the institutionalization index for the first decade. For the second, the Barrientos coup of 1964, the subsequent military junta, and the overthrow in 1969 of President Hernán Siles Suazo—the constitutional successor of Barrientos who was killed in a helicopter crash that year—assured a continued low intitutionalization score.

The military continued divided into the 1970s. General Alfredo Ovando Candia replaced Siles and nationalized Gulf Oil in 1969, but he was compelled to resign under military pressure. Taking the higher echelons by surprise, General Juan Torres formed a leftist, nationalistic government in October, 1970. Torres promoted further nationalization of foreign, especially United States, holdings and organized revolutionary popular assemblies of workers to support his government. Two radically opposed political parties, the conservative Bolivian Socialist Falange, which had bitterly fought the MNR throughout the 1940s and

1950s, allied with the National Revolutionary Movement now a moderate postrevolution party, and conservative military factions to terminate the Torres experiment. As a result, the National Popular Front government of Colonel Hugo Banzer was installed in August, 1971. Political instability continued, nevertheless, with the military split between left and right development programs, and between those who disapproved of the military-civilian coalition government and those who did not. The thwarted mutiny in June, 1974, of "Tarapacá" regiment, for example, involved some twenty army lieutenants. The rebels emphasized in a statement to the press the loss of prestige for the military government because of association with corrupted political parties: "The army is of the people and should serve only the interests of the people and never confront them, harass them, and persecute them, as the governing generals try to do aided by politicians of ill-repute."[15]

Total societal institutionalization in Bolivia has dropped from −.33 in 1950 to −.71 in 1960. The most important explanation for this setback has been a decrease in political party institutionalization from .74 to .13 in the two decades. Postrevolutionary events, as we have seen, included greater military interference in government at the expense of the party system. By 1964 the MNR had splintered into personalist factions of Paz Estenssoro, Siles Suazo, Lechín Oquendo, and Guevara Arze. The deterioration of the MNR has continued into the present decade with power struggles between new rank-and-file and the old-guard politicans—a struggle publicized with the exile of Paz Estenssoro by the National Popular Front in 1974. Before presidential elections scheduled for 1975 were called off political infighting continued strong. The FSB and MNR nearly split the present governmental coalition over the issue of independent electoral slates. The distribution of government ministries and the sharing of political spoils have been the overriding interests that have kept these strange bedfellows between the same political sheets for so long. Public criticism has centered of late on the division of spoils which literally splits public administration and has spawned inefficiency and ever-increasing corruption. Public ministries, functioning no differently from political party secretariats,[16] are a continuing source of public discontent. For example, turmoil at the Bolivian University has rested upon charges that the ministry of education, politically partitioned by the FSB, has often violated University

---

[15]"Un manifiesto de 4 militares rebeldes y respuesta official," *Presencia* (La Paz) June 20, 1974, p. 1.

[16]Samuel Mendoza, "Secretarías Políticas o Ministerios?" *El Diario* June 24, 1973, p. 2.

autonomy by interfering in hiring practices and pressuring the acceptance of FSB-affiliated professors over more qualified but politically unaffiliated ones. As a result, from May 17, to June 17, 1974, faculty and administrative resignations, student demonstrations, and governmental repression led to the temporary closing of the University in La Paz and its invasion by the police. Repression, therefore, for the first half of the 1970s would be higher than the late 1960s score because of incidents similar to closing of the University.

The Bolivian National Revolution of 1952 has irrevocably altered the social and economic structure of the society, but it has failed to create political stability and basic social cohesion. Arguments that the revolution has been stymied or that it is still unfinished, in a sense, ring true.[17] United States recognition of the government and extensive foreign aid—the greatest amount of aid as percent of gross national product in Latin America for the 1950s and 1960s—undoubtedly imposed moderating political conditions. More importantly, foreign aid thoroughly replaced tin imperialism; it contributed so heavily to the government budget that claims of Bolivian economic independence and national sovereignty—ideological and policy cornerstones of the first revolutionary intellectuals—became unsustainable. Possibly, as power corrupts, foreign aid to an impoverished developing society tends to corrupt also. Whatever the explanation, the MNR leadership and its followers had become a staid and corrupt bureaucratic elite by the second decade of the revolution. Leadership renovation remained blocked by old-guard party bigwigs, and factionalism between them could not be contained institutionally.

The *rosca* of the past has been destroyed. A new plutocracy of foreign industrial interests, small- and middle-level mining concerns, and a bureaucratic political clique now controls the country and access to its wealth. The political position of the Indian vis-à-vis the mestizos and the whites has indisputably improved, yet progress for the national majority has reached a roadblock. Hopes of economic improvement have fallen short for most Bolivians as unequal distribution of national wealth and pro-business economic policies of recent Bolivian governments continue. Today the mystique of the revolution is mostly political rhetoric. The ideals and programs of the revolution have been moderated and buried in bureaucratic oblivion by successive regimes. The 1952 revolution should have been the basis for political moralization and social cohesion without precedent in Bolivian history. Possibly

[17]James M. Malloy, *Bolivia: The Uncompleted Revolution* (Pittsburgh: University of Pittsburgh Press, 1970).

postrevolutionary political control and institutionalization, moral asceticism, and revolutionary fervor should have been greater. Undoubtedly, given the constraints of middle-class leadership and extreme economic poverty, revolutionary intensity was difficult to sustain. Having stimulated political mobilization and aspirations of economic betterment, however, which have been difficult to direct and fulfill, the revolutionary experience has left a legacy of discontent and unrest.

PART 3

PATTERNS
OF COHESION

10

QUANTITATIVE ANALYSIS AND HISTORY: HOW DO THEY FIT?

For too long, quantitative and historical tendencies have gone their separate ways in the study of men and societies. Quantitative analysis without history is like a skeleton without flesh; history without quantitative analysis is like formless flesh. Quantitative analysis establishes broad general relationships abstracted from the real world, though it is easily diverted into concern with the elegance of its methodology rather than with an understanding of particular events and situations. History could bring the analysis back to a concern with the problems of the empirical world, but often it is so immersed in the minutiae of the particular that it fails to discern patterns and structure in these events.

The process of analyzing a large number of cases on certain general concepts focuses attention on selected attributes on which people, events, or societies are comparable. Like looking through the wrong end of a pair of binoculars, it obscures the details and emphasizes the general pattern. It then pulls out one or a few aspects, leaving the whole person, event, or society behind, and analyzes only these parts of the whole. By concentrating on a few aspects, it is able to define them carefully, specify the ways in which they vary, and measure the differences. With a few concepts made into variables, the relationships among them can be specified, and the differences and similarities among cases can be systematically compared in order to test the probability that these relationships exist. The result of the process is a statement about the relationships between abstract concepts—a long way removed from the people, events, and societies from which it was derived.

For these abstractions to take on concrete meaning, they must be applied to the world of history. If the theory is verified and informative, it should illuminate the working of history. It should clarify why certain circumstances led to certain phenomena—why a certain kind of person obtained power when he did, why he achieved or failed to achieve his goals, for example. The theory will dramatize the tragic circumstances where well-meaning men become the instruments of death and destruction when faced with forces beyond their control.

Comparative history can accomplish some of what both the quantitative and historical methods can accomplish. By looking at fewer cases, comparative history can keep some of the subtleties and nuances of the phenomena found in history but which are lost in the abstractions of quantitative analysis. It can capture the complex interactions of circumstances and individual dispositions that produce special results. Most important, comparative history can establish and compare the sequences in which events occurred, a comparison that provides the best test of causal relationships.

The method of this concluding chapter is comparative history, but it is done in a loose and somewhat speculative manner, to illustrate its contribution to theory-building rather than for its rigorous application to obtain hard results. To make the comparisons simpler, we have rearranged our cases according to common configurations in our dependent variables. A few countries have consistently produced stable, personalist dictatorships. Three have undergone total revolution. Another three enjoyed relatively high cohesion in one period and then suffered disintegration. Others have been able to increase their levels of social cohesion in recent years. These four configurations do not exhaust the possibilities, or cover all the Latin American countries, but they suffice to show how static relationships, such as those developed in Part I, and historical cases, such as those developed in Part II, can be drawn together to explain the dynamics of how some countries came to have the kind of social cohesion they have had. The comparisons are between the histories of the countries that have had a specific configuration and the other countries of Latin America that have not had the same pattern.

Stable repressive dictatorships—a dying tendency

At the time of this writing, in mid-1975, only one highly repressive personalist dictatorship exists in Latin America—that of General Alfredo Stroessner of Paraguay. At no time since Latin America's independence from Spain have there been so few. Haiti, the Dominican Republic, Guatemala, and Venezuela (as well as Paraguay) had persisting patterns of stable dictatorship in the twentieth century, and one or two of these countries could conceivably reestablish a personalist dictatorship. We have excluded from consideration the far milder and more sporadic dictatorships that have occurred in Nicaragua, El Salvador, Peru, Honduras, Ecuador, Brazil, and Cuba, and the new form of harsh institutional military repression presently existing in Brazil and Chile. There are good reasons to believe that the older form of the stable repressive dictatorship will soon go the way of the dodo bird—into extinction.

A stable repressive dictatorship is one where repression is high—at or near the highest scores attainable under our operationalization—and oppositional violence, particularly unarmed violence, is low or absent. Further, the repression is directed by the dictator himself and is not institutionalized. As a result, when the dictator dies, repression decreases considerably, and violence may increase as the competition for succession develops. After a period, the country obtains a new dictator, who increases repression and reduces violence once more.

The great dictators of this century have been Stroessner of Paraguay, Papa Doc Duvalier of Haiti, Rafael Trujillo of the Dominican Republic, Juan Vicente Gómez of Venezuela, and Manuel Estrada Cabrera of Guatemala. Significantly, each of these dictators had his counterpart in the same country in the nineteenth century: Stroessner had José de Francia; Duvalier had Jean Pierre Boyer; Trujillo had Ulises Heureaux; Gómez had Antonio Guzmán Blanco; and Estrada Cabrera had Rafael Carrera. The recurrence of these dictatorships indicates that the phenomenon is more than a chance occurrence or the result of an exceptional individual. Only five countries have achieved the depths of repression maintained by these dictators, repression with no redeeming social value, dictatorships that neither responded to nor resolved any social problems.

The complete control of a country, even a small country, is an enormous task, and these dictators were men of great ability, devoting long hours of work, single-minded dedication, fantastic memories of people, and totally unscrupulous brutality to the purpose of maximizing their power. They manipulated all the tools of repression themselves and trusted no one, keeping everyone, favorite and opponent alike, in a continuous state of insecurity, with humiliation, imprisonment, or death likely to come when least expected.

None of these dictators granted any privileges to the upper classes. On the contrary, the wealthy and politically aware were those most likely to suffer as individuals. A favorite pastime of the dictators was to humiliate a self-styled aristocrat. They also seized whatever property they coveted. The aristocrat faced potential destruction by the dictator, but he did not have to worry about threats to the structure of power from below. The dictators used the forces of the state to keep the lower classes in their place, and they used the local power structure to maintain social order.

This kind of dictatorship required a special kind of person. A psychologist could identify elements of sadism, paranoia, and lust for power, and trace the origins of these characteristics in the background of the individual. Nevertheless, these dictatorships occurred only in specific kinds of societies, and in these they occurred repeatedly. All but these five Latin American countries have been nearly free of these brutal dictatorships, particularly in the twentieth century. What, then, enabled this particular kind of man to seize power and maintain it in these five countries?

Such a dictatorship was possible only in a society devoid of social values and social structures. These five societies were both amoral and amorphous, exceeding all other countries in Latin America in these characteristics. The situation is completely clear in Haiti, the Dominican Republic, and Guatemala. Venezuela and Paraguay, while sharing most of the characteristics of the others, arrived at their stable repressive dictatorships by slightly different routes.

One looks in vain for any expression of social values in these five societies. The Catholic Church in these countries has never taken a stand on social issues. With some interesting exceptions in Venezuela and Paraguay, no political philosophers have emerged from these societies. The sporadic political parties that have come into existence expressed no social ideology. Governments, whether run by the dictators or by the less repressive transitional regimes, did little to promote the general welfare. They spent next to nothing on education. What little "public" investment occurred came in the form of monumental public buildings for the aggrandizement of the dictator and constructed by firms connected to him. Government was for the benefit of the governors, not the governed. The dictators accumulated enormous sums of money, much of which was kept outside the country. Rafael Trujillo, for example, became one of the world's richest men, while the Dominican Republic remained one of the poorest countries on earth. The transitional governments between dictators were usually no less corrupt, but with less concentration of power, they allowed more persons to feed at the public trough.

Society was also relatively without structures. The wealthy lacked the class cohesion found in some Latin American countries, tending to quarrel among themselves. The Catholic Church was a weak, servile institution, conducting rituals for the oligarchy and ignoring social problems. Labor unions were nonexistent. Political parties, if they existed in name, were meaningless groups with no traditions, no organization, and no ideology. The military, the most organized institution in these societies, lacked a professional tradition and served under the constant supervision of the dictator. In short, these societies were made up of the atomized individuals referred to by Kornhauser in the *Politics of Mass Society,* cited in Chapter 4, and atomized individuals can put up only feeble resistance to a tyrant.

Venezuela and Paraguay form a partial exception to the rule that dictatorships always developed out of an absence of social values and organization. In particular, political writers in both countries defended the authoritarian political system of personalist dictatorship, giving it some positive social value. Laureano Vallenilla Lanz wrote in 1919 of the virtues of *cesarismo democrático,* stating:

> The real quality of Venezuelan democracy since independence has been the predominance of one individual, who derives his origin and legitimacy from the collective will: the will of the popular majority, tacitly or expressed. Our egalitarian instincts, our individuality—still undisciplined, adventurous, free, and heroic—have made it impossible for a caste, class, or oligarchy of any kind to gain control. It is well known that the Catholic Church, limited to a purely spiritual mission and without influence in political life, is subject to the power of the president, who exercises greater power in this respect than did the Spanish king in colonial times.
>
> A democratic Caesar . . . is always the representative and regulator of popular sovereignty. He is the personification of democracy, the nation in one man. In him two supposedly opposite concepts are synthesized, democracy and autocracy. In other words: Democratic Caesarism, equality under one leader, individual power emanating from the people over a collectivity of equals.[1]

[1]Translated and reprinted by Paul E. Sigmund, ed., *Political Change in Latin America* (New York: Praeger, 1970), pp. 225–226.

Vallenilla Lanz's statement is interesting because it confirms what we have said about the weakness of the upper classes and the church, but it makes a virtue of the condition. Paraguayan thinkers, too, considered the advantages of authoritarian rule to outweigh its liabilities. Juan Stefanish's idea of *democracia solidarista*, with its emphasis on man's solidarity with his fellows, provides the counterpart to Vallenilla Lanz's *cesarismo democrático*.[2]

Along with the development of authoritarian social philosophy in Paraguay and Venezuela, came a greater emphasis on institutions. The military formed the institutional base for authoritarian rule in Venezuela, and even managed the succession problem for more than half a century. Paraguay's authoritarian rule has been associated with both the military and political parties, *Liberal, Febrerista,* and *Colorado,* each of which has provided authoritarian rule. The result of somewhat more institutionalized authoritarianism is not less harsh rule, but less arbitrary rule, with some segments of the society relatively secure from dictatorial whim.

Haiti, the Dominican Republic, Guatemala, and Paraguay (but not Venezuela) are together at the bottom of the group of Latin American nations on two sets of data: percentage of population white and mestizo, and number of clergy per 1,000 population in 1912.[3] The two characteristics may be related. In these societies, a racial minority sought to rule a racial majority of either Negroes or Indians. In Haiti, the ruling group was, until recently, mulatto, as the white French regimes were eliminated at the time of independence. The predominantly white church hierarchy never tried to train the illiterate subordinate groups for the clergy, and these societies were therefore extremely short of clergy.

The racial makeup of the population is not important in itself, but it does reflect certain historical conditions that affected the structures and values of society. At the time of conquest or enslavement, the dominant races destroyed the broader social structures of the defeated races. Slavery extracted the Negroes from their African societies, mixed persons with different social heritages, and prevented the formation of any new autonomous organization for blacks. In Paraguay, the colonizing Jesuit orders systematically and totally wiped out the old Indian social structures, placing the Indians in *reducciones,* and giving no instruction

---

[2]Harris Gaylord discusses Stefanish's philosophy in *Paraguay, An Informal History* (Norman,Okla.: University of Oklahoma Press, 1949), pp. 317–320.

[3]Waltraud Morales, who wrote the case study on Paraguay, disputes our general source on racial characteristics for Paraguay. She feels that the Paraguayan population is really more mestizo than Indian and certainly is integrated into society, unlike Indian populations elsewhere.

to their new converts on the formation of social organizations. Then the Jesuits were expelled. The indigenous population was not oppressed as elsewhere and became integrated with the Spanish elements of society, but the traditional social structures were nonetheless destroyed. The conquerors of Guatemala left the Indians more traditional local autonomy, but they allowed no political organization that might have brought together Indians from different localities. In each of these countries, the subjugated race formed the majority, and autonomous organization of these groups might have bestowed the power to resist. Successful domination required the destruction of broader social structures and the continued use of force to prevent the development of any organization of the majorities.

Dominant minority races encourage ideas that tend to legitimize their supremacy through the depreciation of the human worth of the majorities. The process of domination, therefore, destroys the values of a society as well as its structures. Trust, cooperation, mutual assistance, protection of the weak, and the like are values unlikely to develop where people are taught that the majority of the population are no better than animals. Furthermore, the Catholic Church in these societies was too weak or too tied to the oligarchy to propagate more humane values.

The masses in these countries led miserable lives, but they lacked any vision of a better world. Social mobilization, with its exposure to commercial advertising and foreign life-styles, was low. Other Latin American countries with equally low mobilization did not share the same structural and value problems. Except for Haiti and Venezuela in the recent period, the stable dictatorial countries scored relatively higher on welfare than on mobilization, indicating that their populations may have felt less discontent than others in Latin America. Without exposure to alternatives and a long history of cultural suppression, the masses accepted their fate: high infant mortality, constant hunger and malnutrition, no medical services, and crowded, unsanitary housing.

Venezuela's population mobilized swiftly with the oil bonanza that began in the 1920s and continued to the 1950s. By 1970, Venezuela was the fourth most mobilized society in Latin America. Juan Vicente Gómez died a natural death while ruling in 1936, but no stable dictatorships have been established since. General Marcos Pérez Jiménez attempted to establish a personal dictatorship, but after five years of brutal repression, a popular uprising brought him down. The old techniques of rule did not provide Pérez Jiménez with the power he sought. The population refused to be subservient. It is hard to imagine any single man dominating the increasingly complex and educated society of Venezuela in the way Juan Vicente Gómez did only a generation ago.

The societies of the Dominican Republic, Guatemala, Haiti, and Paraguay are not nearly as complex or well-educated, but even they have become much more mobilized in recent decades. The rates of mobilization are lower than in other Latin American countries, but fairly high in absolute terms. Guatemala and the Dominican Republic have undergone "transistor revolutions" to a point where probably half the population had access to radios in 1970. Both countries have cities of well over 600,000, and road development and bus transportation have brought most of the population into some contact with urban centers. Paraguay and Haiti are far behind and changing only slowly, but urban population has doubled in Haiti in the last twenty years. The capitals of both countries are now over 300,000. Guatemala and the Dominican Republic seem to have gone past the point where they can be repressed by noninstitutional means, and Paraguay and Haiti are only ten to twenty years behind.

The governments of all four countries, whether dictatorial or not, will probably have to contend with greater social discontent. How much discontent will depend upon the rate of economic growth, the increase in welfare benefits, and the abilities of the regimes to institutionalize repression. Because welfare is relatively higher than mobilization in each of these countries, except Haiti, discontent is not likely to get out of hand. The institutional structure of these countries resembles the conditions that existed before social revolutions occurred, but unless mobilization greatly outruns economic growth, they are unlikely to reach the point of revolution. The next section will take up the question of how close to revolution they may come.

Social revolutions—will there be more?

Social revolutions happen rarely. In 150 years of independence, the twenty Latin American countries have experienced only three revolutions: Mexico, in 1910; Bolivia, in 1952; and Cuba, in 1959. The rate of social revolution is only one for every thousand country-years. If there are social conditions that lead to revolution, and we assume there are, the particular configuration that precipitates revolution is very unusual. The reason for the rarity of these situations may be that social revolution is, at least, a two-dimensional phenomenon. A country must have the conditions for very low social cohesion—the dimension we have studied—and at the same time have the prerequisites for rapid policy change—a dimension we have not considered here. Because several, but probably different, variables explain each dimension, it is quite exceptional that a nation would have all the conditions to achieve both low cohesion and rapid policy change, and hence, social revolution. Several countries have had the potential for either low cohesion—Colombia and Argentina—or for rapid policy change—Peru and Chile—but did not have the conditions for both at one time.

A social revolution occurs when a society breaks down to the point where government is ineffective, discontent is widespread, and large segments of the population are convinced that the old social system lacks all merit. The severe problems generated by the societal breakdown and conflict require drastic remedies, and groups within the society will prescribe these remedies. If milder means are tried at first, they will soon prove inadequate.

According to our operationalization of social cohesion, Bolivia and Cuba had the lowest scores in Latin America in the 1950s, and they reached their lowest points at the times of revolution. They have a pattern on the violence and repression scores, however, that dramatically distinguishes them from the stable repressive dictatorships. The dictatorships were very much higher on repression than violence, while the revolutionary societies were much higher on violence than repression. The two sets of countries have many similarities—the presence of large numbers of excluded races and weak social structures—but they differed enormously in the levels of social mobilization and on the extent to which mobilization was relatively higher than welfare.

The situations that were conducive to stable repressive dictatorship were static, existing continuously for more than a century in each of the five countries with this form of government. On the other hand, the conditions that brought revolution occurred at only one period of time and were the result of a long process of change. The pattern of change is portrayed in Figure 9. The pattern is abstracted out of the histories of Mexico, Bolivia, and Cuba; it does not, therefore, replicate any one country precisely, but indicates roughly the general timing and magnitude of all three. The magnitudes given are approximate because it was impossible to generate accurate data on each variable for all Latin American countries for all these years. Nonetheless, they demonstrate at a glance how these three countries compared with the Latin American average on the pertinent variables.

The conditions that lead to low social cohesion were established in Part 1 of this book. They are: mobilization greater than welfare; low welfare benefits; and low institutionalization, particularly military institutionalization. For violence to be relatively higher than repression, the situation on welfare minus mobilization must be worse than the score on institutionalization.

Figure 9.   Pattern of Change Leading to Social Revolution in Mexico, Bolivia, and Cuba

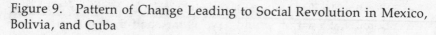
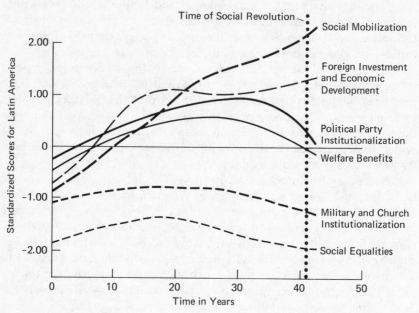

The force that generated the change on mobilization and welfare for these three countries was foreign investment or, in the case of Bolivia, investment in the tin mines by a very few extremely rich Bolivians who were cosmopolitan in their living habits and managed their investments in the same way foreigners did. Total foreign investment in Mexico at the time of the revolution was between $1.6 and $1.9 billion,[4] or more than $100 for every Mexican. Total foreign investment amounted to more than the total national product, a proportion that exceeded the level of foreign investment in any other country in Latin America then or since. Nearly every dynamic sector of the Mexican economy—railroads, banking, utilities, mining, petroleum, large commercial firms—were in the hands of foreigners. U.S. investment in Cuba (and the United States was the principal investor) dominated more of its economy than it did that of any other country in Latin America in 1950, but was still less than in Mexico in 1910. Nevertheless, American firms controlled most of Cuba's public utilities, half of the sugar production, the nickel mines, much of the banking, a large proportion of manufacturing, and the tourist industry. Three families,

---

[4]Wallace Thompson, *Trading with Mexico* (New York: Dodd, Mead, 1921), pp. 96–98.

the Patiños, the Aramayos, and the Hochschilds, owned the large tin mines in Bolivia, and tin mining was the only industry of any consequence in that poor country. The wealth generated by the mines allowed the owners to control much of the banking and real estate as well, but they found it more profitable to invest their earnings abroad.

Foreign investment stimulated the mobilization of these societies. Mining and railroads brought together large numbers of workers where they were exposed to new ideas and allowed to organize. At the same time, the new productive capacity generated urban development to service its needs. The investment also stimulated economic growth, but a large part of the benefits of this growth was sent abroad. The country receiving foreign investment felt the full impact of mobilization generated by the new productions, but received only a part of the welfare benefits. Foreign investment stimulated more wants than it did satisfactions, and the discrepancy between wants and satisfactions depended on the rate of reinvestment. With all profits reinvested, as was likely in the early stages of foreign investment, the growth of the economy was greater than the growth of mobilization, but as repatriation of profits increased, mobilization moved ahead of welfare.

As the repatriation of profits rose, the economy also tended to stagnate. Social mobilization, however, developed an impetus of its own, once started, and continued even when economic growth slowed down. Bolivia and Cuba hit a period of economic stagnation in the 1930s, after which migration to the cities continued, radios were introduced, and, in Cuba, television became prominent. Bolivia had an extra impetus to mobilization in the 1930s from the disastrous war with Paraguay over control of the Chaco. The Mexican economy, on the other hand, was still growing at the time of the 1910 revolution. The much higher rate of foreign investment in Mexico, especially because it preceded unionization and effective taxation of foreign investment, meant that the growing economy benefited the Mexican population very little.

As foreign investment increased in the early stages, the government's revenues also increased. The government could provide additional education and social investments, raising the level of benefits relative to the demand for them. As foreign investment tapered off, the growth in social benefits declined as well. The dizzying rise in foreign investment had another effect that reduced the level of social welfare benefits: the bonanza provided inordinate opportunities for those willing to sell out their nation's resources and for those not inhibited in taking advantage of the new opportunities. It thus promoted corruption in government—a phenomenon noted in all three of these societies. Corruption could be sustained in the early years of prosperity, but once started, corruption developed a momentum of its own, soon leaving few resources to serve the general public. Declining resources and increasing corruption account for the later decrease in the welfare benefits curve in Figure 9.

The growing demands, relative to the possibility of their fulfillment in the economy as a whole, account for the unusual phenomena of declining institutionalization of political parties and the military. Political parties were formed in the early stages of mobilization and waxed in strength with the growth of the economy and greater mobilization. The deepening discontent of the population brought a falling away from the political parties, while at the same time, growing corruption of the leaders undermined their earlier idealism and separated them from the masses. The governments in power at the time of each of these three revolutions received the support of no political party, even though previous governments had been supported by fairly strong political parties. The Mexican dictator, Porfirio Díaz, had taken power with the support of some of the Liberal Party, a party that had instituted rather enlightened government in the nineteenth century, but the fragments of the Liberal Party that remained were all in opposition. The *Auténtico* Party in Cuba, once the party of the idealists of the revolution of 1933, had fallen into complete disrepute and provided no resistance to the nonparty dictatorship of Batista. In Bolivia, the coalition of political parties that ruled after 1947 lost its public support steadily and split.

The military followed a similar pattern and were all in a state of degeneration at the time of revolution. As the governments in the prerevolutionary situation found they were losing control of the population, they attempted to increase the levels of repression, but the militaries, corrupted as they were, could no longer effectively repress. Edwin Liewen describes the Mexican military:

> The Army mirrored the profound social inequalities of civilian life. The officers were completely out of touch with the soldiers and the common people, and they maltreated and exploited both. Opulent in the midst of poverty, unstinting in its use of brutality, lacking in morality and without social conscience, the officer corps epitomized nearly everything the masses resented under the Díaz regime.[5]

The Cuban military had different problems, but equally lacked institutionalization:

[5]Edwin Liewen, *Mexican Militarism* (Albuquerque: University of New Mexico Press, 1968), p. 5.

> Born of mutiny and betrayal, the post-Machado army became the puppet of Batista, a military establishment shorn of traditional ties with the elite, an opportunist, predatory army of professional soldiers of the lower class but devoid of any class loyalties, distrusted alike by the populace and the affluent.[6]

The Bolivian military provided yet another variant of degeneration. It was ideologically split into groups of every persuasion: Socialist, Fascist, old-fashioned liberal, and plain opportunist. Six of the nine men who served as president between 1936 and 1952 were military men, and every administration in this period began or ended with a coup d'état.[7]

The three revolutionary countries clearly fulfilled all the prerequisites for very low social cohesion, which brings with it much violence and considerable repression. These conditions, however, did not insure that a group would come to power that would change governmental policies in sufficient degree to alter the stratification system and warrant the term social revolution. We have not developed a theory that explains why and when societies undergo major shifts in public policy, and what we say on the subject must be considered highly speculative until it is tested further. Our ideas are derived from commonalities that seemed to account for an intense desire for change in these three revolutionary situations.

Before people are willing to experiment with new ways of doing things, they must be convinced that the old ways will no longer work. Under ordinary conditions, people will support only incremental change. What is true for individuals is even truer for governments, which can make policy changes only upon the agreement of an overwhelming majority of the knowledgeable public. Three conditions existed in the three revolutionary societies in Latin America that may have led to the questioning of the values of the old system: the extremely high level of foreign investment; the extraordinary degree of inequality; and the experience of moderate reform that did not work.

High foreign investment, already discussed for its effect on social mobilization and economic growth, had the additional effect of delegitimizing private property. In all three societies, foreign investment had at one time been considered the panacea for domestic ills and the high road for national development. Mexico, Bolivia, and Cuba had received their foreign investment, but not the hoped-for national development. Nationalism supported those who opposed foreign private enterprise,

[6]Ramon Eduardo Ruiz, *The Making of a Revolution* (New York: Norton, 1968), p. 158.
[7]Robert J. Alexander, "Bolivia," in *Political Systems of Latin America,* Martin Needler ed. (New York: Van Nostrand, 1964).

and, as intellectuals raised their voices against these enterprises, no nationals stood up in defense of the foreigners. What began as an attack on foreign investment could easily shift to an attack on capitalism—the most noteworthy practitioners of capitalism obviously were foreign. Without a strong coterie of national businessmen to wage an ideological counterattack, the social system based on private enterprise lost its standing.

These countries also surpassed others in inequality. Land inequality in Mexico and Bolivia was the greatest ever known in Latin America—perhaps in the world (see Chapter 3). Further, land inequality was increasing as the large *haciendas* incorporated more and more of the Indians' communal lands and tricked homesteaders out of their property. Inequality in the ownership of land meant inequality through all of society in these two essentially rural states. Cuba's distribution of land was less unequal, but its level of inequality was exacerbated by extreme differences in living standards between Havana and the rural areas, and very high seasonal unemployment when sugar workers were not needed in the fields.

With inequality high and getting worse, most of the population came to see and feel the injustices inherent in the social system. The Indian peasants of Mexico and Bolivia had lost the traditional rights of their forefathers. Workers in the mines were working themselves to death by the age of thirty, without receiving a living wage to sustain their families. A lesser poverty in Cuba was just as difficult to bear, because those with money had gained it in recent years through government corruption. In these three countries, then, majorities had nothing to lose but their chains.

In spite of the acknowledged inequities of these three social systems, each had tried moderate reform first. Mexico had its period of liberal reform in the mid-nineteenth century, and then turned to Porfirio Díaz and his *científicos* for their brand of "order and progress." Bolivia had experimented with a military Socialist regime in the late 1930s, which, however, did nothing about either the tin mines or the great *haciendas*. Cuba had been thoroughly reformed by the post-1933 regimes. As James O'Connor has pointed out:

> The Cuban economy had already been "reformed" into a state of exhaustion and stagnation. Reform had meant redistribution of the social product, cartelization, the uneven development of the labor movement, irrational labor laws, and so on, and placed clear limits on Cuban economic development.[8]

[8]James O'Connor, "Political Change in Cuba, 1959–1965," *Social Research* 35 (Summer, 1968), p. 316.

None of these attempted reforms had produced the degree of satisfaction with the social system that their authors had predicted. Any government coming to power with the intention of solving the nation's problems would have to do more.

The three conditions—high foreign investment, inequality, and frustrated reform—had fomented numerous ideological tendencies in these countries that claimed to explain the bad situation in terms of the system and that pointed toward forming a new society. Anarchism and a moderate socialism furnished alternatives in Mexico in 1910; by the late 1950s, Latin America was richer in ideologies and Bolivia had proponents of all of them; in Cuba, the writings of José Martí and orthodox communism carried the day. There seemed little connection between the posing of these alternative social organizations and the making of revolution. None of the radical leaders was instrumental in organizing against the old regimes. The Communist Party in Cuba was one of the last groups to join the revolutionary movement. Nonetheless, these groups and ideologies helped to delegitimize the old social structures, direct unrest toward programs, and provide suggestions for new policy alternatives.

Even with institutions corrupted, wants outrunning satisfactions, intellectuals criticizing the old system, and repression completely ineffectual, these revolutions were very bloody affairs. Though none of the three prerevolutionary regimes enjoyed popular support, they did control the official means of coercion, and the narrow clique in government had everything to lose. The clique held out for a long and bloody fight in Mexico; the fight was easier and shorter in Cuba; and the Bolivian revolution took only three days. Policy changes were much less thorough in Mexico and Bolivia than in Cuba. Judged on the basis of the degree of violence and policy change, the three revolutions differed considerably. It is, indeed, surprising that they had so many causes in common.

Two countries in Latin America, Venezuela and Guatemala, had conditions in the 1960s that rather resembled the pattern of development in the revolutionary societies, but both had other conditions that prevented revolution from taking place. Venezuela had the foreign investment that brought with it very high social mobilization, but investment in petroleum had somewhat different characteristics than investment in mining and sugar, the predominant activities of the three prerevolutionary foreign investments. For one thing, petroleum development is highly labor-intensive, limited in its impact on society, and, in addition, continues to be a dynamic sector in the economy.

Venezuela's political parties developed in the 1940s, but were ousted from power in 1948. They continued to improve their organizations and programs while in opposition, however, and when they returned to power in 1958 they had the internal cohesion to put forward a strongly reformist program and to implement it. With a heavy taxation of foreign investment, they were able to mobilize the nation's resources for effective reform. Though revolutionary activity in Venezuela was quite intense in the early 1960s, the system survived because party institutionalization and welfare policy countered the disruptive factors of relatively low welfare compared with high mobilization.

Guatemala's situation was entirely different. It made no changes to counteract the forces conducive to revolution; it neither attempted a strong reformist policy, nor achieved any institutionalization of political parties. The revolutionary activities of the 1960s were not successful, however, because foreign investment was moderate in scale and had little impact on the mobilization of the large masses of the Indian population. Until the Indians go into opposition to the social system, the forces of the old regime are likely to maintain their dominance. Foreign investment, however, continues to pour into the country, and a number of other forces are at work to mobilize the Indians. The guerrilla forces have recognized the need to gain support in the highland areas and have been agitating there. Foreign aid has sponsored Indian education programs for more than twenty-five years now, and the programs are beginning to have some effect. U.S. Catholic missionaries and Peace Corps volunteers have been very active in the Indian areas. These changing conditions are likely to make the old forms of domination of the Indians less effective. Up to now, social welfare has been much higher than mobilization in Guatemala, but the potential for mobilization is much greater than the potential for economic development, given the very inadequate base of human resources. The conditions for social revolution could very easily develop quickly in Guatemala.

The disintegration of cohesive societies

Three countries in Latin America—Brazil, Uruguay, and Chile—fell from among the highest levels of social cohesion in 1960 to among the lowest by the early 1970s. The only parallel in Latin America, or anywhere in the world, is the disintegration of Argentina in the late 1920s and early 1930s, but Argentina's fall was ushered in by a worldwide depression.

Brazil was fourth in Latin America in social cohesion in the 1950s. Citizens could express their political opinions and organize protests with little fear of reprisals from the government, and the government anticipated no armed or violent opposition. In 1964 the military took over the government and progressively removed the right of opposition. As discontent soared, manifesting itself first in demonstrations and then in urban guerrilla warfare, the military regime struck back viciously. By the last two years of the decade, Brazil ranked ninth in violence and fourth in repression in Latin America. Brazil's military repression was completely effective in destroying the opposition, and the country saw little violent opposition in the first half of the 1970s.

In the 1950s Uruguay scored far above all other Latin American countries on social cohesion. There were few societies with greater cohesion anywhere in the world. By the late 1960s, Uruguay had fallen to tenth place, and the situation continued to deteriorate. Strikes and demonstrations flamed into urban guerrilla warfare, and the government met oppositional violence with severe repression until most democratic freedoms were destroyed.

Chile was second only to Costa Rica on our score of social cohesion in the 1960s. Any and every political tendency expressed its view and had an equal chance to compete for political power. An occasional strike or mass demonstration marred the peace, and the government had no qualms about throwing scores of students or workers into jail when they created disturbances, but both government and opposition were very restrained in the means they used to further their points of view. By 1972 demonstrations and strikes were on the upswing. Extremists of both right and left were preparing for a possible armed confrontation. Then, in September, 1973, the military wiped out civilian politics with one of the most brutal take-overs in the history of the world. Chile's social cohesion plunged in 1973 to the lowest in Latin America.

Originally, the governments of these countries were by no means as corrupt or exploitative as those of the repressive dictatorships or the prerevolutionary societies. Public welfare expenditures varied from moderate in Brazil, to high in Uruguay and Chile. All had well-institutionalized professional militaries. Political parties were very well institutionalized in Uruguay and Chile, though much less so in Brazil. The Catholic Church was strong, even if it faced more challenges from Protestant sects than elsewhere in Latin America, and it held at least a moderately reformist view. These characteristics explained the social cohesion these countries enjoyed before the situation deteriorated.

Cohesion, particularly in Brazil and Chile, was based on low political participation. Both Brazil and Chile, for instance, were among the few Latin American countries that excluded illiterates from voting. The traditional system seemed capable of handling the limited demands made upon it by the politically active segment of the population, and the deprived groups remained inarticulate.

Chile and Uruguay, and to a lesser extent Brazil, experienced extraordinary rates of increase in social mobilization from the mid-1950s on, but obtained little or no economic growth. Brazil's economic expansion kept pace with its social mobilization until the early 1960s, but it had a less secure institutional base to withstand any new pressures. All three experienced a great upsurge in political mobilization, stimulated in part by increasing social mobilization and in part by greater party competition. Brazil and Chile, for the first time, found peasant groups organizing and asserting new claims. Voting increased in Brazil by forty percent between 1955 and 1960, in Chile by one hundred percent between 1958 and 1964, and in Uruguay by sixty percent between 1966 and 1971. The vote was only one indicator of more political activity of all sorts. These changes in mobilization and politicalization represented an extraordinary jump in political demands on the governments.

The resources of the governments and the societies had not risen accordingly, however. Uruguay's economic growth, in fact, was negative after the mid-1950s; Chile's was slow and became negative in 1972; and Brazil's highly satisfactory growth rate suddenly reversed itself and became negative in 1963. Without resources, these rather liberal governments resorted to inflationary financing. They each had a tradition of inflation, but now the rate of inflation became astronomical. Brazil's rate went from 38 percent in 1961 to 50 in 1962 to 75 percent in 1963. Uruguay's inflation reached a peak in 1968 at 125 percent and stayed high. Chile's inflation went from a moderate 33 percent in 1970 to a Latin American record of 750 percent in 1973.

The military establishments in Brazil and Chile were, and remain, quite large by Latin American standards. In Uruguay, where the military has not yet taken over completely, it is of moderate size. All three have a highly professional officer corps, which takes pride in its professional and technical standards. None were fraught with political divisions like the military in Argentina or Bolivia, and all projected an image, before their intervention, of apolitical defenders of the constitution. Brazil and Chile had seen some limited military intervention in earlier periods, though, and civilian groups continued to attempt to enlist the support of the military men, the rightists working on the officer corps and the leftists on the enlisted men.

After the late 1950s, the military in Uruguay, Chile, and Brazil, and to a lesser extent in other Latin American countries, had changed the definition of its roles in society, bringing about a new kind of deinstitutionalization. The boundary between military and civilian was dissolved, as military schools and writers expanded their interests and activities to include all aspects of national development. The boundary was not broken by a few ambitious generals, but by the whole military establishment acting as a corporate entity. The successful Cuban insurgency, and especially the execution of military officers by the revolutionary government, sensitized the military to threats from within national borders as well as from foreign enemies. The large United States training missions in these countries, the growing concern with the Cuban challenge to U.S. hegemony in Latin America, and the trauma induced by America's inability to contain the Vietnam insurgency reinforced the national military's fear of the internal enemy. As a result, the military was taught to identify subversives, to fight unconventional warfare and control demonstrations, and to study the social and economic problems that encouraged dissent. Many officers became critical of democratic procedures that allow oppositional parties to question the social system, while offering no resolution to economic and social problems.

In the end, the military, thinking it knew best how to run the country, took over and suppressed all alternative views and political parties and values. Politics became simply administration. The concerns and the interests of the majority became something to control, not something to respond to. Iron rule replaced the more natural cohesion that came from give-and-take and compromise in politics. Government by the corporate military, without concern for civilian organizations, is a new form of government and experience gives us no guide for guessing how it will end.

No other Latin American country is likely to suffer so rapid and severe a drop from a position of high cohesion as have Chile, Brazil, and Uruguay. Costa Rica, the only country that combines high cohesion with liberal democratic politics, is the only candidate. Fortunately, Costa Rica has already passed the transition to high-participation politics, has virtually no military, and is enjoying satisfactory economic growth. The moderately high cohesion countries—Panama, Mexico, Peru, Nicaragua, El Salvador, and Ecuador—lack the tradition of civilian government with a military establishment separate and outside politics. Of these, only Mexico is presently ruled by civilians, and the ruling elite in Mexico have the military corrupted and under control, leaving it incapable of acting as a corporate entity against civilian authority. In the other countries, the military have long been involved in politics and work with, not against, civilians.

The development of social cohesion

Unfortunately, we cannot match the precipitous drop in cohesion in Chile and Uruguay with equal increases in cohesion in other countries. Falling is rapid, but climbing is slow and laborious. Even so,

Costa Rica, Panama, and Peru have made modest advances in social cohesion since the 1950s, and now, with the fall of Uruguay and Chile, are the three most cohesive societies in Latin America. Not far behind are Mexico, Nicaragua, El Salvador, and Ecuador, which, while experiencing some threats to their social coherence during the 1960s, have weathered these storms and maintained a position well above average in Latin America. Venezuela, already discussed in a previous section, has made rather spectacular gains in the last half of the 1960s. How have these countries developed and maintained cohesion? Will they be able to hold their relatively high levels of cohesion, or are we witnessing the rise that comes before a fall?

All of these countries experienced an expanding resource base during the 1960s, one that allowed each sector of the population to improve its standard of living without any group suffering a loss. All except Ecuador had per capita economic growth rates well above the Latin American average of 1.8 percent annually. Panama, Nicaragua, and Mexico had the highest growth rates in Latin America, and Costa Rica and Peru each achieved a solid 2.4 percent per capita annual growth in GNP. With resources expanding, governments had more to spend on welfare for the population, without cutting back on jobs and lucrative contracts for their followers. The three countries that increased cohesion most between the 1950s and the 1960s—Peru, Costa Rica, and Panama—made very impressive efforts to expand education, particularly primary education. Costa Rica and Panama spent more than four percent of their GNP on education in some years—a proportion matched only by Venezuela in Latin America. Mexico and Nicaragua increased their education expenditures during this period, but still spent less than the Latin American average. They made up for lower education expenditures, however, with investments in roads, ports, and electric power generation facilities, and expanded national bank loans to deserving entrepreneurs. El Salvador and Ecuador, which experienced some turmoil in the early 1960s and then recovered, both expanded their educational expenditures more than the average and reached an absolute expenditure somewhat above the average.

None of these countries were highly mobilized socially and were not experiencing high rates of communications change or urbanization. In these, then, there was less pressure on resources. They were far from rich and the majority still lived in abject poverty, but the population was more likely to accept this situation than the citizens of many other Latin American countries.

Can economic growth in Costa Rica, Panama, Peru, Mexico, Nicaragua, El Salvador, and Ecuador be maintained? Our crystal ball looks a little cloudy at this point. We do not have a verified theory of economic growth. We did note, however, that nations overly dependent on outside forces for their growth were more likely to have trouble than those that have generated the dynamism for growth within their own systems.

By this criterion, Panama could definitely be in trouble in the future. Foreign investment in Panama has reached a point higher than that reached anywhere else in Latin America—far higher than it was in Cuba. Its spectacular economic growth of 4.6 percent per capita during the 1960s was almost entirely due to the inflow of foreign resources. Growth may decline when the foreign springs dry up, should that happen.

Foreign investment and foreign aid have also been important factors in the economic growth of the other countries—more so in Costa Rica and Peru, less so in Mexico. Costa Rica and Peru, following the lead of Mexico, have recognized the dangers of economic dependence, however, and are taking steps to limit or control foreign investment and foreign ownership of the means of production.

While it is nearly impossible to predict the future course of economic development in these countries, we can say with some certainty that they will continue or increase their levels of mobilization. The development of transistors means that the number of radios will expand until nearly everyone has this means of communication, and in Panama, Costa Rica, and Mexico, television is also rapidly becoming widespread, with the other countries bound to follow. Population pressure in the rural areas will force migration to the cities in ever-increasing numbers. Only the pace of expansion is in question.

Only Costa Rica and Mexico have a solid institutional base that will allow them to weather many or heavy economic storms. Mexico's total institutionalization is considerably higher than any other Latin American country. Costa Rica scored lower on party institutionalization, but during the last twenty years, its parties have greatly increased their organization and coherence. As noted above, Costa Rica has no military establishment, and Mexico has corrupted and controlled its.

Peru and El Salvador were both very low on institutionalization in the fifties and sixties, which should be taken as a warning. The military in both nations, however, have been ruling with the assistance of political parties. In El Salvador, the military leaders and their civilian allies formed the Party of National Conciliation in 1961, and through it have been able to win elections ever since while allowing some free competition. In Peru, the military cooperated with the *Acción Popular* during the 1960s, and when the military took over the government in 1968, all the political parties cooperated with its reform program. These cases indicate that the separation of the two institutions may be less important than we thought. Difficulties arise when there is antagonism between the civilian and military sectors. Cohesion need not be damaged too greatly by military intervention when it is done in connection with popular civilian organizations, rather than in opposition to them.

Nicaragua and Mexico show another kind of military-civilian relationship which seems to have worked without breaking down the cohesion of the society. In these cases, the political party is the principal organizer, but military leaders cooperate closely with the party. The difference between the two countries is that Mexico no longer has to contend with powerful personalist generals, whereas Nicaragua is dominated by the powerful Somoza family, whose head is also a general.

Of the seven countries presently highest on social cohesion, only Costa Rica has a liberal, democratic form of government, with free party competition and honest elections. The other governments have what might, at best, be described as civilian-military machines that rely upon a combination of graft and patronage, welfare benefits and public campaigning, and coercion to maintain dominance. Frank Brandenburg has described Mexico's government as controlled by a "revolutionary family," a group of some 200 individuals from all sectors of society who share the benefits and cooperate to maintain control of interest groups and the government.[9] The other countries, too, though without the background of revolution, are ruled by a united business-party-military elite that has co-opted some elements of the working class. James C. Scott's characterization of the political machine seems to fit very well, especially Mexico, Nicaragua, and El Salvador:

> What is distinctive about the machine, however, is not so much its control as the nature of the organizational cement that makes such control feasible. The machine is not the disciplined, ideological party held together by class ties and common programs that arose in Continental Europe. Neither is it typically a charismatic party, depending on a belief in the almost super-human qualities of its leader to insure internal cohesion. The machine is rather a non-ideological organization interested less in political principle than in securing and holding office for its leaders and distributing income to those who run and work for it. It relies on what it accomplishes in a concrete way for its supporters, not on what it stands for. A machine may be likened to a business in which all members are stockholders and dividends are paid in accordance with what has been invested.[10]

[9]Frank Brandenburg, *The Making of Modern Mexico* (Englewood Cliffs, N.J.: Prentice-Hall, 1964).

[10]James C. Scott, "Corruption, Machine Politics, and Political Change," *American Political Science Review* 63 (December, 1969), pp. 1142–1158.

The machine is concerned with winning elections and distributes particularistic material rewards to those who can deliver the votes. However, in these countries it also uses coercion selectively to eliminate those who might cause trouble.

The political system that evolves out of machine politics is no one's utopia. Yet it should be considered in the light of certain alternatives. Graft and patronage are far better distributed in this kind of system than in the dictatorial regimes or the prerevolutionary systems. Whereas government policies are used to make cooperative businessmen wealthy, enterprises develop that contribute to the economic growth of the country as a whole. Welfare benefits are higher than in a dictatorship because of concern for the mass electorate. These countries seem as capable of instituting moderate reforms as are the liberal democratic regimes. They use coercion more than liberal democratic governments, but they are relatively immune to the kind of repressive reaction that developed in Brazil, Uruguay, and Chile because they never allow clear ideological cleavages. The political machine has been particularly effective in blunting the confrontations of government-opposition, civilian-military, and left-right political parties. Sharing the perquisites of political office can provide a fairly effective social cement, at least as long as the economy keeps growing.

Colombia, which improved its cohesion more than any country except Costa Rica between the 1950s and 1960s, has been able to put a stop to its horrendous violence and weather a significant guerrilla threat through the development of a strong political machine that incorporated members of both parties under a National Front government. The growing ideological split of the 1940s has been pasted over; dissident groups have been co-opted; labor unions have been manipulated; and those that benefited have delivered the votes. Colombia accomplished the organization of the machine and its improvement in cohesion with a very weak economic growth. As the economic situation improved in the early 1970s, so did the cohesion of the system.

Understanding the future

By the time we begin to figure out the past, the present is upon us and many things in the world have already changed, making our explanations inadequate for an understanding of the future. The early 1950s were much more difficult to predict than the 1960s, partly because of measurement problems, but also because the end of World War II created a world ideology favorable to political freedom and nonviolent political reformism. The economic successes of the Communist countries, the realization that social revolution was possible after the Cuban revolution, and a disillusionment in the international capitalist system with the fall in prices of primary goods, created a new situation in the 1960s which brought much stronger relationships between the variables of this study.

The 1970s introduced some new conditions that may have changed further the relationships between the variables. What caused violence in the 1960s, may now cause repression as the military takes preemptive action. We want to end with a note of caution against holding any explanation of the social world too dogmatically, because all explanations depend on *ceteris paribus*—other things being equal—and in the historical world, nothing ever remains equal. The world will always require constant reinterpretation.

We don't pretend to know what conditions will prevail to make relationships different in the future. All our knowledge is of the past, and we can only predict change on the basis of trends already manifested and passed into history. Perhaps the most important change comes with the learning experience of social institutions and the development of a more general understanding of the human condition.

The world, for better or worse, continues its pace of organization and bureaucratization, bringing with it man's increasing control of the environment and man's growing difficulty in controlling social organizations. Latin American governments with their planning offices and advisory committees, the multinational corporations, the Catholic Church, the U.S. government, and the international organizations have all grown in size, complexity, and bureaucratic experience in the last twenty years and together have become the major protagonists in the decisions that will contest the future of Latin America. These organizations have increased their capability to control economic conditions and to organize the population. They have expanded their intelligence apparatus and communication channels. They have greater power of manipulation of individuals, but they also have established forums for the discussion of social questions and adopted procedures for the conciliation of differences.

Despite the expansion of knowledge and organization, we would stress the ignorance that remains about social questions. The actions of the above-mentioned organizations have been taken with a very limited understanding of their social consequences. Public health has been improved without consideration of the population explosion; labor-saving machines have been installed without thought of unemployment; techniques of interrogation and surveillance have been used without concern for their abuse by the authoritarian state. Science, as it has been developed, has been much more successful in acquiring knowledge of small things than of broader social problems. As a result, change accelerates while control of change lags far behind. In spite of the talk about economic and social planning, the social theory for effective planning does not yet exist. The present study represents our small efforts to understand the social conditions that encourage repression and violence in the hope that both can be better controlled and societies can become more cohesive.

BIBLIOGRAPHY

General

BOOKS AND DOCUMENTS

APTER, DAVID. *The Politics of Modernization.* Chicago: University of Chicago Press, 1965.

BRINTON, CRANE. *Anatomy of Revolution.* Englewood Cliffs: Prentice Hall, 1938.

BURNETT, BEN G., and JOHNSON, KENNETH F., eds. *Political Forces in Latin America.* Belmont, Calif.: Wadsworth, 1970.

CAMPOS, JUDITH TALBOT, and McCAMANT, JOHN F. *Cleavage Shift in Colombia.* Beverly Hills: Sage, 1972.

Center for Intercultural Documentation. *Latin America in Maps, Charts, and Tables: No. 2, Socio-Religious Data.* Mexico, CIDOC, 1964.

CHILCOTE, RONALD H., and EDELSTEIN, JOEL C., eds. *Latin America: The Struggle with Dependency and Beyond.* New York: Wiley, 1974.

COCKCROFT, JAMES D.; FRANK, ANDRÉ GUNDER; and JOHNSON, DALE L. *Dependence and Underdevelopment.* Garden City, N.Y.: Doubleday, 1972.

DAHL, ROBERT A. *Polyarchy, Participation and Opposition.* New Haven: Yale University Press, 1971.

DAHRENDORF, RALF. *Class and Class Conflict in Industrial Society.* Stanford: Stanford University Press, 1959.

DAVIES, JAMES C., ed. *When Men Revolt and Why.* New York: The Free Press, 1970.

DENTON, CHARLES F., and LAWRENCE, PRESTON LEE. *Latin American Politics.* San Francisco, Chandler, 1973.

EASTON, DAVID. *A Systems Analysis of Political Life.* New York: Wiley, 1967.

ECKSTEIN, HARRY. *Division and Cohesion in Democracy: A Study of Norway.* Princeton: Princeton University Press, 1966.

———.*The Evaluation of Political Performance: Problems and Dimensions.* Beverly Hills: Sage Publications, 1971.

FEIERABEND, IVO; FEIERABEND, ROSALIND; and GURR, TED ROBERT, eds. *Anger, Violence and Politics.* Englewood Cliffs, N.J.: Prentice-Hall, 1973.

FRANK, ANDRÉ GUNDER. *Latin America: Underdevelopment or Revolution.* New York: Monthly Review, 1969.

GARDNER, MARY A. *The Inter American Press Association: Its Fight for Freedom of the Press, 1926–1960.* Austin: University of Texas Press, 1967.

GRAHAM, HUGH DAVIS, and GURR, TED ROBERT. *Violence in America.* New York: Bantam Books, 1969.

GURR, TED ROBERT. *Why Men Rebel.* Princeton: Princeton University Press, 1970.

HOETINK, H. *Two Variants in Caribbean Race Relations.* London: Oxford University Press, 1967.

HUNTINGTON, SAMUEL P. *Political Order in Changing Societies.* New Haven: Yale University Press, 1968.

Inter-American Development Bank, *Socio-Economic Progress in Latin America.* Washington, D.C.: Inter-American Development Bank, annual.

JOHNSON, JOHN J. *Political Change in Latin America.* Stanford: Stanford University Press, 1958.

KORNHAUSER, WILLIAM. *Politics of Mass Society.* Glencoe, Ill.: Free Press, 1959.

Latin American Center (formerly Center for Latin American Studies). *Statistical Abstract of Latin America.* Los Angeles: Latin American Center, University of California, annual.

LIPSET, SEYMOUR MARTIN. *Political Man: The Social Bases of Politics.* Garden City, N.Y.: Doubleday, 1959.

LOFTUS, JOSEPH E. *Latin American Defense Expenditures, 1938–1965.* Santa Monica: Rand, 1968.

MECHAM, J. LLOYD. *Church and State in Latin America.* Chapel Hill: University of North Carolina, 1966.

MORALES, WALTRAUD Q. *Social Revolution: Theory and Historical Application.* Denver: University of Denver, Monograph Series in World Affairs, 1973.

NEEDLER, MARTIN, ed. *Political Systems of Latin America.* New York: Van Nostrand, 1964.

NIE, NORMAN H. *Statistical Package for the Social Sciences.* New York: McGraw-Hill, 1970.

Organization for Economic Cooperation and Development. *National Accounts of Less Developed Countries, 1950–1966.* Paris: OECD, 1968.

———. *Stock of Private Direct Investments by OAC Countries in Developing Countries at End of 1967.* Paris: OECD, 1972.

Organization of American States. *América en Cifras.* Washington D.C.: Pan American Union, annual.

———. *Preliminary Study of the State of Siege and the Protection of Human Rights in the Americas.* OEA/Series 50/5/2.8 (September 17, 1963).

PARKIN, FRANK. *Class Inequality and Political Order.* New York: Praeger, 1971.

REYNOLDS, CLARK W. *The Mexican Economy.* New Haven: Yale University Press, 1970.

RUSSETT, BRUCE M. *Trends in World Politics.* New York: Macmillan, 1965.

SCHWARTZ, DAVID C. *Political Alienation and Political Behavior.* Chicago: Aldine Publishing, 1973.

SIGMUND, PAUL E., ed. *Political Change in Latin America.* New York: Praeger, 1970.

United Nations. *External Financing in Latin America.* New York: United Nations, 1965.

———. *United Nations Statistical Yearbook.* New York: United Nations, annual.

United Nations Educational, Scientific, and Cultural Organization. *Statistical Yearbook.* Louvain: UNESCO, annual.

United States Agency for International Development. *U.S. Overseas Loans and Grants and Assistance from International Organizations.* Washington, D.C.: Agency for International Development, annual.

United States Arms Control and Disarmament Agency. *World Military Expenditures.* Washington, D.C.: U.S. Arms Control and Disarmament Agency, annual.

VALLIER, IVAN. *Catholicism, Social Control, and Modernization in Latin America.* Englewood Cliffs, N.J.: Prentice-Hall, 1970.

VAN DEN BERGHE, PIERRE L. *Race and Racism, A Comparative Perspective.* New York: Wiley, 1967.

ARTICLES AND MONOGRAPHS

ADELMAN, IRMA, and MORRIS, CYNTHIA. "An Anatomy of Income Distribution: Patterns in Developing Countries." *Development Digest* 9 (October, 1971), pp. 24–37.

BARRACLOUGH, SOLON L., and DOMIKE, ARTHUR L. "Agrarian Structures in Seven Latin American Countries." *Land Economics* 42 (November, 1966), pp. 395, 397.

BRAITHWAITE, STANLEY N. "Real Income Levels in Latin America." *Review of Income and Wealth* 14 (June, 1968), pp. 113–182.

BWY, DOUGLAS. "Political Instability in Latin America: The Cross-Cultural Test of a Causal Model." *Latin American Research Review* 3 (Spring, 1968), pp. 17–66.

CUTWRIGHT, PHILIPS. "National Political Development: Its Measurement and Social Correlates." In *Politics and Social Life,* edited by Nelson W. Polsby. Boston: Houghton Mifflin Co., 1963.

DEUTSCH, KARL W. "Social Mobilization and Political Development." *American Political Science Review* 55 (September, 1961), pp. 493–514.

DUFF, ERNEST A., and McCAMANT, JOHN F. "Measuring Social and Political Requirements for System Stability in Latin America." *American Political Science Review* 62 (December, 1968), pp. 1125–1143.

ECKSTEIN, HARRY. "A Theory of Stable Democracy." *Research Monograph No. 10.* Princeton: Center of International Studies, Princeton University, 1961.

———. "Authority Relations and Governmental Performance." *Comparative Political Studies* 2 (October, 1969), pp. 269–325.

GERMANI, GINO, and SILVERT, KARL. "Politics, Social Structure and Military Intervention in Latin America." In *Government and Politics in Latin America,* edited by Peter Snow. New York: Holt, Rinehart & Winston, 1967.

GURR, TED ROBERT. "Psychological Factors in Civil Violence." *World Politics* 20 (January, 1968), pp. 245–278.

HOROWITZ, IRVING LOUIS. "The Life and Death of Project Camelot." In U.S. Congress, House of Representatives, 89th Congress, 2nd Session, *International Education: Past, Present, Problems, and Prospects* (Washington D.C.: U.S. GPO, 1967.

KLING, MERLE. "Toward a Theory of Power and Political Instability in Latin America." *Western Political Quarterly* 9 (March, 1956), pp. 21–35.

LOTZ, JORGEN R., and MORSS, ELLIOTT R. "Measuring Tax Effort in Developing Countries." *International Monetary Fund Staff Papers* 14 (November, 1967), pp. 477–499.

MARTZ, JOHN D. "Urban and Rural Factors in Contemporary Latin American Violence." *Western Political Quarterly* 18 (September, 1965), Supplement pp. 36–56.

MIDLARSKY, MANUS, and TANTER, RAYMOND. "Toward a Theory of Political Instability in Latin America." *Journal of Peace Research* 4 (No. 3, 1967), pp.209–227.

MORRISON, DONALD G., and STEVENSON, HUGH MICHAEL. "Measuring Social and Political Requirements for System Stability: Empirical Validation of an Index Using Latin American and African Data." *Comparative Political Studies* 7 (July, 1974), pp. 252–263.

NUN, JOSÉ. "The Middle Class Military Coup." In *The Politics of Conformity in Latin America*, edited by Claudio Veliz. New York: Oxford University Press, 1967.

PUTNAM, ROBERT D. "Toward Explaining Military Intervention in Latin American Politics." *World Politics* 20 (October, 1967), pp. 83–110.

RUSSETT, BRUCE M. "Inequality and Instability: The Relation of Land Tenure to Politics." *World Politics* 16 (April, 1964), pp. 442–454.

SILVERT, KALMAN H. "American Academic Ethics and Social Research Abroad." In U.S. Congress, House of Representatives, 89th Congress, 2nd Session, *International Education: Past, Present, Problems, and Prospects*. Washington, D.C.: U.S. GPO, 1967.

TANNENBAUM, FRANK. "The Hacienda." In *The United States and Latin America*, edited by Herbert L. Matthews. Englewood Cliffs: Prentice-Hall, 1963.

VALLIER, IVAN. "Church Development in Latin America: A Five-Country Comparison." *Journal of Developing Areas* 1 (July, 1967), pp. 471–488.

WOLIN, SHELDON. "Political Theory as a Vocation." *American Political Science Review* 63 (December, 1969), pp. 1062–1082.

Individual countries

ARGENTINA

FERNANDEZ, JULIO A. *The Political Elite in Argentina*. New York: New York University Press, 1970.

FERRER, ALDO. *The Argentine Economy.* Translated by Marjory M. Urquidi. Berkeley and Los Angeles: University of California Press, 1967.

Instituto de Ciencia Política de la Universidad del Salvador. *"La Revolución Argentina": Analysis y Prospectiva.* Buenos Aires: Ediciones Depalma, 1966.

KIRKPATRICK, JEAN. *Leader and Vanguard in Mass Society: A Study of Peronist Argentina.* Cambridge: MIT Press, 1971.

LANDA, JOSÉ. *Hipólito Irigoyen.* Buenos Aires: Macland S.R.L., 1958.

MARTINEZ ESTRADA, EZEQUIEL. *X-Ray of the Pampa.* Translated by Alain Swietlicki. Austin: University of Texas Press, 1971.

PERÓN, JUAN D. *Latinoamerica: Ahora o Nunca.* Montevideo: Editorial Diálogo, 1967.

QUINTERNO, CARLOS ALBERTO. *Historia Recente: La Crisis Política Argentina de 1955 a 1966.* Buenos Aires: Libreria Huemul, 1970.

SABLECORVO. *Argentina y Peru: El Golpe y la Revolución.* Buenos Aires: Editora de Temas Nacionales, 1969.

SCOBIE, JAMES R. *Argentina: A City and a Nation.* New York: Oxford University Press, 1964.

SNOW, PETER. *Political Forces in Argentina.* Boston: Allyn and Bacon, 1971.

BOLIVIA

Area Handbook for Bolivia. Washington, D.C.: U.S. GPO, 1974.

ÁVILA ECHAZU, EDGAR. *Revolución y Cultura en Bolivia.* Tarija: Universidad Autónoma "Juan Misael Saracho," 1963.

ÁVILA, FEDERICO. *El Problema de la Unidad Nacional.* La Paz: Editorial "Universo," 1939.

BARCELLI S., AUGUSTÍN. *Medio Siglo de Luchas Sindicales Revolucionarias en Bolivia.* La Paz: Editorial del Estado, 1956.

BEDREGAL, GUILLERMO. *Bolivia: Imperialismo y Revolución.* La Paz: Editorial "Los Amigos Del Libro," 1970.

CORNEJO S., ALBERTO. *Programas Políticas de Bolivia.* Cochabamba: Imprenta Universitaria, 1949.

DIAZ MACHICAO, PORFIRIO. *Historia de Boliva (1920–1943).* 4 vols. La Paz: Editorial "Juventud," no date.

DIEZ DE MEDINA, FERNANDO. *El General del Pueblo.* La Paz: Ediciones "Los Amigos del Libro," 1972.

REINAGA, FAUSTO. *Tierra y Libertad, La Revolución Nacional y El Indio.* Ediciones "Rumbo Sindical," 1952.

ROLÓN ANAYA, MARIO. *Política y Partidos en Bolivia.* La Paz: Ediciones "Juventud," 1966.

WILKIE, JAMES W. *The Bolivian Revolution*. Los Angeles: Latin American Center, University of California, 1969.

BRAZIL

DULLES, JOHN W. F. *Unrest in Brazil: Political-Military Crises, 1955–1964*. Austin: University of Texas Press, 1970.
IANNI, OCTAVIO. *Crises in Brazil*. New York: Columbia University Press, 1970.
LEVINE, ROBERT M. *The Vargas Regime*. New York: Columbia University Press, 1970.
LOEWENSTEIN, KARL. *Brazil under Vargas*. New York: MacMillan, 1942.
MALTA, OCTAVIO. *Os Tenentes na Revoluçâo Brasileira*. Rio de Janeiro: Civilizacâo Brasileira, 1969.
PAGE, JOSEPH A. *The Revolution That Never Was*. New York: Grossman Publishers, 1972.
ROETT, RIORDAN. *Brazil in the Sixties*. Nashville: Vanderbilt University Press, 1972.
SCHNEIDER, RONALD. *The Political System of Brazil*. New York: Columbia University Press, 1971.
SKIDMORE, THOMAS E. *Politics in Brazil: 1930–1964*. New York: Oxford University Press, 1967.
STEPAN, ALFRED. *The Military in Politics: Changing Patterns in Brazil*. Princeton: Princeton University, 1971.
YOUNG, JORDAN M. *The Brazilian Revolution of 1930 and the Aftermath*. New Brunswick: Rutgers University Press, 1967.

CHILE

CUSACK, DAVID. "Confrontation Politics and the Disintegration of Chilean Democracy," *Sonderdruck aus Vierteljahres Berichte* 58 (December, 1974) pp. 313–351.
MEDHURST, KENNETH, ed. *Allende's Chile*. New York: St. Martin's Press, 1972.
MORRIS, JAMES O. *Elites, Intellectuals, and Consensus*. Ithaca: Cornell University Press, 1966.
SILVERT, KALMAN. *The Conflict Society: Reaction and Revolution in Latin America*. New Orleans: Hauser Press, 1961.

COLOMBIA

CORR, EDWIN G. *The Political Process in Colombia*. Denver: University of Denver Press, 1972.

DIX, ROBERT H. *Colombia: The Political Dimensions of Change.* New Haven: Yale University Press, 1967.

DUFF, ERNEST A. *Agrarian Reform in Colombia,* New York: Frederick A. Praeger, 1968.

————. "The Role of Congress in the Colombian Political System." In *Latin American Legislatures: Their Role and Influence,* edited by Weston F. Agor. New York: Frederick A. Praeger, 1971.

FALS-BORDA, ORLANDO. *Subversion and Social Change in Colombia.* Translated by Jacqueline D. Skiles. New York: Columbia University Press, 1969.

GUZMÁN, GERMÁN. *La Violencia en Colombia: Parte Descriptiva.* Cali.: Ediciones Progreso, 1968.

HOLT, PAT M. *Colombia Today—and Tomorrow.* New York: Frederick A. Praeger, 1964.

MAULLIN, RICHARD L. *The Fall of Dumar Aljure, A Colombian Guerrilla Bandit.* Santa Monica: The Rand Corporation, 1968.

RAMSEY, RUSSELL W. "The Modern Violence in Colombia," Ph.D Dissertation: University of Florida, 1967.

COSTA RICA

BELL, PATRICK. *Crisis in Costa Rica: The 1948 Revolution.* Austin: University of Texas Press, 1971.

MUNRO, DANA. *The Five Republics of Central America.* New York: Oxford University Press, 1918.

CUBA

AGUILAR, LUIS E. *Cuba 1933: Prologue to Revolution.* Ithaca: Cornell University Press, 1972.

BLUTSTEIN, HOWARD L.; ANDERSON, LYNNE C.; BETTERS, ELINOR; LANE, DEBORAH; LEONARD, JONATHAN; and TOWNSEND, CHARLES. *Area Handbook for Cuba.* Washington, D.C.: U.S. Department of Defense, 1971.

BONACHEA, ROLANDO, and VALDES, NELSON. *Cuba in Revolution.* New York: Doubleday, 1972.

Latin American Center, *Cuba 1968.* Los Angeles: Latin American Center, University of California, 1970.

DE LEON, RUBEN. *El Origen del Mal: Cuba, un Ejemplo.* Coral Gables: Service Offset Printers, 1964.

MESA-LAGO, CARMELO, ed. *Revolutionary Change in Cuba.* Pittsburgh, University of Pittsburgh Press, 1971.

NELSON, LOWRY. *Cuba: The Measure of a Revolution.* Minneapolis: University of Minnesota Press, 1972.

PHILLIPS, R. HART. *Cuba: Island of Paradox.* New York: McDowell, Obolensky, 1960.

RUIZ, REMON EDUARDO. *The Making of a Revolution.* New York: Norton, 1968.

SANCHEZ. RAMIRO. *Historia de la Nación Cubana,* Vol. 9. Havana: Editorial Historia de la Nacion Cubana, 1952.

SMITH, ROBERT FREEMAN, ed. *Background to Revolution: The Development of Modern Cuba.* New York: Knopf, 1966.

SUAREZ, ANDRES. *Cuba: Castroism and Communism, 1959–1966.* Cambridge: MIT Press, 1967.

TABER, ROBERT. *M-26; Biography of a Revolution.* New York: Lyle Stuart, 1961.

THOMAS, HUGH. *Cuba: The Pursuit of Freedom.* New York: Harper & Row, 1971.

DOMINICAN REPUBLIC

CRASSWELLER, ROBERT D. *Trujillo: Life and Times of a Caribbean Dictator.* New York: Macmillan, 1966.

DIAZ SANTANA, ARISMENDI. *Desarrollo y Descomposición de la Economia Dominicana.* Santo Domingo: Impresiones MD, 1969.

GUTIERREZ, CARLOS MARIA. *The Dominican Republic: Rebellion and Repression.* Washington, D.C.: Monthly Review Press, 1972.

HICKS, ALBERT C. *Blood in the Streets.* New York: Creative Age Press, 1946.

LOWENTHAL, ABRAHAM F. "The Dominican Republic: The Politics of Chaos" In *Reform and Revolution: Readings in Latin American Politics,* edited by Arpad von Lazar and Robert R. Kaufman. Boston: Allyn and Bacon, 1969.

PEREZ CABRAL, PEDRO ANDRES. *La Comunidad Mulata.* Caracas: Grafica Americana, 1967.

ROBERTS, T. D.; CALLAWAY, SUSAN; CARROLL, MARY E.; MADAY, BELLA; MCMORRIS, DAVID, THEWO, ELAINE; and WEAVER, JOHN. *Area Handbook for the Dominican Republic.* Washington, D.C.: U.S. GPO, 1966.

WIARDA, HOWARD J. *The Dominican Republic: Nation in Transition.* New York: Frederick A. Praeger, 1969.

ECUADOR

BLANKSTEN, GEORGE. *Ecuador: Constitutions and Caudillos.* Berkeley and Los Angeles: University of California Press, 1951.

COCHRANE, JAMES D. "Ecuador: A Present-Day Portrait." *Current History* 51 (November, 1966), pp. 264–269.

GALVEZ, ARNOLD, and JIMENEZ, GLORIA, eds. *Ecuador: Election Fact-book*. Washington, D.C.: Institute for the Comparative Study of Political Systems, 1968.

"La Historia Vuelva a Repetirse." *Visión* 40 (March 11, 1972), pp. 10–11.

MAIER, GEORGE. "Presidential Succession in Ecuador: 1860–1968." *Journal of Inter-American Studies and World Affairs* 12 (July–October, 1971), pp. 475–509.

NEEDLER, MARTIN C. *Anatomy of a Coup D'Etat: Ecuador, 1963*. Washington, D.C.: Institute for the Comparative Study of Political Systems, 1964.

ROUCEK, JOSEPH S. "Ecuador in Geopolitics." *Contemporary Review* 205 (February, 1964) pp. 74–82.

EL SALVADOR

ANDERSON, THOMAS P. *Matanza: El Savador's Communist Revolt of 1932*. Lincoln: University of Nebraska Press, 1971.

GUATEMALA

ADAMS, RICHARD NEWBOLD. *Crucifixion by Power*. Austin: University of Texas Press, 1970.

KEPNER, CHARLES DAVID. *Social Aspects of the Banana Industry*. New York: AMS Press, 1967.

MELVILLE, THOMAS and MARJORIE. *Guatemala, the Politics of Land Ownership*. New York: The Free Press, 1971.

HAITI

GINGRAS, JEAN PIERRE. *Duvalier: Caribbean Cyclone*. New York: Exposition Press, 1967.

RODMAN, SELDEN. *Haiti: The Black Republic*. New York: Devin-Adair, 1961.

ROTBERG, ROBERT I. *Haiti: The Politics of Squalor*. Boston: Houghton Mifflin, 1971.

MEXICO

ANDERSON, BO, and COCKROFT, JAMES C. "Control and Co-Optation in Mexican Politics." *Dependence and Underdevelopment*. Garden City: Doubleday, 1972.

ARRENDONDO MUNOZLEDO, BENJAMIN. *Breve Historia de la Revolución Mexicana.* Mexico City: Impresiones Modernas, 1967.

BRANDENBURG, FRANK. *The Making of Modern Mexico.* Englewood Cliffs, N.J.: Prentice-Hall, 1964.

CARPIO CASTILLO, RUBEN. *Mexico, Cuba, and Venezuela.* Caracas: Imprenta Nacional, 1961.

CLINE, HOWARD F. *The United States and Mexico.* Cambridge: Harvard University Press, 1965.

FAGEN, RICHARD R., and TUOHY, WILLIAM S. *Politics and Privilege in a Mexican City.* Stanford: Stanford University Press, 1972.

GONZALEZ CASANOVA, PABLO. *Democracy in Mexico.* London: Oxford University Press, 1970.

JOHNSON, KENNETH F. *Mexican Democracy: A Critical View.* Boston: Allyn and Bacon, 1971.

KAHL, JOSEPH A. *The Measurement of Modernism.* Austin: University of Texas Press, 1966.

LEWIS, OSCAR. *The Children of Sanchez.* New York: Random House, 1961.

LIEWEN, EDWIN. *Mexican Militarism.* Albuquerque: University of New Mexico Press, 1968.

PADGETT, L. VINCENT. *The Mexican Political System.* Boston: Houghton Mifflin, 1966.

ROSS, STANLEY R., ed. *Is the Mexican Revolution Dead?* New York: Knopf, 1967.

SCOTT, ROBERT E. *Mexican Government in Transition.* Urbana: University of Illinois Press, 1964.

SIERRA, JUSTO. *The Political Evolution of the Mexican People.* Austin: University of Texas Press, 1969.

TANNENBAUM, FRANK. *Peace by Revolution.* New York: Columbia University Press, 1933.

TURNER, FREDERICK C. *The Dynamic of Mexican Nationalism.* Chapel Hill: University of North Carolina Press, 1968.

NICARAGUA

MACAULEY, NEILL. *The Sandino Affair.* Chicago: Quadrangle Press, 1967.

PANAMA

GOLDRICH, DANIEL. *Sons of the Establishment.* Chicago: Rand McNally, 1966.

PARAGUAY

Area Handbook for Paraguay. Washington, D.C.: U.S. GPO, 1972.

CARDOZO, EFRAIM. *Breve Historia del Paraguay.* Buenos Aires: Editorial Universitaria de Buenos Aires, 1965.

———. *Los Tres Heroes del Paraguay: Ayala, Estigarribia y Zubizarreta.* Buenos Aires: no publisher, 1952.

CARUGATI, VICTOR E., and MONTEFILPO CARVALLO, REINALDO. *Diario "La Tribuna."* Asunción, no publisher, no date, although probably published by *La Tribuna* around 1945.

Curso de Introducción a Paraguay, especially lectures of Dr. Adriano Irala Burgos. Given by the Catholic University in Asunción from March 11–23, 1974.

GAYLORD, HARRIS. *Paraguay, An Informal History,* Norman, Okla.: University of Oklahoma Press, 1949.

HICKS, FREDERICK. "Interpersonal Relationships and Caudillismo in Paraguay." *Journal of Inter-American Studies* 13 (January, 1971) pp. 89–111.

LEWIS, PAUL H. *The Politics of Exile: Paraguay's Febrerista Party.* Chapel Hill: University of North Carolina Press, 1965.

PASTOR BENITEZ, JUSTO. *Formación Social del Pueblo Paraguayo.* Asunción: Editorial America-Sapucai, 1955.

PENDLE, GEORGE. *Paraguay: A Riverside Nation.* London: Royal Institute of International Affairs, 1954.

PEREZ ACOSTA, JUAN F. "Migraciones Históricas del Paraguay a la Argentina." *Boletin de la Cámara de Comercio Argentino-Paraguaya* 13 (Buenos Aires, September, 1952), pp. 4–14.

RUBIN, JOAN. *National Bilingualism in Paraguay.* The Hague: Mouton, 1968.

PERU

ALISKY, MARVIN. *Peruvian Political Perspective.* Tempe: Arizona State University, 1972.

Area Handbook for Peru. Washington, D.C.: U.S. GPO, 1972.

CHAPLIN, DAVID. "Peru's Postponed Revolution," *World Politics* 20 (April, 1968), pp. 393–420.

EINAUDI, LUIGI R., and STEPAN, ALFRED C. *Latin American Institutional Development: Changing Military Perspectives in Peru and Brazil.* Vol. R-586-DOS. Santa Monica: Rand Corp., April 1971.

"Gobierno militar del Peru exproprió 8 diarios limeños." *Presencia* (La Paz), July 28, 1974, p. 1.

GRAHAM HURTADO, JOSÉ. "Filosofia de la Revolución Peruana, La Comunidad Laboral," *La Comunidad Pesquera*, Conference by General of Brigade, and Chief of the Audit Committee of the Presidency of the Republic, April 14, 1971, Lima.

HAYA DE LA TORRE, VICTOR RAUL. *Pensamiento Político*. Vol. 2. Lima: Talleres de Industrial, 1961.

JAQUETTE, JANE S. *The Politics of Development in Peru*. Latin American Studies Program, Dissertation Series. Ithaca, N.Y.: Cornell University, 1971, no. 33.

McNICOLL, ROBERT E. "Peru's Institutional Revolution." Latin American Studies, Inderdisciplinary Occasional Papers, University of West Florida, Pensacola, October, 1973.

MARETT, ROBERT. *Peru*. New York: Praeger, 1969.

NEIRA SAMAÑEZ, HUGO. *El Golpe de Estado*. Santiago: Editorial ZYX, 1968.

PALMER, DAVID SCOTT. *"Revolution from Above": Military Government and Popular Participation in Peru, 1968–1972*. Latin American Studies Program, Dissertation Series. Ithaca, N.Y.: Cornell University, 1973.

PIKE, FREDERICK B. *The Modern History of Peru*. New York: Praeger, 1967.

ROZMAN, STEPHEN L. "The Evolution of the Political Role of the Peruvian Military." *Journal of Inter-American Studies* 12 (October, 1970), pp. 539–564.

TRIAS, VIVIAN. *Peru Fuerzas Armadas y Revolución*. Montevideo: Ediciones de la Banda Oriental, 1971.

URUGUAY

ALISKY, MARVIN. *Uruguay: A Contemporary Survey*, New York: Frederick A. Praeger, 1969.

CAMPIGLIA, NESTOR. *Los Grupos de Presión y el Proceso Político*. Montevideo: Ediciones ARCA, 1969.

GILIO, MARIA ESTHER. *The Tupamaros*. Translated by Anne Edmondson. London: Secker and Warburg, 1972.

PENDLE, GEORGE. *Uruguay*. London: Oxford University Press, 1963.

———. *Paraguay and Uruguay*. London: Adam and Charles Lack, 1959.

———. *Uruguay: South America's First Welfare State*. London: Royal Institute of International Affairs, 1952.

RAMA, CARLOS M. *Uruguay en Crisis*. Montevideo: El Siglo Ilustrado, 1969.

SCHURMANN PACHECO, M., and COOLIGHAN SANGUINETTI, M. L. *Historia de Uruguay*. Montevideo: Libreros Editores, 1960.

TRIAS, VIVIAN. *Economía y Política en el Uruguay Contemporaneo*. Montevideo: Ediciones de la Banda Oriental, 1968.

VENEZUELA

ARELLANO MORENO, A. *Mirador de Historia Política de Venezuela*. Caracas: Ediciones Edime, 1968.

CARPIO CASTILLO, RUBEN. *Mexico, Cuba, y Venezuela*. Caracas: Imprenta Nacional, 1961.

LOTT, LEO B. *Venezuela and Paraguay*. New York: Holt, Rinehart, and Winston, 1972.

MERCIER VEGA, LUIS. *Guerrillas in Latin America*. New York: Frederick A. Praeger, 1969.

POWELL, JOHN DUNCAN. *Political Mobilization of the Venezuelan Peasant*. Cambridge: Harvard University Press, 1971.

ROURKE, THOMAS (pseud.). *Gomez: Tyrant of the Andes*. New York: Morrow, 1936.

SILVA MICHELENA, JOSÉ A. *The Illusion of Democracy in Dependent Nations*. Cambridge: MIT Press, 1971.

INDEX

315